GÉRARD DE NERVAL:
THE MYSTIC'S DILEMMA

Bettina L. Knapp

The University of Alabama Press
University, Alabama

To Barbara and George Chimes
whose lives were short, but
whose impress
was deep

I should like to thank Professors Henri Peyre and Nick Lyons for having read my manuscript and offered such fine suggestions, and to thank the latter, as well, for permission to reproduce his poem *The Apodal Swallow.* I also thank my research assistant, Carmen Coll of the Graduate Center of C.U.N.Y., for her help in this project. The first stanza of the poem "Sailing to Byzantium" has been reprinted with permission of Macmillan Publishing Co., Inc. from *Collected Poems* by William Butler Yeats, copyright 1928 by Macmillan Publishing Co., Inc., renewed 1956 by Georgie Yeats; and by permission of M. B. Yeats, Miss Ann Yeats, and the Macmillan Co. of London and Basingstoke. Nerval's sonnets *Les Chimères* have been quoted, for the most part, in the translations of Geoffrey Wagner, from *Gérard de Nerval: Selected Writings,* copyright © 1957 by Geoffrey Wagner, with the gracious permission of the translator and the University of Michigan Press (see chapter 20, note 24).

Library of Congress Cataloging in Publication Data

Knapp, Bettina Liebowitz, 1926–
  Gérard de Nerval, the mystic's dilemma.

  Bibliography: p.
  Includes index.
  1. Gérard de Nerval, Gérard Labrunie, Known as,
1808–1855—Criticism and interpretation. I. Title.
PQ2260.G36Z666   848'.7'09   75-40296
ISBN 0-8173-7608-9

CONTENTS

PREFACE
"NERVALIAN BLACK"

The path to be taken is already marked with these two signs, ulterior landmarks in Bettina Knapp's book, which stamp the great spaces she so admirably explores:

> Love is a growing, or full constant light;
> And his first minute, after noon, is night.
> (John Donne, *A Lecture upon the Shadow*)

Thus it makes possible the transformation of the
unknown into an object, a He or She out of a Thou
that could not originally be experienced but simply
suffered.
(Martin Buber, *I and Thou*)

We must advance in the blackness of transformation: punctuated with periods of *exile,* strangely encircling moments of death.

Instancies of schizophrenic exile were experienced in 1841—in 1853, with language difficulties—a loss of identity and writing ability. In 1842 the instancy of death became known—Jenny's: Aurélia's.

The first instancy of madness seems to anticipate the anniversary of death. The second is the anniversary itself with a decennium added. It is prolonged with the publication of the first *Chimeras*—"written in this state of supernaturalist reverie" that the letter to Dumas evokes.

A whole network of relationships and references are interwoven between these instants or instancies—comparable to those that link Bataille's *The Guilty* with the anniversary of Laure's death ("this fury has led me to my hell").[1]

The Nervalian Inferno permeates—because of its supernaturalist *écriture*—an entire network of exile, aphasia, and death, but not without also encompassing the immense mesh of the narratives captured by an indefatigable ear, sensitive to all the versions that circulate in an inner sea or in the river of its space: "moved myself by the narrative of this passion," he wrote concerning Kaliph Hakim's death. A passion, he adds, "less dolorous probably than the one at the Golgotha," but which he introduces into a great *narrative equivalency,* with those of Icarus, Phaëton or Atys. Comparable also to the component parts of Hölderlin's "clover" through "Bacchos, Herakles and Christ."

When the point of death is reached, the narrative of the passion becomes more precise:

"I have been told many similar things"—

and the momentum of the *versions* in fact constantly accelerates the spiral of the Nervalian Inferno. A spiral that broadens and becomes as exten-

sive as the dimensions of the central accounts of the universal history—
"actually I said to him, the Koran is just a résumé of the Old and New
Testament expressed *in other terms.*"[2] Or, it is condensed at the most vulnerable passages, those dealing with the unconscious: the same can be
said of the unusual parallelism between the discovery of the Kaliph
Hakim in *Voyage in the Orient* and the narrator in *Aurélia.*

> He thought it was his *ferouer* or his double; and
> when an Oriental sees his own ghost, it is the most
> sinister of omens. The shadow forces the body to
> follow it without a day's delay.[3]

... I shudder when recalling a well known German tradition which says that each man has a *double,* and that when he sees it, death is drawing
near. . . . Was it the *Double* of the legends or the
mystic brother Orientals call *Ferouër?* . . . In any
event, *the other* is hostile. . . I thought I heard of a
ceremony taking place elsewhere, preparations for
a mystic wedding which was to be mine, but the
other was then to take advantage of my friends'
and of Aurélia's own error. . . . A dreadful idea
came to me: "man is double," I said to myself.[4]

> The apparition now became all the more menac-
> ing since the *ferouer* was carrying out Hakim's plan
> in advance. Wasn't there a hidden enigmatic
> meaning, a mysterious and terrible sign in the fan-
> tastic Kaliph's plan to marry Setalmulc, whom the
> real Kaliph had himself intended to marry?[5]

There was a double meaning in what those people
told me even though they didn't realize it.[6]

> Terrible night, when the sovereign power took on
> the stature of revolt, when heaven's revenge used
> the armaments of hell.[7]

... I compare this series of ordeals I experienced
with the ancients' descent into inferno.[8]

The series of "ordeals" into the Nervalian Inferno is already considered in terms of a series of narrations which both act upon and are experienced by the author.

"when my friend told me . . ."
"he told me how he had seen himself . . ."
"when he then told me . . ."
"the impression was most acute . . ."[9]

> "I cannot describe the feelings of dejection
> that overwhelmed me . . ."[10]

(Let us note here that the *double,* first a friend, suddenly turning into a dangerous narrator, appears to have been Heine, the sick poet—Marx's friend in Paris at the time of the *Deutsche Französische Jahrbücher*—whom Nerval had actually gone to visit. . . .)

> I was given some paper and for a long time I devoted my energies to representing, by means of a thousand figures interspersed with narratives, poems, and descriptions in all languages . . . a kind of history of the world interwoven . . . with fragments of dreams.[11]

The Inferno in the stories "interwoven . . . with fragments of dreams," is not simply to be looked upon as the geography of a "long illness . . . occurring entirely within the mysteries of the mind," nor as a nocturnal voyage of the nyctalopic Nerval described by Daumal ("from this moment I strove hard to search for a meaning to my dreams"),

—but as an adventure in the very power of recounting *fragments of dreams* and of sketching the thousand *figures interspersed with narratives*—

and in this respect, Gérard is our brother, a precursor and far in the lead in these areas where

"everything was changing shape around me"[12]
"then the monsters changed shape"[13]

"the shadow of the crossed trellises again varied their shapes before my eyes"[14]

coherencies, hidden like wounds, within the plots, advancing more rapidly than surface narratives or carrying forward, ahead of their terminal impress, providing them with the strength and pointing to the dangers, the hold and grip of meaning—these are the elements haunting the Nervalian dark and which make for a night, forerunner far less of surrealism than the supernaturalist reverie stradles in its sovereign power, like a still infantile game, the butt of the jokes of those medics grouped around Gautier and Houssaye at the Impasse du Doyenné, but far from an advanced post:

but rather as part of this ever increasingly ample "Movement of the change of forms," which pursues its course through worldly upheavals and the diaspora of instancies, allying itself with

figures interspersed
with narratives

in *all*
languages   a sort of *history of*
the world blended with

fragments of dreams—

*

*   *

Remarkable is the description that Bettina Knapp develops of the successive groups crossed or constituted by Nerval: from Nodier's "Cénacle" to the *Monde Dramatique* group and the happy circle of L'Impasse du Doyenné. She shows how collective interferences may *activate* and at the same time *accentuate* the solitude of writing.

Nothing delineates with greater detail the Nervalian march than Bettina Knapp's beautiful description. She looks after Nerval as Bettina Brentano von Arnim did over Hölderlin—Scardanelli . . .

JEAN PIERRE FAYE

Gérard de Nerval

THE APODAL SWALLOW
Nerval

Now you are theirs—and they in you,
    suspendu,
hovering above, who once descended, in fire
to fire people: Cain and Tubal-Cain and Adoniram.
Jenny, Marie—and others who were one, all
masters of artifice, perpetual promise,
and country girls, virgin as spring dew,
dancing in a lit glade you knew
and could not know.
                No more
the dark frame envelopes you, the debts
to flesh—O, so recalcitrant—
to this and that and wingless Mammon,
crysallis who turned and spun and saw the pit
beyond Cain and Tubal-Cain and Adoniram,
now leap with mantic joy upon the air,
brave apodal swallow—
twirl, glide over glades you need not touch
not ever,
       suspendu
               hanging
by some mystic cord . . .
what matter in an alley?

NICK LYONS

INTRODUCTION

The nineteenth-century poet, essayist, dramatist, and short-story writer Gérard de Nerval was described by his good friend Théophile Gautier as an "apodal swallow." "He was all wings and no feet," Gautier said. "At most he had imperceptible claws; these enabled him to alight, at least momentarily, just long enough to catch his breath, then to go on . . . to soar and move about in fluid realms with the joy and abandon of a being in his element." It was from these ethereal spheres—sometimes terrestrial—that Nerval not only observed his times but reflected and molded them. His writings had a prophetic cast, expressing certain affinities and mystical tendencies that haunted not only him but future generations as well, and particularly our own.

Nerval belonged to a postwar generation, one born of despair. The tremendous losses in manpower during the Napoleonic wars, and the political débacle that followed, culminating with the Restoration, ushered in an atmosphere weighted down with a corrosive sense of futility and lethargy. Like so many of his contemporaries, Nerval was a man for whom the real world was no longer a source of conquest. Rather, those dazzling secret climes—the inner realm—attracted him and became the source of his fascination as well as the *prima materia* for his literary creations.

Sensitive, deeply disturbed by the political events that had preceded him and that had played such havoc in his personal destiny, Nerval approached his existential experience as one does a mystery, with excitement, fervor, and anguish. His universe encompassed two worlds, which became one in his mind: the cosmic domain of the mystic and the workaday world of the man attempting to earn a living from his pen—dream and reality.

Nerval was one of the first French writers to cultivate the dream visions arising from his unconscious and consciously to transpose these into the written word. His images are archetypal; that is, they emanate from his most primitive depths, the collective unconscious, and are endowed with universal and eternal significance. In *Aurélia,* for example, certain aspects of the "great-mother" archetype are transfigured: the gentle, understanding, compassionate, idealized woman; the deceitful, egotistic type; the shadowy eerie figure who spreads terror wherever she appears in a dream; the flighty coquette. The father archetype is likewise included: the old man who tries to explain the complexities of life to the poet whose inner turbulence has reached paroxystic force; the young man who befriends the poet and attempts to "reason" with him. Rings, amulets, mystical numbers, tarot figures, and alchemical images—such symbols, each with vast ramifications, also appear in *Aurélia.* Cataclysmic events are adumbrated, such as the creation of the world, the flood, the judgment day, but they are less Biblical than they are by-products of the poet's desperate anguish.

In the present work an attempt has been made to evaluate Nerval's dreams along philosophical, aesthetic, and psychological lines. Because Nerval was an inveterate reader, a student of alchemy, the Kabbala, Orphism, ancient mystery religions, Sabbean astral worship, illuminism, and theosophy, preoccupations with mystical matters are expressed in a variety of ways in his dream motifs. Brief descriptions of the tenets of the various religious sects that had aroused his interest are woven into this volume in the hope that this will not only lead to a better understanding of Nerval and his times but will also enable readers to draw parallels between his approach and ours today to questions concerning sin, guilt, redemption, and death (implicit in the cults that came under his scrutiny).

In *Voyage in the Orient,* Nerval delves into the ancient Egyptian mysteries and the secrets of the pyramids. Nerval's actual descent into the Great Pyramid (that of Khufu, or Cheops) during his trip to Egypt becomes an initiation, a *rite d'entrée,* into another sphere of thought and feeling. The significance of initiations in general and their value in terms of Nerval in particular are explicated in the chapters that follow in order to point up the importance of such self-disciplinary practices and their goals: the reshaping and re-creating of the human being.

The implications of certain legends in his *Voyage in the Orient* are also extrapolated. What meanings are we to associate with Cain, Abel's killer, who found his way to the center of the earth and discovered the science of metallurgy, which he passed on to his descendants who, in turn, gave it to mankind? What are the implications today of the man-god Hermes Trismegistus—the father of alchemy, the designer and creator of the pyramids?

Why should Nerval have been so attracted to past civilizations, to legends and to myths? Was it a desire to return to the dawn of history, to the "cradle of civilization," to re-create man's life cycle and, in so doing, his own? Was it his way of reliving the myth of the Eternal Return, which so many people in our society experience vicariously through films, television serials, religious experiences, and psychotherapy?

In the *Voyage in the Orient,* Nerval introduces his own interpretation of the Solomon-Sheba legend—not as it appeared in the Bible but as he projected on it. His version includes a new character—Adoniram—the prototype of all innovators and all artists. Adoniram epitomizes the suffering, inner turmoil, and anguish experienced by all creative people from time immemorial, as they attempt to fashion and give birth to the totally new, whether it be form or idea. It is the leap the artist must take from the Uncreated (the world *in potentia*) to the Created (a concretization of amorphous contents) that makes for both his excoriating pain and the sense of achievement and fulfillment that follows. We learn, too, why the great artist (who is always ahead of his time) can never be understood by his contemporaries, and why he becomes a solitary and lonely figure. In this tale Nerval introduces one of the most exquisite figures of all time: the Queen of Sheba, who is awarded not to Solomon, but to Adoniram.

Voyage in the Orient records a series of drug-encountered dreams, those that Nerval claimed led to the founding of the Druse religion. An effort has been made, in this connection, to explicate the fine dividing lines that exist between the dream, the vision of the mystic, drug-induced hallucinations, and the ravings of the insane. What are the differences and the similarities? Does insanity imply an ability to commune more deeply with the forces of the cosmos? What is the significance of religious visions, as reported by such mystics as St. Theresa of Avila, St. John of the Cross, Meister Eckhart, Jakob Boehme, Moses de Leon, and the Mirkabah mystics? Questions relating to drugs, dreams, and so-called insanity are of extreme import today. As a result of contemporary fascination with the irrational, all types of cults have mushroomed: neo-pentecostal groups, the Children of God, the Campus Crusade for Christ, the Catholics United for the Faith, the hasidic groups, the Krishna Consciousness movement, Ramakrishna's meditative disciplines, satanism, witchcraft, black masses, astrology, tarot, alchemy, the Moonies, and many others. Clubs, metaphysical centers, and college courses on mysticism and the occult have burgeoned. Why this need for "religion"—for the irrational, the emotional, the visceral?

Nerval's short story *The Marquis de Fayolle* relates an exquisite love story, in alchemical terms, with mystical and spiritual innuendoes. It encompasses not merely two individuals but mankind in general—not merely one generation but many. In *The King of Bicêtre,* another Nerval tale, the protagonist encounters his double, which he considers a prognostication of death. Love and death are, then, topics for Nerval's meditations, and for ours as well. What is love? What are its implications, qualifications and needs? Particularly in our times, when family structure seems to be breaking up, what do relationships imply? What is death? An end, a beginning, a transformation?

Nerval's sonnets, *Les Chimères,* examples of some of the most extraordinary poetry in the French language, may be considered a cryptic expression of his life experience; they are his version of *The Inferno, Paradise Lost,* and *Faust.*

There is a sense of urgency and of desperation implicit in all of Nerval's writings. One actually feels the faint cry of despair, the haunting and recurring tonalities of sorrow, and even the panic. Nerval's inability to relate to people on a solid footing, the rejection he experienced by those he most loved, and society's indifference to his plight, encouraged him to seek solace in his inner world. It was there, he believed—in his dreams, in the study of ancient religions, in mysticism—that he would discover an answer to his most pressing problems.

As his suffering grew in intensity, he submerged himself more deeply in the occult. And there were valid reasons for his doing so. Because Nerval's mother died shortly after his birth, he had never experienced maternal love and his relationship with his father was always distant and cold. Whenever Nerval fell in love in later years, he divinized the object of his projections—he adulated the ideal, exquisitely beautiful maternal being whom he so longed to possess. Because of this naïve view of women he neglected to take into consideration their negative side and became not only vulnerable to, but the recipient of, their destructive force. Life became a protracted agony. As a way of release, he began fantasizing about women. Rather than worshipping living beings, as he had done in the past, he resorted to spiritual concepts: figures such as Isis and the Virgin Mary, celestial bodies, a star, a planet. In so doing, Nerval felt safe. He could not be rejected. He would never experience the pain of alienation. But there were devastating side effects, for the course he adopted was tantamount to a withdrawal from life, and it led to a withering away of his conscious world. Nerval's dream realm became the most intense and exciting part of his life experience and his sense of the external reality atrophied. Suicide followed.

Such are the dangers involved in submerging oneself too deeply in the dream world, in the domain of the mystic, or in certain drug-oriented cultures. To become overly fascinated with what is buried within is to neglect what lies without. Narcissus was mesmerized by his own image, which he saw reflected in a pool of water. The rest of the world was blotted out. He saw only himself and, in an attempt to grasp his image, he plunged into the pool and drowned. Likewise, when consciousness is overwhelmed by the forces of the unconscious, dissolution of the ego ensues. One may live on physically in such situations, but one is dead psychologically.

Today, in the last quarter of the twentieth century, more and more people are resorting to all types of extreme behavior in an attempt to experience some kind of quick miracle cure for all their ills. The risks are great. Instead of discovering ways and means of understanding their rage, contempt, despair, hopelessness, and immense sense of defeat, they have been enslaved by exotic beliefs and increasingly alienated from society and from themselves. They are not creative people attempting to bring into the world fresh attitudes and new philosophical ways of looking at life. They are not Adonirams. They are unwilling to pay the price of the creative effort, which includes pain and suffering.

To what can one attribute such an emotional slump? In part, perhaps to man's overly optimistic faith in science, in empirical inquiry, in rationalism and logic. Galileo, Descartes, Kepler, Newton, and Copernicus ushered in an era that led modern man to believe that, given enough time and the right equipment, he would succeed in discovering the mysteries of existence and would conquer nature. Goethe, in his *Faust,* warned of the consequences of such an inflated optimism. Few listened. The march of rationalism, science, and technology was on. Reason was worshipped.

What, psychologically, did such an attitude imply? Man became divided. Just as St. Augustine had, centuries earlier, denied the existence of evil in a God-created world,[1] so modern man was divesting himself of his other half—his irrational side. Evil and the irrational were relegated to baser status. They were not to be mentioned in polite society. Nevertheless, both evil and the irrational are part of a whole, of man and nature. To try to destroy these forces is to kill certain qualities within man and nature, paving the way for disharmony. The more man attempts to extirpate evil and the irrational, the more powerful they become.

The eighteenth century was known as the "Age of Enlightenment." Science was making great strides. Diderot, Voltaire, d'Alembert, and many other philosophers and "Encyclopedists" adopted experimentation as their method of procedure and empiricism as their approach to worldly problems. Yet a strange phenomenon occurred. A concomitant rise of mystical, theosophical, and occult sects took place during this period. Indeed, it reached spectacular proportions. The eighteenth century was also the era of Swedenborg, Martinès de Pasqually, Claude de Saint-Martin, Gall, Lavater, Cagliostro, Mesmer, Restif de la Brétonne, and Count Saint-German (to mention but a few); they founded groups and schools, they wrote books and proselytized. Reincarnation, life eternal, resurrections, correspondences between the living and the dead, transmission of thought—all these matters were raised and answers formulated. For decades the irrational had been unnurtured. Now it catapulted forth. One of the most vicious of all blood baths—the French Revolution—broke out at a time when French rationalism had reached its height, when statues to the Goddess Reason had been erected throughout France.

During the nineteenth and twentieth centuries utopianism, idealism, optimism, faith in the perfectibility of man and in "progress" on all levels continued to feed hope to many. Given the proper social armature, economic conditions, and a rational outlook, man would become All-Good, All-Reasonable; there would be peace on earth and the world would be transformed into a Garden of Eden.

Scientific and technological advances have been enormous, to be sure—beyond man's wildest expectations. Material existence has been facilitated. Many diseases have been eradicated. Better communication has permitted greater ease in travel. But other problems have cropped up: a proliferation of matter, new illnesses, environmental pollution, not to speak of two world wars (and a number of other wars almost as destructive), the atomic and nuclear bombs and man's ability to split the earth and destroy himself.

Today, we find ourselves at a turning point in history. We are more aware, perhaps, of the dangers than nineteenth-century man was. Increased consciousness, however, requires greater courage to face, and then to attempt to solve, our problems. How and where does one acquire such courage, such heroism? What are the supreme values for twentieth-century man? Life, when mass murder is de rigueur? Honesty, when corruption proliferates? Individuality, in a collective world? Progress, when occidental culture is in a state of decay? Organized religions, when they no longer seem to answer the needs of the people? Identity? Security?

There are no short-cut answers. No miracles. The era of the mountebank is over. Too many pills have been dispensed to control anger, anguish, sleeplessness, rootlessness, hypertension, and all the other ills that crop up to plague man in the course of a day. Too many religious cults have proliferated, each promising love, comfort, affection, serenity, identity, security—and happiness.

Gérard de Nerval's writings and tragic life uniquely illuminate many of these issues. His spiritual and often irrational ways are the moving drama of an intensely sensitive poet standing at the threshold of a world that is now too much with us by far.

PART I
THE FIRST DARKNESS

The first darkness is mind, to want to know the how and the when . . .
Antonin Artaud, *Sur les Chimères.*

1 GOD IS THE SUN

*When you have shut your doors and darkened your
room, remember, never to say that you are alone;
for you are not alone, God is within, and your
genius is within.*

Epictetus, *Discourses.*

Gérard Labrunie, as he was called before he added the "de Nerval" to
his name, was born on May 22, 1808, around eight o'clock in the evening, at 96 Rue Saint-Martin in Paris. He was baptized on May 23 and
very shortly thereafter given out to nurse at Loisy, not too far from the
capital.

Gérard's father, Etienne Labrunie, was the son of an upholsterer from
Agen, in the South of France. Strong, vigorous and handsome, with a
high forehead, brown hair, and black eyes,[1] he knew or thought he knew
what he wanted in life. He enlisted in the army at the age of sixteen, in
1792. Three years later, during the revolutionary wars, he suffered a
wound in his left leg and was forced to withdraw from active service.
Strong-willed and not one to wallow in despair, he decided to study
medicine. He must have felt that he would be starting on a new and
positive career, and also that he would be in a position to help both his
country and his fellow human beings. After completing his medical studies, he returned in 1806 to Napoleon's Grande Armée.

A year later, he met and married a "woman from the North," Marie-
Antoinette Marguerite Laurent. Her parents were both active in business, as linen merchants on the Rue Coquellière in Paris. She must have
been a very beautiful young woman, with delicate features and pastel-
like skin tones, because Gérard would later describe her in one of his
works as "resembling an engraving called 'La Modestie' of the Proud'hon
or Fragonard period."[2]

Not long after the birth of Gérard, Dr. Labrunie was named physician
adjunct to Napoleon's Grande Armée, and on December 22 he was attached to the forces stationed on the Rhine. Excited at the thought of
being part of such an illustrious military force, the young couple left for
Germany on April 8, 1810, leaving their son in France, perhaps because
army life was too unstable, too difficult. Dr. Labrunie and his wife traveled to the Danube, the Vistula, the shores of the Baltic, Linz. A hard
worker, he rose rapidly in rank and favor, was named director of the
hospital at Hanover, and then later at Glogau in Silesia. His career was
burgeoning, as was his happiness.

Joy is ephemeral. Life in the army exposes one not only to the rigors
of war but also to the almost constant vision of pain. Perhaps Mme.

Labrunie, gentle and rather frail, was not strong enough to stand the strain. One day, after crossing a bridge heaped with cadavers, she suddenly came down with a fever. She died on November 29, 1810, at the age of twenty-five. The Polish Catholic cemetery of Gross-Glogau in "cold Silesia" became her resting place.[3]

Dr. Labrunie pursued his military career. He participated in Napoleon's Russian campaign, was taken prisoner near Smolensk and was again wounded, this time in the left heel at Wilna which left him with a limp for the rest of his days. After his recovery, he again joined Napoleon's army at Moscow, witnessed the burning of the city, and retreated with his emperor. His escape was almost miraculous but he had to leave his life's possessions—including his wife's "letters and jewels"—at the crossing of Beresina.[4]

Gérard, meanwhile, had been sent to live with his maternal granduncle, Antoine Boucher, a grocer and tobacco merchant, and his wife, at Mortefontaine, in the Valois region, one of the most fertile and beautiful areas in France.

Boucher had many attractive qualities that endeared him to the young Gérard. Brought up in the liberal tradition of the eighteenth-century free-thinkers, he was not only a great reader and a fine conversationalist but a collector as well. From a nearby terrain, the "Clos de Nerval," on the site of an ancient Roman camp, Antoine Boucher had gathered together a collection of memorabilia, including old coins, antique medals, vases. He loved antiquity, particularly the Greek and Roman periods, and enjoyed talking about the gods and goddesses who peopled the heavens in those early days. Though Uncle Boucher also had an affinity for nature, he was no recluse. He enjoyed the company of others. His nature was drawn to both the earthly and the invisible realms, the tangible and the intangible. Young Gérard felt comfortable in his presence. They had mutual interests: both of them loved nature, for example, and responded to the forces about them. One day, Gérard reported in one of his later books, he asked his uncle a rather naïve question about divinity. Antoine Boucher, a pantheist at heart, responded by saying, "God is the sun!"

One of Uncle Boucher's most intriguing characteristics was his passion for collecting. He had amassed a whole group of books which he stored in the attic. Gérard frequently mounted the stairs of the Bouchers' quaint little farm house, with its pointed roof and its dormer windows, and remained, for hours on end, in what he considered to be a treasure trove. He thumbed through, or perhaps even read, some of the volumes. A number of them were quite ancient—torn, yellowed with age; others dated back to pre-revolutionary days; a few were half rotted from the dampness or chewed up by rats. But the printing was still legible. These inanimate objects conjured up a world for Gérard. He discovered books on magic, alchemy, theosophy, the Kabbala, and many other areas of the occult. Though he certainly must not have understood the deeper meanings contained within these volumes, he was drawn to them. It was like tasting something from some tremulously exciting foreign land— some mysterious realm. Years later, Gérard wrote that these volumes, which he had read at a most impressionable age, might have been "unhealthy for the soul."[5] He was unprepared for such extratemporal notions, such flights into astral spheres—planets, galaxies, worlds of giants and gnomes.

Gérard's fantasies were being fed at a rapid rate, not only cerebrally, but physically: he responded sensitively to his surroundings. Mortefontaine, in the Oise district, which was not too distant from Paris, could boast of a magnificent forest nearby—the famous Ermenonville. It was in this region that the much-admired writer Jean-Jacques Rousseau had died in 1778. Ermenonville could also pride itself on an exquisite castle built in the style of Henri IV and set at the far end of a large bright green lawn. Its slate-covered roof, its façade of muted-yellow stone stood out in sharp contrast to the park on the opposite end. A fountain, a brilliant lake, small islands with miniature Greeklike structures in the center, enabling some to find refuge in solitude and study, completed the atmosphere of grandeur and beauty. When Gérard described Ermenonville years later, and its variety in both coloring and climate— shiny and shady, dry and wet, warm and cold—he compared the entire area to Watteau's famous painting *The Embarkation for Cythera*. The wistful, nostalgic, dreamlike quality of Mortefontaine reminded him of a Corot oil.[6]

Aside from the remarkably beautiful surroundings, Mortefontaine held further fascination for the young lad. This heavily forested region had once belonged to the great Charlemagne who had been crowned emperor by the pope in 800. Four centuries later, Mortefontaine and its environs were incorporated into the royal domains. In the fourteenth century, Philippe VI, of the Valois family, gave his dynasty's name to the entire area.

Mortefontaine, near the castle of Chantilly, was also the spot where Gérard had first glimpsed the beautiful Sophie Dawes, a woman who was to make an incredible impression upon him. A legend surrounded her name. She was the talk not only of the town and the region but of the nation. Sophie was twenty-five when the prince de Condé, duc de Bourbon, first met her in London where she had been leading a free and easy life. He brought her back to France and introduced her to society as his illegitimate daughter. The prince found her a husband, Adrien Feuchères, made him a baron and bought him the post of lieutenant colonel, and endowed the couple with a large dowry. When Adrien Feuchères finally discovered the truth—that his wife was the prince de Condé's mistress—he was outraged. He demanded a separation, and it was granted.

Sophie continued to exercise great influence over the prince de Condé and it was perhaps at her instigation that he bought the castle of Mortefontaine for her in 1827. The baronne Sophie de Feuchères, sporting a most fashionable riding habit, cut a beautiful figure as she cantered or trotted through her property, and the natives of the area—including Gérard—would look at her either with rapt admiration or, in the case of the more narrow-minded, with anger and disgust.

Gérard developed a habit during his early days at Mortefontaine that remained with him for the rest of his life, that of walking. He spent hours every day tramping through the vast expanse of greenery surrounding the town. He idled over the region's many ruins, associating them with great periods and daring adventures in French history. He loved to observe flowers in their natural habitat, both wild and cultivated, experiencing keen delight in their beauty, wondering why their faces were always pointed upward to the sun, as if this force were beckoning to them. On hot summer days, he bathed in the fresh streams, cleansing his body and feeling a sense of renewal. Even the dark facets of nature absorbed him. The swamps, the shade of the forest—the hidden and tenebrous areas—held him enthralled and fed his fantasy world.

Gérard was not always alone. He listened enraptured to stories and legends that the townspeople related and to the songs of the region that the young girls sang in their play. Something haunting about the incidents in both the tales and the tunes caught his attention. During feast days, he joined the young people of the town in their dances and festivities; he enjoyed looking at the little girls in their Sunday best—their white lace dresses, their long tresses tied tightly behind them with large ribbons.

Despite the beauty of the scenery, the freedom he was given to wander about, alone or in the company of others, the pleasant friendships he enjoyed, and the communion of spirit he felt for his uncle and aunt Boucher, something fundamental was lacking in his life.

He was a branch growing strong, but weakly rooted.

What impressions concerning his parents could the young Gérard conjure up? Only the fantasies and feelings that his uncle, aunt and cousins nurtured within him. His parents, or those strange beings his relatives called his mother and father, were unreal to him—like dreams emerging from some unknown, exciting, tremulous world. Although his uncle and aunt read him, long after her death, the letters that his mother had written to him from the shores of the Baltic, the Spree, or the Danube, they were like so many intrusions into his inner realm from some strange outside world. They were endowed with magic. Each time he saw them or heard their content, they constellated feelings of joy within him, stimulating his already rich imagination. They aroused his curiosity for other lands, for foreign languages and ways, giving birth to a sense of nostalgia for ancient eras and civilizations. Gérard's fantasy life was being fed on absence—on the void.

In 1814 Gérard's carefree country existence came to an abrupt halt: Dr. Labrunie, retired from the army, suddenly reappeared. It happened quite unexpectedly. One day, as Gérard was playing on his uncle's door step, he saw three officers come by and stop. The first one kissed him with such effusiveness that the lad cried out: "My father, you're hurting me!" From this moment, Gérard would write years later, his "destiny changed."[7]

Dr. Labrunie took his son with him to Paris.

Paris was a thriving metropolis at this period, both politically and culturally. Louis XVIII had been restored to the throne of France in 1814 after the Congress of Vienna. He ruled, supposedly, in the spirit of the Charter—that is, as a constitutional monarch. After Napoleon's brief return to power during the Hundred Days, his subsequent defeat at Waterloo, and his exile to the island of St. Helena in 1815, repressive measures were taken by the French government. The ultraroyalists wanted to ensure the peaceful functioning of their government and to make sure there was no further resurgence of rebellious forces. Until 1816 they ruled in the Chamber of Deputies with an iron hand. Riots, which broke out in Paris every now and then, were quelled immediately. Only after the rage and fear aroused by Napoleon's easy accession to power had been spent could a government with a more moderate attitude emerge.

A relatively temperate view prevailed in French political circles for nearly four years. In 1820, however, with the assassination of the king's nephew, the duc de Berry, the situation again suddenly changed. Revenge and a spirit of bitterness paved the way for reaction. An ultraconservative sweep in the government made itself felt even more forcefully. Proscriptions were the rule of the day: the liberties guaranteed the press under the Charter were revoked; civil rights were abolished; espionage was carried out by both police and secret societies, and property qualifications for voters were increased.

When Louis XVIII died, in 1824, his brother, Charles X, came to the throne and with him came an even more reactionary government. His repressive policies, the indemnities granted by his government to emigres for the loss of their land during the French Revolution, the increased power accorded the Jesuits, including their control over public education, fostered dissatisfaction and finally rebellion.

The Revolution of 1830 was not bloody. It was simply an uprising of the people, students and workmen who seized the opportune moment to express their discontent. The July Monarchy brought Louis-Philippe to the throne. Working men, idealists, humanitarian poets and artists who believed so deeply in progress and evolution, all placed their hopes on this new leader. Their hopes were misplaced. They realized only too late that Louis-Philippe's monarchy was very nearly absolute—that his prime minister, the celebrated historian François Guizot, was to carry out the spirit of his authoritarian reign with dynamism and precision. The conditions of the working class and the poor grew worse; corruption and censorship increased.

Though the change in atmosphere, pace, and mores between Mortefontaine and Paris was enormous, Gérard weathered the storm. His father and he moved into a house on 72 Rue Saint-Martin, where Dr. Labrunie continued to practice medicine, but as a civilian physician. His prospects were good in that working-class neighborhood, and certainly this was one of the factors involved in choosing his location.

Dr. Labrunie was so intent upon bringing Gérard up in a highly disciplined manner that he hired a soldier to take charge of his son. A firm believer in physical exercise, in a Spartan regime, he had his son awakened daily at dawn. The soldier then took him walking for several miles outside of Paris, to the nearby hills where both would eat a large breakfast consisting of bread and thick cream. Dr. Labrunie was convinced that a solid body made for a healthy mind. Such a regime, however beneficial it might be for those of sturdy constitution, had deleterious effects for Gérard. Lack of sleep may have aggravated his already tense nature; overindulgence in physical activity exhausted him, and the extreme rigidity in his upbringing gave birth to fear.

Though Dr. Labrunie tried to do his best for his son, neither of them really understood the other. The father, active, strong, realistic in his outlook, accustomed to the sight of horror, suffering, and death, hardened by the rigors of the war, had no patience with his son: a dreamer, withdrawn and relatively passive in his approach to life. Certainly, there were moments when both father and son discovered a common meeting ground: most frequently when Dr. Labrunie would regale him with stories of army life—particularly the years spent in Napoleon's service. For Gérard, Napoleon was no longer a person; he had become a collective image, a myth.

There were moments, however, when Gérard experienced intense sorrow—the time, for example, when his beloved turtle dove flew away. The incident had vast ramifications because it took place after Gérard had answered one of his father's lady friends rather impertinently. He associated his father's remonstrances, his guilt, and the loss of his bird with the lady involved. His despair was so great that it manifested itself physically. He developed a severe case of scarlet fever. After his recovery, his father, undoubtedly moved by his son's loneliness, tried to console him as best he could and gave him a pet monkey which a captain friend had brought back from a distant land. This animal replaced the lost bird and became the lad's constant companion.[8]

In 1830, when Gérard was twelve, he was enrolled at the Lycée Charlemagne. Here he met the future poet, novelist, and art critic Théophile Gautier. Handsome, gentle, and kind, Gautier was a young man possionately devoted to the arts, ballet, theater, painting, the mime. Perceptive, he saw through the world of appearances, down to the essence of things. It was no wonder that he and Gérard became fast friends. Both responded to beauty, both had become deeply committed to literature, both were haunted by the supernatural and the occult. They must have known, intuitively, that theirs would be a lasting friendship.

In school, Gérard studied the humanities and languages, and also dancing, dramatics, and the rudiments of music. Though he took courses in Italian, Greek, Latin, German, Arabic, and Persian, he had a particular penchant for German. This was understandable. His father, who had lived in Germany for some years, spoke the language fluently and helped his son with his studies. More important, perhaps, was the fact that he associated this language with his mother, who had died and been buried in "cold Silesia."

Gérard was a fine student. There were times when he even seemed rather competitive, at least on an intellectual level. He entered a contest sponsored by the French Academy, which awarded a prize to the best essay written on "A History of the French Language and Literature from 1500–1600." Gérard did not win. He must have been annoyed and even angered by the outcome because he did not accept his failure passively; he wrote a verse satire entitled "The Academy and its Unfindable Members." The prize for Latin verse was awarded to Gérard in his class in rhetoric.[9]

Gérard had begun writing poetry at the age of thirteen—and he looked like a poet. Of medium height and slender build, he walked with grace and ease. There was something arresting about his features: his blond hair fell in soft waves about his face; an expression of tenderness and understanding radiated from his eyes; though his nose was small, it had character; a smile was frequently discernible behind his rather thinly defined lips. He was warm and ingratiating.

Gérard loved to write poetry. Though the themes, the imagery, the very structure of his verses were far from unique—indeed, they were common to the literary trends of the time—they had a whimsical quality worthy of attention. He had filled two notebooks with his verse, and years later he treasured these volumes. They were concrete examples, he wrote, of his youth—something which lived on after this period of his life had vanished into oblivion.

To write poetry was *à la mode*, particularly among the young. Victor Hugo, Alphonse de Lamartine, Alfred de Vigny, Alfred de Musset, and many others had written and were busily at work composing odes, satires, and sonnets. Gérard was impressed and inspired. In 1824 he composed a poem to Napoleon's glory: *Napoleon's Farewell to France,* another, *The Exile's Return,* and in some later verses, the emperor took on the power of a solar god.[10] Napoleon was endowed with an unearthly aura and came to represent everything that was wonderful, powerful, and courageous—to a young lad who unconsciously may have considered himself to be just the opposite.

> Just like the Phoenix, he is reborn from his ashes
> He can dare all, undertake all . . .

Until 1820, the year of Antoine Boucher's death, vacation time had always been spent at Mortefontaine. Gérard looked forward to the rural atmosphere, to the release he enjoyed with his uncle and his Mortefontaine friends. It was a welcome change from the constricting atmosphere of his father's home. Dr. Labrunie's decision to bring two domestics from Mortefontaine back to Paris, Jeanette and Fanchette, pleased Gérard greatly because they were constant reminders of the happiness he associated with the place. Gérard later claimed that he had had a crush on Fanchette and had dreamt about her as his bride and also about the whole fascinating wedding ceremony that such a union would have entailed.

Not only had his uncle's death left a void in his heart, but in 1826 his aunt, Eugénie Laurent, his mother's sister, had died. Gérard had not only associated her with his own mother, but had grown attached to her kindly ways. His aunt and his mother had died at the same age, at twenty-five.

By 1826, at the age of eighteen, Gérard had finished his studies at the Lycée Charlemagne and asked to leave Paris. But he could not go to Mortefontaine because the house in which he had lived there was now inhabited by Uncle Boucher's daughter, Elise, who was in the process of selling it to the baronne Sophie de Feuchères, the woman with that international reputation. Gérard's problems were solved—for the moment—when his grandaunt by marriage (Geneviève Paris), and her second husband (the comte de Saint-Projet) offered him hospitality at their home in Saint-Germain, not far from Paris.[11]

Here Gérard met his two charming cousins, both nieces of the comte de Saint-Projet, Justine and Sophie de Lamaury. They were beautiful, even dazzling. Gérard fell in love with Sophie, or so he would claim in later years. Though Gérard must have smarted at her rejection of him, he enjoyed the company of both young girls, separately and together. The three young people used to take long walks in the forest of Saint-Germain, the fields spread far about. They chatted away, singing the songs of the region, jumping over the streams, counting the rocks. But his infatuation with Sophie went unrequited. Adding insult to injury, she married someone else in 1828.

Gérard was attracted to the castle of St. Germain, with its terrace and galleries, a monument that had once housed the great kings of the French Renaissance, Francis I and Henry II. As he wandered around the castle grounds, examining every nook and cranny, he thought dreamily of times past when life had "seemed" thrilling, when strength, courage, tenacity and passion had been the rule of the day. A longing for some other era, for some other place, grew within him.[12]

It was during his stay at Saint-Germain that Gérard decided to undertake his first important piece of writing and to make his entrée into literature.

The young literati of the 1820s were searching for the intangible. Their works were rooted in discontent. They belonged to a generation living at a crossroads. Values were changing. Politically, the climate had altered too rapidly: monarchy, revolution, the Napoleonic era, the Restoration—and with all the social, philosophical and economic unrest that these rapid modifications of focus brought in their wake. In what could youth believe? What credo could they adopt in such an unstable world? What way of life would be theirs?

Gérard and others like him—Victor Hugo, Alphonse de Lamartine, Alfred de Vigny—had been born too late to experience the fire and frustration that had made for the French Revolution of 1789, the hatred that had inspired the Reign of Terror, the compulsion for conquest that was fostered during the Napoleonic wars. But they felt the emotional aftermath of these traumatic events—and most poignantly. Their personalities grew more complex, less stable; their vision became clouded; their moods vacillated from the depths of despair to extreme elation and exaltation and back again. Nervousness, torment, intensity, passion marked their every endeavor. A cleavage became apparent between the real world about them and the realm of fantasy in which they sought refuge.

As the workaday world grew more and more intolerable, so the need for some strong, courageous figure—a hero—became a necessity. The young people did not recognize that Napoleon Bonaparte was a destructive and negative force—a megalomaniac, a murderer, a man who had thrust France into a series of almost unacceptable humiliations, an instigator of terror and death. Few looked upon his rule analytically. Youth saw in this emperor a bundle of energy, a giant, an eagle—a conqueror who brought grandeur, albeit ephemeral grandeur, to France. Both liberals and idealists believed Napoleon had carried out the real "spirit" of the French Revolution, and that he had introduced real social reforms in the document known as the Napoleonic Code. Napoleon loomed larger than life. Victor Hugo later alluded to this conqueror as one "whose colossal hand built an empire," Gérard, as a "half-God who had been vanquished, but who rose great even" in death.[13]

The disproportion between dream and reality increased as the Napoleonic image took on an ever more mythic vigor. The greater the adulation, the keener the despair with one's earthly lot. Feelings of melancholia, hypersensitivity, and dissatisfaction manifested themselves in a fresh approach to literature. Nature became the repository of all of man's emotions—joys, sorrows, anger, beatitude. Such feelings had certainly been alive before the holocausts. Jean-Jacques Rousseau had expressed them in his novel *The New Héloïse* and in his *Confessions*. Indeed, he had created a new type of lyricism that seemed to embrace the entire cosmos in one fell swoop. Rousseau responded viscerally to nature's moods. And in his turn, François-René de Chateaubriand, whom Hugo labeled the "Sachem du Romantisme," transformed Rousseau's single cry of despair into a collective experience.

Chateaubriand influenced a whole generation of poets and novelists. With the publication of his narrative *René* (1802), attitudes of self-pity, suffering, perpetual ennui, restlessness, and introspection flooded the literary scene. The cultivation of states of morbidity gave rise to what was to be called the *mal du siècle*.

Chateaubriand might have been a painter. He splashed his verbal frescoes with brilliant and somber hues, always reflecting the mood of the character he described—himself, really. His landscapes became dreamscapes, sounding boards for his vague passions and torments. The pain suffered by his hero René was diffused and without remedy; action was meaningless; suicide might provide the only answer. Chateaubriand expressed his torment in a language comparable to groups of musical notations—like heaving waves or infinitesimal ripples, he transformed the emotions and sensations onto the written pages. His words acted and reacted upon the reader's sensibilities.

Pessimism, solitude, negativism swept over the youth of France as other writers added to this sense of futility. Etienne de Senancour's fictional hero *Obermann* (1804), a pessimist, withdrew from society altogether. In solitude, he spent his days delving within himself, attempting to discover his identity. He probed, analyzed, explicated his every motive, thought, whim, and sensation in the greatest detail. But his sick soul was forever confronted with a growing abyss. Strangely enough, the void that Obermann experienced was no longer considered something negative. It was, on the contrary, something to be cultivated! It had the power of arousing delightful and voluptuous sensations. Melancholia was not to be avoided. It filled one's existence with ineffable joy, with a sense of belonging—of belonging at least to the "community" of other suffering souls. Melancholia was to be longed for!

Adolphe, Benjamin Constant's literary hero, had no will at all. Acutely intelligent, he was forever dissecting (and with great lucidity) his own tendencies and emotions. He examined both his inner and outer worlds: one part of him observed the other, and each part prevented the other from acting decisively in any situation. It was as if he were double, a complex of opposites: a man in love but incapable of loving; a man who wanted to leave his mistress but longed to remain at her side. No solace was available to such a person. Indecisiveness, perpetual conflict, and turmoil enabled him to wallow in despair—and to write about it.

Some young people attempted to escape from the prevailing atmosphere of hopelessness and doom by going to the other extreme. They caroused, got "drunk on poetry and love." Known as Bohemians, they sought to be different in all ways. They cut their hair in the *mérovingien* style: a lock resting on their forehead and in the back, their rather long hair, which reached down to their shoulders, cut straight all the way around. Fastidious in their dress, they favored long cloaks, high hats, brightly polished shoes. Habitués of cafés, theaters, and night spots, they also frequented charming little *bistrots* and gaudy dance halls. Instability marked their relationships and attitudes toward life. Joy, romance, and love were their sole concerns. They were mad about life and wanted to live it frenetically, intensely—so long, that is, as their pocket money held out. Their sentimental escapades frequently led to tears, heartache, and suicide. Balzac described their strange ways and their proving grounds (the Latin Quarter of Paris) in such novels as *Lost Illusions.* Henri Murger dramatized their exciting lives in his *Scenes from Bohemian Life,* which Giacomo Puccini transformed into the romantic opera *La Bohème.*

Alfred de Musset was one of these romantics. Always in love, he celebrated his various liaisons in poignant verse. His famous affair with the feminist novelist George Sand rocked Europe. Her rejection of him sent him into a frenzy of despair, but he turned his sorrow into a veritable credo. It was pain that compelled him to write his most beautiful love poetry. Inspiration, he said, resides in the heart. The heart must be touched, troubled, anguished in order to respond, to inspire, to become the fully creative instrument that it is. *"Ah! frappe-toi le coeur, c'est la qu'est le génie!"*

Alfred de Vigny felt quite differently about love. When the flighty and unfaithful actress Marie Dorval cast him aside, nothing—neither religion nor nature—alleviated his sorrow, and he set about preaching a philosophy of stoic resignation. In his poem *The Wolf,* for example, he declared that nothing is more noble than bearing one's pain in silence, nothing more praiseworthy than mastering one's emotions and actions. Only then does man behave with dignity.

Victor Hugo was of yet another temperament. Energetic, fiery, passionate, he defended both the throne and the church. In later years, his attitude would change: Napoleon would be his hero and liberalism his banner. Hugo's verbal prowess had become obvious to discerning readers of his *Odes* and *Ballads* at the very start of his career. A powerful imagination as well as an attraction for the monstrous, for blood and gore, became evident in the fantastic and legendary world he evoked in his novel *Han d'Islande* (1825).

These young romantics—and Gérard, who joined their fold—rejected the ultrarational and cerebral approach to life, art, religion that had prevailed in the eighteenth century. Diderot, Voltaire, the Encyclopedists and the ideologues, were set aside. These eighteenth-century rationalists, who had despised dogmatism and believed science to be the answer to man's problems, and who had cultivated the "fact" and rejected the "a priori," did not meet the needs of the new generation.

French writers, particularly such a one as Alphonse de Lamartine, responded favorably to the works of the English writers of this period— Byron, Shelley, Keats, Scott, Wordsworth—who lived in the realm of emotion, of elective affinities. In his poem *The Lake* Lamartine personified nature and endowed this unique force with new tonalities. The marvels of the universe, as he viewed them in their myriad manifestations—rocks, trees, mountains, lakes, sun, moon—spoke to him, responded to the depth of his feelings. He endowed the visible world with cosmic breath; he expanded man's vision. When reading a poem by Lamartine aloud, one can hear "a soul sighing" from the pain of love or of abandon—the rapture over nature.

English literature was not solely responsible for fostering this new mystique. German aesthetic and philosophical movements also accounted for the change in focus. Mme. de Staël was most instrumental in introducing the new German field of vision into France at the turn of the century. This woman, who combined in her person both intelligence and feeling—reason and passion, who had traveled widely, and who had written widely on philosophical and romantic subjects, became a leading proponent of romanticism. "I cannot separate my ideas from my feelings," she declared. "How can one distinguish one's talent from one's soul? How can one impose silence on feelings that live within us and not lose, at the same time, the ideas that these feelings enable us to discover."

Mme. de Staël had traveled to Frankfort, Weimar, and Berlin in 1803. Four years later she went to Munich, Vienna, and again back to Weimar. She met and became friendly with such figures as Goethe and Schiller and Auguste-Wilhelm Schlegel, who became her son's tutor. It was Schlegel who introduced her in depth to German *Kultur,* who spent long hours explaining to her the philosophies of Kant and Klopstock, the marvels of Lessing. In Weimar she found the intelligentsia to be liberal of mind, open to discussion. Their company was scintillating. The France to which she returned, ruled by Napoleon, whom she looked upon as a dictator, represented repression, bigotry, and decay. Mme. de Staël associated her own liberation and her personal joy with Germany, which became the land of her ideal.

Mme. de Staël reiterated Schlegel's statements in her writings: the South is classical and the North, romantic. The phrase became a slogan, a banner for the romantics. The Northern regions—Germany in particular—Mme. de Staël declared, gave rise to a culture based on pro-

found thoughts and emotions, greater individuality and spirituality. The South—she meant France—was superficial, materialistic, and dogmatic. An optimist, as were many romantics when it came to the political and economic sphere, she believed in the perfectibility of man and envisaged the future of humanity as free and progress as complete.

Literary groups known as Cénacles, in which new ideas were aired, burgeoned in Paris. Poets, artists, critics, musicians—Chateaubriand, Hugo, Musset, and others—were formulating and codifying varied aesthetic, religious, and political credos. The most famous Cénacles of the 1820s were those of Etienne Delécluze, Charles Nodier, and Victor Hugo.

Delécluze, art critic for the *Journal des Débats,* and his friends (including the well-known writers Stendhal and Prosper Mérimée) were liberal and ferociously anticlerical (anti-Catholic).

Mérimée's caustic pen took the church and its clerics to task in both his short stories and plays. *The Theater of Clara Gazul* was a prime example of this kind of writing. He pointed out the materialism of the men of cloth, their power drives, their possessive and autocratic activities in France, Spain, and South America—their lust.

Stendhal's romanticism, exemplified in *The Red and the Black* and *The Charterhouse of Parma,* poured out disdain for the sentimental, lyrical, and overly emotional styles so popular in his day. His approach was sober and analytical. Though his fiction has been considered melodramatic at times, it was acutely realistic, written in a detached, objective, and psychologically penetrating style. Stendhal's cult of individualism, energy, adventure, courage was evident not only in his literary creations but in his intense admiration of Napoleon.

Charles Nodier's Cénacle, the one Gérard frequented, was promonarchy and prochurch. Nodier, who had been named librarian of the Arsenal in 1824, invited young writers and artists to dine at his home once a week, usually on Sundays, where they stayed on far into the night discussing the literary and political themes of the day. Nerval, Hugo, Vigny, Musset, Dumas, and Balzac enjoyed this community of spirit, though Hugo later broke away and founded his own Cénacle.

Nodier was a rather strange human being. A brilliant scholar, he had written on a variety of subjects: linguistics, history, botany, theater. But he seemed to be happiest in his own world of fantasy. The supernatural, the world of dreams, the exotic, and the satanic held sway in his short stories and plays. Influenced by Goethe's ultramelancholic hero Werther, whose unrequited love ended in suicide, Nodier became fascinated with the growth and intensity of feelings, particularly those centered around love. He was haunted by invisible but real forces, which seemed to surround him—by outer-worldly entities.

Nodier was a mystic. Because of his theosophic tendencies, he could be considered a product of his times, the nineteenth century. He did not represent the ideations of the ideologues or the Encyclopedists, but echoed the feelings and sentiments of the Illuminists, a type of underground movement that flourished as a counterpoise to empirical and logical reasoning. Man's arcane world fascinated Nodier—the subliminal regions, the dream, and the parapsychological phenomena. Interestingly enough, there were more books published on the nature of sleep and the dream—the "irrational"—in the eighteenth century—a "rational" era—than at any other period in history but our own.[14]

A world of mystery, magic, and prophecies made itself felt most acutely in the eighteenth century. That it did so is understandable if one keeps in mind the sociopsychological fact that the more one aspect of the human psyche (in this case eighteenth-century rationalism) is emphasized by some, the greater is the tendency of others to seek a balance in its opposite (the irrational). The scientists, the ideologues, the philosophes of the so-called Age of Enlightenment were quite certain that the world about them, the external realm, was the real world. They believed this to be true because their sense perceptions told them so. The goal of knowledge, they claimed, was to learn how to use the organs necessary to acquire greater knowledge. Once this was accomplished, man would acquire more and more power over nature, and over himself as well. One day, man would know *all* the answers.

Others felt cut off from the world about them—now that everything hidden had been brought out into the open and nature had been divested of its myths and hidden secrets. Everything had suddenly become clear cut: each entity, each facet of life, had a cause and an effect; man and the cosmos were open for dissection. But for those who sensed that the universe was not a cut-and-dried affair, feelings of isolation grew and with these feelings a need for comfort. They longed to believe in an all-encompassing divinity, in an eternal, omnipotent and omniscient force. As a result, occult societies grew at a rapid pace. Their credos answered man's need for the sacred. Many lost "souls" flocked to the meeting places—churches and lodges—opened by the Pietists, theosophists, Neoplatonists, Rosicrucians, Masons, Martinists, Swedenborgians, Quietists.[15] These societies, each in its own way, reaffirmed what the Italian and German philosophers of the Renaissance—Paracelsus, Nicolas de Cusa, Giordano Bruno, and others—had posited: that the universe is "a living being with a soul" and that "all beings are united via an essential identity and are merely emanations of the whole."[16]

Nodier's immense knowledge, his constant search into the world beyond the visible and the scientifically comprehensible, fascinated Gérard. Nodier provided a sanctuary for the young writer-to-be whose existential solitude, if not felt more keenly than that of others, was to be experienced in a unique manner.

Gérard had chosen a literary career. His father, Dr. Labrunie, had other plans.

2 HER INNOCENCE SHINES
WITH SUCH RADIANCE

Two souls contend
In me and both souls strive for masterdom,
Which from the other shall the scepter rend.
The first soul is a lover, clasping close
To this world tentacles of corporal flame,
The other seeks to rise with mighty throes
To those ancestral meadows whence it came.
Goethe, *Faust*

When Gérard was nineteen years old and still living with his relatives at Saint-Germain-en-Laye he completed a French translation of Goethe's *Faust.* He had always been fascinated by the Faust myth.[1] One day, when he was still very young, he stopped in front of a book shop on the Boulevard Beaumarchais. A certain volume had caught his eye: Frederick-Maximilian Klinger's novel *The Adventures of Dr. Faust and his Descent into Hell* (1802). The engravings that adorned this edition were terrifying and bewitching, enough to give any youngster nightmares. One illustration featured an enormous Leviathan with wind-blown hair, his eyes and mouth vomiting flames, who held a little twisted and bent Faust between his fingers. The price of the volume—ten or fifteen francs—was far too much for him, and because he could not afford to purchase the book, he returned daily to thumb through its pages. The book dealer, concerned for the condition of his merchandise, decided to place the volume under lock and key. Gérard decided to save his money and purchase it at some future date. At the end of two weeks he returned only to find, much to his dismay, that the shop had vanished: the dealer had died and Klinger's *Faust* had been sold at auction.[2]

There were other reasons which impelled Gérard to undertake a translation of Goethe's *Faust.* In a letter to his father many years later, he wrote: "It is you who taught me German."[3] German had acted as a link between his father and himself, a point of contact between two such different people, perhaps the one way Gérard had of communicating with a man so rigid and armylike. Also Mme. Labrunie had lived and died in "cold Silesia," and for this reason Gérard longed to become acquainted with what he considered to be a mysterious land. His mother had never taken on any reality for him. She had always been a type of fantasmagoria, an evanescent figure. With the passage of time, he endowed her with the characteristics of an "angel." Mme. Labrunie was perfection.

Germany had a variety of alluring features, particularly for budding French poets. Hadn't Mme. de Staël, in her volume *De l'Allemagne,* popularized the philosophical and aesthetic renaissance taking place in Germany at this period? Weren't German poets and artists also rebelling against the stress placed on science and technology and the industrial advances taking place in their land? They too despised the sordid conditions of everyday life, the ugliness of their cities, the poverty and destitution they saw about them. They were likewise overwhelmed with feelings of melancholia and an intense desire to escape.[4]

Philosophers and poets such as Novalis, Schelling, the two Schlegels, and Tieck believed that nature was a living organism and not merely a mechanism capable of being reduced to its various components or elements. Unable to face the ugly realities of the industrial civilization rising up around them, the young German romantics began living in a dream world. Some became lotus-eaters; others fed on art, music, poetry, and philosophy. The intensity of their suffering, the turmoil they experienced and described in detail in their works, fostered a new aesthetic, a fresh way of viewing life.[5]

Novalis and Tieck, among other German writers, established what has been called an "autocracy of the imagination." In opposition to the eighteenth-century ideologues and Encyclopedists, they distrusted the world of appearances and longed to commune with a profounder realm in which the Divine would make His presence manifest. They believed that Man's Fall from Paradise as related in the Bible, which had led to his earthly existence, was tantamount to a separation from God. Because man was no longer "one" with Divinity, he had become divided and so belonged to two spheres: the world of matter (the earth) and that of spirit (the Divine realm). Life on earth for the poet then became a long search, a way to experience that primordial unity with God or the existence he had known before the Fall, before his birth.

To be united with divinity could be experienced, they suggested, during certain moments in life—in periods of ecstasy or illumination when the individual, divested of his identity, flows into the All or the Universal Force.[6] Man's earthly existence, therefore, consists of an unending desire for oneness with God or with the Cosmic Soul. Life (the birth of man) is looked upon as a separation from God, and so death, in this context, becomes a return to Him. From such a vantage point, death is not to be feared or treated as something ugly. It is merely a *rite de passage,* an initiatory process into another existence.[7] The cosmic way then consists of perpetual flux, of eternal Becoming, a series of "assimilations" and "dissolutions." Everything in the cosmos is subject to metamorphosis and, therefore, engenders perpetual communion with the All, or with God.

The poetry of Novalis is a superb example of the new emphasis placed on the cosmic realm and a concomitant devaluation of the world of "reality," or of "appearances." Novalis had lost his beloved fiancée Sophie von Kühn when she was very young, and his life had been transformed into a veil of tears. "I am surrounded by an ineffable feeling of solitude since Sophie's death," he said. "The entire world is dead for me."[8]

With time, however, Novalis came to look upon Sophie's death as part of a universal process. She was, in effect, fulfilling her destiny, permitting herself to progress through a series of stages, successive reincarnations that would lead eventually to a "higher reality." Death, for Novalis, became not an end, nor was it something to be evaded. On the contrary, "Death was to him but the Gate of life." In *Hymns to the Night,* Novalis wrote: "A union even in death—is a marriage—which gives us a companion for the night. It is in death that love is the sweetest; for he who loves, death is a wedding night—the secret of most tender mysteries."[9] Since existence was eternal and limitless then man's earthly sojourn became an "infinitesimal" part of the Whole, a passing from one form of being to another.

In *The Disciples at Sais,* Novalis describes nature as a vast "self," as, paradoxically, both independent and yet related to the Whole or to the Infinite. The poet, by means of his art, may be able to come into contact with the Infinite because his imagination can transcend the illusory world of appearances via a descent into self. "Every descent into self— every glance inward—is at the same time an ascension—assumption— a vision of real external reality."[10] It is within these inner regions that primordial unity may again be experienced.[11] During such moments, the individual experiences the *numinosem;* and mundane images are thrust out of his mind, which is freed from concern with the superficial and yet capable of remaining active and perceptive. In such a contemplative state, the poet becomes conscious of his vision or intuition and his mind dips into the ineffable, that world which transcends feeling and sight—that central region of the soul which unites the individual with the Eternal, with the All.

That Gérard felt a particular affinity for the poetry of the German romantics is quite understandable. Their metaphysical notions, as expressed by Novalis, opened up new worlds for him, permitted him to delve into the realm of eternal Becoming, of the "universal Soul." It gave Gérard, so lonely an individual, a sense of belonging, of being part of the whole.

Gérard's rapprochement with Goethe's ideations were even more intense. Goethe not only believed in a universal soul but that all things— both visible and invisible—were endowed with life, each instant, each object, each spatial configuration. "The eternal lives in all things; only in appearance and in certain instances does it become immobile . . ."[12] Unlike many romantics, however, Goethe felt that poetry, as well as any art form, was an act of volition. In the creation of the work of art, inspiration and intuition were necessary but not sufficient; the poet had to use his will or his reason to control, to fashion, what lived *in potentia* within the unconscious. The writer must, therefore, struggle with form, must tame the elements that emerge helter skelter from his subliminal realm.[13]

Goethe's *Faust* is a dramatic presentation of a myth, that of an aged scholar who had spent his life in the pursuit of knowledge and had finally come to realize that he had by-passed life, that he had never known love. Since myths are conglomerates of archetypal projections emanating from the collective unconscious they are frequently able to reveal the unconscious situations of the creator of the myth as well as the psychic condition of those who project upon it.

What are the psychological implications of the Faust myth in terms of Gérard? Faust, let us recall, who had been so well versed in theology, law, medicine, alchemy, magic, longed for infinite knowledge.[14] He became a symbol of man's hubris, his eternal desire to equal God. In ancient times the Tower of Babel and Prometheus myths illustrated the restrictions placed upon man by a higher power and the punishments meted out to him each time he insisted upon destroying the cosmic balance by altering the role he played in the universe. Faust's unquenchable desire to know all, his restlessness, and his constant search is his way of denying the finite world and, in so doing, rejecting the laws of nature.[15] If man were to discover the secrets of nature's mysteries (birth, death, immortality) he would be destroying the peaceful coexistence of all cosmic creatures and as such would not be fulfilling his specific function on earth. From such a point of view, Faust may be looked upon as a destroyer, as a daemonic force, bent on divesting nature (or God) of its omnipotence and omniscience.[16]

Faust is likewise a symbol of the man who has repressed his instinctual life, rejected his human qualities. His one-sided life has been spent in intellectual pursuits. When he realizes how little he really knows, how narrow his world has been, he longs to enlarge his collective experience—to know joy and sorrow, the flesh and the spirit, the great and the small.[17]

Two figures in the drama represent Faust. Wagner, his assistant, stands for Faust's intellectual half, the part of himself that seeks to know all. Mephistopheles represents Faust's unconscious negative qualities—those aspects of himself that he had rejected and that are alluded to in Jungian terminology as the "shadow."

Wagner says, "Though I know much, I want to know everything."[18] As his influence over Faust becomes more pronounced (or as Faust's thinking function usurps greater power), his attitude becomes increasingly one-sided. As a result, tension (libido, or psychic energy) is created between his cerebral and instinctual halves, making his situation virtually untenable. Faust is a man possessed: a victim of imbalance. Only through a dissociation or destruction of his present "thinking" orientation (that is, of what Wagner represents) could he begin to live in harmony with himself.[19]

In Faust's attempt to experience the Absolute, that is, the whole of life's experience, he divests himself of his "wisdom," those forces which had maintained some semblance of equilibrium within. When he evokes the *Spiritus Mundi* but fails to conjure up those forces that could bring him fulfillment a feeling of uneasiness invades his being.

Faust leaves his lodgings and wanders about the town. He is depressed, suffering from a type of deflation: the realization of the vast amounts of knowledge he has not yet grasped. Though the citizens of the town look upon him favorably, remembering how his father had helped them through the terrible plague, Faust knows the medical man's limitations only too well.

Back in his study, Faust begins translating the Gospel according to St. John: "In the beginning was the word. . . ." A dog enters, its shadow increasing in size until it invades the entire room. Faust attempts to understand this phenomenon in a scientific and analytical manner but is unable to do so.

Whereupon Mephistopheles emerges and introduces himself as "the spirit of destruction." His goal: to abolish Faust's one-sided attitude and to permit him to experience life in all its unity.[20]

Gérard quotes Mme. de Staël in his preface to *Faust* and declares Mephistopheles to be a "civilized devil," devoid of claws and a tail, an alluring and attractive force and therefore all the more difficult to recognize and consequently more dangerous.[21]

As Faust's shadow, Mephistopheles represents his opposite, both physically and emotionally. While Faust yearns for beauty and love, Mephistopheles' notion of enjoyment is being carefree and irresponsible. Mephistopheles brings Faust "down to earth," enabling him to live physically by providing him with the beautiful Gretchen. He describes Faust: "There is nothing terrestrial about him, neither does he drink nor eat. His spirit is always spanning space . . ."[22] Faust in such a context is an abstraction, representing the "symbol of aspiration."[23] Mephistopheles likewise encourages Faust to deny the Christian notion of asceticism, which had been instrumental in Faust's rejection of the physical world.

With Mephistopheles, Faust goes to a tavern where a witch gives him a brew that rejuvenates him. He now sees himself as a young and handsome man and is beside himself with excitement. He has a vision of Helen of Troy in a mirror, and Mephistopheles tells him that "With that drink in your body, you'll see Helen in every woman."[24] Never having experienced human relationships with his senses or his feelings, Faust doesn't know how to handle himself. Like a child eating sweets for the first time, he seeks complete and immediate gratification.

Faust succumbs to the world of his senses (or of "illusion"), seduces Gretchen, and experiences his opposite side. Divested of his cerebral "wisdom," he has lost all perspective and become a passive agent. He now identifies as completely with his instincts as he had previously identified with his cerebral side.

Faust looks upon the naïve Gretchen as an "angel," a manifestation of some divinity, as purity personified, as the Immaculate One. Without insight, unable to discriminate or to individualize, he is, in this respect, like Epimetheus, the "afterthought." Gretchen is not an angel; she is a simple country girl brought up in a conventional manner to be devout and good.

For Faust, Gretchen has become a collective image, that of the eternal feminine. But she is an object for him, and as such no real relationship can come of their meeting. Faust seduces her, makes her pregnant, and kills her brother. Only when he learns that Gretchen has murdered her baby and been imprisoned for doing so does he suddenly become conscious of the role he has played in her life.

But Faust experiences consciousness in revolt and anger. His immediate reaction is to blame Mephistopheles for his plight. But the more Faust reviles his enemy, the more potent a figure Mephistopheles becomes. He "accuses" Faust of having wanted to possess what he was incapable of handling. "Why do you consort with us . . . if you can't go through with it? You want to fly and then you get dizzy. Is it you or we who make the advances? Who destroyed her? I or you?"[25]

Unable to accept blame for his own acts, Faust becomes all the more irate. He is ready to kill Mephistopheles, who then replies: "You are looking for a thunderbolt? It is well that it wasn't given to you miserable mortals. To crush the first innocent person they meet, is the way tyrants relieve themselves of embarrassment."[26]

What is Faust trying to kill when he seeks to destroy Mephistopheles? His own negative qualities, which have run wild. He is outraged by his own blindness, by the fact that he had been victimized by his subliminal forces, that all objectivity, vision, and perspective had been destroyed. For the first time, his polarities have come into focus: his former cerebral attitude and his present hyperphysical way. He sees himself divided and in so doing experiences consciousness. It is at this point that he asks Mephistopheles to take him to Gretchen.

For Gérard, Gretchen assumes the greatest importance, for she represents to him an aspect of the feminine principle, or archetype.

This archetype, as we have seen, was first experienced by Faust in a negative manner: the witch who gave him the magic brew that transformed him into a handsome young seducer. This negative transcendental force also gave him the necessary equipment to bring him to his senses. When Mephistopheles took him to the Witches' Sabbath at Blocksberg, following his liaison with Gretchen, Faust experienced the extremes of lust, rioting, and instinctuality, but he soon became bored with it all and, finally, aware of the wrong he had done.

As represented by Gretchen, the feminine archetype stands for purity, spirituality, and earthiness as well. She is more sensitive than Faust and feels the two warring factions within his nature. She is also repelled unconsciously by Mephistopheles and experiences this aspect of Faust because she lives a natural existence; she is close to the earth and understands intuitively that Mephistopheles will be a threat to her.

In psychological terms, Gretchen is an "anima" figure. The anima may be defined as an autonomous complex that represents man's unconscious inner attitude toward woman. Anima figures as they appear in dreams, myths, and literary works of all types are usually the repository for feelings or notions that are not discernible in man's outer attitude. They are, therefore, highly revelatory of both the author's feelings and the inner unconscious state of those who project onto such figures.[27]

The fact that Faust was unable to see Gretchen as she really was indicated that he was identifying with this anima figure. The ego (or conscious attitude) and the persona (the mask used to adapt to the environment), were not properly differentiated. Since no rapport between the ego and the persona existed (they were identical), no relationship was possible between the conscious and the unconscious attitudes. The ego was not autonomous (independent or objective) in its attitude, as it should have been. Rather, it was dominated by the persona. As such, the ego could not relate to the "processes of the unconscious" and therefore the anima held sway. Because the anima remained unconscious, no application of the thinking or rational function within a being could be forthcoming; it was experienced in projection on a real person. One who is the victim of anima projection is doomed to suffer great passions and great disappointments; there is little possibility for such a person to adapt to the object of his projection in a conscious manner since his ego does not experience this persona objectively.

Faust, then, was a man who had become identified with his persona, his handsome, physical self.[28] Lacking perspective, he remained subservient to the anima, becoming its tool; and he failed to build any kind of relationship with the beloved object before him, Gretchen. Faust's conscious adaptation to the anima figure was not possible so long as he remained unconscious of his problem. If he could have distinguished between the object of his affection and the real earthly Gretchen, his former attitude would have been depotentiated, its power would have diminished, and the projection would have vanished.[29]

Judging from the manner in which Gérard described Gretchen in his preface, i.e., as perfection, she had become an angel for him, too. She was an anima figure par excellence. She is not, Gérard declared, the typical heroine of melodramas. On the contrary, she is a type that one may meet with rather frequently in real life and is all the more touching for this very reason. She is superior to the "vulgar loves" of Don Juan "and to Manfred's Astarte."[30] Gérard called her speech to Faust in the prison scene "heart rending" and "unique" in the theater.[31]

Gérard had already met Gretchen types in real life: the little girls of Mortefontaine with whom he so enjoyed singing and dancing. They stood for purity, beauty, and harmony—all those angelic qualities that emerge with blurred vision. Gérard's cousin Sophie, for whom he had felt such affection and whom he had wanted to marry, was also an anima figure: she too spelled perfection. All these types represented Gérard's prevailing function, his feelings. Because he was unaware of his unconscious longing to possess an ideal creature, Gérard was forever transferring the "angelic" feminine figure of his imagination onto real people or imaginary situations.

Like Faust, Gérard failed to create any conscious relationship with his inner processes. An identification between his ego and persona prevailed, making him passive in his relationships with women. The Gretchen type was all his heart desired. She was beautiful, radiant, fresh, sincere, tender—an ideal soul. This kind of transpersonal force had entered Faust's life as a sacrificial being, an agent that would enable him to experience life on both physical and spiritual levels.

So far, Gérard's anima figures remained unconscious. His relationships with women had been experienced only in terms of projection. He played a passive role in all these encounters; he had not yet become capable of understanding the flesh-and-blood woman in a love situation. Unable to differentiate between the ideal and the real, he was forever endowing women with divine traits, and what real woman could ever live up to such an image?[32]

Normally, the first bearer of the anima image is the mother. In Gérard's case, there had been none. Normally, during the child's maturation, he struggles to separate himself from the mother image and to create and develop his own faculties and personality. Gérard was never faced with this type of conflict, which is so necessary for a person's future psychological independence. His unconscious goal was in fact the reverse: he wanted to return to the mother, or to relate back to whatever object symbolized maternal warmth, beauty, and self-sacrifice.

Thus far in Gérard's life the Gretchen figure had been an ideal one. It should be remembered that Gretchen had mothered her own sisters and brothers and had, therefore, represented the kind and gentle maternal principle. The picture did not change, however, when Gretchen killed her child. Gérard could also identify with her because his own mother had "rejected" him when she left for Germany without him and again when she died.

As might be expected, Gérard also associated his mother (the maternal female principle) with death. In this case, the maternal principle became the personification of an unconscious fear which Gérard experienced three times in his life.

> The fever which led to her death gripped me three times in my life, at periods which may be divided into regular and periodic intervals. At these periods, I have felt my mind struck with the images of mourning and of desolation which had surrounded my cradle.[33]

Gérard could readily sympathize with Faust's "horrible torture" and with his subservience to Mephistopheles, who had transformed him into a "fugitive, an exile. . . ." The question arises whether Gérard would or would not remain victimized by his own anima problem.

3 ONE OF MY LITERARY TUTORS

*This earth is merely a passage way where
souls gather to test themselves, and if
your soul, as faithful as it is devoted,
remains married to mine during the years
which time has measured out for us, all
of eternity will be ours.*
    Charles Nodier, *Franciscus Columna.*

Gérard's translation of *Faust* was very well received by both the critics
and his friends and gave its author a sense of accomplishment. It had
even been purported that the great Goethe himself praised Gérard's
translation in a conversation with his friend Eckermann: ". . . despite the
fact that the translation was for the most part in prose . . . I can no
longer read *Faust* in any other but the French translation, which gives
it renewed novelty, freshness, and spirit."[1] Hector Berlioz, who was to
base his musical composition *The Damnation of Faust* on Gérard's translation, expressed his admiration in the following terms: "The marvelous
book fascinated me immediately; I could not put it down; I read it constantly, at table, in the theater, in the street, everywhere."[2]

Gérard was twenty. He had published his first book, had acquired
something of a reputation, and was invited to the Cénacles that were
flourishing all over Paris. He was drawn to the one headed by Charles
Nodier at the Arsenal, which was frequented by such writers as Balzac,
Gautier, Hugo, Lamartine, Musset, Sainte-Beuve, and Vigny, and by
such artists as Delacroix and Goujon.

Though Nodier was twenty-five years Gérard's senior, the two were
meant to understand each other. They had common interests: Nodier
had written an adaptation of *Faust* for the theater; in fact, it had been
said that it was he who first introduced this medieval character to
Gérard. Nodier and Gérard could discuss the esoteric implications of
Faust; few people in Paris were so well versed in alchemy and magic as
they. There was also an affinity of personality: Nodier was soft-spoken,
deeply sensitive, a man who felt his way into situations. Always understanding of the problems of others, his tenderness and his gentleness
endeared him to many young people.

Nodier was born out of wedlock in 1780 at Besançon and was not
legitimatized until 1791. His father, a forceful, dynamic, and rather dogmatic man who had been mayor of Besançon, had presided for a short
period over the criminal tribune of that city during its Reign of Terror.
In later years, Nodier recalled with horror some of the particularly ex-

coriating spectacles he had witnessed as a child of fourteen, and he inserted some of these terrifying episodes in his short stories: the rolling heads, the pathetic cry of the person who knows his life is about to end, the sharp cut of the knife as it severs the flesh and the neck bone, the blood flowing into the gutters. Such traumatic experiences might have accounted, at least in part, for the hypertension Nodier later developed. But there were other causes, too.

Nodier's family life, ever since he could remember, had been particularly unpleasant. His mother, whom he never mentioned in his writings or, apparently, in his conversations, had been a housemaid. She was a brusque, ignorant, and unfeeling woman, and Nodier had always disliked her intensely. Yet fate acts in strange ways because it was from his mother that he inherited Addison's disease.[3] Nodier suffered from other ills: insomnia and periodic fevers, which were not to abate with the passing of years. On the contrary, the opium that he took every now and then seemed to aggravate his condition.

Nodier's sense of isolation was instrumental in the affinity he felt with Goethe's fictional hero Werther. As a young student, Werther had committed suicide because of an unrequited love. Though Nodier did not follow Werther's example, he had been tempted to do so for ten long years. Instead, he changed his life's focus. His attraction for Chateaubriand's literary character, René, also a despairing young man who suffered from an obsessive ennui, or *mal du siécle* as it was called, taught him to analyze his despair, his feelings of inertia that paralyzed his every move. "At twenty years of age," Nodier wrote, "I saw all, I knew all, I forgot everything." He had been victimized by "all sorrows and consumed in useless hopes . . ." At this age he realized for the first time— and accepted the situation—that "he was not meant to know happiness."[4]

Though a devout Catholic, Nodier did not find salvation in a conventional approach to worship. His needs were more complex. The writings of such mystics as Jakob Boehme, Emmanuel Swedenborg, Claude de Saint-Martin, Martinès de Pasqually, and Jacques Cazotte stimulated his imagination and helped him to develop his own comforting credo.

Nodier had known Jacques Cazotte, the author of the popular work *The Devil in Love* (1772). A friend of his father's, Cazotte used to visit the family at Besançon and speak openly of the elementary spirits that peopled his universe. He was a firm believer in alchemy, magic, the power of charms, transmigration of souls, and magnetism. A whole new world had been opened for the young Nodier, as he sat breathless at the edge of his seat.[5]

It has been claimed that one evening shortly after the publication of *The Devil in Love* a "grave" looking gentleman "draped in a brown coat" was admitted to Cazotte's room. The stranger began making all sorts of "bizarre" motions with his hands, those used as signs of recognition by members of certain secret societies such as the Martinists or Masons.

Cazotte, who did not understand the esoteric meaning of such antics, grew impatient. When the stranger finally realized that Cazotte was not a member of either the Martinist or Masonic orders, he was dumbfounded. How could Cazotte have described these secret rituals so precisely if he had never been exposed to them? How could he have depicted certain gestures known only to those who had risen to the First Degree? "What!" he asked, "those evocations amid ruins, the mysteries of the Kabbala, the occult power over air, the striking theories implicit in the power of numbers, the will, the fatalities of existence—could all these things have been imagined?"[6]

The author of *The Devil in Love* was not a member of any occult society at that time. It was one of those inexplicable coincidences. Later, however, Cazotte was so taken with the tenets of the Martinist Order that he joined the sect.

Martinès de Pasqually was the founder of what later became known as the Martinist Order. Its beliefs were a composite of the Kabbalistic rites of the eleventh century, early Gnosticism, and Neoplatonism as prescribed by the Alexandrian spiritual leaders of the ancient world.[7] According to Claude de Saint-Martin, Pasqually's disciple during the early years and later head of the order, man had fallen out of God's favor after committing the original sin—that is, when Adam and Eve ate of the fruit of the Tree of Knowledge. Once cast out of the Garden of Eden onto Earth (or Matter), man became subject to misery, disease, and death. Because he had once been part of God, however, he longed to return to his primordial paradisiac state of being. To do this, man must listen to certain "inner signs" and to his "inner voice"—God's way of acting through him. Man can hear God's dictates when he descends into himself and practices certain arcane exercises, which both Pasqually and Saint-Martin taught the members of their order. Once a withdrawal into self had been experienced by the neophyte as fully as possible, he became "reintegrated" into God, or reentered the state of primordial unity.[8]

For the Martinists, intelligence and will are the only active forces in nature capable of "modifying phenomena." If man masters these agents he can descend within, which is tantamount, in mystical terms, to an ascension toward God and a higher order of things. Man, in complicity with God, is capable of carving out his own destiny.

The Devil in Love centers around the power of the Devil. This destructive element within the cosmos is forever standing in man's path, preventing him from becoming reintegrated in the universal essence. Man, therefore, must be strong and fight his way through this evil by means of certain magic formulae, secret rituals, and a whole series of ascetic practises.[9]

Cazotte's novel enjoyed a tremendous success. The young in particular were impressed with his visions, the magic and mystery that permeated so many of his scenes. They felt that Cazotte's talent was unique because he was capable of describing both people and situations "in their fantastic element."[10] Unlike many of his contemporaries who wrote fantastic tales because they enjoyed cultivating this art form, Cazotte actually believed in his dream visions; they were warnings, signs, portents of something taking place in another frame or sphere of existence. It was reported that Cazotte not only predicted the events surrounding his own death, but the deaths of the others present on that fateful evening. He was one of the nine elected to save the monarchy, he declared, and his death on the guillotine, he further affirmed, had been revealed to him. The facts corroborated his predictions. He looked upon himself as a martyr, as a Christ figure, who had spent his life fighting for the cause of righteousness and goodness and against the evil that had permeated his society.[11]

Like Cazotte and other mystics, Nodier also believed in reincarnation and was haunted by the thought that death was a return to the Eternal, to the All, life being merely a differentiation of the One. Nodier longed to transcend the world of appearances, of matter. But he was not only a dreamer. In a sense, he was a rather practical man who lived a conventional life. He married in 1808 and had several children, only one of whom, Marie, survived. Marie, who was gifted in a multitude of ways, attracted people to her; beautiful, charming, intelligent, and a fine musician, she became the focal point of her father's existence.

Nodier was a hard worker and his knowledge was vast. He was forever writing on a host of subjects: articles and drama criticism for newspapers and magazines (the *Journal des Débats,* the *Quotidienne,* for Chateaubriand's paper, *Le Conservateur*); books on natural history, *Dissertation sur l'usage des antennes chez les insectes* (1789); works on philology, *Dictionary of French Onomatopoeias* (1808), *The Army's Secret Societies* (1815); fantastic tales, *Smarra* (1821), *Trilby* (1822), and much more.

Nodier was appointed librarian at the Arsenal Library in 1824. It was in this elegant building that he was to make his home.[12] The Arsenal was far from being a gaudy building. Its lines were sober and graceful. Its superb staircase on the ground floor set the tone for the entire building. A rather spacious house, the ground floor included a corridor, a dining room and pantry. The second story, perhaps more grandiose, included Mme. Nodier's bedroom and her husband's, a living room, a study, and a library.[13]

According to Dumas, Nodier led a double life. On week days he was both librarian and bibliophile; on Sundays, he was transformed into a man of the world, the leader of his Cénacle. His life was full. Not a minute was wasted. His nights were consumed in writing literally until dawn; only when daylight began shining through his shutters did he go to bed for several hours sleep, after which he breakfasted and attended to personal matters.[14] To keep awake during the day, he resorted frequently to stimulants. White wine acted as a catalyst.

Nodier went to the theater often—to the Variétés or to the Porte-

Saint-Martin, the Ambigu, the Funambules—after which a short stop at a café and then home again.[15] Nodier adored the theater. His favorite actor was the ebullient Talma, who cut such a noble figure on the stage and had been highly regarded by Napoleon, too. Nodier was also drawn to the performances of the famous pantomimist Debureau, the first to create the character of the sad clown, Pierrot. Nodier was friendly with Guilbert de Pixérécourt, known as the "King of Melodrama"; he went to Guilbert's plays and even coined another name for this popular playwright, "the Corneille of the Boulevards."[16]

Everyone looked forward to Sunday evenings at the Nodier's. Alphonse de Cailleux, a museum director; the baron Taylor, administrator of the Théâtre-Français; Augustin Soulié, Nodier's colleague at the Arsenal; Francis Wey, whom Nodier treated like a son; Dumas—all were frequent visitors, as were Gérard and Gautier.[17] Sometimes Nodier told stories by Scott, or his own, in a clear and elegant manner, gesticulating from time to time, his long slender hands enacting the dramatic events he recounted, while his face mirrored a sense of excitement or serene melancholy. On some evenings he injected a note of terror into his surroundings, as he described, in the minutest detail, Dr. Polidori's *The Vampire.* He loved such stories, and the English Gothic novels as well, which were the rage of Paris. Who hadn't read the works of Horace Walpole, Anne Radcliffe, and *The Monk* by M.G. Lewis?[18] These stories, so immersed in blood and gore and the supernatural, could when properly narrated send chills up the spine of any listener: the gloomy backgrounds of the ancient English or French castles, the open tombs, the candles burning deep into the night, the underground vaults, the vampires who came at unexpected moments bent upon sucking the blood of their innocent and usually very beautiful young victims. Nodier had also written tales of horror: *Jean Sbogar,* which featured hideous reptiles with human faces, headless giants, a monstrous universe of cruelty and instinctuality. Nodier claimed that some of his stories had been told to him by persons who had experienced the incidents recounted.[19]

At other times Nodier told fantastic tales in the manner of the German writer Ernst Theodor Hoffmann, whom Nodier considered a visionary, and whose fascination with the world of magetism, the occult, and the supernatural stirred Nodier's already well-developed imagination. It was the inner domain that Hoffmann investigated, exteriorized, and then dramatized—the realm of dreams, nightmares, hallucinations, madness. Hoffmann lived in the workaday realm, and the world of fantasy and was always a prey to interludes of great terror and inexpressible joy.[20] Hoffmann's dreams, as revealed in his stories, were usually tormented, disquieting, ushering in moods of disenchantment, nostalgia, and malaise. According to Sainte-Beuve, a devotée of his work, Hoffmann was endowed with a sixth sense that enabled him to understand man and nature, obscure relationships, phenomena that escape all scientific explanation.[21] Hoffmann was one of the first to discover a relationship between music and somnambulism. Music, it seems, sets the unconscious into motion; it provokes dreams and visions, expands vistas, and, because it is a catalyst, it leads directly to sleepwalking.

Hoffmann's tales swept Paris like lightning. In his essay *The Fantastic in Literature,* Nodier praised such stories as *The Devil's Elixir* (1816) and *Night-Pieces* (1817), which had caused a whole generation to tremble and to dream. Gérard was inspired to translate some of Hoffmann's tales; Loève-Weimar, the future diplomat, also rendered some of them into French. Gautier wrote stories in the manner of Hoffmann, which gave him an opportunity to bring to life certain torments that accompanied a corrosion within his own soul.

Nodier knew just how to make both readers and audiences shudder. In his own fantastic works—*Smarra,* or *The Night Demons*—he brings to light the horrors confronting those who sleep: the presence of ineffable beings who hover about and suck the blood, the very life, out of anyone within their grasp. Such beings as Nodier delineated were not relegated to fiction. He believed that relationships between the living and the dead were not only possible but were in fact taking place all the time; that resemblances between certain people, though separated by centuries, were examples of reincarnation and also of another phenomenon: the dead are in love with the living or vice versa and procreate when united. Animals were endowed with souls; they understood man's world but on another dimension. How else, he reasoned, could the unparalleled devotion of dogs after their master's death be explained?[22]

Sometimes, when Nodier told one of his fantastic tales, a world of feeling took possession of him. His dreams, transmuted into the story line, were lived out in his daily existence. There were deep ties, he said, between the dream and the waking state: during the sleeping hours, the thinking faculty makes its way into the unconscious via images. In the preface to *Smarra,* or *The Night Demons,* he wrote: "Ulysses' descent into hell is a dream. . . ." Reality has a way of living out its own strange existence, he implied in his tale *The Crumb Fairy,* when the main character, Michel, remarks: "My impressions during my waking or sleeping hours are at times confused, and I am not really worried about sorting them out, because I cannot decide which are the most reasonable or the best."[23]

During the course of the Sunday-evening gatherings Nodier would call upon Lamartine or Hugo to speak. "Enough prose for the moment," he'd say. "Now let's have some verses!"[24]

Lamartine was greatly concerned with the impression he was making upon others. He was always conscious of how he looked and what he said. When he wanted to appear noble, his attitudes and mannerisms were imposing. The artist David d'Angers, also a habitué of the Nodier Cénacle, remarked that Lamartine had perfected the art of seating himself. "The undulations of his body," he declared, "had the supplety of a serpent."²⁵ At the Arsenal, Lamartine read his famous poem *The Lake:* standing erect, one hand pressed over the buttons of his jacket, his voice was singularly moving. Sometimes he wrote verses to Nodier's lovely daughter Marie, about springtime, youth, always mentioning her charm and beauty.²⁶

Musset also joined in. Lamartine described him as "nonchalant," his "elbow resting on a cushion, his head posed on his hand, his hair flowing," his eyes "dreamy rather than dazzling."²⁷

Victor Hugo and his beautiful wife Adèle were often present, as was Sainte-Beuve. Indeed, Nodier looked upon Hugo as a close and devoted friend. He helped the young poet considerably by writing critiques of his first novel, *Han d'Islande.*

Loève-Weimars, director of the newspaper *Le Temps,* later to become a diplomat in Russia and Bagdad, added further lustre to the already brilliant coterie.

Delacroix, Fourier, and the religious sociologist Pierre Ballanche, who defended the doctrine of palingenesis, also made their presences known at the Arsenal.

But when Balzac entered, a titan stalked in! The entire house trembled with energy and excitement. Speaking in fervent tones, his hair like an animal's mane, Balzac gesticulated fervently as he described one of the characters from his latest works, *La Maison du Chat-qui-pelote* perhaps, or *The Elixir of Long Life,* sometimes including some piquant details in what were otherwise mysterious and occult events; for he, too, believed in the transmigration of souls.²⁸

It was usually about ten o'clock in the evening that Marie, Nodier's daughter, would accompany herself at the piano and sing both old and new French songs. She also played contre-dances and waltzes while some of the guests danced. Others watched her agile fingers fly over the keyboard. Louis Boulanger, one of the most popular song writers of the era, injected a note of humor and wit into the fun.²⁹

Nodier retired rather early to his rooms. His wife, always solicitous of his health, made certain that his bed chamber was heated and that coals were placed in his bed even before he was ready to retire. It has been said that while Nodier lived in the fantasy world most of the time, Madame Nodier had become *his reality.*³⁰

After his daughter's marriage (1830), Nodier suffered a type of depression. He felt he had lost his main attraction. More important, he could no longer see his daughter daily and the void gnawed at him. He became more and more introverted. His dream world began intruding more insistantly upon his real life because his dream brought with it the joy he needed to survive.

Nodier was troubled not only because he felt he was beginning to lose his memory but also by what he felt was Hugo's defection when Hugo established his own Cénacle and his own circle of friends and disciples. Hugo had usurped Nodier's place and had become one of the most popular figures in the literary world in Paris. No longer the center of interest, Nodier lacked the stamina and enthusiasm to continue the Arsenal gatherings.

Nodier exercised a lasting influence on Gérard, who referred to him later on as "one of my literary tutors."[31] Nodier had aroused his interest in the dream and the nightmare, in poetry and history, in religion. But it was not merely the man's erudition that had so impressed Gérard, but also his modesty and the gentleness of his ways. Gérard compared Nodier to Lucius Apuleius, a man who had been initiated into the cult of Isis and had found illumination amid "the debris of mythologies."

Nodier had quested his entire life for an answer to his existence—for a valid explanation for his suffering, for his solitude and the spirit of restlessness that encumbered his being. Gérard also thirsted for this knowledge.

4 THE LITTLE CÉNACLE

When still young and more audacious,
I dared fix my eyes for an instant on the glory:
A black spot remained in my avid gaze.
Gérard de Nerval, *Le Point Noir.*

Gérard had to settle matters with his father. Dr. Labrunie had vetoed
a literary career for his son, insisting on the more secure and remuner-
ative profession of medicine. Gérard, who was financially dependent
upon his father, had no choice but to comply, and enrolled in medical
school, attending classes at the Clinic Hôtel Dieu. In order to add to his
pocket money he worked, from 1828 to 1830, in a printing firm and
then as a clerk to a notary. Though his days were busy, they were not
always pleasant. During the cholera epidemic that struck Paris in March/
April, 1832, in addition to his regular activities, Gérard helped his father
care for over a hundred patients.[1] Severe pressures were put on him
because of the growing shortage of doctors and the rapid progress of
the disease. People were dying and Gérard, always deeply affected by
his surroundings, wondered ever more insistently on the meaning of
life, which seemed to vanish with such ease.

Gérard always yielded to his father's demands. Nor was he one to com-
plain, though in a letter to a friend he did express his marked preference for writing over medicine. To make life more palatable, he might
have imagined himself a nineteenth-century Faustian type. After all,
Faust had also been a man of science and perhaps, like him, Gérard
would meet his Gretchen, too.

A basic conflict, however, was in the offing. Gérard had officially entered the realm of science but was wedded to the world of the artist.
Poetry was more suitable to his temperament; his imagination, the intensity of his feelings had to find literary expression—some meaningful
outlet. Yet, there was something within him that prevented him from
overtly confronting his father. As the months passed, a progressive sense
of fatality began plaguing him, something he felt but could not articulate.

Gérard did have moments of respite—when he was with his friends.
Gautier, Dumas, and other romantics had become increasingly drawn
to the Middle Ages and to the Renaissance, and so had Gérard. Valor,
creativity, enthusiasm had seemed to erupt in every facet of life in those
olden days. An inveterate reader, Gérard regaled his friends when re-
citing poems by such sixteenth-century poets as Ronsard, Du Bellay,
Baïf, and Belleau in a clear, soft, perfectly modulated voice. Frequently,
he sang these verses, interspersing the light and graceful color tones
with intricate rhythmic effects.

Gérard wrote a number of poems in the manner of Ronsard, *Odelettes* (1832–1835), or little odes, which focused on themes that had preoccupied both the Renaissance poets and Gérard—the *carpe diem* theme, for example, which aroused such feelings of melancholia over the fleeting nature of life—the end to all beauty and joy. Not all of Gérard's poems depicted somber moods, however; some were flooded with gaiety. Like the Renaissance poets, Gérard felt a profound affinity with nature that comforted him in moments of solitude and was ever present to assuage his pain.

Fantaisie (1832) might be compared to a delicate carving. Though the theme interwoven in the poem—time and music—is abstract, the poet's vision is concretized in a magnificent brick castle—its stained-glass windows casting a reddish hue over a park and river, while in a window above, there stands a beautiful lady in ancient dress; her hair is blond and her eyes are black, and he recognizes her from a previous life.

> Il est un air pour qui je donnerais
> Tout Rossini, tout Mozart et tout Weber,
> Un air très vieux, languissant et funèbre,
> Qui pour moi seul a des charmes secrets! . . .

> There is a melody for which I would give
> All of Rossini, all of Mozart, and all of Weber,
> A very ancient melody, languishing and funereal,
> Which for me alone holds secret charms!

Le Point Noir (1831) is of particular interest because of its prophetic and metaphysical innuendoes. It relates the experiences of a young boy staring at the sun and the black circles that become visible to him after he looks away. The colors play an important role in this poem; they are like a series of barometers measuring the poet's emotions. The sun, a fiery red, becomes the poet's dynamism and spirituality; the blackness of the circles are manifestations of his despair, an intimation, perhaps, of his unhappy destiny. The image of the eagle at the end of the poem stands for man's courage, for it alone is capable of looking at the sun directly and is unaffected by its intensity.[2]

Gérard read Byron, Scott, and Thomas Moore (as all good romantics were doing at this period), and he even composed an adaptation of Moore's verse (*Irish Melody*, 1830). Nor did he neglect the German poets and dramatists. His *German Poetry* (1830) includes translations of works by Klopstock, Schiller, Goethe, Burger, and others. These German poets, he felt, wrote from their depths, drawing on their own roots, on their national history and legends. They did not give primacy to the word alone, but to the idea, the feeling, the atmosphere.[3]

The young French romantics did likewise. Hugo had demonstrated this most dramatically in his novel *Notre Dame de Paris*. A return to the past was of collective interest for the romantics; for Gérard, however, it had a special meaning. To regress into by-gone eras did not merely mean to conduct historical research, to seek geological or archeological finds; for him it was an expression of a fundamental restlessness, an inability to live in the present. In returning to the past there was the possibility of recreating one's life, of modifying one's destiny. Wasn't this the function of myth?

Gérard wanted to change—to be different than he was: stronger, more outgoing. He would change his name. It was stylish to do so. Many of his friends had adopted pseudonyms: Pierre Borel had become Pétrus Borel; August Maquet was now known as MacKeat; Théophile Dondey, as Philothée O'Neddy. Gérard would call himself Gérard La Brunie de Nerval. He took the name from a piece of land at Mortefontaine that had belonged to his maternal grandparents, the "Clos de Nerval." There were interesting asides in the choice of the name. The letters in Nerval spelled out his mother's maiden name in reverse "Lauren[t]"; it also included the letters in his father's name, "La Brunie." By adding the Nerval, Gérard unified what had been divided and so mother, father, and son were together once again, at least in name. Some of his friends understood what he had in mind—those who already knew.

Though Gérard La Brunie de Nerval lived a frenetic existence, what with his classes in medicine and his literary work, he was no recluse. He enjoyed the company of his friends. Gautier, whom he had known since his Lycée Charlemagne days, and always so thoughtful and considerate, was present when Nerval needed him. So was Dumas—sure of himself, adventurous in his writings and amours alike.

Nerval's friendships depended upon his moods. There were moments when he preferred to be alone, taking long walks about Paris. Amid the bustle of the Parisian streets, ideas emerged. He jotted down a sentence or two, a word, a fleeting thought, in a red notebook that he always carried with him.[4] There were times, however, when Gautier saw him from a distance and realized as he came closer that Nerval's eyes had been invaded by an "absent look," as if he were deeply entrenched in some remote world: "his blue eyes glimmered like stars, his thin blond hair, already lighter now, looked like golden smoke surrounding a porcelain cranium."[5] On these occasions, Gautier approached his friend slowly, spoke to him in soft tones, quietly ushering him back to the world of reality.

Gérard had the capacity to make friends. He was always welcome at Nodier's Cénacle, and at Hugo's. There was something ingratiating about him. Sober in his manner, discreet in his conversation, and gentle in his ways, people enjoyed being with him. He had no enemies. Everyone wanted to help him. He inspired pity.

After Nodier had put a virtual end to his Cénacle, Gérard, Gautier, and some other friends decided to begin their own Cénacle, in 1830, to be known as Le Petit Cénacle. The official meeting place was the atelier of the painter Jehan du Seigneur, located at the corner of Rue de Vaugirard and the Rue du Regard. It was a simply furnished studio, with some chairs, a bed, and a hammock; some drawings hung on the walls.

A whole group of creative, joyous, and sometimes quite rambunctious young people joined the Cénacle. Differ as they might over political and even aesthetic ideologies, they were compatible. Philothée O'Neddy, author of *Fire and Flame,* was forever in a state of inspiration but was always, for some unknown reason, putting off writing his magnum opus. The seventeen-year-old, Roman-born lithographer Célestin Nanteuil, who later drew charming illustrations for some of the works of Hugo, Dumas, and Gautier, looked like an "angel" to his friends.[6] Auguste MacKeat, who was said to have ghostwritten several of Dumas' novels, had a fertile imagination and was forever helping others (including Gérard) in their literary ventures. Pétrus Borel, more than anyone else, stood out in this group.

Passionate and dynamic, Borel was an outspoken partisan of the romantic movement and a Jacobin in political life. Architect, painter, and poet, he had one great hatred—the materialistic bourgeois. When he entered Du Seigneur's atelier, his very demeanor commanded respect. There was a Spanish haughtiness about this tall, thin man—an aristocratic, even autocratic, manner. His dark brown beard, his moustache and his bright red lips gave him a somewhat Oriental look. His friends called him the "lycanthrope," the wolf man, because he was so clever and, at times, cruel. He often spoke in riddles and paradoxes, and was frank but never vulgar.[7]

Dumas was impressive because of his extroverted personality. He regaled his friends with adventure stories of crime and passion. Gautier, thin and sickly at this period, was more reserved, except when he broached the subject of politics. He was an imperialist.

Nerval could always be distinguished from the rest. They dressed in outlandish costumes—flamboyant reds, greens, with large capes and high hats. Nerval wore a simple suit of Orléans cloth in the summer and a black tail coat in the winter. His shirts and collars were always white. He spoke in soft and well-modulated tones. Judging from the medallion made of him by Jehan du Seigneur, he was rather handsome. His hair fell in ringlets about his head; his forehead was broad, his nose, slightly aquiline. He looked like the Roman emperor Nerva, whom he claimed as his ancestor.

The members of the Petit Cénacle did not always gather at Du Seigneur's studio. Sometimes they met at a cabaret, the Petit Moulin Rouge on the Avenue de la Grande Armée, not far from Napoleon's triumphal arch. The chef was a Neapolitan and his food was sublime: macaroni, noodles, spaghetti, meats of all kinds, piquant sauces, velvety wines—all helped create and sustain an atmosphere of gaiety and insouciance.[8]

This was *"la vie bohème."*

On one occasion, legend has it, Nerval brought a skull from his father's collection. It had belonged to a drum major killed in the battle of Moskowa.[9] Nerval exhibited it to his friends, then filled it with wine (or, by some accounts, with water from the Seine) and passed it around the table. Each one drank from it. Some may have been repulsed by the idea initially but their revulsion readily disappeared when they heard that Hugo's monstrous character *Han d'Islande* always drank from the skulls of his victims—and Han had become a hero figure for these romantics.

Nerval was so impressed with *Han d'Islande,* indeed, that he decided to adapt it for the stage. The horrendous and grotesque monster must have been modeled after one of Anne Radcliffe's or Monk Lewis' ghastly apparitions—or even after the monster in Mary Shelley's *Frankenstein* or perhaps Goethe's Homunculus. Hugo's monster was designed to terrify all people of all ages. His head was enormous; a low forehead, thick eyebrows, a large pudgy nose, eyes circled with mauve, a huge gaping mouth, an ear-shattering voice that sounded more like the frenzied growl of an animal than the tones of a human. Scenes depicting caves, masked men, subterranean vaults, cadavers, poisonings, tortures, demons, killings, skeletons rattling their chains—all the gothic trappings that Hugo could think of were included in this "shattering" work. And readers were attracted to this macabre novel as bears are to honey.

For some unknown reason, Gérard's theatrical version of *Han d'Islande* was not produced. But neither Hugo's work nor his own disappointment dampened Nerval's enthusiasm for the theater. As Gautier phrased it, the theater "is the luminous center around which most diverse ideas converge" and the only place "where the poet can reveal himself to the crowd."[10] Nerval was convinced that the theater would solve his financial problems. If he could just write one successful play he would be able to escape his father's domination. Such an idea was not preposterous; there were many successful dramatists among the romantics. Dumas had won fame with *Henry III and His Court* (1829), *Antony* (1831), and other plays. Hugo was about to begin his battle for recognition in the theater. In 1827 he had written a preface to his play *Cromwell* in which he stated that French plays had been reduced to a series of sterile and servile imitations of classical theater. Nothing original was taking place in the dramatic arts—save for Dumas' works. Inspired by Shakespeare and the German romantics, Hugo proclaimed free expression for the theater. "Everything that exists in nature exists in art," he wrote. No subject should be taboo; no action lacks decorum. All human emotions should be expressed on stage, from the sublime to the grotesque. There should not be just one action or one decor. Nor should the time allotted to the events be limited to twenty-four hours. The "unities" of time, place, and action, which had been adhered to by the classicists ever since the seventeenth century, should be abolished.

Three years after *Cromwell,* Hugo wrote *Hernani.* He wanted to introduce Parisians to a new diet, to a world in which the past would be resurrected in all its grandeur and horror. His language throbbed with dynamism—with metaphors, antitheses, images. Hugo had a battle on his hands, and Gautier, Borel, and Nerval were on his side. The so-called Battle of Hernani was waged on opening night, February 25, 1830. The young romantics arrived dressed in outrageous colors, as attested to by Gautier, who wore a pink doublet, bottle-green pants, a black jacket, a grey topcoat with a green-satin lining, and a black ribbon tied around his neck.[11] Nerval, as usual, wore black and inconspicuous clothes. Nerval distributed bits of red paper on which the Spanish word *Hierro* had been written. Gautier was given six pieces of paper, which he handed out to others who had joined their forces; Borel was given some. Hugo's partisans gathered in military style in the galleries of the Théâtre-Français. The battle between the romantics and the classicists began on stage, then extended throughout the theater. Shouts and fighting broke out, litter was thrown. Hugo and his group won the day!

No wonder Nerval was filled with rapture and excitement when thinking of the theater. Here was a world where passion reigned, where action, audacity, and life could still be experienced to the utmost.[12] Nerval's fascination for the theater was without bounds, but his talents in this domain were slim. His play *The Prince of Fools* was either never completed or was lost. This same fate befell his *Lady from Carouge, Villon the School Boy,* and *Tartuffe at Molière's. Lara* or *The Expiation,* which he wrote together with MacKeat, was submitted to the reading committee of the Théâtre-Français and was accepted but never produced.[13] A similar fate met his play *Nicholas Flamel,* based on the life of the medieval alchemist.[14]

Nerval's life was varied and active in the early 1830s. In order to earn some extra *sous* and still remain in touch with the theater, he started writing drama reviews for *La Tribune romantique, Vert-Vert,* and *L'Artiste.* This meant that he spent less and less time on his medical studies and more and more on literary activities. To relieve his fatigue he could always count on his friends at the Petit Cénacle. In the autumn of 1831, he and his group were having such a glorious time singing and shouting in the streets that they were arrested and sent to Sainte-Pélagie prison for the night.[15]

Despite his friends' and his jocular attitude, Nerval discovered that France, politically, was not a free country. Authorities were nervous whenever any group of people congregated, and in July, 1831, it was decreed that all political gatherings were to be forbidden. The following year, in February, Paris was in a state of frenzy because of rumors that the royal family was to be kidnapped at a reception at the Tuilleries. When the police saw some carousers—Nerval and his friends—on the Rue des Prouvères, they immediately hauled them into prison, convinced that they were plotting to overthrow the government. Nerval's second stay at Sainte-Pélagie, in February, 1832, was not as unpleasant as he had anticipated. In fact, he used the opportunity to observe prison conditions and to come into contact with certain political infractors.[16]

The theater and poetry, the cabaret with its wine and merriment, were not Nerval's only activities.[17] His short story *The Enchanted Hand* was written during this period. It is Hoffmanesque, with magic, alchemy, and mystery imbedded in the story line.[18] The style is stark, the details vivid and accurate. The tale takes place in seventeenth-century Paris and opens on Place Dauphine.[19] An underlying note of distress may be detected in *The Enchanted Hand*: "Your horoscope prophesies death and nothing can undo such a course," the magician says to the protagonist. Did Nerval sense something about himself that he could not as yet rationally understand?

5 THE PSEUDO-BOHEMIAN

*Not to be loved and never to have
the hope of being loved.*
Gérard de Nerval, *Letters to Jenny Colon.*

The year 1834 marked a turning point in Nerval's life. On January 19 his maternal grandfather Laurent, a warm-hearted and practical man who had worked until the very end in his linen shop, died. This sad event, though painful, had its compensatory side: Nerval inherited thirty thousand francs. After having lived on four hundred francs a year doled out to him by his father—certainly not a sufficient sum to live on away from home—his grandfather's legacy seemed like a fortune.[1]

Nerval was given only a small sum of money immediately after his grandfather's death (the rest of the estate took some time to settle, since it was to be divided between Nerval and his aunt Eugénie's son, Pierre-Eugène Labrunie); nevertheless, events moved swiftly. Nerval's first act of independence was to move out of his father's house, to 15 Rue de Vaugirard in April and then to 6 Rue du Paon in July, the latter the home of his friend Célestin Nanteuil, a member of the Petit Cénacle. By September Nerval had made up his mind to travel.

Italy was fashionable. Most romantics and preromantics—Goethe, Chateaubriand, Lamartine, Byron, Shelley—had made a cult of Italy, the land of art, romance, music, and of the sun. Like Faust, perhaps, Nerval also longed to see other lands, to broaden his knowledge. More important, he wanted to come into contact with the ancient statues and monuments about which he had read so much—to touch, to feel, to enjoy the forms and colors of paintings that he had only seen in reproductions, and to listen to the heartbeat of Italy and see its lush and savage landscapes.

Nerval first traveled to the South of France (to Avignon, Vaucluse, Aix), then to the French Riviera (Antibes, Nice), then to Italy (Livorno, Florence, Rome, Naples, Pompeii), and finally back to Paris via Marseilles, Nîmes, Agen, his father's birthplace, where he had some relatives.

The South of France was, for Nerval, a land of enchantment. Here an intriguing culture had flourished during the Middle Ages; here the troubadours, those bards of old, had accompanied themselves on their rotes and sung in soft, melodious tones to their lady loves. Their approach to poetry centered on eternal fidelity, unswerving courage, and a profound admiration sworn to the lady of their choice. The cult of the *Domina* as an immaculate figure had been supreme in this land.

Nerval's trip through France and Italy might be looked upon as an act of liberation. It was not. Nerval was far too filled with guilt and anguish to enjoy fully or even really to benefit at all from the excitement that comes with the discovery of fresh lands. The object of this guilt was Nerval's father. Gérard had not had the courage to inform Dr. Labrunie of his projected trip to Italy. He merely mentioned his intention of going to the South of France, to Agen in particular to see his father's family. Once en route, Nerval enclosed a group of letters to his father in an envelope sent to his friend Jehan Du Seigneur, asking Jehan to forward them to Dr. Labrunie at appropriate intervals. "I'll tell him that I went to Italy only after my return," Nerval explained. "It would have frightened him."[2]

Was Nerval actually trying to spare his father worry, was he fearful of confronting him, or was it a bit of both? Nerval's relationship with his father had not changed with the passing of years. He could not relate to him on adult terms. Financial dependency had cowed Nerval emotionally. His father, a rather taciturn man, was not easy to approach. Had he been told of his son's trip to Italy, Dr. Labrunie would certainly have become angry. "Why spend the money traveling?" he might have said, and understandably so. Dr. Labrunie's army pension was only 420 francs a year, which was not sufficient to live on. As a physician in a bourgeois neighborhood he was able to earn enough money to support himself and his son. Still, funds were scarce, and Dr. Labrunie was a practical man.[3] Nerval, who could not bring himself to speak openly to his father of his plans or of his future hopes, must have justified his inability to face him by simply stating that he wanted to spare his father unnecessary worry.

Other difficulties also intruded upon Nerval's peace of mind during this trip. He had never had any practical experience with money and was incapable of arranging for anything that smacked of finances. He tried to plan for all eventualities before his departure by giving some negotiable stocks to Du Seigneur and asking him to sell these at various intervals and send him money orders. The plans did not work out. He had to eat the least expensive foods (pasta, bread, cheese, and fruits) and to economize on his modes of transportation, taking stagecoaches and riverboats, and even walking a great deal of the time. Nerval was so overwhelmed by material responsibilities that his trip no longer seemed a joyful experience. By the time he arrived in Naples, his shoes were worn, his clothes frayed, and he barely had enough money for a meal.[4] Whatever sentiments of rapture might otherwise have been inspired by the landscape, they were mitigated by fear, anguish, and guilt.

Every act of liberation is necessarily followed by pain. As independence of spirit strengthens, however, one's torment usually either disappears or diminishes. In Nerval's case, it had the opposite effect. Fear of his father's criticisms and anxiety about his dwindling funds superseded all else.

Once back in Marseilles a sense of "relative" security returned; in France, on terra firma, he breathed a sigh of relief. He was annoyed with what he considered to be Du Seigneur's negligence and wrote him so. Why had he not received the funds he had requested five weeks earlier? Had unforeseen events prevented the fulfillment of an obligation? Was Du Seigneur "sick or dead?" Was "Paris buried under an earthquake?" "Was the stock market destroyed?"[5]

Nerval did not bear a grudge. He was too elated over his return to France. In fact, he was in such high spirits that he decided to play a prank. He still had five *sous* in his pockets and would—by some sleight of hand—transform himself into a dandy, a Don Juan. At the station he gave two of his *sous* to a shoeshine boy and three to some urchins to carry his luggage to the luxurious Hôtel des Princes. Nerval then made his grand entrance, the urchins preceding him. Both the hotel clerks and the director noticed him. An aristocrat, they must have thought. Nerval was given a room, food, and the finest treatment—all on credit. At dinnertime, he had an even more amusing experience. At the next table sat a military man, slightly "demented" or senile, and his wife. She was forever trying to prevent her husband from drinking too much, but could not counter his wishes in too overt a manner or he would react violently. When he ordered champagne, which the doctors had forbidden him, she offered it to the few people in the dining room. Since Nerval sat right near her, she kept filling up his glass. Her husband, annoyed at the attention his wife paid Nerval, left in a huff. As for Nerval, he was thrilled by what he interpreted as a show of affection on the lady's part. "I don't look like Anthony, I know it, but in comparison with that old man, I am absolutely formidable."[6]

This incident took on important proportions because Nerval related it in both his letters and in a short story, *Octavie*. It is understandable that he should have misinterpreted the display on the part of the lady in the dining room. Nerval had not yet, so far as we know, experienced any kind of real relationship with a woman. He had been enamored of the little girls of Mortefontaine, infatuated with his cousin from Saint-Germain-en-Laye, but these loves were always experienced from a distance. The young ladies involved were objects of adoration, not really flesh-and-blood human beings with whom he could establish any real rapport. Deprived as he had been of maternal love, he did not know how to cope with women, or how to explain certain situations. Therefore he overreacted with the lady from Marseilles, mistaking casual remarks for profound and passionate statements.

The conviction that a beautiful lady had been attracted to him enhanced the rest of his trip. There were other reasons, he thought, mystical reasons, for his encounter with this woman. After all, everything that happens on earth is destined to happen. This lady had been placed in his path for some mysterious reason. *Nothing happens by chance.*

Upon his return to Paris, Nerval did not move into his father's house. He went to live instead, at least temporarily, with an artist friend, Camille Rogier, the future illustrator of Hoffmann's *Fantastic Tales,* who lived in a small and cluttered attic studio on 5 Rue des Beaux-Arts. Neither Rogier nor Nerval could afford better quarters. Nerval's grandfather's will had not yet been settled and the heir still had to watch his finances carefully.[7]

When certain funds did become available, Nerval, Rogier, and Gautier, together with Arsène Houssaye, the future director of the Comédie-Française, rented an apartment near the Louvre, on the Impasse du Doyenné (today the actual Place du Carrousel).

Though in the middle of Paris, the neighborhood surrounding the Impasse du Doyenné was almost countrified. One could hear the cocks crow, the goats bleating, the birds humming and chirping. Not far away stood a church in ruins, with its three pillars reaching up to the sky, lending an atmosphere of gravity to the area. Old and dismal houses on either side of the Impasse gave the street a rather sinister look, at least according to Balzac's description of it in *Cousine Bette:* "the tenebrous atmosphere, the silence, the glacial air, the cavernous depth of the ground" reminded him of "crypts, of living tombs."

The Impasse du Doyenné might have been "deathlike" to Balzac, but to Nerval and his friends it spelled heaven. Joy, excitement, frivolity—and work—would fill their lives. For Nerval, it symbolized final liberation from his father, or so he thought.

The apartment was located on the second floor and consisted of six bedrooms, two studios, a vestibule, an immense drawing room, and some worn furniture abandoned by the previous tenants. The drawing room, with its rococo ceiling and its large paneled walls, was really the pièce de résistance. Camille Corot, a frequent visitor, painted an Italian landscape on the walls. Théodore Chasseriau, one of Ingres' fervent students, decorated another section of the wall with depictions of "Diana taking her bath."[8] Gautier put his stamp on the wall with a scene he called "Lunch on the Grass" in the style of Watteau.[9] Other visitors drew naiads, dryads, nudes, and landscapes.

Gavarni, the illustrator for the witty and satirical *Charivari* and future editor of a fashion magazine, paid frequent visits to Nerval, Gautier, and Houssaye. Other creative young people, coming from what seemed to be all parts of Paris, enjoyed merry-making with Nerval and his group and believed that happiness and success were within their grasp.

Nerval, Gautier, and the other bohemians, poor for the most part, overlooked the squalor of their quarters. Gautier's mother, fearing for her son's health at one point, used to send provisions from Neuilly to fill usually empty larders. The wealthy Roger de Beauvoir, stylish in his dress and aristocratic in his ways, would come and bring wines and delicacies of all sorts. The atmosphere at the Impasse inspired Beauvoir to write an ultraromantic novel, *The Procope Café* (1835), for example, and plays in which insouciance and gaiety reigned.

When Dumas visited, everyone knew a "storm was brewing," and no sooner "had he entered than he left." He was always busy, tremendously active, his imagination in a state of perpetual effervescence.[10]

And no one was ever bored when Edouard Ourliac came. Charming, humorous, Ourliac was endowed with a rare talent for satire. A devotee of Voltaire, he seemed able, with grace and ease, to imitate his master's acerbic wit. In his novels, *The Protestant Archbishop* (1832) and *Jeanne the Black* (1833), Ourliac demonstrated his fine talent for character analysis. Later, as a journalist for the *Figaro, L'Artiste,* and *La Presse* he knew just how to inject the right amount of causticity in his remarks, to hurt or to annihilate someone he did not favor.

Alphonse Esquiros, another visitor, was a poet and novelist, and author of *The Magician* (1837). In later years, his idealism ran rampant and he was converted to socialism, writing such works as *The Gospel of the People* (1840), believing most fervently that mankind's lot on earth would one day mirror paradise.

Nerval had never known such happiness, such freedom. He took an interest in his surroundings, in the decor of his room and the apartment.

By 1835 he had received the rest of his inheritance and decided he would spend it as he saw fit. He had fine and expensive tastes. Sometimes he acted impulsively. One day he saw a Renaissance bed for sale, legend has it, which had belonged to Marguerite de Valois. The price: eight thousand francs. He bought it on the spot. It was so large that to get it into the apartment, the entrance had to be dismantled. Gérard, most ceremoniously, placed the bed in the center of the drawing room and his own mattress at the foot of his precious possession. When asked who would occupy the bed, Nerval answered, "my imagination."[11] Nerval looked upon his bed—this objet d'art—as something sacred, and upon the entire area, as his "sanctuary."[12]

He made other purchases, not so enormous but equally magnificent: a Médicis console, two buffets, a Louis XIII armchair, tapestries depicting the four seasons, two paintings by Fragonard for which it is said he paid only fifty francs.[13]

Though a sense of camaraderie existed between Nerval and his friends, something prevented him from participating in the earthly pleasures that the others knew. He was not one to carouse with the young ladies, dancers, actresses, models, and midinettes who were forever adorning the apartment on the Impasse du Doyenné. Nerval was more withdrawn, more secretive and solitary. Nevertheless, now that he was no longer living under his father's aegis certain tensions seemed to have disappeared. Nerval no longer had to be punctual; no routine had to be followed, no accounting of the day's activities had to be given.

Nor did Gautier's life always take on the golden glow of joy. He and

Rogier had fallen in love with the same girl—"Cydalise No. I," they called her.[14] Rogier painted her portrait in her "taffeta" dress; Gautier immortalized her "in the pure crystal of a sonnet."[15] But Cydalise No. I suffered from consumption—a fashionable disease at the time— and spent most of her days lying in a hammock that hung in the drawing room of the apartment. As the men's passions grew, so did their jealousy. Only when the beautiful demoiselle died of tuberculosis did a reconciliation between Gautier and Rogier take place—over her death bed.[16]

Suffering must have taken its toll on Gautier: he began losing weight; his friends, Nerval in particular, grew concerned. Nerval informed his parents about the well-meaning treatment conferred upon Gautier by the doctor in charge, but indicated that no visible signs of improvement had been forthcoming. The doctor kept Gautier in bed and applied suction cups to his back and chest. When Nerval explained the situation, the Gautiers permitted Nerval to change the course of treatment. "Get up . . . and come and have supper with us," he told Gautier, who was so weak at this point that even Nerval was terrified. As the diet of good food and good fun continued, however, Gautier snapped back to good health. What had touched Nerval most deeply in this incident was the attitude displayed by the Gautiers. "They loved their son," commented Nerval, perhaps wistfully, and this is "a rare thing."[17]

Dinners, festivities of all sorts, costume balls, theater parties—all took place at the Impasse du Doyenné. Nerval's mood was so optimistic that he even exchanged his shabby, worn and shapeless black clothes for tight-fitting, greenish trousers, a form-fitting jacket with a high collar, patent leather shoes, and light gloves.

A dandy—he would command attention.

The year 1834 was to be momentous. Nerval was twenty-six years old. He had a fairly regular post as critic for *Vert-Vert* and *l'Artiste,* work he enjoyed. But something unexpected and highly significant happened one evening at the Variétés theater. On stage, Nerval saw what he considered to be the most exquisite, the most perfect actress of them all: Jenny Colon—blond, with long soft curls about her face, a fine figure, a slender neck, blue eyes, a remarkably white skin, and a velvety voice. Nerval could not stop looking at her.

Indeed, Nerval was in love—instantly, madly, passionately. Night after night he returned to the Variétés theater and sat in the same box "in the full dress of a suitor"; she consumed his entire existence. Nerval began to live for the Variétés performances, the lights, the theater—and the illusion her presence on stage created.

Nerval's courtship of Jenny was unique. Timid, particularly when it came to women, he did not go backstage and introduce himself as was customary after the first, second, or third performance. He sat on the edge of his seat, admiring and worshipping her from afar. He sent her exquisite bouquets but never signed the notes he tucked into them.

Nerval made inquiries into her life and took seriously—as a sign of some mystical bonds—the coincidence that both he and Jenny had been born in 1808. His conviction that they were destined for one another was unswerving. It had been written in the stars.

Jenny Colon, a native of Boulogne-sur-Mer, was the daughter of an acting couple and had, since her earliest days, performed in theaters all over France. At fourteen she appeared on the stage of the Opéra-Comique in Paris; at twenty, she toured Scotland and married an actor, Lafon, at Gretna Green. It must have been a spur of the moment decision because the marriage was soon annulled. A Dutch banker entered her life at this time, doing away with all of her financial burdens. By 1828 she was in Paris and had devloped into a fine actress and beautiful singer, a "threat" to any woman. Though her repertoire was varied, the plays in which she performed were for the most part mediocre: *The Week of Loves* by Dumanoir, *The Modiste, The Prima Donna, The Comrade at the Pension* by Ancelot.

As for her character, she was no prude nor was she timid or withdrawn. Confident of her attributes, her talent and her beauty, she knew she could charm almost any man. Nerval was easy prey.

To be enamored of an actress in the 1830s, when romanticism was in full bloom, was stylish. Victor Hugo—with his wife's knowledge—was already passionately in love with the gorgeous Juliette Drouet, a liaison that lasted nearly fifty years. Pétrus Borel was infatuated with Lucinda Paradol; Alfred de Vigny suffered from his passion for Marie Dorval, whom he compared in his anger to "a woman impure in mind and in body."

The difference between Nerval's relationship with Jenny Colon and those of his friends with their respective actresses was immense. While Hugo, Borel, and Vigny had declared their love overtly, whether joyfully or with pain, Nerval's adoration remained a secret. He did not inform his lady love of his feelings. In fact, he did not even meet her until months after he had fallen in love.

Little is known about their relationship. No one knows exactly when they actually met or what was said at their meetings. Introverted by nature, Nerval tried to hide, even to dissimulate, all facts connected with his liaison—if in fact there had actually been one. Gautier, Nanteuil, Borel—all remained silent on the subject, unwilling to betray a confidence. Only the sparsest facts have come to light.

Nerval's epoch-making adventure blossomed only in his world of fantasy. As he watched her from his box at the Variétés theater, Jenny the Woman began to slowly disappear, to be replaced by Jenny the Divinity, the *femme inspiratrice,* the anima figure. Like the bards and troubadours of the Middle Ages, Nerval vowed his love to her for eternity. Even that was not sufficient. In his dreams he played a modern knight in shining armor—he made her an international star. He would assure her good fortune by writing a "great" play.

Nerval's fantasizing was not merely in the abstract. The inheritance he had received from Grandfather Laurent would be put to good use. He would take Balzac's "wise" advice and found a magazine whose main purpose would be to celebrate his beloved's talents and beauty.

Thus *The Dramatic World* came into being. It would include articles on all aspects of the theater: sets, choreography, acting, playwrighting, costuming, designing, lighting. It would be published weekly, at a price of four *sous*.[18] Everything about the magazine would be elegant: the finest paper would be used, the printing would be artistically set, the illustrations would be beautiful.[19] Frédéric Soulié would help with the editing and Gautier, Dumas, Berlioz, Musset, Karr, Janin, Nanteuil, Rogier, Gavarni would contribute articles or illustrations. *The Dramatic World* could not fail.

The first number was published on May 5, 1835. Everything in the issue was designed to honor Jenny Colon. Gavarni drew an exquisite sketch of her in one of her costumes. Her blond hair curled neatly about her head was a suitable frame for her large eyes, her small but straight nose, her lips, which wore a most engaging smile; her short bouffant dress underscored her captivating figure. She was in every way the essence of femininity.[20]

Nerval believed that Jenny was too great an artistic and musical talent to continue at the Variétés. He felt she was fit for the opera. With her fine voice, only the right type of criticism and publicity were needed to bring about such a change. Though Nerval himself refrained from writing articles in her praise, he asked Gautier and other friends to do so. When finally he found the courage, he proclaimed the following: "This young woman with an open, smiling, amiable, and resplendent face is Jenny Colon; she exudes happiness and gaiety. Jenny who was seen on this same stage as a child; beautiful, fresh, mischievous, dressed in the costume of a little Savoyard, receiving so many bravos and candies, was seen twelve years later at the same theater, where she received such beautiful and deserving applause."[21]

Nerval had become Jenny's defender and would fight for her reputation under any circumstances.[22] When Jules Janin, critic for the *Journal des Débats* and a friend of Nerval's, denigrated her both as a woman and as an actress, Nerval countered Janin's remarks with unparalleled courage. The passive, withdrawn and timid man had turned into an heroic defender. If others, friends or acquaintances, ever called Jenny coquettish, superficial, flighty, materialistic, or anything else not complimentary, he rose to the occasion with brio.[23]

The theater is a world of illusion. Jenny's life was based on her ability to create such "illusion" and to transform fictional lives into stage "real-

ities." Because Nerval "adored" her, he unwittingly yielded to the world
of fantasy, identifying with the lovers in the plays in which Jenny performed. No living relationship could ever emerge from such an unreal
situation.

Nerval lived in a state of euphoria; he sang the praise of his beloved.
The Dramatic World functioned, and he had moved out of his father's
life. On November 28, 1835, Nerval gave a fantastic ball, to fête, perhaps, the new magazine and his beloved. "Le Bal des Truands," as it was
called, was an event that no Bohemian in Paris could or would ever forget. The guests were drawn to the Impasse du Doyenné from the re-
motest areas of Paris. They had been asked to come in costume and
arrived in the most outlandish and daring ones. Rogier's attire was the
most splendid of them all: he wore a Venetian robe of green damask
embroidered with a silver and gold chain hung from his neck.[24]

Nerval never forgot "Le Bal des Truands." Years later, he wrote: "We
gave balls, suppers, costume parties. . . . How happy these times were."[25]

Nerval's worship of Jenny continued. He went almost nightly to the
Opéra-Comique, watched her every move on stage, thrilled to her bell-
like and "delicious" voice, the realism of her gestures, the charm of her
stance, the variety of her facial expressions. Did he wonder why such a
great star should act in such dull plays and operas as *A Daughter of Eve,
the Estates of Blois*?[26] The greater his ambition for Jenny Colon grew, the
more out of touch he was with reality.[26]

The Dramatic World could not survive on enthusiasm alone. Neither he
nor his friends knew the slightest thing about business. As a result, Nerval not only lost the money he had invested in *The Dramatic World* but
incurred debts. More painful to him, certainly, was the fact that he felt
he had lost face with Jenny. He had wanted to offer her fame and fortune. Now he could do neither.

During the dismal months that followed Nerval continued to see her
either alone or in the company of friends, though no one knows how
frequently. His idealization did not falter with his altered circumstances.
She was still his goddess, the supreme being who reigned over his life
and destiny, his "mystic wife." As an anima figure, she joined his former
platonic loves: the little girls of Mortefontaine dressed in their freshly
washed white-lace dresses, the beautiful cousin at Saint-Germain-en-
Laye. Jenny incorporated them all. She was for him the Virgin Goddess,
the essence of purity, beauty as well as that Maternal, all-loving Queen
of the Night.

As the living incarnation of the Divine Mother and Wife, she ruled
his world. His studies in the occult, as a child and under Nodier's tu-
telage, only reinforced what he had already sensed: Jenny was destined
for him for all eternity, and if he could not possess her in this world,
she would surely be his in the next. Why not? It had happened to the

young Francesco Colonna who had to give up his beloved Polia because she was of noble birth and he was not. This Renaissance man had written in detail about his love in *The Dream of Poliphilo*. The certainty of his eventual union with Jenny sustained Nerval during the trying months ahead. Not only had the magazine been wrenched from him, but he would have to confront his father who would certainly look down upon him with contempt.

Still another dream vanished. After eighteen months at the Impasse du Doyenné, Nerval and his entire entourage were evicted. The noise was too great; there were too many disturbances. When Balzac—whose own ill-fated enterprises became notorious—asked Nerval how he had come to lose his possessions, how a world of beauty and loveliness could have been dissipated so easily, Nerval answered in Balzac's own terms: "Misfortune."[27]

Though *The Dramatic World* had failed and nothing real seemed to have come from his relationship with Jenny Colon, Nerval was determined to write a "great" opera for her—one worthy of her talents. It would be based on the legend of Solomon and the Queen of Sheba. The latter was an object of fascination and mystery; an aura surrounded her name. She must have constellated unconscious tendencies within Nerval.

Always meticulous in his literary pursuits, Nerval did not approach his libretto haphazardly. He spent weeks and months reading all he could find about the Queen of Sheba: Oriental tales, Biblical stories, the Talmud, the Koran, the mysteries of Zoroastrianism, La Peyrère's history of the seventy pre-Adamite kings, Héberlot de Molainville's *Oriental Library*, works on Lilith, on the Persian bird Hudhud, on Hermes Trismegistus, and many others.

Jenny became synonymous with the Queen of Sheba. Nerval visualized her donning her regal robes and precious jewels, arriving in Palestine from some remote country in Arabia. The very ambiguity of such a figure added lustre to the entire picture. What did the Queen of Sheba symbolize? A woman coming from some "strange" and distant land was the bearer of new elements, new traditions, new ways. She was linked to the wisdom of the great King Solomon, the builder of the most magnificent temple of all time. According to Biblical tradition, when she arrived in Palestine, she and Solomon exchanged gifts and a while later she returned to her land, gave birth to a son who was then given back to his father to be educated in true Hebrew tradition. At the proper time, the son would be sent back to his native land to spread the doctrine.

For Nerval, the Queen of Sheba had taken on the qualities and power of an archetype, a transpersonal figure. As such, she was indeed illusive, her origin and identity clothed in mystery. It had been theorized that the Queen of Sheba came from Yemen and that her name was Sheba (others called her Balkis or Makeda, Neghesta-Azeb, the Queen of Noon). What of her religion? It has been associated with the Sabbeans, star worshippers from southern Arabia, known for their trade in spice and gems, who believed in a creator-god who remained inaccessible to man except through the intermediary of spirits.[28]

Nerval completed his libretto. His hopes were high when he presented it to the well-known opera composer Giacomo Meyerbeer. This German-born musician, who had already won accolades for *Robert the Devil* (1831) and *The Huguenots* (1836), seemed pleased with Nerval's libretto. He asked him to make certain changes.[29] After the modifications were made Nerval returned the libretto to Meyerbeer who smiled with what Nerval interpreted as satisfaction. Days passed. Each time Nerval went to see the composer, Meyerbeer would greet him cordially, but he never committed himself. Taken aback, Nerval interpreted this hesitation as a rejection. There were perhaps reasons for Meyerbeer's attitude: the well-known dramatist Eugène Scribe had written many librettos for Meyerbeer and perhaps the composer, fearful of accepting the work of another, procrastinated.[30]

Though Nerval's plans for an opera based on the Queen of Sheba did not materialize, he did write a short play for Jenny Colon: *Corilla*. Like Jenny, the female protagonist was an opera star. She was loved by Fabio and Marcelli, the former who is in love with an illusion, she discovers, and the latter, with himself.[31]

To supplement his income, Nerval decided to work full time as a drama critic. He made friends easily and since he already had a reputation among the literati, he found himself in a fortunate position. Alphonse Karr, editor of the *Figaro*, asked him to write for his newspaper as did Nestor Roqueplan, editor of the *Charte de 1830*. Gautier procured him work on Emile de Girardin's *La Presse;* other journals and papers accepted his contributions every now and then: *La Revue de Paris, La Sylphide, Le Prisme, Revue des deux mondes, Le Temps, l'Illustration, Le Mousquetaire, Vert-Vert.* Nerval would be able to keep body and soul together.

No matter how arduous his work as a drama critic became, Nerval still nourished the idea of writing a "great" play for Jenny Colon. He found the perfect solution: he asked Dumas to collaborate with him on an opéra-comique to be called *Piquillo*. It could not possibly fail, he thought—not with Dumas' name associated with the venture.[32] Yet it did. It opened on October 31, 1837, and closed just twenty-five nights later. Nerval attributed whatever fine criticisms it received to "the talent of our prima donna, Mlle. Jenny Colon."[33]

To make matters even worse, Jenny announced her marriage on April 11, 1838, to the flutist (who was also her tour organizer) Louis-Marie-Gabriel Leplus. According to some observers Nerval accepted her mar-

riage rather well—as part of his earthly destiny; he continued to be convinced that she would be his in the next world. He, therefore, continued
to immortalize this "radiant" creature in a series of letters that he wrote
to her but probably never mailed. *The Letters to Jenny Colon,* which are
part of the great epistolary literature of France, were of course not published when written. Six of the letters appeared in the *Sylphide* (December, 1842) under the title "A Novel to be Written," as missives said to
have been composed by the Chevalier Dubourjet, who had died in
Santo-Domingo. Eighteen other letters to Jenny Colon were not published until October 15, 1902.[34]

These letters are fascinating not only because of the purity and simplicity of the language but because of what they reveal about Nerval's
state of mind. Jenny is depicted as an anima figure, as the representative
of an unconscious inner attitude with respect to the feminine principle.
As such, she is both collective and individual, mortal and immortal, human and divine, personal and transcendental. The themes running
through the letters may be divided into three motifs, each relating to an
aspect of the anima figure: (1) The theme of sacrifice, (2) The mother-
and-child motif, and (3) The son-lover motif.

Why has sacrifice become such an important factor in most religions?
It indicates the abolition of an attitude inimical to life. Psychic energy,
usually expended on a conscious level in dealing with everyday situations, is withdrawn and flows into the unconscious. Sacrifice involves
regression, and as such, it disrupts the instinctual foundations of the
personality.[35]

What was Nerval sacrificing and what were its implications? For Nerval, sacrifice meant the annihilation of everything he felt to be incom-
patible with his existence. By withdrawing into his world of fantasy, he
was weakening, sacrificing his ego. The ego, the center of consciousness
standing between the inner and outer worlds, must adapt to both. In
Nerval's case, the ego was losing its power and found itself incapable of
relating to external reality. Nerval was aware (at least to a certain extent)
of what was happening to him, and even wrote in his letters: "I could
write such a beautiful novel for you if my thoughts were calmer!"[36] What
escaped his comprehension were the destructive side effects resulting
from a progressively weakening ego.

The unwitting sacrifice of Nerval's ego made him a prey to his unconscious and, as such, a victim of oscillating moods. He was either in
a state of anguish, torment, he confesses in his letters to Jenny Colon,
or so dazzled by her image that he could barely stand the intensity of
the flame she had ignited within him. "There is a ceaseless storm of
thoughts in my head, which dazzles and fatigues me; there are years of
dreams, of projects, anguishes which would like to compress themselves
into a sentence, into a word."[37] Because he was a victim of his moods,
he could never take a firm stand. He was either too rash or too reserved

toward Jenny Colon. Discomfited by his timidity, he deprecated himself for not having the courage to declare his love openly; and when he did exteriorize his feelings, he was ashamed by the banality of the words he chose to express them in. Discouragement sometimes turned to annoyance. He blamed his misery on her "indifference," thereby transforming her into a negative figure bent upon hurting him.

Any man who sacrifices his ego, unwittingly or not, falls under the spell of his anima figure. He becomes tempestuous, passionate, fearful of his own inner fire, frightened at the thought of offending his beloved, never knowing how to rectify certain situations or calm his "agitation." The more he seeks to change his ways, to alter his fits of moodiness, the less power he has over himself and the more he admires what he considers to be her "courageous" and "patient" attitude. Jenny had become Circe, captivating him into submission. Her superiority was such that Nerval looked upon her not as a mortal woman but as a deity who dispensed her kisses and her justice on her own terms.

> My God, my God, I thank you! Your eye met mine, your hand holding mine. You knew it would be. And what difference does it make if I couldn't speak a word to you . . . a few hours of sweetness and a night, a whole night.[38]

Nerval became helpless, like a child to be cared for and guided.[39] His relationship then took on a mother-child motif and anima-Jenny was experienced on an infantile or adolescent level. He described his disappointments when she treated him unkindly and his ecstasy when she bestowed favors on him; when he exteriorized his passion overtly he begged for forgiveness. Indeed, Nerval had regressed to a veritable childlike state and even questions himself: "Am I a child? even though I love you with all the rashness of a child!"[40] As a maternal figure, Jenny filled a void in Nerval's heart—she became, symbolically, the mother he had never known. He begs her to listen to his anguish and torments, to comfort him with her understanding acceptance and love.[41]

As a child, Nerval also berates this mother figure for having neglected him, but to show his unbounding love, he confesses his willingness to die for her. However, to Nerval death represented eternal sleep, a realm where pain and turmoil were nonexistent, where love was reciprocated, spiritualized, divinized, immortalized. By many romantics, including Nerval, death was envisaged in the form of a woman—a mother figure who takes the poet in her arms, cradles and comforts him, disperses his torments. "Death," Nerval writes, "appears to me as crowned with pale roses, at the end of a feast; I sometimes dream that she awaited me, smiling at the bedside of a woman I adored, not at night, but in the morning; after the inebriation of happiness, and that she said to me: Come on young man! you had your night as others have their day: now, come and sleep, come and rest in my arms; I am not beautiful, but I am good and helpful, and I do not give pleasure, but eternal calm."[42]

Psychologically, Nerval is already dead in that he has surrendered totally to his anima. She wields her power over him and because of this he remains lifeless, until those times when she seeks to stir him into activity. When she withdraws her affection or attention, he withers and dies, as do all victims of the Great Mother archetype.

In this regard, Nerval is playing out a nineteenth-century version of the ancient Son-Lover myth, that of Cybele and Attis, the son who ended by castrating himself. Nerval's utter submission to Jenny has transformed him, in these letters, into an object of her desire or disdain. Indeed, when overwhelmed by her kindness, he sometimes loses control over his speech and aphasia momentarily takes hold of him. Such speechlessness implies that the unconscious has taken over the conscious personality, making it incapable of adapting to real situations. The dream images that emerge under these circumstances are so potent, so charged with energy, as to dictate his ideations, his attitude, his manner of relating to people. The anima figure feels for him, decides his course.

The anima is usually a compensatory figure and as such possesses those faculties and qualities which the individual lacks in his conscious attitude. In Nerval's case, she stands for the mother, wife, and mistress. She offered him rapture, excitement, passion. To become independent requires an intense struggle comparable to Siegfried's fight with the dragon. Nerval had never been capable of asserting himself with either his friends or his father. He was loved by all who met him, perhaps, for this very reason—as one who was amenable in all ways, who was willing to go along with others, who was never a source of conflict.

Nerval's affective relationship with Jenny, rather than diminishing with the years, was exaggerated and became transformed into a myth.[43] And he refused to change his stand: he "did not try to have this beautiful idol whom I have loved from afar, descend from her pedestal."[44] Instead of depotentializing her after her marriage to another, he places her even higher, declaring that he had never really loved her as one mortal does another, and that his love transcended worldly limitations: "It is your soul I love above all."[45]

Anima implies soul, that eternal living corpus, the transpersonal value given to an image that imbues it with force and vigor and infuses it with life. As Dante had his Beatrice, Nerval had his Jenny. But how would Nerval continue to function in real life, now that Jenny was married? How much attention would he devote to this anima image? How much life would he blot out because of it? How would his weakened ego cope with situations and people? And would he ever be able to relate to real women?

6 THE ARTFUL PANDORA

*This is the Hypnerotomachia of Poliphilo, which
teaches that all things human are but a dream, and
in which many things are set forth which it is
salutary and meet to know.*
Francesco Colonna, *The Hypnerotomachia.*

Now that Nerval's love for Jenny Colon could not be realistically experienced, it dominated his unconscious. Every woman he met, every female figure he created in his short stories, poems, or dramatic works, would in some way be associated with her. When, for example, he went to see a troupe of Hindu dancers on August 12, 1838, he saw Amany, the most beautiful of all, as an avatar of Jenny Colon.

Nerval was so deeply moved by the Hindu dancing troupe, the Bayadères, that one may well ask why. Certainly his projection onto Amany accounted for some of his responses and the beauty of the other dancers was also impressive: their undulating forms, the host of symbolic gestures woven in space, and the oral accompaniments to the visual feast—the metallic bells that sounded so tremulously at various intervals, followed by harsh, shrill sounds that broke up the harmonies. Something that Nerval noted in the critique of the performance deserves close examination.[1]

Nerval suggested that when viewing the Hindu dancers he had come face to face with a "primitive race." A past, not merely his own but that of man in general, intruded upon the present—as if linear or eschatological time had been obliterated and the eternal present came into being suddenly, forcefully, and dramatically. With the past looked upon as a present reality, a host of new associations, fresh feelings also came into view—in which Nerval could wander about ad infinitum.

Nerval associated freely as he watched the performance: the songs, the music, and the dancers, as they wove their way across the stage, all reminded him of Biblical times and, strangely enough, of Scottish clans colliding with one another. A feeling of timelessness and spacelessness took hold of Nerval, to such an extent that he felt he was a witness to one of Vishnu's incarnations—and like the Hindu worshippers in the midst of a trance he experienced a momentary eclipse of the self, a weightlessness, as though he had evaporated or had been dispersed into the atmosphere.

Amany, the tallest of the group, infused the entire ambiance with a cosmic quality. She sang and danced with an ethereal quality that marked her every delicate gesture. It was as if she had enticed the world into herself, had succeeded in captivating unknown forces into her orbit—

divinities and demons alike—into quiet submission. Nerval looked upon the spacial designs she wove as visual transcriptions of Ariadne's monologue bewailing Theseus' desertion of her, or the song that the Queen of Sheba might have sung when greeting King Solomon. Amany's eyes were her most arresting feature. They glowed within: the two orbits symbolizing light, the spirit illuminated and, Nerval suggested, "the face seems to find refuge" in the eyes. Mobile and fluid, they had become living forces, breathing substances. All her feelings and thoughts are "concentrated in the eyes, the most beautiful in the world."[2] It was via Amany's eyes that Nerval followed the transformation taking place within her soul and, in so doing, felt a parallel sensation within his own. As for the rest of her face, save for the opening and closing of the mouth, it was "calm and serious like an antique mask."[3]

A metaphysical aura descended on the performers. The petulant and vigorous steps and poses, the animal chants, the incantations, prayers and rhythmic effects became outerworldly, reminiscent of Shiva's dance of creation. According to Hindu myth, it was the god Shiva who succeeded in transforming energy (visible in the form of circles of flames which surrounded him) by uniting space and time—thereby creating the world. For Nerval, Amany had been transformed into a goddess who ushered in a world of mystery and magic before his very eyes.[4]

The oral aspects of Hindu drama also captivated Nerval. Music is a pattern given to heretofore disparate manifestations of the universe. It is a transformative agent with the power of changing the inaudible into the audible, nonthought into thought and its expression in the word. In this sense, music represents both the undifferentiated world of the spirit (the sound and thought-word not yet come into being) and the differentiated realm (the sound and thought-word that have come into being).[5] According to certain mystics, namely the medieval Spaniard Abraham Abulafia, a state of nonthought (which he calls "a music of pure thought" and compares to musical harmonies) may be ushered into existence via meditative practices. His method, which he terms *Tseruf,* is described as follows:

> And from the ear the sensation travels to the heart, and from the heart to the spleen (the center of emotion), and enjoyment of the different melodies produces ever new delight. . . . And the secrets, which express themselves in these combinations, delight the heart which acknowledges its God and is filled with every fresh joy.[6]

Abulafia goes on to associate the "music of pure thought" with the alphabet.

Pythagoras also spoke of a "music of the spheres," which he viewed in terms of numbers. The Greeks believed that music had been given to man by Orpheus who, with his lyre, had succeeded in dominating nature in all of its forms: animal, mineral, and vegetable. Nature became associated with music and because of this link, the instrumentalist (or the poet, the creative individual) could experience nature from within, thereby making for the miracle of the word—the transformation of the inaudible sound into the audible thought.[7]

Schopenhauer described "wordless sounds" that ushered in a new realm in which he could travel about freely through space and time. Hermann Hesse, in *The Magic Bead Game,* also delineated such states of pure thought which, when severed from the senses, succeeded in creating harmonies within the human being:

> The ear drank in the fugue; it seemed to him that he was hearing music for the first time in his life. Behind the music being created in his presence he sensed the world of Mind, the joy-giving harmony of law and freedom of service and rule . . . his face softly glowing from within. . . .[8]

Nerval, ever since his earliest days at Mortefontaine, had always been receptive to music. Indeed, his love for Jenny Colon may have been attributed in part to her talents as a singer. Nerval also gave primacy to tonalities in his poetry: "There is a melody for which I would give all of Mozart, Rossini, and Weber. . . ." Music had an assuaging effect on him; it acted as a release mechanism for feelings he could never express overtly and always tempered with an overly cerebral or intellectual approach. Music fed what was starving within him, rounded out what had become sharp and cutting.

Nerval was so captivated by the Bayadères dancers and Amany in particular that whenever he strolled about Paris he stopped in front of shops with Oriental figurines on display, associating these statues with the dancers he had seen. One day he came upon a statue of Amany executed by Auguste Barre and marveled at the perfection of the work: its inner glow, its serpentine contours, the grace of its lines—the "nobility that reigns in its pose."[9] This statue became a source of mystery and excitement; it seemed to take on a life of its own, moving, breathing, sighing. It was as if the entire Orient were alive before Nerval, and he commented on "the richness and the divine pleasure of the imagination."[10]

Amany's corporeal image and the fact that she was lost in space were not the only factors involved in Nerval's attraction to her. It was her mobility. Paradoxically, though she did not move, she represented a world in flux, the realm of becoming. The contradictory forces encapsulated in this statue—human and inhuman, mobile and immobile—formed a *coniunctio* and merged before Nerval's eyes. The intense activity he projected onto the statue of Amany awakened a corresponding creative desire within himself. The rebuffs he had received at the hands of the critics did not affect his zeal because he had decided to alter his course, so far as the dramatic arts were concerned: instead of writing a light and gay work, he would reveal the inner workings of a world that had always haunted him—that of the alchemist.

Before Nerval could set to work on his next play, *The Alchemist,* he and Dumas had agreed to coauthor the drama *Leo Burckhart,* based on the life of the well-known German dramatist August von Kotzebue.[11] The research involved in such an undertaking was vast and since Nerval was such a meticulous worker, he and Dumas decided to take a trip to Germany to discover the details *sur place.* In the fall of 1838, Nerval joined Dumas in Frankfurt, the city in which Kotzebue had lived and had been assassinated.[12]

Shortly after Nerval's arrival in Frankfurt, Charles Durand, the editor of the *Journal de Francfort Français,* introduced him to Alexander Weill. A former rabbi, Weill was well versed in the Kabbala, and it has been suggested that it was he who initiated Nerval into its mysteries. Weill also acted as Nerval's guide during his stay in this city, taking him to the university, the gardens, the palaces, the Taunus forest nearby, and also introducing him to the nightlife, with its taverns, dance halls, and theaters. Weill was also helpful in practical matters, seeing to it that some of Nerval's articles were placed in the French newspapers of the city. The funds earned from this work, together with the articles he had promised to send the Parisian newspapers *Le Messager* and *La Presse,* would help cover Nerval's expenses.

Nerval and Weill became fast friends, so much so that he convinced Weill to move to Paris. He would be far better off in France, Nerval declared, than in Germany, where he earned his living as Durand's personal secretary and by translating German and English short stories into French.

> "You must come to Paris with me" Nerval said. "To Paris. . . . I would die of hunger with my Alsatian accent." "I assure you," answered Nerval, "outside of Hugo, Gautier, and myself, everyone in Paris speaks a kind of hodgepodge like yours. To be Alsatian and Jewish at once is an infallible combination: with your Hebrew, your Greek, and your German, you will be able to present yourself at the Institute. No one will understand you and you'll pass for a great scholar!"[13]

Nerval and Dumas attended to their research with diligence. *Leo Burckhart* was completed in Paris. But before it was to open, Nerval was already at work on *The Alchemist.* His attraction to alchemy is perfectly comprehensible. After all, the alchemist's goal was to discover the secrets of matter and in so doing, to transform base metals into gold. Wasn't the writer's task similar?

The classical alchemist, with his melting pots and retorts, delved into unchartered realms, attributed certain laws and images to a variety of chemicals and elements. He projected onto matter contents within his own unconscious. Faust, for example, was in the process of *descensus and infernos* when he tried to conjure up the Spirit and discover life's arcane substance. The alchemist's desire, suggested C.G. Jung, parallels a process going on within himself, an unquenchable thirst to become acquainted with the occurrences within his own inner world.[14]

Just as the alchemist projects aspects of his own unconscious onto matter and attempts to discover the "spirit imprisoned" within the substance he is studying, so the poet (or any artist) participates actively in the creation of the work under his consideration by choosing the exact word, line, or sentence to express the thought, feeling, or idea. The confrontation of the human element (either the poet or the alchemist) onto the material entity in question (either a rock, chemical formation or in the case of the writer, the blank page, the pencil or pen) engenders energy or fire. The ensuing friction between mind and matter makes for the alchemist's discovery and the poet's work of art. The well-known alchemist Gerhard Dorn wrote: "Within the human body there is hidden a certain metaphysical substance, known to only the very few whose essence is to need no medicament, for it is itself corrupted medicament."[15] This medicament, or medicine, is an arcane substance that Dorn defines as *veritas*. "There is in natural things a certain truth which cannot be seen with the outward eye, but is perceived by the mind alone [*solamente*]. The philosophers have known it, and they have found that its power is so great as to work miracles."[16]

When approaching the subject of alchemy, Nerval was in effect carrying on an inner dialogue between his concept of the work he wanted to write (the differentiated realm) and the world *in potentia* (the undifferentiated realm before the idea has manifested itself) that lies buried within him. Nerval's creative activity required a descent into self or into his own chaotic world, which alchemists have termed *nigredo* (black). Though *The Alchemist* was based on a story by Grazzini, the characters and incidents reveal, in a slightly veiled manner, his own torments.

There are three main characters in *The Alchemist:* Fasio, the sculptor-alchemist; his down-to-earth and loving wife, Francesca; and the courtesan, Maddalena, endowed with angelic features, but who turns out to be a female devil who drives Fasio on to acquire more and more material wealth by creating gold.

The two women represent contraries: purity and seduction, love and passion. They are anima figures, to be sure—autonomous or split-off complexes endowed with energy, each bent upon destroying the other, each seeking to become the dominant power. If *The Alchemist* is a projection of certain elements within Nerval's unconscious, one suspects he was experiencing this same inner conflict. Whereas Nerval's previous anima figures (Gretchen in *Faust,* the little girls of Mortefontaine) had been for the most part pure and simple, when he met Jenny Colon, the figure was expanded to include a more regal and sensual type of femme fatale in the Queen of Sheba myth. In his letters to Jenny, Nerval's anima image included the mother-child and the sacrificed-child motifs. In *The Alchemist,* fascinatingly enough, all these facets are included in the two main characters, an indication that Nerval was beginning to express such potent forces in dialogue form.

A very interesting study on Nerval suggests that he had had (or was having at this time) a liaison—whether spiritual or physical is not known—with a beautiful actress, Esther de Bongars.[17] If Nerval had established a relationship with her, it could have accounted for the introduction of the dual female figures in *The Alchemist:* Jenny and Esther might have been experienced in projection.

The Alchemist was first performed on April 10, 1839, at the Renaissance Theatre and *Leo Burckhart* opened on April 16 at the Porte Saint-Martin. Nerval's spirits ran high—and with reason. One of the most celebrated actors in France, Frédérick Lemaitre, played Fasio in *The Alchemist* as well as an important role in *Leo Burckhart.* Lemaitre, who had portrayed Othello and Hamlet, and roles in Hugo's and Dumas' works, was so popular a figure among theatergoers that whenever he strolled along the street crowds were sure to follow. He was the idol of the boulevard theaters, the star of melodrama. Handsome, tall, powerfully built—he radiated virility. Ida Ferier, Dumas' mistress and future wife, as attractive as she was dynamic, played Francesca in *The Alchemist.*

Everything should have gone well with so fine a cast and theater. It did not. Critics felt that *The Alchemist* was contrived, that the happy ending was artificial and unwarranted. The play netted Nerval twelve hundred francs. As for *Leo Burckhart,* the director had so skimped on the decors that the entire play lost point and force. It was performed only twenty-six times.

Nerval's sense of failure must have caused him great suffering, particularly vis-à-vis Jenny who, though married, was still his ideal and the one person he wanted to serve. His friends—Hugo, Lamartine, Balzac, Musset—were already famous, adulated, while Nerval was still struggling and unsuccessful. Was fate against him? Was something in his destiny bent upon destroying him? A great deal of time had been spent writing *Leo Burckhart* and *The Alchemist* which had depleted him and he had not been able to devote many hours to his activities as a journalist. The result was that he was again in dire straits. He was forced to publish anything and everything. *Leo Burckhart* was printed in *La Presse* and also in book form, with an appendix he had written on German universities. His articles on his travels were also published in newspapers and magazines. Nerval was so pressed for time that he asked his good friend August Maquet to help him meet a deadline: September 17 and 18,

1839. Nerval would give him the plot-line of the story he had in mind, *The Singular Biography of Raoul Spifame,* and Maquet would write it.[18]

Nerval's Hoffmannesque story, *The Singular Biography of Raoul Spifame,* not only inspires fear but is one of the earliest expressions of the dual personality theme that in time took on greater and greater importance in his literary works. The events depicted in the story take place in sixteenth-century France. Raoul Spifame, a young man whose father has sent him to Paris to study law, has worked hard and received his degree. One day he sits in court observing the events. Suddenly, King Henry II walks in; their eyes meet and both are astounded by their resemblance as is everyone present: "It seemed to King Henry II that a portrait had been placed opposite him which reproduced his entire person, transforming only his splendid regal vestments into black clothes."[19] The similarity was disturbing for Raoul because, according to certain beliefs, when you are confronted with a person who looks just like you, it is a sign of imminent death. After the incident, many at court begin mocking Raoul, addressing him as "Your Majesty" or "Your Highness" and bowing and scraping every time he comes by. As the days pass, Raoul's actions alter. He seems to have lost his identity and walks in the streets, stopping passers-by, informing them of his ideas concerning governmental reforms. Raoul is put in an insane asylum and suffers a high fever, after which his reason breaks completely. By day he sits in a chair, at night he informs the guards that his real life is beginning because of his "extraordinary dreams." A new world opens for him in which he identifies completely with Henry II and thinks he is living at the Louvre, riding at the head of his army, speaking to his counsel, presiding over splendid banquets when, in fact, he is living in an asylum. At times, Raoul becomes conscious of "a second personality" and experiences it most shockingly one day when he is given an antique mirror of polished metal. As he looks into it, he suddenly sees the king in the mirror, talks to him, rises in his presence; but when he extends his hand to greet the monarch, he touches only the mirror, which falls and shatters. After he suffers another bout with high fever and delirium, the authorities decide to place another mental patient in his room, a man who thinks himself a great poet. When the poet arrives and sees Raoul, he falls on his feet, certain he is in the presence of his monarch. The King-Raoul gives him a pension and his old clothes, which the poet takes for regal vestments. Each thus reinforces the other's fantasy. The two make their way out of the asylum and, once in the street, Raoul again speaks of his new political philosophy: he suggests new laws, the abolition of capital punishment, the suppression of certain taxes, additional food for the poor. And the populace greets Monarch and Poet with frantic applause. Finally, the real king arrives. Touched by Raoul's gentleness, he permits him and his poet to live out their lives in a charming castle.

The first time Raoul sees Henry II he was visibly shaken by the ominous prognostication that such resemblance entails. Such a feeling of death is understandable. When a person with a weak ego sees his double before him it is as if his wholeness (or, strictly, his own personal property) had been split off into component parts and given to someone else. When such a situation occurs in primitive societies, it is interpreted as a loss of soul, or death.[20] The same may be said in Raoul's case. Though physical death did not ensue, psychological demise surely did, since the supremacy of unconscious forces annihilated the conscious attitude.[21]

Psychologically, what happened to Raoul? Whenever he fantasized or permitted his resemblance to Henry II to cloud his objectivity he was in effect reacting to his vision as an observer. Rather than interrogate himself on the similarity existing between himself and Henry II, rather than sounding out his inner attitude, he accepted or endured his vision. The mirror image (that of the king) had become, therefore, acceptable to his conscious mind and, as such, had become something real. So far as he was concerned, he was the king. Once the conscious mind consents to live out such a hallucination (confusion of identity), the unconscious is in the ascendency. The more activated the unconscious becomes, the more psychic energy it needs to function, the more it withdraws from consciousness. When libido flows inward at such a rapid rate, a depression may ensue and one's physical stamina is lessened (hence the fevers that Raoul suffered during his internment in the asylum). Each time he went through a traumatic experience (the first incarceration, the shattering of the mirror) it was manifested physically in the form of a fever or other discomfort. The transformation may be likened to an alchemical change.

In alchemical terminology, a diminution of psychic energy from the conscious mind that leads to an inability to differentiate between exterior and inner reality implies a unification of that which must be differentiated if it is to live an everyday existence. Such an occurrence indicates a unification of base and noble metals—in psychological terms, a *coniunctio* between superior and inferior functions. Raoul, as Henry II monarch of France, associated the highest function (the collective role of the monarch, the patriarch and father principle) with that of the plebeian Raoul (the realm of feeling, the individual who attends to his own subjective needs). The king, who generally represents universal or archetypal man, the ruling or governing principle within a being, stands for supreme consciousness, self-control, and judgment. In this particular story, the king represents the unlimited power principle, whereas Raoul (lawyer, feeling type) seeks to help humanity and stands for individual morality, kindliness, and justice. To unify these frequently opposing principles is impossible in the world of reality. An ideal is of necessity an abstraction; to experience it realistically is to concretize it, thereby divesting it of its limitless nature as an amorphous content. The double image (monarch and plebeian, collective and individual) is united in Raoul's fantasy life, indicating the destruction of the differentiating principle within his personality (that is, his ego). Only within the unconscious could the ideal and real become one, and so what could have been constructive if carried out on a realistic level (Raoul's reforms in terms of man's governing principle or his conscious mind) has become an agent of destruction, driving Raoul insane.

The king-lawyer unification may also be looked upon as an *imitatio Christi*. The king-lawyer is a Christ image, a monarch and reformer, who seeks to bring joy and happiness to mankind. To succeed in his task he must sacrifice his reason as Christ sacrificed his life to redeem man. To his basic dialectic of the king-lawyer (Christ principle) is added a third force: the feeling function in the guise of the poet, a projection of Raoul's personality as well. Emotion and feeling are necessary if a populace is to be aroused. The poet injects such sensations into Raoul's outlook, which had until now been a series of cerebral and abstract notions. Because of the poet's persuasive powers the real Henry II, deeply moved by the image of king-poet, provides them with a castle.

The mirror episode is significant. It is a visual manifestation of the split that had taken place within Raoul's personality. The mirror per se may be looked upon as a unifying force in that it concretizes, fixes and holds Raoul's dream, thereby making it real. The first time Raoul looks into the mirror he is fascinated by his image as king. In this case, we may consider the mirror as life's adversary since it not only enables but encourages Raoul to continue living in a world of make-believe, regressing even more deeply into his unconscious and so decreasing his ability to function in real life. Because of his progressive withdrawal from life, his ego has deteriorated completely. The mirror, which paved the way for such unification, has become synonymous with his conscious mind: it is also a passive instrument. Once the shaking of the hands was accomplished and the mirror shattered, reality was activated and the dream destroyed. Raoul was so traumatized by the incident that he became delirious and withdrew still further from reality.

Interestingly, Nerval introduces his readers to a patriarchal society for the first time. The real King Henry II permitted Raoul and his poet to live out their fantasies, indicating his acceptance of the situation. Such an outcome may reveal a desire on Nerval's part to have his own father not only tolerate his flights into fancy but to help him bring his endeavors to fruition.

Nerval wrote another tale at this period, *The Devil's Portrait* (Oct. 23, 1839), which is also Hoffmannesque in style,[22] and which is even more revealing of Nerval's inner frame of mind. On a December night, the narrator meets a friend of his at Charing Cross, a painter, Eugène. Eugène tells him that he is not well, that he cannot sleep and is deeply tormented. It seems that his father, a doctor, had forced him to study medicine, but later, realizing his son's penchant for painting, had permitted him to study both. One day, Eugène meets Sir Thomas Wilkinson and is invited to his home. Eugène falls in love with his daughter Laura, an exquisite girl with the perfection and harmony of a Greek statue. Eugène's father, meanwhile, dies and leaves his son penniless. Mr. Wilkinson and his daughter leave for Paris and Eugène has neglected to ask them for their address. He rushes to Paris and spends two months looking for them. He decides in desperation to paint Laura's picture; perhaps if someone sees it in a gallery, he thinks, they may tell her about it. Laura happens to walk by one day. Eugène sees her and as he walks toward her she responds with "icy coldness" and then glides out of the store. Abashed, he faints. Sometime later he is reminded of a painting, *Satan's Fiancée,* which he had once seen in a vault in the Church of Santo Giorgio in Venice. He leaves for Venice, locates the painting, and recognizes the image of Satan's fiancée as Laura. He returns to England and it is at this juncture that he meets his friend, the narrator of the story. Eugène confesses his pain and the thought of Laura as Satan's fiancée pursues him "into my very dreams." Subsequently, the narrator does not see Eugène for a few days and becomes worried; he goes to Eugène's lodging only to discover that he has taken laudanum and died.

In *The Devil's Portrait* Nerval introduces us to still another anima figure: a combination of seductress (the Laura he saw in Paris) and the pure and naïve type of girl he had first met in London. Though Nerval had characterized these types in *The Alchemist,* never had the polarities been so precisely incised. In *The Devil's Portrait,* the negative anima figure not only appears as a temptress, an enticing Circe type, but as a virulent, destructive, and overpowering force, closer to the Greek Lamia figure. Such a negative figure, who enjoys dominion in the unconscious, prevents him from adapting to exterior circumstances, if only in terms of his own painting. He can only portray her, can only see her, and when she vanishes he must either find her or feel cut off from his very being. When an anima figure dominates an individual to such an extent, it indicates autonomous activity within the unconscious, which frequently may be understood as revelatory or anticipatory of things to come.[23] Had Eugène been able to take heed of what was happening to him, had he tried to understand and objectify his attitude toward his anima figure, he would have become aware of the tragic fate in store for him. Inability to halt the course of events indicated a passivity within his personality leading to his own destruction.

There are autobiographical elements in *The Devil's Portrait.* Eugène's father was a doctor who wanted his son to study medicine; after his father's death he had extreme financial problems. Gérard's father likewise wanted his son to become a doctor and though Dr. Labrunie had not died, he had stopped supporting his son financially and in a sense had cut himself off from his life. Nor is Nerval a balanced and objective artist. Like Eugène, he too is a prisoner of his anima and is incapable of controlling his element. The fact that Eugène neglected to ask Laura for her address in Paris indicates an inadequate association with reality, an inability to adapt to external circumstances. That he rushes to Paris and searches frantically for Laura reveals his inability to function without his anima figure. Indeed, his personality crumbles, which signifies that her autonomy over his psyche is very nearly complete. In his painting, Eugène concretizes his vision of her in an attempt to recapture the lost anima figure, and thereby to immobilize and immortalize her. When she passes by the art store in Paris he cannot stand the pain of being divested of his anima figure. Some uncontrollable force compels him to go to Venice to find a certain painting in the vault of a church. The painting, in this instance, represents a treasure (knowledge) and will, he believes, permit him to understand the mystery of Laura. The church vault may be likened to Eugène's subliminal realm, and it is associated with a religious edifice (*religio* = linking back); it represents an attempt on his part to delve within himself, to unravel the riddle of her origin within himself. For some, such knowledge leads to illumination and a confrontation with the problem highlighted; for Eugène, it brings death, the total submission to his unconscious, to the she-devil or the femme fatale.

Nerval had not yet come to such an impasse.

It is strange that Nerval picked the name Laura to depict the she-devil. Petrarch had given this name to his beloved, who symbolized his aspirations and occupied the focal position in his life. Schiller also wrote a series of poems to his equally perfect Laura. Since Nerval's Laura was a totally negative figure, one might conclude that for Eugène she was never associated with spiritual growth as she had been with Petrarch, nor with lyricism as she was with Schiller. Nerval's Laura is a diabolical aspect of the psychic function, an independent and therefore dangerously powerful element.

Love for Dante was also associated with fate—an *amor* from which he could not free himself. Though the woman Dante loved existed in reality, she acted as a catalyst, compelling him to give her permanency in the world of art. Laura might have stimulated Eugène's artistic talent, but she also overwhelmed and subjugated it. An artist needs freedom of imagination to ferret out the riches that lie within his unconscious and to bring them forth in viable form. Since he was unable to come to grips with his anima figure, it ensnared and strangled him. What other possible outcome was there but suicide?

Both tales, looked upon as an expression of Nerval's psychic state, are distressing. In the first story, we are confronted with a man who loses his identity and goes insane; in the second, a man who is dominated by a woman and commits suicide. In both cases, the hero is unable to cope with reality. *The Devil's Portrait* is the more forthright reproduction of

Nerval's unconscious in that it analyzes, symbolically, his entire male-female orientation. Nerval experienced women on two levels: either as angelic abstraction or as "she-devil."

Had he lived in the twelfth or thirteenth centuries Nerval would surely have been in tune with the times—centuries during which courtly love was so popular an expression of an emerging feminine principle in a society previously dominated by a patriarchal orientation. Man's deep need for redemption during the Middle Ages was manifested by a rejection of sensual love and an acceptance and longing for sublime, gentle, and refined relationships. Such an attitude would have appealed to Nerval. In the nineteenth century, however, his shying away from relationships with real women, his withdrawal into a fantasy world, might have been misunderstood by women, who might have interpreted such passivity as distaste. Unwilling, perhaps, to pursue a friendship that could come to naught, they shied away from his company. He, in turn, experienced a further distaste for reality and a greater attraction for his subliminal realm. The misunderstanding seemed complete.

After Nerval's disappointments in the theater—*Leo Burckhart* and *The Alchemist*—it seemed that a trip to Germany might alleviate his tormented soul. He looked forward to a change of scene and thanks to Gautier, who introduced him to Jean-Louis Lingay, secretary to Guizot, the prime minister of France, Nerval was sent on an official mission to Austria, and a small sum of money was put at his disposal. Nerval's task would be to inform the minister of the interior and the minister of instruction of Austria's commercial and political attitude toward France as echoed in the press, the books published, and in human relations.

Armed with a goal and with a government subsidy, Nerval, now thirty-one years old, left for Germany on October 31, 1839. He went to Lyon, Geneva, Lausanne, Berne, Zürich, Lake Constance, Lindau, Augsburg, Munich, Salzburg, Linz, and finally Vienna, where he remained three and a half months.

Nerval was captivated by the charm and beauty of Vienna. The city was a living corpus; a center of culture, excitement, and creativity, particularly in the musical sphere. The inner city, with its tortuous streets, high houses, St. Stephen's Cathedral, the imperial palace, glittered like a jewel. Schoenbrunn Palace was a vision to behold: the immense rooms, the luxurious furnishings, and the thick gold inlay. Even more breathtaking, according to Nerval, was the Marie-Theresa pavillion situated on the nearby hill. Its architecture seemed unreal; the lawns, which unfolded like "immense sheets of greenery,"[24] looked as if they had emerged from some fairyland.

Nerval met the French ambassador, M. de Saint-Aulaire, who had also translated *Faust* and who invited him to the fashionable embassy parties—gala affairs at which the most aristocratic, gifted, and famous people of Europe were present. At one of these affairs he met the great Franz Liszt. Dignitaries were also at the embassy parties: the princes Dietrichstein, Schwarzenberg and Esterhazy, the Marshal Duke de Raguse and the Belgian violinist Beriot, alluded to as a second Paganini. Even Metternich, the chancellor of Austria whose reactionary politics had dominated European diplomacy ever since the Congress of Vienna, made his presence known on certain occasions.

Nerval was so impressed by the people he met that he wrote his father: "Here I am, just as you were in 1809, experiencing the great moment of my life." Indeed, Nerval's trip to Vienna would usher in a momentous experience. It was in Vienna—the city of music—that he met the pianist Marie Pleyel.

Jules Janin, editor of the *Journal des Débats* and close friend of the celebrated Marie Pleyel, had written Nerval a letter of introduction to her. But Nerval lacked the courage to give it to her or even to have it sent. She was a woman "courted by so many dukes, princes, and great artists" that he almost despaired of ever meeting her.[25] Nerval waited and was finally introduced to her at an embassy party.

Marie Pleyel, whose name had been Camille-Félicité-Denise Moke, was Parisian-born (1811). Her Belgian father and German mother were well aware of her talents as a child and had her study with the finest teachers of the time: Herz, Moscheles, Kalkbrenner, and later, in St. Petersburg, with Thalbert.[26] She married Camille Pleyel in 1832 and took the name Marie. In Leipzig she met Felix Mendelssohn and played with his orchestra. They were very close friends and it has been intimated that their relationship had been more than platonic. In 1830 Berlioz fell deeply in love with Marie Pleyel. Auber admired her beauty and talent. Liszt called her the "goddess of the piano" and introduced her to Viennese audiences; indeed, in a letter to Countess d'Agoult, Liszt wrote: "She has a magnificent talent, unquestionably she is the best pianistic talent existing."[27]

Marie Pleyel had a reputation as both an artist and siren. When Nerval finally met her, he was transfixed. "Her face, her eyes, her voice, her smile" moved him to the very marrow of his bones. Her beauty—the deep blue eyes, the black hair parted in the center—combined both "romantic" and "Spanish" traits. And when Nerval, already keenly receptive to music, listened to her play the piano, he was deeply inspired and experienced a type of enthusiasm he had never known before.[28] So reserved in the past, when it came time for the parlor games at the embassy, Nerval joined Marie Pleyel in charades and the general festivities.

Life took on a rosy hue. Vienna was a dream and he had a new star to worship.

When not at the embassy, Nerval went to operas and cabarets, and amused himself to such an extent that he had no time to attend to his work. He did not write the articles for *l'Artiste* nor did he accomplish any other creative work. "I can do nothing here," he wrote. "The Viennese drinks, eats, waltzes, and the foreigner visiting has but only tasted of this regime that he turns into a Viennese himself." Excitement buoyed him. Wherever he went, love was in the air. In his letters to friends in Paris, he tells of the blondes, brunettes, the types of women he met—and intimates that he was successful on several occasions. He praised the openness of the Viennese women and castigated the French ladies who "make you suffer for three months" before granting their affection. "In Vienna, three days are sufficient. . . ." In Vienna, one sings of love, "one is madly in love, not with one, but with all women at the same time. L'odor di femina. . . ."[29] The Strauss waltzes, the tea gardens, the exquisite parks, the entire atmosphere contributed to Nerval's state of elation.

Whether Nerval was actually successful with women is a moot question. Scholars, for the most part, believe that the women he mentioned, Katty and Vhabby in particular, were not his friends at all, but rather the mistresses of Gautier and Weill. Nerval sometimes attributed women belonging to other men to himself and he probably felt that there was nothing wrong in doing so. The fact that he mentioned women in the collective ("one is madly in love, not with one, but with all women at the same time") tends to corroborate such a point of view, reminding one of his seeming inability to establish individual relationships.

An enigma also exists with reference to his allusion to the Archduchess Sophia. Certain scholars believe he was enamored of her. She was a beautiful, regal woman. But had Nerval ever met her? Was he alluding to the real Sophie or a spiritual figure, the Gnostic's Sophia, the symbol for divine wisdom? Or to the beautiful and sensual Sophie Dawes whom he had seen, or so it is intimated, when a young boy at Mortefontaine?

One of Nerval's most cryptic works, *La Pandora,* was written about his Viennese venture. Here he talks of the great pain he suffered because of La Pandora's coquettish nature, her sadism, her indifference. She loved to kiss him, he said, when he wore his black suit because it reminded her of priestly garb (as she put it, "I adore priests").[30] Most scholars believe that Pandora, though obscured under all types of alchemical symbols, was Marie Pleyel. If so, who is the other female mentioned "but the beloved memory of the other protected me against the charms of the artful Pandora"?[31] No one yet has been able to unravel the mystery of these identities. Was "the other" a spiritualized vision of Jenny Colon who protected Nerval against the "artful" Pandora? Or was it another?

Did Nerval write *La Pandora* in alchemical symbols in order to hide a very profound sorrow, or something he had just discovered about himself? We know that Marie Pleyel thought of Nerval as "a tender poet."

In her letter to Jules Janin, she wrote: "I very much like the tender poet whose soul is incapable of dreaming up any evil. I have spoken to him *frequently* about you, and when I was sad because I had not received any news from you, he consoled me with a most perfect kindness."[32]

How far Marie Pleyel's relationship went with Nerval is not known. According to Dr. L.H. Sebillotte, Nerval did have a liaison with Marie Pleyel but discovered that he was impotent and was overcome with deep sense of shame and failure. Whether his inadequacies manifested themselves only with those women he loved and idealized and not with the "others" is a mystery.[33]

Nerval's association of Marie Pleyel with Pandora revealed his negative attitude toward her. Pandora, endowed with beauty and charm, had been given to Epimetheus as a wife; because of her curiosity, she opened a forbidden jar and out flew all the evils of the world: troubles, disasters, diseases. She quickly put the lid back on but only Hope remained. Pandora represents the serpentine, sirenic, demoniac side of woman. In *La Pandora,* Nerval describes himself dressed in black and being embraced by Pandora when he wore the guise she liked and repudiated by her when he changed his outer appearance. Nerval associates himself with Epimetheus, a man who sacrificed his ego, who yielded to the other world, and though attempting to relate to external objects (people) Pandora, on his own terms, he yielded to them. In *La Pandora,* Nerval is living out a myth, the negative female principle that may be associated with the alchemical enigma written by Nicolas Barnaud and that Nerval included in his work: "Neither man, nor woman, nor androgyne, nor girl, nor young, nor old, nor chaste, nor mad, nor prudish, but all of this together." Pandora was all of these things to Nerval. Now that she had rejected him—and he had been overcome with shame when discovering his own weakness, he would have to find another path in life, another route to fulfillment.[34]

7   FAUST REVISITED

Tell me, what is Destiny preparing?
Goethe, *Poem to Charlotte von Stein.*

Life in Paris was arduous. Financial stresses obliged Nerval to work very nearly around the clock. Articles, short stories, and criticisms had to be churned out daily. To add to his burdens, Gautier departed on May 11, 1840, for Spain, and Nerval had to take over his column in *La Presse* until October 15. This represented additional work, but additional income as well. In a letter to Jean-Louis Lingay (June 23, 1840), Nerval complained of the difficulties involved in completing his daily assignments; they left him little or no time for his own projects. He was alluding to his translation of Goethe's *Faust*, part II; it was far more complex than part I and had taken Goethe nearly ten years to write—from 1822 until the year of his death in 1832.

Faust's world was that of the mystic, the alchemist and the magician—where past, present and future were fused; where the living could penetrate the world of the dead and vice versa; where pantheism reigned and "God was everything." For Nerval the doctrine of reincarnation, implicit in *Faust,* meant that suffering souls on this earth could vanish into another sphere of existence only to take on human form again, to reenter the life cycle with their beloved. Nerval needed the comforting doctrine of reincarnation to pursue his daily existence—he needed faith. He had always suffered the torments of the believer who rationalizes and who finally disbelieves—a residue of his rationally oriented upbringing. Everything that rested on faith alone was questioned and finally perhaps even ridiculed.

Nerval's struggle between faith and reason came out into the open on one occasion, at Victor Hugo's home on Place des Vosges. During a discussion of religious subjects, someone questioned Nerval and he answered in a most significant manner:

"But Gérard, you have no religion!"

"I, have no religion? I have at least seventeen."

Nerval returned to *Faust* because there was something about this work that filled an aching void within him. Faust, in part II, conquers death; he experiences beauty, glory, and redemption. Such an outcome to worldly existence was enviable—a goal that Nerval in his own way might also achieve. Moreover, Nerval looked upon Goethe as a sage, neither overly involved in religion nor totally rejecting it. Unlike Voltaire and the eighteenth-century philosophes, Goethe was not an adversary of mysticism, alchemy, or any of the occult arts. He shared the rationalistic views of Enlightenment—but with moderation. He was like an "arbiter," resolving whatever tensions remained between the scientific views of the world and the cosmos and the deeply religious outlooks. Goethe did not bring about a "fusion" between these two polarities, but because of Goethe, Nerval wrote, in his lengthy preface to part II of *Faust,* "antiquity and the Middle Ages extend their hands to one another without overwhelming one or the other; matter and mind are reconciled and admire each other."[1]

Goethe had long been involved in a wide variety of secret religious orders. He had been a member of the Amalia Lodge of Freemasonry in Weimar (1781) and of the Order of the Illuminati, an organization to which many well-known men belonged. A rather militant group, the Illuminati had been founded to combat certain "nefarious activities— such as the practice of necromancy—as carried on in certain regressive occult societies. Abuses in Germany and later in France, around 1756, had taken place during false séances, where the practitioners of these secret arts would take advantage of the sorrow of others to obtain sums of money. Sham alchemy was also practiced throughout Europe. Instead of seeking spiritual enlightenment in the hermetic works of such people as Jakob Boehme, they sought to become simple gold makers.[2] Nor did these charlatans immerse themselves in the monistic concepts of Swedenborg who, like Boehme, based his ideology on primordial unity and a series of correspondences that existed between the spiritual and material universe.[3]

Nerval responded to the emphasis Goethe placed on such ancient mystical religions as Pythagoreanism, Gnosticism, Orphism, astrology, and the stellar cults. Goethe had even read his own horoscope at the outset of his autobiography: two negative constellations, the Sun in direct opposition to the Moon and Venus, in opposition to Aries. Astrologists interpret such signs as indicating deep emotional conflict between the abstract and concrete, the spiritual and the material. Goethe had searched for a balancing of the opposing forces within him, "an equilibrium which was forever being threatened by emotional turmoil."

Like the Neoplatonists, Renaissance and later philosophers (Kepler, Paracelsus, Nicolas de Cusa, Giordano Bruno, Pascal, Leibniz, Swedenborg), Goethe believed that the universe was a living entity filled with souls that were linked to one another, each soul being an emanation of the wholeness of the universe. The manner in which the various souls acted or counteracted was governed by universal sympathy, the implication being that nothing is isolated in the cosmos and that everything has a cause and effect upon particles or atoms within the universe. Man is a privileged creature in the hierarchy of the chain of beings because, unlike other cosmic entities, he is capable of thought. He can experience reality or truth while still alive. By contemplation (or through some inner experience, a descent into self) man may perceive the "other" world, giving him a new vision of the whole or the all.

Unlike many of the Renaissance metaphysicians and the Illuminists, such as Claude de Saint-Martin, Goethe felt that, whereas the universe was divine to begin with, it did not "presuppose a creator"; for him, all laws, order, and commandments were self-contained. Each individual, therefore, is capable of fulfillment; every instant is justified by its own being; life's goal is to achieve the highest state of perfection, or in Aristotle's words, *entelecheia* (entelechy). Once this state has been reached, the person or entity is gently reblended into the universal organism and becomes encapsulated within one of the spheres surrounding the earth. These spheres are structured within a hierarchy ranging from the lowest to the highest.

According to Aristotle, entelechy is a "dynamic principle enabling man to realize that which he is inherently capable of becoming." Faust and Goethe believed that all nature was equipped with a dynamic quality, enabling it to accomplish its mission of perfection. Each being was a form *in potentia* capable of ascending and realizing itself in its most ideal form or state.[4] Goethe describes *entelecheia* in the following manner.

> Every Entelecheia is a piece of eternity, and the few years during which it is bound to the earthly body does not make it old. If this Entelecheia is of a trivial kind, it will exercise but little sway during its bodily confinement; on the contrary, the body will predominate, and when this grows old the Entelecheia will not hold and restrain it. But the Entelecheia is of a powerful kind, as in the case with all men of natural genius, then with its animating, penetrating, and ennobling power upon the organization, but it will also endeavor with its spiritual superiority to confer the privilege of perpetual youth.[5]

Goethe's belief in *entelecheia,* or the theory of *élite* souls, led him to consider that all in the cosmos was in a state not only of becoming but of ascension.

Goethe, Nerval wrote in his preface to part II, was not fearful of death. How could he be, since it would lead to another sphere of existence and to his ascension? Rather, Goethe sought to define the meaning of death. The past, for him, remained eternally present in the form of "intelligence," or "shadows" that reside in a series of concentric regions outside the finite material world. In this new frame of existence these shadows carry out their work and fulfill themselves still further.

> For him, as for God probably, nothing ends, or at least nothing but matter is transformed, and the centuries pass and are conserved in their entirety in the state of intelligences and shadows, in a series of concentric regions, spread around the material world. There, the phantoms again accomplish or dream of accomplishing actions which had been revealed to them formerly by the sun of life and in which they proved the individuality of their immortal soul.[6]

Goethe had been influenced by the Akasic Record, an Eastern doctrine that affirmed that everything that happened on earth and within man's mind had been indelibly recorded on the Akasa, a type of ether believed to encircle the world. According to sixteenth-century visionaries, if man disciplines himself in the practice of clairvoyance for many years, he will be equipped to perceive through Astral Light certain signs within the Akasic Record.[7] Dutoit-Membrini, in his *Divine Philosophy,* defined Astral Light as a kind of sensorial experience, like a third eye of knowledge that emanates from sidereal influences and permits an individual to experience divine illumination. Just as the body originates from the "powder of the earth," he suggested, so the soul is made up of starry substances. The stars act strongly upon each person and each of us must try to understand and determine the outcome of these influences.[8] Hermes Trismegistus, the founder of alchemy, wrote in his *Poimander* that all planetary powers, either in the form of parts or of elements of the planet, are present in the soul before it even comes into being. Because of this "link" there is a connection between man on earth and his "astral sources" in the cosmos. The planets and the stars affect man's very existence—his cosmic fate (*heimarmene*).[9]

To believe in the Akasic Record is to conquer death. Such a philosophy and its sister mystic faiths attempt to do away with the concept of death as an end. Ever since man was placed on earth, he has refused to accept the thought of death as a finale. Hermes Trismegistus, Pythagoras, Orpheus, the Platonists—all believed in the continuity and eternity of life and looked upon it as an ever-transforming process.

For the ancients, time was not considered in a linear manner, that is, with a beginning or an end. It was believed to be cyclical or eternal, and, therefore, not subject to the laws of the finite universe. Time was not conceived in terms of past, present, and future. Rather, it was looked upon as eternally present, experienced in every material entity—and basic to the soul. Since eternal time was implicit in the soul's very make-up, it never died. It merely ascended to astral spheres. Hermes Trismegistus believed that by divesting man of his worldly garments (or untying or loosening the bonds or knots of matter which forever hold man captive on earth) through a certain series of initiations, his eternal soul would ascend, but in a different form, after which it would be regenerated. Participants in ancient cult practices varied in their descriptions of the mystical journeys undertaken by the soul. Believers in Isis and in Mithraic cults, for example, were convinced that the soul assumed either human or animal forms, depending upon the success of the initiatory process in each case.

In a letter to Falk, Goethe wrote: "I am certain that I have been here as I am now a thousand times before, and I hope to return a thousand times." To Charlotte von Stein, whom he loved, Goethe suggested: "How well it is that men should die, if only to erase their impressions and return clean washed." A poem written to this same woman underscores his palingenesian convictions.

> Tell me, what is Destiny preparing?
> Tell me why we two have drawn so near?
> Aeons since, you were my sister, sharing
> Kin with me, or else my wife most dear.
> Everything I am, my every feature,
> You divined, my every nerve could thrill,
> Read me at a glance—no other creature
> Knows me as you know, nor ever will.[10]

When Faust, in part II, descends to the Realm of the Mothers (which may be interpreted as a descent into Self, into the collective unconscious, or into another sphere of existence), he emerges from these primal depths, renewed—and Helen of Troy appears as a spiritualized force whose beauty exists not only outwardly but inwardly as well. Nerval suggests in his preface:

> If it is true, as religion teaches us, that one part of us is immortal and survives the decomposed human being, if it is preserved independently and distinctly from the rest and will not merge in the universal soul, there must exist in the immensity of these regions or planets, a place where these souls preserve a form which is perceptible to the vision of other souls, and even those who have are disengaged only momentarily in the dream, from terrestrial ties, via magnetism or ascetic contemplation.[11]

Gérard had discussed regeneration and reincarnation many times with his friends Nodier and Gautier. They believed that souls, already formed by God, could once again make their presences known to certain types of individuals and would, in this way, be able to "love" them once again.

> It would be consoling to think that nothing which has struck one's intelligence ever dies, and that eternity preserves within its breast a type of universal history, visible via the eyes of the soul, a divine synchronicity, which would enable us to participate one day in the science of He who sees the entire future and the entire past in one glance.[12]

Nerval believed that one could attract souls toward one, that one could make contact and communicate with the departed.

> Now it would be possible to attract souls back into the domain of created matter, or at least formulated by God, a brilliant theater where they had played, each one, a role which lasted a few years, and have given proof of their strength and love? Would it be possible to condense in their im-

material and unseizable mold, a few pure elements of matter, which would enable him to relive a visible existence which would be more or less long, reuniting and shining upon one another suddenly, like light atoms running around in circular fashion in a sun's ray?[13]

Goethe had always been an admirer of sincere alchemists, those whose intent was to "spiritualize" values in matter. He had come into close contact with the greatest occult scientists and scholars of his age not only in Frankfurt, his native city, but in Weimar, Strasbourg, and Leipzig.

Goethe was not interested in the "practical," gold-making side of alchemy. But he was preoccupied with it as a healing or medical science. He had recovered dramatically from a rather mysterious sickness in 1769 and attributed his cure to various chemical substances that he had been given. After this incident he began studying certain properties and correspondences between mercury (which alchemists associated with the spirit), sulphur (associated with the soul) and salt (associated with the body). He hoped in this manner to find or establish some kind of balance between his own physical and spiritual realms. Goethe both marveled and wondered why alchemists, early men of science, had attributed certain unusual names and properties to the chemical elements: to mercury, for example "divine winged Hermes . . . manifest in matter, the god of revelation, lord of thought and sovereign psychopomp . . . living silver, quicksilver . . . which glistens and animates within."[14] In so doing, the alchemists personified and also deified chemical elements, implying that within such substances there lay an entire "world-creating spirit" that had been "concealed or imprisoned in matter."[15] To discover or to isolate this spirit, hidden in matter, was the goal of the true alchemist and what fascinated Goethe.

Faust's odyssey in part II, or his search for Self (God, the infinite), may be looked upon as a series of alchemical experiments or a "succession" of alchemical "states" occurring in an ascending process.[16]

The great alchemists of old were not only scientists but philosophers and mystics. Father Zosima (third century), Albertus Magnus, Roger Bacon, Raymond Lully, Paracelsus—all were interested in the transmutability of chemical elements, and also in perfecting man, transforming him into a higher and more perfect being.[17] The scientific activities of the alchemists gave rise, therefore, to mystical notions concerning unity, diversity, and theories of correspondences and reincarnation. For example, chemical combinations first viewed as distinct substances were observed to recombine under certain conditions and, interpreted from a mystical point of view, indicated a union of opposites.[18]

The goal of alchemy was to create a *coniunctio* from opposing polarities such as the original four elements (earth, water, air, and fire). Though the techniques used by the alchemists varied somewhat, they had a com-

mon desire: to divest the baser elements of their impurities by means
of a series of experiments and, in so doing, to return to primal unity
during which time the philosopher's stone would come into being. From
a metaphysical point of view, such an experience would indicate oneness
with God. The philosopher's stone was defined as the substance from
which *all* emanates and was looked upon in a metaphysical terminology
as a new unity or "Centrum" (the Self or God) that encompasses the
Alpha and the Omega, a term used by Christ to describe himself and
which implies universality.

The path leading to the creation of the philosopher's stone was difficult, involving (usually) four steps that the alchemist described in terms
of color.[19]

1. *Nigredo,* or blackening process, which was comparable to chaos: to the
   massa confusa before the separation of the elements; a state in which
   matter is reduced to a liquid condition;[19] or as "a quality of the *prima
   materia.*"[20]
2. *Albedo,* the second step, is a whitening stage resulting from the washing of the elements in question (*ablutio,* baptism). It has been called
   the "silver" or "moon" condition, which is to pursue its upward journey until it reaches the solar status.[21]
3. *Citrinitas,* or yellow state, was omitted by the alchemist after the fif-
   teenth century. This color embodied the "Sun" or "good" aspects of
   the elements prior to actual union or the transmutation process as it
   progresses in an ascending hierarchy.[22]
4. *Rubedo* comes into being when the fire, with which the alchemist heats
   his elements, rises to its most powerful intensity, when the elements
   turn red, and all impurities have thereby been extracted from them.
   The union of opposites now comes to pass and the philosopher's stone
   has been created. The notion of the philosopher's stone varied with
   each alchemist. For some, it contained the elixir of life; for others it
   was gold or the *prima materia* out of which gold could be produced.
   It was also looked upon as a spiritual or mystical substance from which
   the new man, known as the *homunculus,* would be molded. The homunculus, referred to by the Gnostics as Anthropos or the Divine
   Original Man, was capable of transcending the old divisions of time
   and space, birth and death, and could unite with a higher form.[23]

The four-part alchemical process corresponds to four different psychological stages in the development of the human personality in its attempt to experience harmony and balance. The *prima materia* or *nigredo*
stage has been compared to man's "primitive" nature, the state of unconsciousness. He is unaware of his conflicts, needs, and desires and
either lives in a state of paradisiac ignorance or is overcome by his troubles and is perpetually prey to inner chaos and turmoil. Such a state,
depending upon its acuteness, leads to *un abaissement du niveau mental*
and in some cases, may make a person virtually helpless. As self-knowl-

edge deepens, so the individual becomes more conscious of the conflicts within him, with a concomitant lightening of color (in common parlance, "light dawns"), comparable to the alchemist's *albedo* and *citrinitas* stages. As the turmoil reaches a peak of intensity (*rubedo*), a union of opposites takes place—not because the individual has become unaware of his conflicts but by virtue of his knowledge of them. Man has been delivered from the domination of his instincts, but he has not rejected them: his physical and spiritual halves are working in harmony. He has understood what has been happening within him and has assimilated the component parts and polarities within his psyche. This last stage is comparable to man's highest earthly spiritual state and has been looked upon by alchemists as the "quintessential element born out of the purification of the four elements composing the physical nature of man."[24]

How did the alchemical process manifest itself in *Faust,* and what did Nerval project onto this work? That Nerval concentrated his efforts on certain episodes, namely those dealing with the Realm of the Mothers, the entire Helen sequence, and Faust's redemption at the end, while neglecting or relegating other passages and scenes to mere résumés, is good indication of the trend of his thinking at this time.[25]

The Realm of the Mothers

Let us recall that Mephistopheles had told Faust to descend to the depths—to the Mothers—to get Helen. Before his journey, however, Faust experiences a deep sleep, and when he awakens he has forgotten his past misdeeds. Mephistopheles gives Faust a key (that of knowledge) and warns him to "take hold and not to undervalue it."[26] In the Realm of the Mothers Faust confronts all types of shapes and shadows, a world in flux, constantly forming and transforming itself. This formidable, frightening, and horrendous world, alchemically, may be alluded to as *nigredo;* psychologically, it is the collective unconscious, and the "primal darkness" of the Gnostics. Here Faust touches the tripod with his key to call up both Helen and Paris from the night of death (or disintegration). Since Faust is experiencing the *nigredo* stage he is thrust into a *massa confusa,* where all is chaotic, undifferentiated, unknowable—where, psychologically, conflicts are experienced at an unconscious level. In this state of *disiunctio* transformation of the arcane substance inherent in all matter takes place.[27]

For Faust, who possessed a healthy ego,[28] a descent into the Mothers, though at first sinister, was both profitable and inspiring. In this realm all man's riches (his imagination, inspiration, and the like) exist in undifferentiated form. For Nerval, whose ego was weak and whose character so introverted, such a journey into the world of the Mothers might prove to be disastrous.

In the Realm of the Mothers, Faust (like Prometheus, in this instance) brought about the rebirth of Helen and Paris. In terms of modern scientific terminology, such a feat meant that Faust had solved the mystery of matter or had gained the knowledge of nuclear fission, fusion, and all the rest. By combining certain atoms and reshuffling others, he accomplished the reincarnation of those celebrated lovers of antiquity. But when Faust saw Paris kiss Helen he became angry; Faust wanted her for himself and justified his feelings by saying that he tried to rescue Helen from her abductor. He grabbed her and then touched Paris with his key. No sooner had Helen been seized than she dimmed and vanished; Paris exploded. According to certain mystic sects, Helen was called an *eidolon,* a reflection or "lower soul" (a higher soul never descended into matter) into which Faust had injected energy. The psychological implication of Faust's possessive act indicated that he had not succeeded in uniting the feminine or feeling side of his nature (as represented by Helen, an anima figure) to his masculine thinking principle (the knowledge of matter). Indeed, at this point, feeling has been so undervalued that is has vanished in the Realm of the Mothers.[29]

Faust's second attempt to deal with matter and with the feminine principle occurred in his home. Wagner, Faust's assistant, has just fashioned a little man, a homunculus, whose power is all spiritual. The homunculus represents "radiance" and suggests "enlightenment." He may be considered, therefore, a type of *anthropos* or primal man, a very helpful individual according to Chaldean legend. Wagner's homunculus, however, is not free; he remains imprisoned in his alchemical vessel. It is only when Faust begins his search for beauty (Helen) that "the glass booms and blazes." When the homunculus sees the incarnation of the feminine principle in Galatea he is so deeply affected that the spiritual attitude activates the "indwelling" principle within the homunculus. Such a confrontation shatters the homunculus' glass protection. Symbolically, the image indicates an extremely cerebral and, therefore, no longer creative or positive life attitude. Faust's attitude in terms of the homunculus image must be broken up so that a new frame of reference may come into being—new depths experienced. This is exactly what occurs in Goethe's work.

Faust's experience with the homunculus may be equated with the alchemist's second step, *albedo,* the whitening stage that appears after the washing of the elements. *Albedo,* which has been looked upon as "daybreak," has definite visual associations in terms of the dialogue's allusions to rivers, streams, and seas. Now Faust begins to understand the worlds in collision within his own being: the cerebral and rational approach to life and the volatile, irrational feeling principles. Unless thinking can work in harmony with feeling, a break within the psyche will occur.

Helen emerges once again in all her beauty. Now she begins talking of her past and cannot believe she has been the cause of so many destructive acts.

> Looms this from some past life? Or am I seized and crazed?
> Was all this me? Is still? and ever shall I be
> The phantoms scare or them that lay proud cities waste?
> My maids now shudder, but the eldest, you alone
> Stand there unmoved: then give me words of truth and sense.[30]

Helen is so distraught by her past misdeeds that she faints.

In Greek mythology, a faint was equated with a deep sleep or with bathing in the waters of Lethe. Helen's sleep has also been interpreted as part of an initiation ceremony, a *rite d'entrée* that will, according to Platonic theory, permit her to recollect her past.[31] In *Phaedrus*, Plato wrote:

> . . . this is the recollection of those things which our soul once says while following God—when regardless of that which we now call being she raised her head up towards the true being.

Psychologically, Helen's faint represents a regression into a void, *nigredo*, where she experiences her "essential" being and observes "the radiant child of light" (her past).[32] In so doing, she has become capable of looking beyond herself, her present identity, her past, the "House of Fathers." In mystical terms, she has experienced cosmic time, the eternal present. She has completed her initiation and has reawakened into a new sphere of existence.

Kneeling before her, Faust declares that he worships her and will be her servant and defender. He takes a seat beside her and they figure as king and queen. A *coniunctio* has taken place, that of Sol and Luna; opposites have been united in a mystical coitus, instinctive energy (the sexuality they both had known in the past) has been transformed into a spiritualized one. The ritual of marriage (Sacred Marriage, which the alchemists celebrated in terms of their chemicals and the Greeks relived at Eleusis in "silence, darkness, and in perfect chastity") takes place. An offspring, Euphorion, is born from this union—a "Divine Child."

These events reveal the passage taken from the *citrinitas* to the *rubedo*. Faust and Helen (now the royal couple) symbolize matter progressing in an ascending order and red (royalty), the energy needed to give birth to Euphorion (a new attitude) and unity to two disparate facets of the cosmic body (man and woman) and of the psyche (thinking and feeling).

There seems to be something defective in the union of Helen and Faust because Euphorion, like Hermes, was born a thief. He robs, then jumps from boulder to boulder, carrying his golden lyre with him. Flames burn violently on his forehead and these stand for spiritual power.[33] After a while, Euphorion, like Icarus, begins to soar through the air, only to fall dead and dissolve. He wanted too much, and too quickly, as Faust had at the outset. It is from the "other" world that he speaks to his mother.

O Mother, in this desolate realm
Leave me not alone!

Helen vanishes and joins her son, leaving her garments and veil with Faust. Mephistopheles says to Faust: "Hold fast to what little is left to you. . . . It is no longer the goddess you have lost, yet it is godlike. Turn this priceless gift to your account and raise yourself aloft."[34]

Though Faust's marriage to Helen was far from perfect, it enabled him to experience his feeling principle and paved the way for his ascension and redemption.

Faust's Redemption.

Faust is now floating away on a cloud and has a series of visions: a woman lying on another cloud who reminds him of his "heart's earliest treasure"; Gretchen in this image, but spiritualized as she makes her way to heaven, "like beauty of soul, grows and does not dissolve and rises into ether, drawing the best of my inner self after it."[35]

At the end of the drama, Faust[36] is transformed into Dr. Marianus, a spiritualized being who has shed his earthly vestments and can see beyond the material world of illusion. Psychologically, Dr. Marianus stands between consciousness and the psychical state or "paranormal" phase, when revelation or hallucination take place. Dr. Marianus is a visionary, a seer. His soul is redeemed by the Mater Gloriosa.

The Mater Gloriosa has been associated with Sophia, whom the Gnostics consider the World Soul or the All-Mother. Sophia, a very complex entity, is believed to be the "intermediary between man and God," and as such, has been called the "Mother of the Living, the Shining and Merciful Mother." She has been associated with the Virgin Mary, Isis, Juno, and Helen. Faust's contact with women has been experienced in an ascending order: Gretchen, the instinctual woman, or the one who has fallen into matter; Helen, the spiritualized but fleeting representation of imperfect joy; the Mater Gloriosa (Sophia) or perfect or absolute purity, the link between man and God.[37]

Dr. Marianus prostrates himself in adoration before the "Virgin, Queen of Motherhood," and his soul ascends into a world of divine reality and love—the World Soul.

All that is transitory
Is but a symbol:
The incompleted
Here is perfected;

> Here is indescribable
> Will be accomplished.
> The All-Mother leads us
> Upwards and on.[38]

Faust's ascension may also be looked upon from the point of view of the anima.

1. Gretchen represented the earthly, biological, sexual, Eve-like phase of man when he looks upon woman as an agent to be fertilized, a collective entity.
2. Helen represents the sexual Eros, but on an aesthetic or romantic level where vision is concretized.
3. Eros has reached the heights of religious devotion; spiritualization of woman in motherhood, a union of opposites.
4. Faust's soul is received by the Mater Gloriosa or Sophia, the Eternal Feminine, Wisdom that transcends the holy and pure—and becomes absolute *truth*.[39]

Such a fourfold experience as Faust had known was a quest that Nerval himself perhaps sought to experience and to some extent already had. He longed for the Gretchen types when he was young, and perhaps even when looking at Jenny Colon and Marie Pleyel. But something (psychological, physical, or both) may have prevented him from any prolonged relationship or consummation of a union. Such an inability might have been attributable in part to the fact that he, like Faust, longed to experience spiritualized Helen and the Mater Gloriosa. Whereas Faust had plunged into the Gretchen episode physically and could, therefore, continue on to the second phase of his development, Nerval had merely skirted the outer fringes of life.

Nerval was projecting his own disjointed unconscious onto Goethe's work and was trying to live out the Faustian drama vicariously. Whether this was an "escape" from life is a debatable question. But surely Nerval, in his relationships with women, was cultivating his ultraspiritual half more than his earthly side.

Now more than ever he was convinced that a soul that longs to come into contact with another is capable of attracting it to its own sphere of existence, "to implant some element of matter in the way of the souls that would then render it perceptible." Nerval observes that "Helen is a phantom for others, a shadow—but for FAUST SHE IS REALITY AND HE LOVES HER." The reason Helen vanished the first time, and disappeared to be with her son, the second, Nerval reasoned, was because their love had not reached a sufficiently spiritual level to remain eternal.

Helen's emergence into Faust's time (her reintegration into matter), was accomplished, Nerval observes, with "the rapidity of a dream," as if clock time had been arrested, fixed, turned back, or even broken, marking a century for each hour. Time in this sense may be viewed in terms of space or distance—as a series of never-ending concentric circles that enclose all the planets and themselves as cyclical or cosmic time.[40] In cosmic time, which has no past, present, or future and cannot be measured spatially, no thought, sensation, or experience, whether spiritual or physical—no composite of atoms—ever vanishes. Whether dead or alive, Paris and Helen roam about "ruminating their past lives." Faust meets them by means of the "immense aspiration of his soul, which is half disengaged from the earth" and succeeds in "attracting them outside of their circle of existence" and bringing them to his.[41] Faust, writes Nerval is

> voluntarily outside of the solid, outside of the finite, outside, one could even say, of time. Does he rise? descend? It's the same thing, since our earth is a globe. Is he going toward the people of the past or the future? They all coexist, as to the diverse characters of a drama which has not yet unfolded, but which has nevertheless come to fruition in the author's mind.[42]

Because Helen has been reincarnated and has succeeded in reentering a sphere closer to the earthly one she has defied her destiny and escaped the Fate of the Greeks or the Gnostic's *heimarmene*.[43] She succeeded in transcending her destiny, Nerval observes, because she had abstracted herself from the finite realm in which her husband and she had lived as individuals and had become an eternal type (an archetype) to be recognized by all men in all centuries as an aspect of the eternal feminine.

By escaping from her individual self or cycle (as the original Helen of Troy) she assumed eternal or collective qualities (Helen's eternal beauty as a woman), and this permitted her to reappear in the Middle Ages and become queen to a man whose genius represented an entire epoch. Those who, according to Goethe, possess an *élite* soul, that is, have made their mark on their time and civilization, have earned "prolongation outside of duration" and so possess the "cohesion" needed to escape "confusion" and "nothingness."[44]

That a literary figure assumes collective importance is an expression of a trend within man's development; when an individual (such as Nerval) attempts to live out such a myth vicariously it may encourage him to become what he is not—to consider the symbolism of his act and not the act per se. The consequences could be destructive, creating still further disharmony between the individual's spiritual and earthly sides. Because Nerval could not experience love—either with Jenny Colon or Marie Pleyel—on an earthly level, he justified his failure by attempting a spiritual ascension and living almost exclusively in a fantasy world.

By the fall of 1840—Nerval was now thirty-two years old—he felt he needed another change of scene. Belgium was near enough and yet sufficiently distant for him to rest so he planned to visit Lille, Coutrai, Antwerp, Liège, and Brussels. To make such a trip financially possible, he asked the French government for an assignment, which was granted him—to study literary infringement of French works being published in Belgium.

Nerval had planned to relax during most of his stay but he did take some work with him, poems by Heinrich Heine that he had promised the author he would translate. They were already good friends; Gautier had seen to that some time back, when he introduced the two shortly after Heine's arrival in France. Heine had fled from his politically conservative country and no sooner had he moved to Paris, in 1831, than he fell in love with the city, its life, and its people. He married a charming French girl, Juliette, who devoted her every waking moment to him.

Nerval had spent lengthy hours discussing Heine's poetry with him. Though the words were not difficult to translate, the tone, the rhythms, the sheer musicality of Heine's verses were almost impossible to render in another language. In Belgium, Nerval kept writing to him, asking him for his opinion on certain choices of words, certain expressions. It was fortunate that Nerval had this type of work to do because the weather was particularly poor during the fall and winter seasons. It was cold, misty, damp, and very windy much of the time. Nerval complained of frequent headaches. When these passed, they were followed by a type of ennui.

But he had his distractions. In Liège he loved to walk around the medieval city with its spires and colorful houses, and to watch the free-flowing Meuse River wander down the large valley. In Antwerp he visited the Rubens museum, the Cathedral. In Brussels he was intrigued by the Renaissance windows of the church of St. Gudule, called the "Church of the Miracles," with its intricate carvings on the façade of the edifice. In Brussels Nerval also attended séances in magnetism, which were quite popular at the time.

Perhaps the real reason for Nerval's trip to Belgium had nothing to do with a much-needed vacation. He had learned that Jenny Colon was scheduled to open there in *Piquillo* in October. His ennui might have stemmed from the fact that the opening was postponed to December 15. Nerval would simply have to wait. Moreover, December 15, for someone so deeply interested in numerology, struck a foreboding note. It was on that day that Sophie Dawes, the baronne Sophie de Feuchères, a woman he said he had seen and worshipped as a young man at Mortefontaine, had died in London.

Despite such lugubrious associations, Jenny Colon thrilled Nerval in *Piquillo.* He was so enraptured by her performance that he looked upon her as he had on those very first nights he saw her at the Variétés theatre in Paris, when he had sat glued to his seat night after night. It was as if time had stood still.

Again, he thought of coming to her aid, of publicizing her success in Brussels. He asked a friend of his in Paris to insert some blurbs in *Le Siècle*, *Le National*, and *L'Artiste* praising Jenny Colon's talents in *Piquillo*. Some days later, Jenny's coartists were informed of the situation and became enraged. The situation caused much embarrassment to both Nerval and, certainly, to Jenny Colon.

The most surprising event of all was the invitation Nerval received from Marie Pleyel. She had returned to Brussels to be with her mother and to perfect her piano playing before going on a European tour, and she suggested that Nerval come to a little gathering at her home. On this occasion he is said to have met Jenny Colon once again.[45]

The shock of such a confrontation was highly disturbing. Shortly thereafter, Nerval suddenly returned to Paris; he said that an "imperious duty," "a debt to be paid," compelled him to do so.

8   THE ABYSS

First of all, what is me?
Gérard de Nerval, *The Golden Ass.*

When Nerval returned to Paris in February, 1841, ostensibly to pay a debt, he was in a state of extreme agitation. He had been unable to find any kind of release from a mounting state of anxiety. His financial burdens, which if anything had increased, had assumed in his mind insurmountable proportions. He had to write twice what he had before and to attend either theatrical or operatic performances almost nightly. Extreme frustration resulted. Yet he did find the time to write a story, *The Golden Ass,* in collaboration with two friends (or so scholars believe), Edmond Texier and Arsène Houssaye.[1]

That Nerval borrowed the title, *The Golden Ass,* from the tale by Lucius Apuleius is indicative of his state of mind. Apuleius had been born in Madura (A.D. 125), a small Algerian town. He studied in Carthage and then in Athens, traveled extensively, became a fine lawyer and lecturer, and wrote volumes on natural science, poetry, philosophy, and the drama. Lucius married a woman older than himself (she was forty, he was twenty-nine) who helped him in his work.[2] More important was the fact that he had been initiated into the Eleusinian mysteries and, later in life, into the Isis cult; he had remained untouched by the young Christian sects growing up around him, and looked upon them as rather peculiar. Mithraism, and the Dionysian, Egyptian, Eleusinian, Isis, and Serapis mystery cults continued to flourish during the second century A.D., but relatively few people had actually been initiated into these groups or found fulfillment in them; most had become nonbelievers, substituting some kind of rational or nihilistic philosophy for the religion of their ancestors. As for the lower classes, they were swept up by magic, superstition, palmistry, soothsaying, and astrology. The old world's religious framework was breaking up, paving the way for the spread and growth of the new religion that was to reach its apogee in the Catholicism of the Middle Ages.

Nerval's world was somewhat similar to that of Apuleius. Catholicism, which had been losing ground ever since the Reformation, had given birth to many rival religious sects both Christian and non-Christian. Occult groups such as the Masons, Rosicrucians, and Swedenborgians, practitioners of Mesmerism and Theosophy were cropping up all about, each convinced it offered a panacea for man's earthly problems. The Age of Enlightenment and the French Revolution sounded the death knell of organized religion. Nerval felt the fissures in Christianity and experienced most deeply, as did many in his generation, the notion of a decaying civilization and the birth of a new life. How would Nerval cope with these new forces? How would he experience their power in his inner world?

Nerval's *The Golden Ass* may shed light on this problem. He called his protagonist Peregrinus-Proteus. The historical Peregrinus, who was born in Parium in A.D. 105 and died at sixty in Olympia, was a Cynic. (According to Lucian, who wrote a tale on *Peregrinus' Death*, he had been a Christian once, but he had been excommunicated for profanation and had thereafter become a Cynic.) At the Olympic games he informed the populace that he intended to throw himself into a fire, hoping his audience would stop him from following through on his threat. The crowds gathered but no one intervened. Not wanting to go back on his word, he cast himself into the flames and perished. Peregrinus must have represented to Nerval some aspects of his own cynicism toward revealed religion, his skepticism of pat solutions to life's immeasurable problems.

Proteus, the last half of Nerval's protagonist's name, may be associated with the Greek sea god of whom both Homer and Vergil spoke. He was supposed to know everything that had taken place in the past, was taking place in the present, and would take place in the future, but he was extraordinarily reluctant to reveal the details of his knowledge. To pin him down, one had to tie him up during his slumber in some cave by the sea. Even when so caught, he would try to escape by transforming himself into another shape—serpent, leopard, fire, water. But, if truly caught, he would return to his original shape, reveal his secret, and then jump into the sea.

Proteus' capacity to assume any shape must have fascinated Nerval and may have come to represent the variety implicit in the created universe as well as within its counterpart, the human personality: man's lionlike nature, his serpentine ways, his fiery notions, his leopardlike qualities. André Gide admired the Proteus type, the person who could adapt to all circumstances and situations, be ready for any change in life, be forever *disponible*. For Nerval, such transformation had mystical connotations. It not only pointed the way to reincarnation, to transmigration of souls, but to regeneration. It underlined the link between the conscious and the unconscious and man's continuous journey from the rational to the irrational—one world to another, one shape to another.

Not only was the choice of Peregrinus-Proteus significant, but so were the events in the tale. The story opens with the marquis de Morangles sitting next to his dead friend. Suddenly his friend rises up and tells him that he is not the person who had died two hours earlier but, rather, "a poor Pythagorean, skeptic, cynic, epicurean, mystic, apocalyptic philosopher who will one day play the lead role in the mystery of the last judgment."[3] The marquis is stunned as he listens to the man telling him of his incarnations over the past sixteen centuries. "Such is the law of transformation!"[4] One day, he said, optimistically, he would discover the secrets of reincarnation and then his body would be able to choose its final abode. The marquis and the reincarnated Peregrinus-Proteus decide to travel and listen to the prognostications of the popular philosophers of the day as they settle all worldly problems. They attend a socialist congress and listen to the words of a "great" humanitarian whom scholars have identified as Charles Fourier (1772–1837). Fourier's disciples looked upon him as a type of messiah and his works (*The Theory of Four Movements*, 1804; *The Treatise on the Domestic Agricultural Association*, 1882, among others) as a veritable Bible. Fourier believed that both individualism and a competitive system were not only an imperfect way of life, but an immoral one. Only by giving free expression to man's real nature, by indulging his passions and his desires, would happiness and virtue result. Misery and vice, he declared, were caused by the unnatural constraints society imposed upon man. A united effort on the part of all people would pave the way for a harmonious world. Countries should be divided into departments or *"phalanges,"* each having its own common buildings and lots for cultivation. In accordance with this credo of liberty, he suggested that any member of the group would work in any field he wanted and could pass from one task to another at will. Modestly enough, Fourier felt that his social contribution was comparable to Newton's in mathematics and science. Newton had discovered gravitation based on the belief of harmony and attraction between material bodies; Fourier had established a similar concept in terms of four great departments within the world; society, animal and organic life, and the material universe.[5]

The marquis de Morangles and Peregrinus-Proteus then listened to another self-styled savior of mankind—the founder of Evadism. Evadism became popular during the early years of the reign of Louis Philippe. The story of its founder, Ganneau, again points up man's eternal naïveté, his need to believe in something—anything. When a young man, Ganneau had not only been a dandy, sporting beautiful clothes and spending considerable sums on material possessions, on gambling, but had also been very interested in the science of phrenology. Since his father was a hatter, always fitting people for size, Ganneau had developed his own theories concerning this new science. One day, the story goes, Ganneau, who had set himself up in practice as a phrenologist, was visited by a beautiful young woman. Preoccupied with a gambling loss at the time, he was unaware of the woman's charm. His voice, melodious and soft spoken, just droned on and he continued stroking the back of the patient's head trying to understand what phrenologists have labeled "the bump of amorousness." Suddenly, she cried out, put her arms around his neck and said: "I love you!" Ganneau was struck by his patient's beauty; several weeks later she left her husband and she eventually married Ganneau. They were happy together until she became ill and died. Ganneau was so depressed that he toyed with the idea of suicide. One night, however, he had a vision. She came to him and asked him to continue his life on earth and to found a new religion, which would help mankind, based on certain theories in which she believed.[6]

Evadism was the result.

According to Ganneau, the Virgin Mary was no longer to be looked upon only as Christ's Mother but also as his wife. Mary's celestial image (as Christ's mother) was thus united with that of her earthly counterpart, Mary the whore, Mary Magdalene. Both Mary and Christ are, therefore, personifications of what is, paradoxically, both united and separate—the Androgyne. Ganneau, as Le Mapah, was androgynous. "Mapah is androgynous, the man who is both father and mother."[7] Indeed, the word *mapah* is composed of *papa* and *mama*. The Evadists, French off-shoots of Swedenborgians, believed that antagonism between man and woman just did not exist and that beings were free; that God had become man in Christ and had been incarnated again in the French people, and had been killed at Waterloo. Le Mapah reasoned that the word *water* in Waterloo, one of the four basic elements named by Heraclitus, and *loo*, Dutch for "earth," the second of the basic elements, represented the world.[8]

Ganneau set up the Apostolic Seat of Evadism on the Quai de Bourbon on the Île Saint Louis in Paris. Here his followers—mostly artists, sculptors, writers, and poets—would meet and listen to their god, dressed in a spectacular costume (long blue smock of a workingman, a felt hat, a woman's long cloak), preach his doctrine of mystical unity. Le Mapah's eloquence, his hypnotic eyes, his lyrical language, his sensuality, the grace of his gestures, and the elegance of his demeanor caught the attention of some of the most notable men of his day, including Balzac. Ganneau's long auburn hair, which reached half way down his body, lent a "heavenly" quality and dignity to his features. Whenever he spoke in public, he was usually accompanied by a woman who was (or so she claimed) in a somnambulistic trance. Sometimes Le Mapah claimed that he was Louis XVI and the woman beside him, Marie-Antoinette.[9]

Though Nerval mocked both Fourier's and Le Mapah's lucubrations, he was fascinated by their prognostications of cosmic harmony, reincarnation, and mystical unity. Nerval's reactions toward parapsychological phenomena were always ambivalent. At times, he believed, at other moments, he did not. That he should have taken the trouble to attack these doctrines as he did—certainly in a humorous vein—indicated a fundamental rapport with them.

As the days continued, Nerval felt more and more alienated from society and from himself. He seemed to be living a game, trying to create an illusion—that he could remain solvent, that he was capable, like anyone else, of earning a living. His mounting sense of isolation triggered an increasingly dynamic process within his unconscious. He began experiencing hallucinations, visions. At times he saw his mother, or the person he imagined her to have been. At other times he thought Jenny Colon, Marie Pleyel, the baronne de Feuchères, the beautiful archiduchesse Sophia from Austria appeared to him as real as they were in life, but with the added attraction of belonging to him alone.

These women, divested of their individual qualities, their flesh-and-blood natures, their assets and frailties, assumed mythological proportions. They were archetypes, aspects of the eternal feminine, endowed with the attributes of Isis, Astarte, the Queen of Sheba, Gretchen, Helen of Troy. Now, there were days when Nerval could no longer distinguish dream from reality. Worlds had merged.

Nerval's friends—Jules Janin, Théophile Gautier, Edmond Texier—noticed a change in him. He was in a constant state of excitement: his speech had accelerated tremendously, his words bubbled forth. He was forever expounding his ideas on mysticism, religion—Evadism, Swedenborgianism, Pythagoreanism, Oriental and Occidental mystery cults—and always broached them in extreme detail. Frequently, he identified with the various figures he mentioned and adhered to the dogmas they preached—at least temporarily. The "Golden Verses" of Pythagoras, the mysterious numbers of the Kabbala, from which he quoted frequently, took on profound significance for him. Orpheus' descent into the underworld became for Nerval a premonitory journey, a prelude to his own inner descent. Isis took on all the radiant beauty and mystery implicit in an eternal and universal goodness. Soon, Nerval observed, she would lift her veil for him and permit him to experience the ultimate in life. The Egyptian *Book of the Dead,* the occult works of Persian and Chaldean mystics, the Vedas—all became part and parcel of Nerval's universe. Indeed, he came to look upon himself as a hierophant, an initiate whose ascetic practices would enable him to traverse and explore the abysses within the universe.

One rainy night (actually at about one o'clock in the morning), Hippolyte Lucas, poet, novelist, dramatist, journalist, and a friend to Nerval, met him on the street. Nerval was returning from the theater and seemed beside himself. He had knocked on his door, he told Lucas, and had been refused admittance by the concierge. Now he was looking for a hotel in the vicinity, where he could spend the night. Lucas invited him to his apartment, which was not far off, and Nerval accepted. Lucas lit a fire as soon as they got in, and both men chatted and drank Rhine wine.

Nerval was excited and spoke eloquently, Lucas reported, about his trips to Germany, his plays, his future plans. When it grew late, Lucas gave Nerval a blanket and told him to sleep on the couch. At about four in the morning, Lucas awakened. He had heard a strange noise. He looked up and saw in front of the fireplace what seemed to him at first glance to be a "phantom." He called to it. It was Nerval. "If I were superstitious," Lucas said, "you would have frightened me, you look like a shadow."

Nerval had gotten cold during the night, he informed Lucas, and was trying to light a fire. But spirits do return, he told his friend, and he pointed to Hamlet's father as a superb example. Nerval further postulated that correspondences exist between heaven an earth (as Swedenborg had intimated) about which most people are unaware. Nerval then began discussing certain aspects of the occult sciences displaying, according to Lucas, great depth and knowledge. Lucas went to bed again and awakened the following morning to find Nerval reading. They breakfasted and finished the Rhine wine. Nerval's mood had altered considerably. Instead of the exhilarated, energetic, spirited Nerval of last evening, Lucas was faced with a "somber and taciturn" person who "didn't speak any more." Nerval left and thanked his host in his usual courteous manner. Lucas remained deeply concerned.

On another occasion, Nerval was walking down the street at about midnight and stopped in front of a certain house. As he looked up at the number in front of it—thirty three—he saw a woman with "a pallid complexion" and "cavernous eyes" walking toward him. He associated her with death and was convinced that the incident—a hallucination according to Nerval's friends—was an omen of his own impending death.

This notion, which Nerval felt so acutely, may be explained not only as a physical demise but a psychological one as well. What kind of death was confronting him? Was it the death of his literary career because he was dispersing his energies on relatively unimportant dramatic criticisms? Was it the death of the relating principle within him—which permitted him only slimly to communicate with others? Was it the realization that he needed some outside stimulus to arouse his imagination and creative powers? Was he beginning to question the worth of his own talents as a writer? Did his feeling of imminent death stem from what some scholars have termed his sexual impotence?

All of these may well have contributed to the progressive deterioration of Nerval's ego. His anguishes, fears, frustrations cascaded forth. Periods of exhilaration were followed by prolonged despondency then superseded by extreme optimism, joviality, conviviality, and, strangely enough, emerging feelings of power. Nerval's quixotic state, the unaccountable rapidity of his speech followed by sudden apathy and dejection, startled and worried his friends.

According to Edmond Texier and Jules Janin, Nerval's condition reached a crisis on Rue Miromesnil during a Mardi Gras celebration on February 23. Nerval had been visiting someone on that street and had suddenly been gripped with a desire to smash the glasses and chairs.[10]

Moments later, his mood changed. He left the house in good spirits, humming a tune and walking down the street as if riding on a cloud. His friends wanted to follow him but he insisted that he wanted to walk alone—that he was following a certain star and did not want to lose track of it.

As he walked he heard shouts of joy all about him. People in bizarre costumes and masks were feasting the celebration. Liquor flowed. Suddenly, and for no apparent reason, something must have frightened Nerval. He felt like a stranger, alienated in the midst of this gaiety, exiled from his reverie. The masked people must have become part of a grim reality; they had become transformed into demons and spirits.

Psychologically, what had happened to Nerval? The processes of organization and correlation, always associated with perception in normal people and which emanate from the unconscious, had vanished. The masked beings appeared to him as distortions and his paralyzing dread of what surrounded him must have prevented him from responding or even expressing his feelings in any coherent way. He felt trapped, caged. He was so terrorized by what he saw that he must have attempted to get rid of his fear by removing his clothes in the middle of the street—each article of clothing represented a terror. When someone attempted to stop him, he fought him off. His strength seemed to have doubled, as though his entire body had been injected with some kind of "electricity," making him capable of "overthrowing everything that approached him."[11]

The night watch finally stopped Nerval. He was taken to the police station by force and remained there until the following day, when he was taken to Mme. de Saint-Marcel's rest home on 6 Rue Picpus. Nerval's acute phase, of what has been diagnosed as schizophrenia, lasted thirteen days and was characterized by periods of aphasia and cataleptic exhaustion.[12] By March 5 he had apparently improved enough to be granted permission to read and write, and to go into the park next to the rest home. All he needed, he stated in a letter to his father, was lots of rest and good food.

According to his friend Alexander Weill, Nerval's condition was far from normal. After spending four hours with him one day, Weill left the rest home deeply frightened and depressed over Nerval's future welfare. Years later, he described his meeting with Nerval in an article published in *l'Evénement.* One morning, Weill wrote, he received a note from Nerval written in pencil: "I had a bout with ecstatic fever and am now on Rue Picpus, now. . . . I must talk with you. Come as soon as you can. I need you."[13]

Weill, led into a glass-paneled room in the middle of a garden surrounded by iron fencing, saw Nerval pacing up and down. In one hand he held a book, in the other, some cloth. Nerval was most cordial. He explained his condition in detail and told Weill that he had been placed in a rest home so that he could have some peace and quiet. After a few moments he asked to see Weill's fingernails. "You know," Nerval affirmed, "I am acquainted with the occult science of palmistry. I see that you descend from very high people, as I do, but in order to make certain I must see your feet. Take off your shoes and your socks and I'll tell you about your origins."[14]

Weill realized that the man could no longer distinguish fact from fiction. Since he did not want to excite Nerval he complied with his wishes. Nerval examined each toe separately and with utmost care. Then he showed him his own feet. "I am the son of King Joseph, the Emperor Napoleon's brother. This secret was told to me by my mother who was in Danzig with him. The coldness that my father always displays toward me is proof of this fact."[15]

Such conclusions were not idle fantasies. Nerval had been meditating upon his genealogy for some time, long before he had been taken to the rest home. He had drawn up elaborate charts proving his regal ancestry. On his paternal side, he maintained, the Labrunies descended from the celebrated Paladins, the knights of the German Emperor Otto. Three of these knights had settled in France: in Poitou, Périgord, and the Nîmes region. According to an etymological study, the name Labrunie was of German extraction: *brennen*, to burn . . .[16] Associations could also be made between Labrunie and Brunhilde—the fact that Nerval's mother had married an army man and had followed him to battle was comparable to the obligations of the German Brunhildes and their heroes. In a letter that Nerval wrote on March 14 he included a group of archaic and pseudo-archaic words of German, Latin, and Gothic origin as well as certain esoteric signs with Eastern and Near Eastern symbolism. He then signed his name as followed: "D.G. Labrunüe Dye Nâwoe."[17] On another letter, two days later, his signature read: "G. Nap. della torre Brunya e Pallazza."

Nerval's friends, Théophile Gautier, Alexander Weill, and Francis Wey (who worked for the government and would later invent the *roman feuilleton*) became deeply concerned. They observed Nerval carefully, listened closely to each of his prognostications, and always acted toward him with understanding and sympathy. Whenever they could, they attempted to ease his anguish, to lessen his burdens. Wey reassured Nerval that he could receive future work from the ministry of interior and promised him more government missions.[18]

After his release from the rest home on March 15, Nerval experienced a period of lethargy. He felt he was living a peripheral, unreal existence and was disturbed by his inability to comport himself as others did. His turmoil increased and the same symptoms reoccurred: extreme motility of speech, frenetic physical activity. His unconscious had become an autonomous force; it was in a state of hyperstimulation—an endless series of disparate images kept floating into consciousness. No sooner were these images consciously recognized than they vanished, pushed aside perhaps by the next influx of visions emanating from his subliminal depths.[19] By March 20 Nerval's condition had become so alarming, his regression into his inner world, so complete, that he was taken to the famous rest home of Dr. Esprit Blanche. Nerval was suffering once again from aphasia. He had moments of stupor when he felt nothing but a type of impersonal lucidity: he knew what was happening to him, was aware of the events taking place, but could not exteriorize his will to the outside world. He could only experience life inwardly. He had been cut off from any contact with the outer world. Yet his intelligence— a type of "motion-picture lens"—functioned and seemed able to record "everything which came within its focus," but always on a passive level.[20]

Nerval was particularly fortunate in being able to go to Dr. Blanche's rest home. Dr. Blanche not only enjoyed an unusual reputation as a most understanding physician, but also as the practitioner of the most advanced treatments for mental patients. His clinic was a beautiful eighteenth-century building situated high above Paris—on a hill in Montmartre where many windmills still dotted the horizon. Dr. Blanche made his home in this clinic because he believed that close contact with the patients, and the re-creation of a family situation, would be beneficial to them. Kindness and understanding—together with rigorous discipline—were included in his method, and he trained his staff accordingly.

Half of the building housed Dr. Blanche's wife, his son, servants, and less serious mental patients; he placed the more difficult and even dangerous patients on the other side, where they were always under close surveillance. A large garden, also divided into two sections, surrounded the building. Dr. Blanche rejected all violent procedures in the care of his mental patients. He felt that harsh methods were deleterious to the sick and undermined their confidence, an important factor in restoring them to health. Dr. Blanche always attempted to win their affection and confidence in order to establish some kind of communication. Sometimes, when he felt it important, he instilled in some of his patients a sense of fear because, he reasoned, "fear is capable of repressing the patient's fury."[21] He also felt that the mentally sick have an acute sense of justice and should be treated within the framework of their phobias. He was adamant concerning physical therapy: he obliged all of his patients (those capable, of course) to walk in the park, to exercise, and, when called for, to indulge in hard manual labor. Meals were taken in common. Two large tables were placed parallel to each other; Dr. Blanche and his family ate at a third. Perfect order was maintained during meals. If there were any disturbances, Dr. Blanche's aids would settle the disputes. Sometimes straitjackets were necessary, and in serious cases Scotch baths were prescribed (that is, hot and cold showers used alternately). These were designed to shock patients out of their torpor or fury.

Dr. Blanche's wife played an important role in his treatment of patients. She was always on the premises, comforting those who needed comforting—the perfect mother image. Patients identified with her, responded to her warmth. When she became ill in 1832 and had to leave the rest home for quite some time, patients, such as the poet Antony Deschamps, who himself suffered from periodic bouts with mental depression, felt so deeply about her that in one of his poems he called her "the angel of the house."[22]

Nerval reacted favorably to the kindness shown him at Dr. Blanche's rest home. Though he improved, he still harbored a deep sense of shame; his attitude toward his sickness was one of rejection. When writing to his friends, he mentioned his minor "relapse" and referred to his sickness in a flippant manner—a slight torment, nothing more.

Nerval was released from Dr. Blanche's rest home on November 21. He was given three hundred francs by the minister of the interior and of fine arts to help finance trips to the South of France, Belgium—and perhaps to the Middle East.

PART II
VOYAGE IN THE ORIENT

Dust thou art, and unto dust shalt thou return.
Genesis 3:19.

9 DEATH—TIME

The ruins of Time build mansions in Eternity.
William Blake, *Letter to William Haley.*

We know little of Nerval's activities during the months following his release from Dr. Blanche's rest home. It is believed that he left Paris on
December 23, 1842. A friend from Bordeaux, Joseph Fonfrède (reputed to be an Egyptologist, though there is no evidence of this), accompanied him. They arrived in Marseilles on December 28, in Alexandria on January 16, and in Cairo, where they remained for three
months, on February 6. Nerval reacted to his new surroundings with
intense excitement. He experienced the sensation, he wrote, of slipping
back into time, of penetrating some mysterious reality. He was so enthralled that he began dressing like an Egyptian and even shaved his
hair. He first set up quarters at a small hotel, but soon moved into a
French neighborhood in Cairo, and finally, in March, took a house in
the Coptic quarter and hired a servant. He socialized with the French
consul, Gautier d'Arc; with Dr. Nicolas Perron, a specialist in ancient
civilizations; with Clot Bey, a former European adventurer who had
become a Muslim lord; with the director of the polytechnical school; and
with the former director of the Paris Opera, among others.

Nerval kept careful notes of his personal experiences in Egypt and
the other countries he visited. He frequented libraries, read widely in
history and ancient religions: Héberlot de Molainville's *Bibliothèque orientale,* W. Lane's *Modern Egyptians,* the works of Silvestre de Sacy, Abbé
Terrassons' *Sethos,* which detailed initiation procedures in the ancient
Egyptian mystery schools, and many more volumes. His notes furnished
him with material necessary for the many articles he was to write in a
variety of magazines and newspapers: *L'Artiste, Revue des deux mondes, La
Silhouette, Le National,* and others.[1]

Scholars such as Pierre Martino, Gilbert Rouger, and Jean Richer have
pointed out the many factual errors in Nerval's articles: historical in-
accuracies, misinterpretations of religious ideologies, and the like. But
Nerval was neither an historian nor a philosopher. He was a creative
writer. Like Corneille and Racine, who based their works on so-called
historical facts, and altered these for reasons of plot and characteriza-
tion, Nerval took liberties. His *Voyage in the Orient* should be examined
primarily as a subjective and meaningful creative work that reveals not
only Nerval's extraordinary literary style but also his imagination and
inner peregrinations.

Voyage in the Orient is an odyssey—that of Nerval's soul. It is his initiation into a deeper sphere of existence—that of death, an aspect of life

that had preoccupied him ever since he was a child, when he had equated it with separation. His mother's demise had instilled a void within him, a certain *Angst*. The deaths of his grandparents, of his aunt, of the baronne de Feuchères, who represented his youth, were also important departures from life. The most heart-rending of all must have been Jenny Colon's death on June 5, 1842, from—so it is claimed—the strain of her many tours and repeated pregnancies. Though he knew they would eventually be reunited, her death gnawed angrily at his already troubled existence.

Adding to Nerval's *Angst* was an additional fear, that of recurring insanity. To be declared a schizophrenic—Nerval's disease, though the word had not yet been invented—meant that he was capable of experiencing two worlds, that of the unconscious, which is timeless and spaceless, and (when cured) that of the rational mind, with its limitations. There was always that terrible threat: the inability of consciousness to remain dominant in his life. This submersion of consciousness into the unconscious meant, to all intents and purposes, the death of Nerval's rational existence. Was there a link, he might have wondered, between mystic delusions and religious hallucinations (Ezekiel, Paul, Loyola, Theresa d'Avila) and his own madness or inner visions, which also encompassed cosmogonies and cosmologies? Did withdrawal into the unconscious imply a deeper inner vision into past experiences? Anterior existences?

Like so many men of his age, Nerval was a divided human being. He wanted to believe in divinity, in an afterlife, in metempsychosis; but he was very much a product of eighteenth-century Enlightenment, of scientific attitudes that devaluated and even destroyed such metaphysical notions. Hadn't Voltaire written that the study of metaphysics was an insufferable waste of time, that metaphysics "contains two things; the first, what everyone who has any common sense at all already knows; the second, what no one will ever know."[2] Christianity in particular, as observed in nineteenth-century France, no longer offered Nerval an answer to his torments. He needed a new spiritual orientation, something that would fill the void within him. His Voltairian side, the part of him that questioned every belief, credo, and point of view, that analyzed and eventually depotentialized faiths centuries old, had to be rooted out if he were to survive emotionally. He needed a religion to stem the tide of his conflicts, to calm his doubts, to comfort him, to give him the security he so desperately sought.

Why should Nerval have assumed that by studying ancient religions and civilizations he would be attacking or at least confronting the problem of death, and at the same time, that of life? Had something already died within him? Or had it never come to life? Because he had been deprived of a mother's love, his feeling function, his instinctual side, had never been developed. Whatever was natural to Nerval was either repressed or viewed in a cerebral manner, always masking, rejecting his own feeling function. The only time he could ever relate to feelings were in his descriptions of nature—again cerebrally conceived. His writings such as his early poems and odes, his short stories, his travelogues, which touched upon flowers, meadows, trees, the sky, a running brook were accurate, profound, and always tinged with something tremulous, some instinctual force that never quite dared show itself, that stirred only in his subliminal depths. This feeling, this Eros quality had been stunted. The result: Nerval's scientific or thinking function had become highly developed whereas his feeling function had remained dormant, coming to life only through the word—the image. Because of this split within his own personality, his relationships with people (particularly women) were marred by excessive timidity and awkwardness; this might have contributed to what Dr. Sebillotte has termed Nerval's impotence. The question that Nerval might have posed, at least unconsciously, was whether his feeling function could ever be revived. Could the cerebral approach to life—his mask, his protection from the terrifying workaday world—be integrated into his personality, thereby balancing it and making life more bearable?

Plutarch's "The Great God Pan is Dead" could easily apply to Nerval. The Greek philosopher meant that man had become severed from nature. Symbolically, it indicated that man had become divested of his "natural" and "creative" function. He felt at a loss, deprived. Nerval's overly sensitive and highly strung nature felt this void acutely. It was as if he were living at the edge of a great chasm, an abyss, into which he was in mortal danger of falling.

Nature, for most nineteenth-century men, was no longer the generative force it had been for the ancients. In the early days man had looked upon nature as a realm of mystery and magic. A tree, a flower, a mountain were not simply objects for study or observation. They were filled with spirits, divinities, and they had an hypnotic and enticing effect upon people. Men related to these various forces, felt themselves a part of them, not cut off from them. The romantic poets, and Nerval also, felt an affinity with nature. Their feelings overflowed into it whenever they described lakes, shrubs, sunsets. They were convinced that their loneliness would be dissipated through the living force of nature. Poets such as Lamartine found solace in the vast expanse surrounding them by projecting their anguish onto "mother" nature. Though Nerval believed he could calm his turmoil by returning to the scenes of his childhood, by immersing himself into nature, he never really gave of himself spontaneously, instinctually. His approach was always restrained, reserved, secretive. Nature was his refuge from a world he could not face. The fear of being hurt encouraged him to withdraw still further into nature, which was now viewed in terms of his own childhood, his national past, man's history. In this way, Nerval associated nature with time. More important, every withdrawal from the workaday world reduced his ability to relate to the people about him.[3]

The question now arises as to why time, as measured by the ancients, might be associated with death (both physical and mental), and why it also might offer Nerval an answer to his own problems.

The ancients measured time in terms of cyclical events. They looked upon each day as a conquest over night, as an eternal beginning, as a cycle or circle, to be understood and experienced. There was no beginning and no end. The concepts of past, present, and future were nonexistent. Living close to nature, the ancients had become one with the cosmos and had placed themselves within the endless series of cycles. No split existed between them and nature, no consciousness of themselves as separate entities from the forces surrounding them, from the world of phenomena. And death, for the primitive, was one of the organic phenomena, one of the personal changes. It was not looked upon as a separation or as an end. Fear did not enter the picture, as it had come to do for the "civilized" man of the nineteenth century.

The Greeks also looked upon their world as circular, "returning perpetually upon itself, self-enclosed, under the influence of astronomical movements which command and regulate its course with necessity." Pythagoras, the Stoics, the Platonists regarded cycles of time (*aiones*) as similar situations recurring over and over again. There was no single or unique event in life; nothing took place only once. Even an event such as the condemnation of Socrates would be enacted over and over again during the course of subsequent cycles or circles. Time consisted of an "eternal return." Since the universe moved in a continuous series of circles, according to Plato any change indicated a fall rather than an ascension to an Ideal state. There was no concept of improvement or progress. Change, on the contrary, was looked upon as a "degenerescence," and time as a "hierarchized vision of the universe." What man experiences on earth is merely a reflection of a superior or ideal truth. According to Aristotle man may say that he lived "after" the Trojan war, but since he is part of the circle of life that continues in its circular course, the event will occur again and one might just as well say that he lived "before the event and not after it."[4]

With the advent of Judaism and Christianity, eschatological consciousness (or historical time) was born. Past, present and future became distinct phases of existence and the belief in "temporal consciousness" altered man's relation to the cosmos and to himself. He emerged separate from nature. With such a cleavage, death was looked upon as a fearful experience, a problem, something that inflicted pain—as a separation or an end. Time, no longer measured as a circle, became a straight line.

Such "temporal consciousness" came into being when the concept of creation *ex nihilo* was adopted by the Hebrews in the Old Testament. In Genesis, for example, it is stated that the world was created in seven days out of chaos or nothingness. The world had a beginning and, per-force, it would have an end. The notion of *aeternitas* or of the *aión* gave way to the belief in *sempiternitas*. The greater man's consciousness of his identity and individuality became, the more fragmented was his exis-tence. Divisions into centuries, decades, years, days, hours, minutes, sec-onds followed.

The belief in an end after death was inherent in early Judaism. With the passage of years, man severed himself more and more from nature. Without nature's strength and support and her eternal qualities, man found himself alone. He could no longer face the idea of death as a void, as an end in itself, as a cutting off from life—not the idea of an eternal God and mortal man, born from dust and returning to it.

The more intolerable the belief in death as an end to life became, the greater was man's longing for an afterlife. Another realm was created by the Hebrews (resurrection), by the Neoplatonists (the realm of es-sences, of perfection), by the Christians (hell, heaven, limbo, resur-rection).

With the advent of science, technology, and the worship of reason (during the French Revolution), there arose another stumbling block. Man discarded the precepts offered him by organized religion: the no-tion of Christ's resurrection and the belief in transcendence, paradise, and hell. Once again man became entrapped by time. Time became syn-onymous with death and death was a finale.

What remains for people who have either voluntarily or involuntarily lost their faith—lost the religion that had helped them face life and death? The stoic is convinced that man must think about death at all times so as not to fear it and to overcome its negative characteristics. The nihilist is determined to accept the "meaninglessness" and the "fu-tility" of life. The atheist becomes his own god, the molder of his own destiny. What of a man such as Nerval, who needed the comfort of belief to bolster him, to unite what was constantly being pulled apart within him?

Nerval was a type of archaeologist—a man searching into the collec-tive past in the hope of finding his own identity, his own raison d'être, his own sense of the meaning of life and death. His genealogical inves-tigations had made him the descendent of Napoleon's brother, of the German Knights of the Emperor Otto; he wanted to investigate still fur-ther, into an even more remote area and era—to the cradle of civilization.

Nerval's *Voyage in the Orient* may be divided into four sections, each depicting another spiritual and intellectual experience—a further de-scent into the world of reality and self-awareness.

10 THE HYPNEROTOMACHIA

Like every real dream, the Hypnerotomachia is Janus-headed; it is a picture of the Middle Ages just beginning to turn into modern times by way of the Renaissance—a transition between two eras, and therefore deeply interesting to the world of today, which is still more transitional in character.
C.G. Jung, *Foreword to The Hypnerotomachia.*

One of the most arresting sections of the first part of *Voyage in the Orient* deals with Francesco Colonna's *The Hypnerotomachia,* a favorite of Nerval's. *The Hypnerotomachia,* which signifies "dream, love and strife," is far more than a mere idealization and spiritualization of women; it is a mystic vision in which death becomes a positive entity—an entrée into a world of infinite dimension, where unity, beauty, and joy exist in an eternal present.[1]

The Hypnerotomachia relates Colonna's dream visions, which center around his great love, Polia. Colonna, born in Venice in 1433, became a painter and fell in love with Princess Lucretia Polia of Trevise; because of the vast differences in their social standing, however, their marriage became an impossibility and, Nerval notes, because no altar "celebrating Christ . . . the God of equality" would bless such a union, Colonna entered the Dominican order and Polia became a nun.[2] Each studied philosophy and religion; each lived a dual existence—their daytime lives apart and their nighttimes dreaming of a life together. In their "double dream," wrote Nerval, they "surmounted the immensity of space and time."[3] Colonna recorded his dreams in a book that he bequeathed to Polia. His visions took him through many dangerous and harrowing experiences and concluded finally with nuptials at Cythera, celebrated under Venus' star.[4]

That pagan and Christian customs should have been fused in Colonna's book of dreams is understandable. Colonna was a humanist and humanism was a composite of opposites, a blend of the Christian and the pagan, the materialist and the spiritual, the classical and the modern. The humanists had resurrected antiquity, which the medieval theologians, considering paganism detrimental to the spread and domination of Christianity, had attempted to crush. Despite the suppression of classical cultures, however, knowledge of ancient civilizations was extensive, though slanted, always subject to the church's dogmatic interpretations. As the church became more and more secularized, new ideas infiltrated. Salvation was no longer a certainty and, therefore, the link between man's earthly existence and the world hereafter was broken. Absolute answers vanished and the humanist found himself floundering in a world in which rigid dogma was falling asunder. The humanists turned to the pagan world for substitutes. They admired beauty, spontaneity, and nature. The ascetic, guilt-ridden world of the Middle Ages, with its sharp distinctions between good and evil, could not satisfy the Renaissance man.[5] This did not mean that church dogma was cast aside; rather, it initiated intense inner conflict. The humanist experienced the pleasures of antiquity with accompanying feelings of remorse and anxiety. Humanists such as Colonna sublimated their love, sensuality, and inner feelings of joy in their poetry, painting, music. In the arts the new *Zeitgeist* was born, and life itself began taking on a rosier hue. The somber, deathlike tonalities of the Middle Ages retreated in favor of a more brilliant, less guilt-ridden frame of reference.

Polia's love for Colonna, or those emotions she aroused within him, paved the way for his return to classical antiquity and with it the consummation on his love through a spiritual marriage. The pagan world in Colonna's visions became a land of grace, beauty and freedom. Guilt and remorse intruded upon his dream world, however, in the form of a series of dangerous ordeals—like an initiation rite: overcoming wolves, passing through forests, and similar challenges. Once he had fought off the frightening forces placed before his path, he gained admittance to the eternal realm of bliss, where he met his Polia in a land divested of such artificial concepts as past, present, and future—and death.

Because Colonna had succeeded in going through an inner metamorphosis, he was able to unite what had been severed in the external world: his feeling and thinking functions. During his life, his feeling function had been rejected; it had been considered sinful. His cerebral attitude, therefore, predominated in all of his worldly attitudes. Such an inner transformation has led some scholars and psychologists, most notably C.G. Jung, to believe that the *Hypnerotomachia* was an alchemical document. Its first translator into French, the alchemist Beroalde de Verille (1600), believed that Colonna's dreams were replete with symbols behind which were hidden important secrets. The uninitiated, he claimed, should not have access to such works for they would be incapable of understanding them and might even misinterpret and condemn them. Colonna's lengthy architectural descriptions, Verille maintained, were detailed accounts of the alchemists' most solemn symbol, the Hermetic vessel within which were hidden the directions for transmuting matter into the philosopher's stone.[6]

The alchemists, as we have seen in previous chapters, were intent upon creating the philosopher's stone and thereby bringing about a spiritual rebirth within the psyche; that is, they were interested in the cre-vient to both her "charms" and her will. Such "courtly love" revealed an ation of a new man. To achieve this goal they had to transform what was imperfect (imbalanced) into something perfect (in harmony with itself and the cosmos). Because the universe consisted of four elements, conflict and tension arose among them and the cosmos was, therefore, in a state of becoming; according to Heraclitus, fire was its center. When Heraclitus spoke of fire, however, he did not mean merely that which burns in the ordinary sense of the term. He also meant, for example, the fire of grapes, which turns into wine and alters one's frame of reference (fire water); the fire of feeling (warmth, passion); the polarities in the seasons; the dynamic process(es) experienced by physical organs (liver, heart, spleen, lungs, kidneys)—among other things. Modern psychologists have added the various states that an individual experiences under different circumstances—anger, joy, thought, care, fear. By mixing and warming matter, the alchemist altered its previous state, proving that differentiation exists within the original substance, albeit in a potential state. His task consisted, then, in the "reblending of nature" and, by his so doing, the "reforming" of matter, reshuffling the inner contents that he projected onto it.[7]

Colonna accomplished this transmutation in *The Hypnerotomachia*, by focusing his unconscious visions on Polia and overcoming the dangers placed in his path. Such a process caused an inner struggle; the tension expended, altering his body chemistry, and making possible his "spiritualized" and "divine" union with Polia.[8]

The austere tendencies in *The Hypnerotomachia* (his journey, the tribulations, the guide) may have been gleaned from his readings in Dante's *Divine Comedy*. The group of poets with whom Dante had been associated in his youth, the *fideli d'amore*, considered love from two points of view: a combination of the rational way of thinking (influenced by the precepts of Aristotle and Thomas Aquinas), and the more affective path (as taught by the Neoplatonists, St. Augustine, and Christian mystics such as the pseudo-Areopagiticus). Love was something that reflected and grew out of God. Earthly love represented a step in an ascending hierarchy: love vowed to a mortal woman would lead to divine love. Such a notion could include both physical and spiritual passion. In this case, the woman becomes double: on the one hand, personal, physical, and mortal, and on the other, collective, abstract, and transcendental, in that she represents pure intelligence, the Idea, and an eternal force in God.

Without Petrarch's love sonnets to Laura, Colonna might never have written his *Hypnerotomachia*. Petrarch had been exposed not only to Italian humanism but also to a new trend in male-female relationships arising in France. The cult of the woman—of the virgin—had become popular in the twelfth and thirteenth centuries, transforming woman into an ideal and powerful figure. The man, as a result, was usually subservient to both her "charms" and her will. Such "courtly love" revealed an emergence of the female principle in society, the first glimmer of the Renaissance, and with it, the demise of the patriarchal, male-dominated world of the Middle Ages.[9]

One of the earliest and most remarkable women to arise in this new female-oriented society was Marie de Champagne, who created a "court" in which love cases were discussed and tried. Andreas Capellanus wrote a treatise, *De Amore,* in which well-known women judged certain situations involving love. The verdicts pronounced were an attempt on the part of women to find a common denominator between the rational principle (cerebral quality as represented in a patriarchal society), which included a sense of obligation and responsibility, and the feeling principle (the affective side prevalent in matriarchal groups) where love and emotion became dominant forces. Love, in certain cases, as witnessed by the Tristan and Isolde legends and the "Lays" of Marie de France, was looked upon as both a wonderful feeling and as a dangerous and fatal disease. The guilt experienced when love got out of hand would, in a Christian society, have to be paid for if redemption was to take place. Suffering, many poets felt, was the only manner by which sinful love could be expiated. The need for redemption ushered in a desire to cast off the "vulgar" sensuality associated with physical love and to experience a more "refined" and "purified"—a "spiritualized"—relationship. The verses of the troubadours and poets of France at this period, those of Bernard de Ventadour, for example, were symbolistic, even secretive. Indeed, their women became so etherealized, so devoid of reality, that a tension—of which they were unaware—developed between their idealized concept and the real females they encountered in daily life.

Colonna's Polia really existed for him. He was a catalyst,[10] the vehicle that enabled him to create his work of art and in so doing, to recreate himself. A catalyst, in alchemy, neither blends with nor becomes part of the chemical ingredients that are in the process of being transformed. It remains separate and distinct. Polia, though living in some remote region in Colonna's mind (or in Italy), acted upon the object in question (Colonna the monk), transforming an overly cerebral, ascetic, sin-ridden man into one who could feel love, contentment, and inner joy.[11]

What did Nerval project onto Colonna's *Hypnerotomachia?* Uppermost is the concentration on the cult of the woman, the beloved—not in terms of mortal love but as an eternal and spiritualized experience. Such a view took Nerval out of his finite world, where time and death were synonymous and plunged him into the infinite cosmic domain. The cult of the woman could also redress (as it had for Colonna) an inner imbalance between Nerval's repressed affective side and his overly developed cerebral orientation. But, whereas Colonna had struggled to overcome the terrifying obstacles placed in his path, Nerval, so far as we know, had not.

The woman for Nerval frequently took on divine attributes: she was unique, an astral force like Isis, Venus, Astarte, Rhea, or the Virgin Mary. The woman was the possessor of innumerable mysteries and encompassed purity, modesty, motherhood, understanding, and tenderness. Great artists such as Dürer, Van Eyck, Fra Lippo Lippi, Raphael, and Rubens had also been affected by the cult of the madonna. They painted women as a *mater dolorosa,* a *mater gloriosa,* a *vagina dentata* with all of her evil aspects (rage, jealousy). At the end of *Faust,* thus, the chorus mysticus sings *"Das Ewig Weibliche zieht uns hinan"* ("The eternal womanly nature draws us upward").[12] For Christians, the Virgin Mary had to become the offshoot of all mother goddesses. Even the objects attributed to her had their counterparts in antiquity: the "starry mantle of Aphrodite Uranos, the dove of Ishtar."[13]

The female goddesses alluded to frequently by Nerval were Isis, Venus, and the hyperdulian Virgin Mary who presided over "all the forces of nature in the three regions of heaven, earth and the underworld." And he continued:" Venerable goddess, who loves the shadows . . . visible and invisible . . . from whom all things emanate, for you give the laws to the entire world, and you order even the Fates, sovereign of the night!"[14] They were forever fruitful. As Euripides observed: "Earth bears all things and takes them back again." Aeschylus wrote in *The Suppliants:* "Mother Earth, Mother Earth, avert his fearful cries!"[15]

If Nerval identified with Venus, Isis, and the Virgin Mary as "earth mothers," he would, of necessity, experience feelings of regeneration. The mystery cults, as religions based on feeling, served to arouse these emotions, thereby permitting an integration of this force into an intellectually oriented way of life.[16] The difference exists between the spiritual experience of the ancients and the Christian conceptions. In the former, union between the votary and the deity in question took place after an attempt was made on the part of the "mystai" (the earthbound initiate) to raise himself through a ritual or purification act to enlightenment or union with God. The Christian, after his ascetic trials and prayers, waits for God to descend and instill divine grace within him, thereby freeing him from sin and redeeming him.[17] In both Colonna's vision and Nerval's identification with it there is a compromise: a perpetual assent and descent of the divine figure and of the initiate. Such vertical activity enables him to blend an overly earthbound attitude with an overly spiritualized orientation.

Where would such a remolding of view lead Nerval? Practically speaking, he would acquire new knowledge and fresh material for his short stories and articles. Psychologically, his already poor adaptation to the world of reality would be increased. By identifying with Colonna, Nerval once again sought refuge in a world of fantasy in which he believed supreme happiness existed. By withdrawing from everyday life (without the struggle waged by Colonna), where Nerval knew only despair, he focused his dream experience on whatever transcendental force he idealized. The process worked as follows: Nerval would take the earthbound woman as his point of departure, endow her with all the divine attributes of a goddess (Isis, Venus, the hyperdulian Virgin Mary), and then place her in the sphere of perfection. Since mortal women are prey to the vicissitudes of time, they cannot hope to compete with such an idealized vision. Only further alienation from the world could possibly ensue from such an attitude on Nerval's part.

11 DESCENT INTO THE PYRAMID

Egypt is a vast tomb . . .
Nerval, *Voyage in the Orient.*

Nerval's journey to Egypt was tantamount to a trip into time; it may be viewed as a psychological and metaphysical desire for rebirth. By returning to the "cradle" of civilization, Nerval was attempting to revive elements that had either died within him or had never really been brought to life. Rebirth requires an initiation period that is usually fraught with terror.[1] Nerval's initiation in Egypt consisted of two steps: the first centered around the feminine principle, and the second, a descent into the pyramid (or Self).

Women were described by Nerval from the very outset as the representatives of a culture filled with "enigmas and mysteries," a land of "serious and pious" people. The fact that women walked about veiled, retaining their baffling quality, provoked and encouraged his reverie: "This certainly is the land of dreams and of illusion!"[2] Only women's eyes were visible and these, he observed, were "dangerous"; they mirrored the soul—fascinating and haunting. Because they remained incognito, they were looked upon by Nerval not as individuals but as collective figures—remote, reserved, and mysterious. As archetypes, these women became stepping stones for his illusions, his idealizations, like figures walking and stalking about in anonymity.

On Nerval's first night in Egypt he fell asleep in his room to the sound of "strange music," "vague sounds" of bagpipes, "a hoarse *viole* that worked strongly on my nerves."[3] The harmonies and cacophonies ushered in a flow of memories: Burgundian and Provençal Noël hymns, secular music, ancient and modern sounds. Nerval awakened from his dream-reverie, went to the window, and saw men chanting, drumming, and lighting torches. His guide informed him that he was witnessing the beginning of a wedding ceremony.[4]

It is significant that Nerval's stay in Egypt should begin with a marriage ceremony: a union of sexes, a fusion of Occidental and Middle Eastern cultures, of past and present. The cymbals, drums, castanets, the glitter of the torches, the many slaves accompanying the cortège, Nerval wrote, was like a theatrical decor. What really held his attention was the object of this pageantry—what he called "the red phantom," the veiled bride. He was tantalized by this apparition, which seemed to "slip" or "glide" before him, looking larger than life under the "pyramid-shaped diadem" encrusted with "sparkling stones" that she wore on her head.[5]

Nerval's vision of the "red phantom" had alchemical overtones. The color red implies *rubedo* (fire), the warmth of nature, the redness of her moonlike aspects and the fourth phase of the alchemical process before the *coniunctio*. This bride is sacred. She is like those other female celestial figures (from Venus to the Virgin Mary) to which Nerval frequently referred, bedecked in their cult objects: star-filled mantles, diadems of precious stones, rays shining forth from them. The "red phantom" described by Nerval is about to be initiated into a sacred mystery, that of marriage. Her husband, dressed in gold and red, becomes in this ritual a complementary figure to his wife. The gold he wears has an equally interesting alchemical meaning: it represents higher value, the spirit or sun in man. A union then between the spiritual forces (masculine, Sol) and the natural (earthly, feminine, luna) forces within the cosmos is about to take place.

The alchemist has a distinct advantage over Nerval (or any layman) because he projects onto matter and can keep on doing so as long as he pursues his experiments. A person like Nerval, who was forever projecting onto people and situations (in this case the marriage ceremony), could be divested of the object of his transference because it was external to him. Rather than attempting to integrate the forces that such a projection symbolized, he kept transferring to outward entities and thereby left his personality fragmented and weakened. So long as the object or people upon whom he transferred his feelings were available, all was well; but if they were to vanish, a dislocation of the personality could well ensue.

Nerval was fortunate to be able to project onto the women he saw in Cairo, to remain an observer and not a participant in such a marriage ceremony. When he was invited to enter the bride's house, which would have involved him actively in the ritual, Nerval declined, perhaps fearful of experiencing the "red phantom" as an earthbound person in her natural surroundings and thereby destroying his idealization of her. Distance made her inaccessible to him—alluring, seductive, exotic not only in her dress and her demeanor but in the very language she spoke. "One man will possess the secret of this beauty or of this unknown grace; one only will be able to pursue his ideal in peace and consider himself the favorite of a sultan or a fairy . . . and besides, doesn't every man have the right in this happy land, to renew more than once, this day of triumph and of illusion."[6]

Nerval's desire to remain uninvolved was underscored when friends suggested that he take a slave girl and marry her. Nerval refused to do so on the ground that he did not want to go through a religious ceremony (either Coptic or Christian) entailing a consecration that he would have to break when he left the country—this despite the assurance that he could leave the girl or obtain a divorce from her at any time.[7] He rejected all attempts to link him to another human being. He may have thought that to accept a real woman would be stultifying. How much more beautiful it was to dream of remote, beautiful, and comforting divinities!

Nerval did take a Javanese slave girl to live with him, but their relationship must have been asexual. Why a Javanese? Why not an Arab girl? Perhaps because she came from an even more remote land and stood out from the rest. Perhaps because Nerval's attraction "for the unforeseen" or for exteriors: "the metallic brilliance of her eyes, the whiteness of her teeth, the distinction of her hands and the length of her dark mahogany hair. . . ."[8] Like Baudelaire, Nerval was mesmerized by outer vestments, by the visible and sensual aspects of the woman, for these are stepping stones to the dream, to enchantment, and to escape— particularly in Egypt, where the climate is hot and heavy and dulls the senses.

The magic and mystery associated with the women of Egypt and their habits was manifested in the harem, a world in itself. Seductive, always able to entice men, women were kept in captivity (it may be supposed) to prevent them from annihilating the masculine principle. The Egyptians—the men, that is—had an ambivalent attitude toward the female, being both attracted by their charms and fearful of their power. One of Nerval's friends, Suleiman-Aga, affirmed that women "bring out the worst in men, they encourage his acidity, [and his] egotistical and cruel nature," they "destroy fraternity and charity . . . [and] cause quarrels, injustices and tyranny." Women are to be enjoyed at certain times, declared the Muslim, as objects to be tasted with delight and then pushed aside when one is satiated. Forced to live separately in harems, these *vagina dentata* types could do little to challenge man's power. Austere rituals accompany a man's visit to the harem, and precisely because his access is surrounded with difficulties, his pleasure is heightened.[9] It is in the harem (the matriarchal world) that man's initiation begins and that he tastes the bounty of nature.

Nerval's life in Egypt had for him the lustre and excitement of a fantasy world. It was, he wrote, as if he were living out the marvels of *The Thousand And One Nights.* The customs, the thinking processes, the reactions of the Egyptians were the reverse of those he had known in Occidental lands. What the French labeled fantasy, hallucination, and even madness, the Egyptian considered very real. When Nerval told an Egyptian, "I see in my dreams all the spirits, the giants unleashed before me, since Solomon's time," the Egyptian understood him and agreed with him. When Nerval made such a statement to Dr. Blanche or his friends in France they looked upon it as "the product of an overexcited mind." Every spirit or phantom experienced during the sleeping hours, every ecstatic vision of beauty, had the lustre of reality for the Egyptian. It is quite understandable that Nerval should have been so taken with this land, where his world of unreality had become reality.

The solar disc—the sun—first made Nerval aware of the vast differences between the Occidental and the Middle Eastern cultures. In Paris, he wrote, the mornings took on greyish color tones, the furniture was "angular," and "the imagination strikes against the window pane like an imprisoned insect."[10] Egypt stood for the sun bursting forth "at the edge of the sky, preceded only by a vague white gleam."[11]

It was through the sun that Nerval was first introduced to the death-and-rebirth mysteries. The sun, a totality, a composite of opposites, contained both aspects of life—the red and the black, "the black sun of melancholia."[12] Because this celestial disc was a totality, it could be looked upon as a god, a life-giving and death-dealing force: radiant, dazzling, spreading joy in life, making for fecundation and growth in nature, but also blinding, scorching, a source of destruction and devastation.

The individual who encounters the blackness within the sun is experiencing what psychologists and metaphysicians have called the "creative void." It is defined as that area "beyond the state of consciousness which permits the individual to undergo a *numinous* (or religious) experience— or an aesthetic or psychological revelation."[13] Nerval's understanding of the black aspect of the sun indicated that he had stepped beyond consciousness and had penetrated the collective unconscious, where man's creative faculties reside. Once his subliminal world had been stirred by such penetration, consciousness could then step in, capture whatever images it sought, and direct and formulate these in the work of art. The collective unconscious, from a metaphysical point of view, may be compared to the "void" (the same void from which, according to the Bible, God created heaven and earth) where the spark of creation lives *in potentia.*

Because of its godlike characteristics, the sun stirred something within Nerval's unconscious, which in turn activated his creative forces. The dynamism he experienced enabled him to recount in vivid and moving terms his experiences within the Great Pyramid, as he relived the Osiris death-and-resurrection mystery—which is Everyman's drama.

The Egyptian god Osiris (Good) had been killed and cut up into small pieces by his brother Set (Evil), a divinity who has been described as one who "irritates the eyes, dries up the lungs, [and] casts clouds of insects on the fields and orchards."[14] Isis, Osiris' wife and sister, searched all over the world for her husband's parts, gathering them all together except for the phallus, which had been eaten by the oxyrhynchus fish. She restored him to life in another realm and then gave birth to their son Horus, who ruled the upper world henceforth, while she and her husband became the lords of the underworld.[15]

Though the Egyptians had been converted to Christianity, Nerval stated, the people still "celebrated the mysteries of Osiris." The "ecstatic visions," the sight of the god who had been killed and reborn, "The

Living God!" provoked extraordinary visions for both laymen and whirling dervishes.[16] The past had *not* vanished; indeed, it had remained alive and vibrant and had given birth to innumerable religions, philosophies, and sciences: Moses, Orpheus, and Pythagoras (among others) had been initiated into the secrets of the mystery schools; mathematics, astronomy, alchemy, astrology had been taught in this land.

The death-and-resurrection of Osiris was the focal point of all worship in ancient Egypt; understanding this was the goal of all learning. The Egyptian Pharoah spent his terrestrial sojourn preparing for his death—building and providing for his eternal life. Little interest was placed in worldly possessions. Aside from the Pharoahs' palaces, Egyptian dwelling places were neither ornate nor sumptuous. People considered their homes as temporary abodes in which to house the body during its brief earthly sojourn.

It was toward the resurrection of the human being, in the manner of the great god Osiris, that life on earth was lived. Hermes Trismegistus, the founder of alchemy, said that the goal of this royal art consisted in "freeing or transforming spirit which is concealed in substance, the *prima materia* or *vilis*." Being dead and buried, therefore, is looked upon as a *primary* condition and virtually as the starting point for the work required to assure rebirth.[17] According to some psychologists, death may indicate a "maternal yearning," not only as a personal mother, but as Mother Earth who "receives the dead back into herself." Such a vision of the Mother archetype encompasses her dual role in life—the mysteries of birth and death, a return to the earth.[18]

In Egypt, death, not life was stressed. The dead man was provided with a tomb and riches he might need during the course of his "night journey." The notion that life no longer exists in a grave was considered untrue by the Egyptian. Life did exist, but in an unmanifested state; it was a world *in potentia*, which burgeons forth when properly cared for. Socrates said ("Gorgias"): "Well, life as you describe it is a strange affair. I should not be surprised, you know, if Euripides was right when he said: Who knows if life be death, and death be life? And perhaps we are actually dead, for I once heard one of our wise men say that we are now dead, and that our body is a tomb."[19] Heraclitus' dictum was interpreted by the Gnostics as implying a descent of the soul into the physical and imperfect world where it remained imprisoned for a time: "We live the death of the Immortals, they live ours."

Nerval's fascination with the pyramids was immeasurable. Enormous interest in the pyramids had been kindled. In 1789 Napoleon was reputed to have said "Soldiers, forty centuries are looking down on you."[20] In 1799 the Rosetta Stone was dug up by an unknown French soldier, and in the early 1820s it was deciphered by Jean-François Champollion. In 1817 Battista Belzoni discovered several tombs in the valley of Biban el-Muluk near Thebes, including that of Sethos (Seti) I, and in 1818 he opened the tomb of Chephren, in the Second Pyramid, and investigated the contents of the royal burial chamber.[21] The German-born Richard Lepsius, arrived in Egypt the same year Nerval had, 1843. Lepsius and his group unearthed monuments dating from the Old Kindgom, discovered traces of many unknown pyramids, and studied 130 mastabas, oblong buildings that housed both cult rooms and burial chambers.[22]

When Nerval stood in front of the Great Pyramid of Gizeh he expressed a desire to see Mozart's Masonic opera, *The Magic Flute*, performed at that very spot. In this work the humblest ascend, through pain and sacrifice, from one level of illumination to the next, all leading to purification and joy—to union with the Queen of the Night.

Before Nerval's descent into the pyramid, a sheik whom he had met in Egypt related the following legend concerning the origin and building of the great Egyptian pyramids. "Some authors believe that the pyramids had been built by the pre-Adamite king, Gian-ben-Gian; but according to more popular tradition here, Saurid, the son of Salahoc, who lived three hundred years before the flood, had a dream one night. He saw the world upside down—. . . men falling on their faces and houses on men; the stars were colliding into each other in the sky and the debris from their confrontation covered the earth." The king told the priests and wise men of his dream and the smartest of the priests informed the king of a dream that *he* had had, and predicted that there would be a deluge of water and fire. The pyramids were, accordingly, constructed in an angular shape so as to sustain the shock of the falling stars and planets, and were set with specially built blocks that would prevent penetration by either fire or water. In these pyramids the king, the illustrious people of the land, and all the great works of science and art were to be conserved for posterity. The first pyramid was reserved for the princes of the family. The second housed the idols related to the stars and planets. (The ancients believed that these bodies were living beings, attached to them in spirit and to the earth as well, and could, therefore, influence the course of man's life. They were forever giving offerings to the celestial bodies in order to win their favor: they built tabernacles to the planets and stars; they wrote books on astrology, history, physics, treatises on precious stones and science.) The third pyramid would contain the tomb of kings and priests, all of whose bodies were embalmed so they could be resurrected after a certain interval of time, depending upon the course of the stars.

The origin of the pyramids, then, was closely linked to astral bodies. The ancients believed that constellations had their earthly counterparts, which influenced both their destinies and their personalities. Many personified and deified these constellations (lion, bear, Orion) and in this manner identified with them and felt a bond between themselves and the cosmos. When the king dreamt of colliding stars and planets, it was very real for him. So-called "civilized" man had abolished these old beliefs and built his new cosmology with angels, floods, saints; he could no longer believe in the divinity of the stars, planets, in gods of trees, water. Thus he was cut off from the cosmos. And yet these primal forces still lived within him as symbols, and emerged frequently in his dream world—as demoniac, erotic, panic-type images.

According to other Arab historians (such as Ibrahim ben Ebh Wasuff Shah) the pyramids at Gizeh were built when "the Heart of the Lion" had reached "the first minute of the head of Cancer." Aby Zeyd el Balkhy postulated the theory (based on an ancient inscription) that the Great Pyramid was built when the Lyre was in the constellation of Cancer "twice twenty-six thousand solar years before the Hegira," or about seventy-three thousand years ago. The traveler Ibn-Batuta said that the Egyptian Hermes Trismegistus, "having ascertained from the appearance of the stars that the deluge would take place, built the pyramids to contain books of science and knowledge and other matters worth preserving from oblivion and ruin."[23]

Nerval looked upon the outer configuration of the pyramids, with their ascents and descents, and saw them as linking spirit and matter— as a manifestation of the sun's eternally circular pattern. On his way into the pyramid, Nerval met a Prussian "son of Voltaire,"[24] who may be looked upon as representing Nerval's own rational principle. Together they penetrated the pyramid, an arcane realm that Nerval described with utmost accuracy: the enormous crevices between the marble slabs, which made walking difficult; getting down on his belly to pull himself through sand and cinder-covered areas onto a gallery with a very deep well. . . .[25]

All the difficulties involved in the descent of the one hundred fifty steps into the pyramid were part of the ancient initiation ceremonies.[26] These took place as follows: The ancient Egyptian acolyte begins his trials with a purification rite; then he sits in a chariot that races down the center of the pyramid, a ride entailing great danger. The priests greet him and ask him to jump or rush into a well one hundred feet deep. If the neophyte hesitates, the priest considers this an indication of "prudence," since fear is part of life, acceptable within the human personality, and must be confronted so one can deal with it. The priest then gives the hierophant a lamp, which helps him to descend the well. Pieces of iron stick out from inside the wall at intervals and help him on his way down.

At the bottom of the well, he sees a gallery enclosed by an iron fence. There, three men wearing the masks of the Dog God Anubis begin taunting and threatening him. He is not frightened by these apparitions, however; he fights them and continues on his way. He then arrives at a heavily forested area; no sooner does he set foot here than the entire place is illuminated, like a "vast fire." The neophyte crosses the flaming stretch of land (he is burned only slightly) to a river, across which he must swim. Giant wheels in the center of the river create tremendous currents. As he swims about, trying to make his way to the other side, he is pushed here and there and is soon exhausted. A ladder emerges from the water but no sooner does the initiate try to climb it than the rungs come loose and fall into the water. A strong wind adds to his torments. Just as he is about to despair, two large rings appear in front of him. If he is perspicacious, he grabs hold of them and hoists himself up through an open door. Once this part of the initiation is completed, he is permitted to glimpse an immense veiled statue of Isis.

The most difficult section of the ordeal is yet to come, however, for now the initiate must fast for forty-one days, consuming only a few ounces of bread and a cup of Nile water at night. He is allowed to talk and to question the priests and priestesses who live in these subterranean cities, "to observe the mores of these mystical people who had renounced the world."[27] He spends another eighteen days in complete silence, during which time the holy ones analyze and criticize the initiate's actions during the course of his life. Twelve more days are spent behind the statue of Isis, during which he begs "the goddess to appear to him in a dream."[28] Finally, after three months of suffering, the initiate is permitted to look upon the sacred Isis in all her dazzling beauty.

"Then his astonishment was at its height, upon seeing this cold statue whose traits had come to resemble those of the woman he loved, the most, or the ideal he had conceived the most perfect beauty to be."[29] As the acolyte attempts to touch her, to concretize what is spiritual, to fix what is in a state of flux, she vanishes in "a cloud of perfume."

The initiate is then invited to the most sumptuous repast. His only regret "is having admired for but one instant this divine apparition, which had deigned to smile at him."[30] But, as Nerval added, "his dreams would return her to him."[31] The initiate falls asleep and is carried to an area of beauty and perfection, a paradise[32] with luxurious vegetation and spectacular shaped trees. According to Nerval's Prussian friend, the bas-reliefs on the pyramids were over four thousand years old and featured a woman offering a man a forbidden fruit while a snake or evil spirit looked on.

The only element lacking to the acolyte, was, Nerval added, the presence of "a woman, an innocent virgin, so young that she seemed herself to have emerged from a morning dream." The acolyte did have a vision; he dreamt he possessed a beautiful girl "with the admirable traits of Isis herself." He thought he would be permitted to keep this companion as a reward for having passed his test; but he was forbidden to touch her. Should he fail to control himself, he would be condemned to wandering about the world for the rest of his life, spreading the doctrines he had learned in the pyramids. If he did not succumb to temptation he would be considered the equal of kings and would be looked upon as sacred.

Every year the priests and neophytes donned the masks of Osiris and reenacted his "passion" in ritualistic ceremonies. The rite was called "the opening of the mouth," dirges were sung, such as the "Lamentations of Isis," infusing a living quality into him who had been divested of cosmic breath. Herodotus, Plutarch, Origen, and the church fathers, among others, had written in detail of these Egyptian mysteries. They considered them the most sacred and profound dramatic ceremonies ever to be performed over the dead. These mysteries were not only an initiation into the void but also a confrontation of the mystai with the four elements: earth, water, fire, air. If the mystai, therefore, endured these trials, he experienced an inner transformation and an illumination. He became capable of seeing that transcendental light within himself.

What was the acolyte experiencing that made such a profound impression on Nerval? The acolyte was in effect reliving the mystery of death and rebirth; symbolically, he had to die in order to be reborn. As an initiate, he was returning to the very source of life, to the prenatal darkness, the void that was to be followed by the great illumination, or a highly creative period. Only with darkness can there be light; the seed grows in darkness; darkness is the very *principia vitae* of all that exists. Isaiah wrote (45:23):

> And I will give the treasures of darkness, and
> hidden riches of secret places, that thou mayest
> know that I, the Lord, which call thee by thy name,
> am the God of Israel.

Blackness implies deep introversion, a withdrawal into self, into a solitary realm—the void—where ideas and feelings germinate, take root, and are finally excised.[33] Such, perhaps, is what Nerval experienced in this descent into the Great Pyramid—through projection.

There were other factors involved in Nerval's journey. According to the Prussian rationalist, Moses had failed in his attempt to pass the test and for this reason was angered and delivered his people out of Egypt. Triptolemes, Orpheus, and Pythagoras had also been unable to complete their ordeal and founded three religions respectively: the mysteries at Eleusis and at Samothrace, which worshipped the Greek fertility goddesses known as the Cabiri and the Orphics.

The fact that Moses had left Egypt to found a new religion indicated that the rituals practiced by the ancient Egyptians no longer answered a need within him. He took the seeds that had germinated in darkness and brought them to light, nurtured them in the desert, and developed a new and fructifying force in Judaism. Moses may be looked upon as a revolutionary. He broke with the past in order to build a new orientation for himself and his people. He created the first—probably—monotheistic religion.

Orpheus, considered the founder of the Dionysian mysteries, intro-

duced the "un-Greek doctrine of sin, atonement, stain and purification"[34] to Greece; his followers restrained the maenadic elements in the
early mystery cults. Orpheus "ennobled" man through the divine arts
of music, and entered Hades to bring back his beloved Eurydice but
failed in his mission; his lamentations at his loss were so poignant as to
have stirred the rocks in the forest.[35] The followers of Orpheus were
convinced that the divine soul must return to its source; that the body
is the prison and tomb of the soul, which longs for liberation and which
will experience it after a series of reincarnations and purifications.

Orphism was one of the earliest religions to sanctify the notions of
pain and suffering. Suffering is brought to an individual (man or god)
by a superhuman force or being and, as such, makes him worthy of
redemption. Osiris was dismembered; St. Anthony's flesh had been torn
from him by demons, his limbs dislocated, so that the profane man could
be destroyed and his spiritual half live on in the liberated soul.[36]

What is perhaps the most arresting aspect of Orphism and must certainly have aroused Nerval's interest was the fact that Orpheus also experienced a dismemberment, as had Osiris and, in another fashion,
Christ. Such a destruction of the human body may be looked upon (as
in the case of the sanctification of suffering) as the soul being torn from
its earthly prison in its attempt to ascend and win final purification.[37]
Osiris, Orpheus, and Christ had all descended to Hades; only the last
two reemerged.

Mystery cults, whether those of Osiris, Orpheus, Pythagoras, or Christ,
have several factors in common:
(1) purification ceremonies (catharsis)
(2) initiation when the acolyte becomes associated with other initiates
(3) the trials
(4) the young man becomes a seer and must impart his vision to others
    who have not experienced this deepest arcanum.
(5) The initiate severs relations with the noninitiated since each expe-
    riences life on a different level and the ordinary person can no longer
    communicate with the acolyte or understand him
(6) The initiate is dead to profane existence and has been reborn to
    eternal life.[38]

When Nerval went to Egypt and descended into the Great Pyramid
he experienced a parallel process within his own psyche. In a letter he
wrote at the time he said that he "felt rejuvenated by ten years."[39] Such
a feeling of elation is clearly understandable for one who has experienced the mystery of death and rebirth, not merely intellectually but
physically, with all the emotions concomitant with such an initiation.

Nerval was, of course, most attracted to the Isis part of the acolyte's
initiation. He saw this divinity as wife, mother, healer, guardian, sister,
mourner, and, indeed, as a *Mater Gloriosa*. What he experienced through
Isis was a visual manifestation of his soul as seen through projection

onto this transcendental cosmic entity. Isis, as representative of infinite beauty, glory, and perfection, had gathered unto herself the attributes of all celestial creatures, namely the Virgin Mary. This Isis-Virgin Mary would lead Nerval, he believed, through all disparate realms, through the world of entanglements, into the calm and serenity of her own mystic realm: "oh divinity! whose color tones are not pale like those of the moon, but scintilate at a distance and cast golden rays on the world like a sun of the night!"[40]

Isis also taught Nerval that life and death were but two sides of a totality—that physical death need not be feared. For Nerval, such a view had enormous psychological ramifications. If a dissolution of the ego (insanity) should ever again occur, he could equate it with an inner descent—a descent into the pyramid, an initiation into another transpersonal realm. Such an inward journey might yield fascinating fruits. For within death (blackness), within the unconscious (eclipse from life), creativity is still taking place; it might lead into another sphere of existence. "Happy is he who, having beheld these things, descends beneath the earth," says Cicero in *De Legibus,* for "he knows the end of life and the Zeus-given beginning."[41]

12 AN IMITATIO CHRISTI...
THE KALIPH HAKIM

A dream (should I worry about a dream?)
Entertains in my heart a chagrin which gnaws at it
I avoid it everywhere, everywhere it pursues me.
Jean Racine, Athalie.

Nerval felt younger, more vital, and generally better in Egypt. "When I set foot on this maternal land, and plunged myself once again into the venerated origins of our history and beliefs, I was going to stop the course of my years, I was again a child in the cradle, young again right in the heart of eternal youth."[1] It was as if his descent into the Great Pyramid and his reliving of the mystery of death and resurrection had infused him with a new sense of time.

But something else stirred within him. He had discovered—perhaps before his arrival in Egypt, though the notion had been reinforced here—that dreams could not only be of great importance to him and to his literary creations but that they sometimes revealed important messages. In ancient times, the Egyptians, Babylonians, Assyrians, Hebrews, Christians, and many more religious sects believed that God (or the gods) made His (their) will known through dreams; examples of such revelations are found in *The Book of the Dead, The Bible, The Koran,* and *The Vedas,* among other sources. Nerval's stay in Egypt inspired him to write the story of the Kaliph Hakim, the founder of the Druse religion, whose credo had come to him through a dream. The analogies Nerval could draw between the incredible happenings revealed to saints, wise men, and prophets in their religious revelations and his own dreams might permit a redefinition of insanity. Where does one draw the line between the ascetic who lives in the desert and "experiences" the Godhead all about him and within him, and the troubled man whose dreams convince him that he, too, is in communion with God?

The Druse religion is hermetic, its origins veiled in mystery. The Druse lived in Egypt, then settled in Syria, Lebanon, and Safed. They practice a dual form of worship. They are allowed and indeed encouraged to worship the state religion, thus avoiding any discrimination and persecution. But on the inside, they adhere to their own secret doctrine. Persecution and proselytism are not practiced, and it is one of the few religions that does not relegate Christians, Jews, and Muslims to eternal damnation simply because they do not adhere to Drusean doctrine. And contrary to custom in other ancient religious sects, Drusean women are taught to read and write.

The Druse's messiah, the Kaliph Hakim, appeared A.D. 1000, some four hundred years after Mohammed. Like Christ, he was incarnated in the body of a man. His birth, also like that of Christ, had given rise to certain astrological movements: at the hour of his entrance into the world, the planets centered around the signs of Cancer and Saturn and a comet appeared in the East, where the beast of the Apocalypse was to have come down.[2] According to the *Dictionnaire oriental,* which Nerval read assiduously, Hakim belonged to the Fatimides race, which had conquered Egypt in 970 and was said to have descended from Ali and Fatima, Mohammed's daughter. Hakim possessed certain extraordinary traits, wrote Nerval: "he had a lion's face, a voice that vibrated like thunder, and one could not bear the brilliance of his somber blue eyes."[3] According to some scholars, Hakim had red hair, which made him an even more powerful figure—like fire; his hair tones resembled those of the solar disc.

Hakim was reputed to have been extremely cruel. He compelled Christians to convert, and had them whipped and tortured and, if they still refused, had their heads cut off. An ascetic, dressed in white, Hakim, forbade all feasting and joys. He adhered to the law of simplicity decreed in the Koran. Sex was repugnant to him. His only passion was his sister Sitt-el-Mulk, whom he kept imprisoned in the palace for fear she would escape. Angered at his sister's desire to seek distraction, he had all women's rights suppressed and compelled them to conceal their faces.[4] About 1014, two Persians came to his palace and were instrumental in helping him formulate his credo.

Hakim claimed to be in direct communication with God and that he was the incarnation of the divine intelligence. In 1016, he revealed his powers to the people in the Cairo Mosque. Anger and hostility on the part of the populace greeted him. A Persian mystic, Hamza ben Ali ben Ahmed, a felt-maker by trade, was made Hakim's vizier and committed his creed to writing. He won many converts for Hakim but, as Nerval observed, "the powerful inheritor of the Fatimides obtained less power over souls than the carpenter's son in Jerusalem and the camel driver Mohammed at Medina."[5] In 1020, Hakim was assassinated on the orders, it is believed, of his sister. His followers were told that he had merely withdrawn to another world in order to meditate and that, in due course, he would reappear.

Nerval likened the Druse beliefs to those of Christianity, but a Christianity "without Jesus, because the Druse believe the apostles delivered a 'false messiah' to the people, the real one was hidden among them— Hamza—who bore the name of one of the disciples, Eleazar."[6] The Druse believed in one ineffable, incomprehensible, indefinable god who created the first creature, the "universal intelligence" that manifested itself in the person of Hamza. Only Hamza can communicate with deity. He has been incarnated several times on this earth: as one of Jesus' disciples, Eleazar; as Salamel-Faresi, when he was brought into the world in Mohammed's time; and again during the periods when Enoch, Noah, Abraham, Moses, and Pythagoras lived. His last incarnation was revealed in the person of Kaliph Hakim. Whenever he was incarnated (whether in Egypt, India, Persia, Palestine, Yemen, or Tunis) he performed some "grandiose action," always with the purpose of ridding the world of the evil engulfing it—fighting either the Islamic evil spirit Eblis; or Methouzael, the king of the giants at the time of the Flood; or Nemrod during Abraham's stay on earth; or the Pharoah when Moses led his people out of bondage from Egypt; or Antiochus and other sinister figures. The Druse believed that the coming of the Messiah in the person of the Kaliph Hakim had been predicted by the stars in the thousand-year cycle.[7]

Five ministers are in charge of directing the divinity's commandments, and were, of course, also created by him: the angels Gabriel, Michael, Israfil, Azariel and Metatron. These ministers represent: intelligence, the soul, the word, and the left and right wings. Three other ministers, but of an inferior order, were also brought forth: the soul, the overture, and the phantom. When needed, they intercede in human affairs; "the human face is led astray and falls too easily into forgetfulness of their obligations; the Supreme Being and his angels turn themselves into forgetfulness of their obligations; the Supreme Being and his angels turn themselves into men and only by human means, to reestablish order in things."[8]

Unlike Christians, the Druse believe neither in original sin nor in hell or paradise. Reward and expiation take place "with the return of the soul into other bodies."[9] Beauty, wealth, and power are given to the elect. The unfaithful return to earth in the form of slaves, as sick and suffering people. When a person dies, the "fleeing" soul is magnetically drawn into the body of a child being born and the stars regulate this "exchange of destinies." A pure life enables a Druse to ascend the hierarchy of reincarnation. If he rises to the ninth degree or sphere, the full mystery of his creed, including insights into previous incarnations, is revealed to him. All Druse may elevate themselves (through virtue and study) to the highest rank of the Ockals, or Akl (spiritual class). Those who are unable or do not feel the need to experience the arduous trials of the initiation process, remain Dhahel, or Ignorant.[10]

Though Nerval drew heavily on such works as Silvestre de Sacy's *Mémoire sur la dynastie des assassins et sur l'origine de leur nom* (1809), the *Dictionnaire oriental,* and many other volumes dealing with the founding of the Druse sect, his interpretation of Kaliph Hakim's life transposed facts.

Nerval sees Kaliph Hakim as a man profoundly wronged and misunderstood by society. Hakim's visionary experiences had been of the purest, most noble, and spiritual kind. The lot of the superior being, however, is to suffer, to be reviled at the hands of the "lesser" people. But when the rabble murdered Hakim, they merely destroyed the "profane" in man, his mortal half. The saintly individual lived on as a regenerated being. Hakim's incarnation into matter was looked upon as a type of initiation, a purification—and those who believed in him, worked for him, were likewise worthy of sanctification.

Though Nerval sees similarities between the Druse religion and the Egyptian and Christian mysteries, he also sees differences. Hakim is depicted as a mortal man and his conflict consists in the struggle between the desires of his earthbound self and his quest for spiritual fulfillment. Hakim is depicted neither as a mythological figure (as was Osiris) nor as the son of God (as was Christ). Hakim's suffering, his inability to communicate with the world, could easily be equated with the pain every man experiences when attempting to ascend the spiritual scale. Nerval could easily identify with Hakim's anguish, introverted existence, and vision of realms of eternal beauty.

When Nerval first introduces him in his narrative, Hakim is disguised as a poor man frequenting the *okel,* a den where men gather to talk, drink, and smoke hashish. Hakim has extraordinary eyes: "dark blue, like those of sapphires with an undefinable power; they both frightened and charmed at the same time" and were "a mirror of his soul." Two forces are at work in Hakim: he is kaliph but dresses as a poor man.

Yousouf, a Sabbean, enters the *okel* and by some inexplicable power, is drawn toward Hakim. That Yousouf was a Sabbean is highly significant. The Sabbeans, a sect originating in Yemen, worshipped the sun in the form of the goddess Shams and believed that the stars and planets regulated their lives. It is thus understandable for Yousouf to be destined to meet Hakim. It is likewise comprehensible to have Nerval will it so, since he believed in the meaningful nature of strange encounters, *fatum.*

Yousouf encourages Hakim to taste hashish, promising that paradise will be revealed to him if he does. The kaliph, at first averse to such a suggestion, believes that ludicity and objectivity must always be maintained: one must be master of one's thoughts and emotions and not their slaves. The conflict between the rational and the irrational course is registered in his face.

> The stranger fixed his somber azure blue eyes on him, the skin of his forehead contracted into violent wrinkles, to such an extent that his hair line followed the undulations; at one moment one would say that he wanted to throw himself onto the unsuspecting young man and tear him to pieces; but he controlled himself, his traits relaxed and, suddenly changing his mind, stretched out his hand to the cup and slowly drank the green powder.[11]

After imbibing the drug, Hakim's vision expands, the barriers erected between the conscious and the unconscious vanish, and he experiences feelings of exaltation, rapture, and frenetic excitement similar to those Nerval had known when entering Dr. Blanche's rest home.

> He appeared to be a prey to extraordinary excitement; swarms of new thoughts, unheard of, inconceivable, traversed his soul like fiery whirlwinds; his eyes sparkled as though lit up from within, by the reflection of an unknown world, a superhuman dignity revealed its demeanor, then the vision was extinguished and he let himself rest indolently on the floor.[12]

Analogies may be made between Hakim' feelings of ecstasy and those described by certain saints and theologians in their tracts (St. Theresa d'Avila, Ignacius Loyola, St. John of the Cross). Though the church fathers did not (to our knowledge) use hashish or other such drugs to cultivate their visions, they did indulge in practices equally conducive to hypnotic states and visions: special rituals, chanting, praying, counting. Monk Gregory of Sinai discovered a system "for the attainment of the light of Mount Tabor" and put his neophytes through a series of procedures that included a baptism (the bath of rebirth), penance, ascetic practises of all types, sacramental acts.[13]

What were the contents of Hakim's visions? First, he was overwhelmed by the sensation that he was "God's equal," that his perception went far beyond the crude and material aspects of the visible world, that his eyesight had been so sharpened that it made contact with his soul. Yousouf now intervened and explained in religious terms that the spirit had been freed from the strangulation of the body and enjoyed in the atmosphere of "space and light" its ability to converse with other spirits; but the mortal experiencing such "startling revelations" is dazzled as he peers through the doors that open onto eternity.

Hakim's feeling of equality to God has psychological import: under the influence of a drug (or insanity), a person may experience the collective unconscious in too forceful a manner. As a result the ego loses its mediating position, ceases to be capable of acting as a regulator of activity, and is overcome by the subliminal world. It identifies with the total personality, or the Self, rather than with the conscious personality. If the Self is the "God principle" in man, when the ego identifies with the total personality, the individual looks upon himself as God, and all rapport, all perspective, between his outer and inner situations vanishes. Is there, then, only a fine dividing line between those who claim to have been divinely inspired (Hermes Trismegistus, Moses, Mohammed, Christ, Orpheus) and ordinary mortals who are said to be suffering "delusions of grandeur"?

Yousouf now relates a dream that he once had, which keeps reoccurring as he lies relaxed in his little boat on the Nile River. "As though in the depths of infinity, I perceive a celestial face, more beautiful than all the creations of the poets, who smiles at me, with a penetrating tenderness, who descends from the heavens to come to me. Is it an angel? A Peri? I do not know. She sits down beside me in the little rowboat and its crude wood is suddenly changed to mother of pearl as it floats down the river."[14]

Yousouf then tells Hakim that he saw a woman near the island of Reddah with similar characteristics. Though she was of flesh and blood, she was endowed with "celestial brilliance," and when she lifted her veil he was allowed to see the glittering stones of her garments. He took her bejeweled hands into his and caressed them, but then noted that his own hands were scratched by the sharp edges of the precious stones. He was sure that he was experiencing reality, not a figment of the imagination: how else could his hands have become scratched? He threw himself at her feet and expressed, in the most "burning and sublime manner," the full extent of his love for her. Each word had "immense significance," each word enclosed "universes of thoughts, mysterious phrases, the echos of vanished worlds vibrating within him."[15] Yousouf was certain he had seen the woman before, in some anterior existence, and had therefore succeeded in fusing past and present into an eternal time— and all this through love.

Nerval identified with Yousouf's vision, which revealed his craving for the infinite, his yearning for warmth and understanding, his need for elevation. Yousouf, when experiencing this type of dilation of the mind, was flooded with feelings (as represented by his deep projection onto the beautiful female figure). His entire being felt the warmth of acceptance. The fact that he was scratched by her jewels may have been a forewarning of the dangers involved in approaching such a powerful figure. Yousouf's dream sequence encouraged Nerval's belief in the transmigration of souls, his preoccupation with the time-death motif— time as a cyclical and not as a linear event. Love is also envisaged as a fatal or destined happening and for this reason is experienced in this narrative by Yousouf, the Sabbean, the believers in celestial bodies and their regulating powers.

In analyzing Yousouf's vision one is struck by the constant reference to "light," "glitter," "rays," "brilliance." A rapprochement may again be made between the visions of the mystics and Yousouf's world. Words such as "celestial light," "flamboyant," "fire," were noted by St. Hildegarde in her writings: "Shade of the Living Light, Brightness, My Soul has always beheld this light, The Brightness which I see is not limited space and is more brilliant than the radiance round the sun." Theresa d'Avila described herself as being so filled with joy that her "face was shining and rosy, and her eyes shone like candles." The Pseudo-Areopagite's spiritual writings are actually a series of hymns to light.[16] Divinity appears to the Parsees, Manichaeans, Mandaeans, and many Gnostic sects through haloes or in luminous rays of light or fiery images focusing upon Him.[17] In Genesis I we read (1–3):

> And the earth was without form, and void; and darkness was
> upon the face of the deep. And the Spirit of God moved upon
> the face of the water.
> And God said, Let there be light: and there was light.
> And God saw the light, that it was good.

Mystical visions frequently follow certain steps, as do initiations. The first indication of inner knowledge resides in blackness (as it did for the alchemist), such as that experienced by the neophyte during his initiation in the Egyptian pyramid rites. Such blackness would be tantamount to the state of regression. The artist also experiences this phase before the "spark" of creation has ignited. Once creation begins, it grows and is measured by the light of *gnosis* (knowledge). Such knowledge permits the visionary to describe his dream, the artist to concretize his insights. Blackness was experienced by Hakim before his vision; Yousouf may be looked upon as another aspect of Hakim, his "double," as we will later learn.

Hakim describes his ideal female figure to Yousouf. Shame concerning his "monstrous" love had overwhelmed him and he had remained silent about his passion. Now, however, the hashish has given him the courage to express his innermost feelings: his love for his sister Setalmulc. He justifies his passion by saying that it is evil only to those who measure such a relationship "in terrestrial terms." His love for his sister is not sensual, he declares, but totally spiritual. Therefore, his love takes on the stature of cosmic grandeur, it is "indefinable," an "affection as profound as the sea, vast like the sky, as God could experience it."[18] She is "the wife of my divine soul, the virgin destined for me during the first days of creation." Union with his sister, he concludes, would permit him to create a "definitive god, more powerful than all those which have already become manifest under a variety of names."[19] Hakim then tells of his life on earth when man had first been created, of the Garden of Eden, of his past incarnations.

Hakim's incestuous love, when explained in terms of "spirit" and of "divinity," is comparable to relationships implicit in other cosmogonies. Isis and Osiris were both husband and wife and sister and brother. Incest was not limited to divine spheres in Egypt, where Pharoahs married their sisters to ensure that the throne stayed in the family. In Greek mythology, gods and goddesses were forever procreating via mother, sisters, brothers. If incest is looked upon symbolically, as a union of similar matter or as a unification of oneself with the "essence of one's own self," a coalescing of inner polarities (male and female) takes place. All conflict (as between male and female, outer and inner, conscious and unconscious) is eliminated; all tensions, energy, and dynamic qualities vanish. When matter, unaffected by outside force, remains at rest, stasis sets in. Such a situation can lead only to degeneration and disintegration.[20]

After Hakim had expressed his passion to someone else (after it had become a psychological reality), he felt stronger about his position in the world and his ideations. When a bearded man calls the Sabbeans to sacrifice a white rooster and black calf in honor of Hermes and Agathodaemon, Kaliph bursts out in anger. The colors of his eyes change from blue to black, his face contorts, and his voice rages like a lion's roar. All those present shudder as he labels them "unfaithful," "idol worshippers." When they ask him about his god—Christ? Mohammed?—Hakim answers, with dignity: "I adore no one since I myself am God! the only one, the true, the unique God, the others are only shadows."[21] The crowd, enraged by such arrogance, pounces on him. Yousouf slips into the melee and guides him to safety on his little boat on the Nile. The Kaliph gives him a ring and tells him that if he should ever want something from him, his wish will be granted.

This incident could be looked upon as the fate meted out to all revolutionaries, innovators, and original thinkers whether in religion, poetry, politics, arts, sciences, or medicine. One who seeks to bring in the new is subject to immolation by the masses. In the story of the grand inquisitor, in *The Brothers Karamazov,* it is said that should Christ reappear again among men he would meet the same fate as he had before. To reject the status quo, to cast off old ways for new, mysterious, and dangerous ones requires courage, strength, perseverance, and a spirit of sacrifice. The fact that the Kaliph had the courage to confess his identity (God) only when under the influence of hashish indicated a fundamental weakness within his psyche. Rather than possessing the lionlike personality that Nerval had believed him to have, he was inwardly meek, self-effacing, and undeveloped. The disguises he wore (those of a poor man) when meeting Yousouf in the *okel* and on other occasions, suited his inner personality far better than the regal robes he donned as the Kaliph.

Hakim was in the habit of going on his donkey to his observatory at Mokatam, in the country. There he would try to understand the course of the holy planets, as had his ancestors who were well versed in the kabbalistic sciences. He wanted to learn about his personal destiny and to dwell on the spiritual aspects of life (the observatory was a type of religious edifice, high and pointed upward)—to relate to the infinite. But to dwell on cosmic matters as intensely as Hakim did is to steer one's thoughts away from earthly matters, daily preoccupations, to see things in a collective manner, symbolically, and not specifically, individually.

When Hakim left the observatory, immersed as he was with a sense of the infinite, he would don slave's garments and walk among his people, listening to their talk and profiting from his experience.[22]

The fact that Hakim wore a slave's garment might be an indication of his slave's mentality. He was a man unable to master any part of his being; he was always succumbing to influences around him: either human or in the form of hashish or the power of his inner visions.

Nerval included a blind stranger motif in his story of Kaliph Hakim. A famine had broken out in Egypt, and a blind stranger who claimed to be an alchemist approached Hakim. When he told Hakim to save his people, the Kaliph ridiculed him. He is blind, he taunted, how can he say such things to a man he has never seen. "All men are blind vis-à-vis God," answered the stranger. It is with his "inner eye" that everything becomes visible—that he knows that Hakim is capable of performing miracles. The Kaliph is now convinced that he not only has the right to order people but must direct and punish humanity: it is his divine obligation to do so. He goes toward the city, gets hold of the baker who sold bread for gold, and orders him beheaded. At this instant, Yousouf rushes into the crowd and Kaliph must grant him his wish: that the baker's life be spared.

The blind stranger motif appears in many legends and fairy tales—Tiresias, Cassandra, Oedipus. The function of the blind seer is to warn man of his vagaries, of destructive situations. They are catalysts who force the people involved to act openly, thereby enabling them to reassess or reevaluate their lives. The blind stranger who came up to Hakim was an alchemist who transformed base into pure metals—or man's earthly life into a divine condition.

Hakim failed to understand the import of the blind man's message. He lacked the depth necessary to comprehend divinity as totality—as representing both good and evil. In fact, Hakim is unable to distinguish either force. He has become a power-driven man who tries to rectify an economic state by slaughter. His rage for power was so great that all lucidity, all judgmental and discriminatory faculties vanished. It was Yousouf, Hakim's double (his feeling principle) who saved the situation.

On another occasion, again under the effects of hashish, Hakim enters his palace. His slaves are terrified by his "physiognomy illuminated with rays" by "his demeanor both uncertain and stiff, his gestures which are strange." He walks through the dark corridors, inner vaults, filled with carvings that resemble a "grotto of stalactites" and the reds, greens, azure colors and gold encrusted all about, are like a series "of exploding tints," like "glass mosaics," an epiphany. He arrives at his sister's room and sees her as if she were a "beatific vision," like the "queen of vanished empires, whose Gods were their ancestors." And "her eyes made others lower theirs, as though they were contemplating the sun, a golden pallor, heightened at the cheek by two clouds of make up, her mouth a dazzling purple burst out like pearl-filled pomegranates." When Hakim beheld her it was as if his earthly body had vanished and his godlike nature flooded his entire being. "His coloring reflected the light of another world. It was indeed the Kaliph's features, but illuminated by another spirit and another soul. His gestures were those of a phantom and he looked like his own specter."[23]

The Kaliph had to all intents and purposes left the earth for spiritual climes—had transcended his personal existence and taken on a collective life. Reality could no longer be experienced on an individual basis with responsibilities, remorse, or other earth-bound attitudes, but rather as a state without moral ties. When Hakim tells his sister that they are to be married ("such is my sacred will") he believes that such an incestuous relationship is his divine destiny, a marriage of opposites that will form a godlike totality. Divinity's views may not be considered in the light of earthly man's needs and desires. Like all gods, Hakim considers himself to be justice; he *is* the law and all is permitted him in a transcendental world not bound by the moralistic and limiting notions that rational man has imposed upon himself in his differentiated world in order to maintain some semblance of order.

Setalmulc did not live in a godlike realm. She was repulsed by her brother's desires and later, in secret, called Argevan, the grand vizier, to her side. He had been made regent of the empire when Hakim was proclaimed Kaliph at the age of eleven, and had always retained his power. Hakim reigned outwardly; Argevan was the power behind the throne. When informed of Hakim's plan, his bony cheeks grew taut, his countenance darkened and became even more austere; the sinister "Tau" sign appeared on his head—"the sign of fatal destinies."

The grand vizier, with his "austere," meditative countenance, represents the father figure in the narrative and stands for moral righteousness, justice, the status quo, consciousness, prohibition, and moral commandments—as opposed to the irrational and instinctual side of man in the person of the hashish-smoking Hakim, who has no regard for law, custom, and the consequences of his own acts.

In his observatory, Hakim consulted the stars once again and noted with shock and anguish that the planet Saturn had become livid and pale and that Mars was aflame. He knew he was in danger. But rather than face the possible bloodshed that might occur should he confront his enemies (as a great ruler or hero would have done), he sought release from his responsibilities. Resorting to disguise once again, he dressed as a fellah, and met Yousouf, to indulge in hashish. Dazed by the drug, Hakim suddenly screamed out: "Eblis! Eblis!" (the Arab Satan), whereupon Argevan appeared. He ordered his men to take Hakim to Moriste, a combination prison and insane asylum. There, in his cell, Hakim realized that it would be wiser not to divulge that he was God, that "divinity" had been imprisoned in his body and that he was the "incarnation of the Supreme Being." To adhere to a path of silence wouid be difficult in view of the "incontinency of the imagination," but a necessity if he were ever to be released.[24]

Nerval's identification with the Kaliph is obvious: misunderstood, doomed to suffer, student of astrology, an evil destiny, the silence he had decided to maintain in the asylum. Such was the course that Nerval had chosen when in Dr. Blanche's rest home. To tell others about one's fantasies and visions—the Isis figure that Nerval had seen—would have led both doctors and friends to declare him insane. Instead, he re-pressed his thoughts and remained on the well-beaten path. Hakim, though he began a similar course, lacked Nerval's resolve. One day, the doctor who was caring for him brought a great Syrian man of science to visit him, Avicenna (980–1037). Hakim was so impressed with this man's knowledge and the depth of his wisdom that he yielded to his impulse and spoke out: "Oh, you who see me now, as Aisse (Jesus) had once been, abandoned under this form and in his human powerlessness to hell's plans, doubly unrecognized, as both Kaliph and God, under-stand fully that I must leave this unworthy place as soon as possible. If you are for me, make yourself known; if you do not believe in my words, be cursed."[25] Avicenna looked at the doctor in charge and affirmed that Hakim's reason had abandoned him.

During the days of incarceration, Hakim listens to the inmates as they relate their stories—the powerful positions they had held in anterior existences, their lives on earth during the reign of the pre-Adamite kings. But as the days flow by, the inmates gather about Hakim, as if sensing he was their leader. But there were times during this painful period when Hakim himself began doubting his own divinity "as had the Son of God on the Mount of Olives."

That Hakim should have compared himself to Christ (or that Nerval should have, since he identifies with the story's protagonist) is under-standable. The Christ figure symbolizes suffering and the nobility of such a state. Nerval further suggests a similarity between the insane and the criminals and Christ's followers, who likewise did not come from an élite class, but were "*gens de mauvaises vie*, tax collectors and publicans," the rabble.[26] Were those rejected by society visionaries, then?

Hakim, who had won the confidence and admiration of these crimi-nals and insane persons, so aroused them that they broke down the doors. The guards, who were "struck by fear," thought the hand of des-tiny was at work. "It is Allah, coming to judge the world!" they cried out. As Hakim walked to the mosque with his followers, "a superhuman radiance encircled his face." Muslims, Christians, and Jews bowed before him, declaring him to be the real Messiah—or the real anti-Christ that the scriptures had predicted would appear a thousand years after Christ. Hakim spoke to his followers, told them he was their Messiah and that he appeared to man each time "the power of heaven loses its control over souls, whem virtue becomes a crime, wisdom becomes folly, glory becomes shame."²⁷ He encouraged his followers to set fire to the city— as had happened before in Gomorrah, Enochia; mankind must be punished for its sins, purified to earn redemption.

Argevan tried to stop the fire and the war that broke out between Hakim's followers and his own. In the carnage that ensued, Hakim, described by Nerval as being "endowed with second sight," saw Eblis leave his mortal trappings and call upon his demons to help him kill Argevan and his followers. After Argevan was killed, the Old Man reappeared and told Hakim: "Lord, this is enough! stop the destruction in the name of your forefather Moezzerdlin." Hakim put an end to the carnage and thereafter spread the doctrine of toleration and law.

Hakim told his sister that their wedding would take place in secret because the masses were not yet ready to accept something so alien to their ways. Though the stars warned Hakim of the nefarious events awaiting him, he comported himself like a god, "conscious only of his eternity," and remained undaunted at the thought of his mortal and perishable coverings. One night, while returning to the palace after having consulted the stars, he saw all types of lights and festivities going on. He entered in secret and saw his sister sitting next to a man (the replica of himself) bedecked with precious stones. To see one's double, according to Arab tradition, is to see one's own death. Hakim withdrew into the shadows. Soon a young Arab and a gigantic Ethiopian carrying a large knife left the palace. The Arab kneeled down and the Ethiopian took out his knife and it looked as if he had chopped the young man's head off. Much to Hakim's surprise, however, the head had not fallen off. The Ethiopian whispered something in his ear. The Arab made his way toward the Nile. Hakim recognized him as Yousouf, saying "We look like brothers."²⁸ Yousouf told him that Setalmulc had asked him if he loved her enough to die for her and when he answered affirmatively, he did not realize he would be asked to kill Hakim. Hakim did not punish his sister for her treachery. But one night, as he went to consult the stars, three men pounced on him. One was his "brother," who helped Hakim fight the other two. Both Hakim and Yousouf were killed. His followers were told that he had withdrawn into the desert to meditate and formulate his doctrine.²⁹

Yousouf may be looked upon as Hakim's double or his shadow. It is he, with the help of hashish, who becomes the catalyzing agent, the force that compels Hakim to reveal his visions, his divinity, and to force these into consciousness. Without Yousouf, Hakim's inner world would have remained hermetically sealed. Whenever Hakim attempted to deal consciously with his inner revelations, he was forced to confront an entire society structured on relatively stable customs and he did not have the courage to fight for his doctrine. Because he lacked the strength to face the situation lucidly, he failed to deal well with problems generally.

Hakim recognized Yousouf as his double only when he saw him sitting next to his beloved sister, winning her affections, something that he had been incapable of realizing. Yousouf represents the feeling principle, which is capable of insinuating its way into people's hearts, the one who had first suggested to Hakim that he take hashish permitting him to "open" up, to express his inner thoughts, to communicate with others. Because he had been so accustomed to repressing and suppressing his emotions, he did not know how to cope with them when they emerged. When approaching others, his manner was awkward and impatient, and finally became ruthless and cruel.

Hakim could function well in the mental institution because it was a cloistered, regressive atmosphere in which he could let his fantasies roam unchecked and no one would condemn him for them. So long as Hakim's ideations remained imprisoned (in his unconscious) and un-articulated, life could be lived within limitations. Once Hakim external-ized his thoughts (spoke them out in a real situation), he collided with social law and values. Unable to relate to these, he was finally destroyed by them.

The real *agent destructeur* in this tale was the love Hakim bore his sister. Had he not been subjugated by this anima figure, had she not ruled him totally, he might have been able to come to grips with himself and the world at large. He might have understood his sister's mortal and limited notions (incest taboo), her anger at being imprisoned and restricted. Because of his passivity, encouraged by the hashish he took, his fate could be likened to those of other male lovers: Attis, Narcissus, and Hippolytus.

Hakim in many ways is an offshoot of Nerval himself. The theme of the unfortunate destiny, of the double world (sane and insane), of the utter submission to the female principle, the obstacles confronting him in the world of reality were also Nerval's.

13   THE QUEEN OF SHEBA
AND ADONIRAM

Love is a growing, or full constant light;
And his first minute, after noon, is night.
John Donne, *A Lecture upon the Shadow.*

The Queen of Sheba, as woman and legend, had fascinated Gérard de Nerval ever since 1835, when he undertook to write a libretto for Meyerbeer. Although the project remained unrealized, the haunting vision of this regal figure grew in intensity with the passage of years. Now that he was in the Middle East, Nerval investigated aspects of the myth upon which the Masons, the Rosicrucians, and the alchemists have built entire philosophical and cosmogonic systems.

Nerval's version of the Queen of Sheba story, later published in *Voyage in the Orient,* differs from the Biblical tale as related in II Chronicles and I Kings 10.[1] According to the Bible, Solomon was widely known for his statesmanship, "judicial shrewdness," and ability to govern. He had divided his country "into twelve districts, apart from Jerusalem, which was apparently governed directly by a viceroy."[2] His scientific learning, his poetic inspiration, and his wealth were equally remarkable. He traded on sea and on land, with African kingdoms, and with King Hiram of Tyre, from whom he received gold, wood, ivory, and peacocks in exchange for horses, slaves, and copper from his famous mines at Edom. Solomon built a palace that took thirteen years to construct and a temple on Mount Moriah in seven years, "where the Lord appeared unto David" (II Chron. 3:1). The furnishings, the metalwork for these buildings were fashioned by Tyrian craftsmen and were, the Bible tells us, a marvel to behold. The architect of both the temple and the palace was Hiram (I Kings 7:13) or Huram-abi (II Chron. 2:13), the latter the son of a Syrian who came from Tyre and a woman from the Naphtali tribe.[3] Hiram was "skillful to work in gold, and in silver, in brass, in iron, in stone, and in timber, in purple, in blue, and in fine linen, and in crimson: also to grave any manner of graving, and to find out every device which shall be put to him, with thy cunning men, and with the cunning men of my lord David thy father" (II Chron. 2:14). Hiram constructed a "molten sea" which, according to the Bible, was an enormous poollike structure filled with water and resting on twelve brass oxen "an handbreadth thick." Its brim "was wrought like the brim of a cup, with flowers of lilies: it contained two thousand baths" (I Kings 7:26).

The Queen of Sheba, hearing of Solomon's wisdom and wealth, went to Jerusalem to see if his reputation rested on fact. "And when she came to Jerusalem with a very great train, with camels that bare spices, and very much gold, and precious stones: and when she was come to Solomon, she communed with him of all that was in her heart" (I Kings 10:2). After having asked Solomon certain questions to test his wisdom, she was even more impressed by his spiritual depth. "Happy *are* thy men, happy *are* these thy servants, which stand continually before thee, *and* that hear thy wisdom" (I Kings 10:8). "Blessed be the Lord thy God, which delighted in thee, to set thee on the throne of Israel; because the Lord loved Israel forever, therefore made he thee king, to do judgment and justice" (I Kings 10:9). Sheba gave Solomon gold and precious stones. He gave her "all her desire, whatsoever she asked, besides *that* which Solomon gave her of his royal bounty" (I Kings 10:13). Sheba then returned to her land and bore a son called Melinek. Solomon reigned in Jerusalem, over all Israel, for forty years and then he "slept with his fathers, and was buried in the city of David, his father . . ." (I Kings II: 42–43).[4]

For Nerval the two most important figures are the Queen of Sheba, whom he also refers to as Balkis,[5] and Adoniram, a character that he (Nerval) created, who is the master builder of the palace and the temple (perhaps based on Hiram). Solomon, who is alluded to as Soliman in Nerval's tale, is no longer the wise monarch of antiquity, no longer a type of anthropos figure, or semidivine personage, who understood the language of the birds, but rather a materialistic, deceitful, greedy, and lustful monarch.

Soliman is denigrated by Nerval. His face is marked with "perpetual serenity" and though he is old, there are no wrinkles; he wears only an expression of "the immutable peace of ineffable quietude." Everything he dons is of gold: his clothes, shoes, and crown, as well as his throne. He looks like "a golden statue, with his hands and mask of ivory."[6]

To lower further the image of Soliman, Sheba comments on the sumptuousness of his palace, the riches it contains, and expresses in subtle terms her disdain for his excessive use of gold, the heaviness of the ornamental detail. Most shocking of all, to her, is the fact that it took him seven years to build the temple and thirteen for the palace. She has praise only for the architectural genius who built these monuments, whom she does not know.

Sheba criticizes not only Soliman's excessive materialism but also his attitude toward women, as expressed in Ecclesiastes: "And I find more bitter than death the woman, whose heart *is* snares and nets, *and* her hands *as* bands: whoso pleaseth God shall escape from her; but the sinner shall be taken by her" (7:26). As for Soliman's poetry in the Song of Songs, it is contrived, cerebral, obscure, and filled with sophisms and contradictions. Poetry, she maintains, must come from the heart.

According to the Bible, the Queen of Sheba asks Solomon certain questions in order to test his wisdom. In Nerval's version, her three questions are answered only after the high priest, Sadoc, tells his monarch the answers he had bribed one of Sheba's followers to reveal.

Despite her distaste for Soliman, Sheba decides to entertain him by showing off her magical powers. With her ring she calls her birds and has them cluster over her and Soliman's heads like a canopy, sheltering them from the sun. As the thousands of birds fly above them (scarlet, black, all hues of blue), Soliman is awed of Sheba's power and kneels before her. She is worthy, he tells her, of commanding both kings and the elements. She gives him her precious ring as a gift.

Nerval's rendition of the bird incident is in sharp contrast to the Biblical account. Solomon understands not only the language of the birds (and of other animals), but also rules over a whole group of demons with whose help, it is said, he built the temple (I Kings 4:29–34). Because God was satisfied with the temple that Solomon had built in his honor, the Midrash Bereshit rabbi says, "The power over the animal world, lost by Adam through his sin, was regained by Solomon." In the Talmud it is stated that "Solomon before his fall was lord over all the terrestrials and celestials." According to certain Arab legends, Solomon's birth was so grandiose an event as to recall that of a Messiah: "The child Solomon is born with a radiance of light in his face, Eblis [i.e., Satan] and his hosts melt as lead of iron melts in fire, the angels come down on earth to assist at birth, the earth is laughing in joy, the wild animals bow toward him and the tame ones come near."[7]

In Nerval's legend not only is Sheba invested with magical powers, but she also has an augural bird, the Hud-Hud, or Hoopoe, bird. This bird has been described in legends as having a long slender bill and "an erectile tuft of feathers on his head."[8] Arabic and Persian lore claim that the Hoopoe bird can perform stunts of magic and foretell the future.[9] In the Koran (Sourate 27) we read:

Solomon succeeded David. He said: "Know, my people, that we have been taught the tongue of birds and endowed with all good things. Surely this is a signal favor.

Solomon marshalled his forces of djinn and men and birds, and sent them in battle array. . . .

He inspected his birds and said: "Where is the lapwing? I cannot see him here. If he does not give me a good excuse, I shall sternly punish him or even slay him.

Sheba's Hoopoe bird has a black beak, red cheeks, gray eyes, and plumes of gold. It is faithful to its mistress and good to all whom it loves. Whenever the queen is faced with grave problems, she consults her bird. It was said that if the bird should ever alight on a man's hand, Sheba would know that he would be her love.

Sheba—"the Queen of Noon," "the Queen of the South," "the Queen of the Morning," or "the Divine Balkis"—is creative and mysterious. She arrives in Soliman's kingdom from Yemen (known in ancient times as Sheba) with sixty elephants, camels, Abyssinians, Ethiopians, and with caravans filled with incense, perfumes, gold, precious stones, ivory, ebony, and costly garments. (Jer. 6:20, Ezek. 27:15,20,22) A Sabbean star worshipper, she regulates her life according to the movements of the sun and the planet Venus and refuses to continue her journey at night when her deity is absent. With the first rays of the sun Sheba enters Jerusalem, the city of gold, and greets the divine body—the sun.

Although Sheba is always mistress of herself, she is also complex: active, calm, volatile, reserved, naïve, clever, cerebral, emotional, cruel, and tender. Her eyes are mysterious and revealing, her face "ardent and clear like newly molten brass." She represents all that is pure, exciting, and novel, and reminds Soliman of the ideal and "the mystical face of the goddess Isis." Dressed in white, in a diaphanous gauze gown, she appears like a cloud "a lily lost in a cluster of jonquils."[10] Her beauty was dazzling, Nerval wrote, like that of a goddess. She represents a new order, as contrasted with Soliman's traditional beliefs and reactionary doctrines.

Adoniram, the artist-creator (Adonai-Lord, Adon-man, or a combination of both), is of unknown origin and in this respect is unlike the Biblical Hiram. He possesses a "strange and fascinating beauty" and has godlike qualities. He is withdrawn, introverted, rebellious and perpetually dissatisfied with his artistic endeavors; he is searching for some superior force that will enable him to create the greatest masterpieces of all time. The artist-creator, whose mind "boiled like a furnace," lives in a world of his own and dreams of gigantic artistic structures—of the impossible.[11]

Adoniram is the prototype of the romantic artistic creator: suffering, somber, mysterious, misanthropic, secretive, and audacious. He is of course misunderstood by the populace, upon whom he looks with "disdain," considering their concepts limited, their vision superficial. He "participated in the spirit of light and the genius of darkness." He belongs to the world of the spirit, where imagination is fomented by the perpetually turbulent waters of the unconscious. He is indifferent to women, while they in turn tried to avoid the fire in his eyes. His one thought, his one passion, is creation. His sole companion, Benoni, is a child artist who came from a Phoenician family.[12]

Adoniram's thoughts forever revolve around the past—pre-Biblical and even pre-Adamite times—when the world was ruled by a series of great kings.[13] After the pre-Adamite monarchs, however, the world started to degenerate: diversity, contradiction, lack of discipline led to laziness and a withering of the imaginative faculties. When Adoniram, who worked night and day preparing his creative pieces, saw his workers feasting at Soliman's reception honoring the Queen of Sheba's arrival, he turned aside in disgust. People, he thought, should not indulge themselves in this manner; they should not feel satisfied with past accomplishments—in this instance, the construction of the palace and the temple, symbols of Soliman's vanity. These monuments are ephemeral; a spark could reduce them to cinders, conquering armies could raze them. Only Cain's descendants, Adoniram believed, were worthy of admiration.

According to certain Kabbalistic, Masonic, and Rosicrucian traditions, Cain, together with his sisters, withdrew to the south after he had killed his brother Abel. There he founded a city, Enochia, which he named after Enoch, his first-born. Alchemists have likened Enoch to the Hermes of the Egyptians and the Mercury of the Greeks. Cain's daughters, according to the Kabbala, were loved by the angels Aza and Azael. Because of this infraction of the rules, the angels were cast down from heaven, "imprisoned" in matter, and their divine natures covered by earthly bodies.[14] Their union with mortals engendered a race of giants, the "mighty men of old," the "men of renown" mentioned in Genesis: "There were giants in the earth in those days; and also after that, when the sons of God came in unto the daughters of men, and they bare *children* to them, the same *became* mighty men which *were* of old, men of renown" (6:4). As for Cain. he toiled, he searched, he dug into the earth, and finally he came upon fabulous metal mines. After discovering the secret of welding metals, he bequeathed his knowledge to his descendants Tubal-Cain.

Cain's descendants, Adoniram felt, had created such extraordinary works in metal that the forms they molded were unnameable—so remarkable that they frightened God, who caused the earth to tremble when he looked at them. The extraordinary city of Babylon, Adoniram maintained, with its wondrous Hanging Gardens, had been built from cast-off materials used by the artisans of Enochia. The pyramids themselves, he declared, had been built by Cain's descendants, and for this reason would last for all eternity. Adoniram himself dreamed of building a sphinx so incredible it would make Yahweh turn pale.

Adoniram's contemporaries were mediocre artists. A true artist does not copy nature, Adoniram claimed; he searches for "unknown forms, unnamed beings, incarnations in front of which man steps back . . . faces capable of instilling respect, gaiety, stupefaction, and terror."[15] The Egyptians and Assyrians, both closer in time to Cain's descendants, were audacious artists who wrenched their creation out of the rock. Their minds leapt forward; their imaginations were undaunted. The Hebrews on the other hand, are controlled by matter; they are "servile" imitators of nature and, therefore, art has been lost to them.

When Sheba meets Adoniram, it is as if two worlds have blended into one, as if friction and opposition have ceased to exist. As he speaks to Sheba, Adoniram's voice takes on strange tonalities. Since she knows nothing about him other than the fact that he had built the palace and the temple, she cannot understand the intensity of his reaction to her or hers to him.

Adoniram tells Sheba that he has learned the art of sculpture by hammering, cutting, and incising rocks right out of mountains—by forcing his scissors into the earth's crust. One day, as he was walking about, the earth seemed to open up before him. Rock upon rock just fell away. He investigated the gaping maw and discovered a cave, a buried city with vaults and arcades, a forest of stone that had, seemingly, remained in the same state for thousands of years. Colossal figures, a series of "giants" seemed to emerge from the darkness, like those that had disappeared from the earth centuries before. Animals could also be delineated in the inner city and looked like nothing he had ever seen—terrifying specters carved out of man's wildest imagination. Adoniram remained in this dead city, observing these phantoms of bygone kingdoms and learned from them the *tradition* of his art.

When he is alone with Sheba, Adoniram advises her openly that to marry Soliman would be like blending the blood of a racially pure person with that of a slave. Does a lion lie with a domesticated dog? he asks. Soliman's race is impure—he has intermarried with all peoples; his Hebrews, once courageous, creative, and warlike, have been reduced to a shadow of their former selves, and they are effete, lazy, and unimaginative. Once peace had settled on the land, it brought luxury and sensuality—a preference for gold over iron. Sheba—whom he refers to at times as Balkis—is the daughter of a patriarch and should not sully herself by such a marriage.

Adoniram stands with Sheba and Soliman before the thousands of people of Jerusalem. Sheba, testing his power, asks him to call his workers together. Undaunted by what seems an amazing request, he makes the *Tau* sign (a Masonic symbol) and within seconds a "human sea" swarms toward him—men from distant valleys and planes, divided like armies into columns of one hundred thousand artists, thirty thousand iron workers, eighty thousand stone-cutters and masons, seventy thousand transporters of materials, thirty-three hundred intendants. The queen is perplexed. How can Adoniram call so many workers to him with such speed? Does he have some extraordinary power at his disposal? She humbles herself before his "sublime" and "occult" ways and gives him a necklace of precious stones.

Soliman, displeased by this behavior, is jealous of the artist's youth, his beauty, his vitality, but mostly of his creative powers. He strikes back at Adoniram by condemning everything he had previously praised: he calls Enochia, built by Cain, a "criminal city" (compare Gen. 4:17), and the art of moulting metals, discovered by Tubal-Cain and carried on in the shadows of darkness of the earth, an imperious art. Then he praises his own ideas and accomplishments: the simple, pure, and orderly lines of his temple, the unit of its plan—the very antithesis to Adoniram's night realm with its horrendous monsters and idols.

In a play of wills and in an attempt to right a wrong, Sheba dwells on the topic of idolatry. One can idolize routine: for example, Soliman's traditional ways that had once brought order out of chaos but that now have become destructive and offensive forces. As for Soliman's artistic endeavors, whether in poetry or the sculptures he ordered his artists to make during his reign, they were staid hieratic figures borrowed from the Egyptians, but without the spark, the lifeblood, the creative élan that the originators of this art had possessed.

The dichotomy between Soliman's old, routine ways and the Sheba-Adoniram creative force becomes accentuated in a series of events, as, for example, when Soliman feasts the Queen of Sheba at Mello. From his villa, situated on the top of a hill—an "aerial" domain—one is able to observe green and fertile valleys interspersed with palm and pine trees as well as a series of white tombs, all symbolizing most dramatically the differences between the two ways of life. Mello, at the top of the hill, stands for the spirit; the valley of Josephat represents fertility, life, and death—the cycle of existence. During the course of this meeting Sheba reveals the story of her ancestors. She came from Yemen, a once arid and sterile country that her people had transformed into one of the world's richest kingdoms. For two centuries they dug rivers, elevated mountains of granite higher even than the pyramids, excavated "cyclopean vaults under which entire armies could march, built aqueducts, canals, industries, and prairies, and planted forests."[16]

Soliman stops her with a counterargument. One should not attempt to reverse the order of nature by creating artificial civilizations, by bringing industry and commerce to a land unable to support such additions. Judaea, he declares, was arid and should not be encouraged to include more inhabitants within its boundaries than it can feed. If all of Yemen's artificial lakes were to dry up, Soliman asserts, Sheba's people would be burned by the sun. "One must not tempt God nor correct his works. What he does is good."[17]

Sheba, who stands for the new, the active, the aggressive, and the creative principle, believes that Soliman's doctrines would force society to remain in swaddling clothes; would hold mankind down and would prevent independence of thought. Man is a builder of palaces and towns; he can work in copper, gold, and metals of all types. God gave his creatures the "genius of activity" and this should be developed and used to benefit both body and spirit.

The "molten sea" episode is perhaps the most extraordinary in Nerval's narrative. Adoniram had dreamt of building a molten sea—an immense brass vase—a feat, if it could be realized, that would verge on the miraculous.[18] The time is now ripe to test his work before the queen, Soliman, and the populace. Adoniram dons the white apron of the architect and commands his workers to carry out his carefully laid plans. As the work begins, Sheba declares that he looks like a divinity of fire commanding a cataclysmic event to begin its life. The boiling metals start "breathing," the open furnaces groan, the massive brick towers are like flames reaching out into the atmosphere; the world about them takes on a variety of colors—reds, purples, blues, oranges, white—the flowing brass flashes through the darkness of the night as a creation that defies spatial limitations comes into being.

Suddenly, Adoniram's helper, Benoni, discovers three workmen standing where no man should have been. He realizes they have betrayed his master. Benoni runs to Soliman and informs him of the treachery, but it is too late to stop the flow of molten metal. As the mass of burning metal pours forth with volcanic speed, torrents of brilliant colors sweep over the area—blood red to gold. The populace is immobile, stunned. Silence clothes the city. Adoniram sees a shadowlike figure cross the bed of molten metal and, convinced it is a saboteur, plunges the iron hook he was holding deep into the intruder's chest, then hurls the body with superhuman force all the way to the city's ramparts.

Adoniram's experiment is underway and the entire area is liquid fire. The frenzy and excitement abate when the mold, into which the metal had run, suddenly cracks. The experiment fails. With this realization, Adoniram lets out an inhuman scream—a wail that rends the earth—the pain that only an artist-creator knows when unable to realize his dream. Adoniram attempts to combat the flow of the liquid metal, to war with the elements—fire and water—but to no avail. Detonations are heard like a series of "furious volcanoes," reminiscent of that terrible night when Sodom and Gomorrah had been destroyed.

Dishonor has been heaped upon Adoniram. He leaves the multitude and withdraws into his own working area. There is a strange figure that seems to be moving about, and Adoniram hears his name pronounced three times. An apparition then comes into view, a huge human form that rises and comes toward him, carrying a hammer. He leans toward Adoniram and speaks: "Awaken your soul, arise, my son. Come, follow me. I have seen the evils that have befallen my race, and I have taken pity on it."[19]

It is here that Adoniram's descent into the abyss begins—a descent into the world of the past or, psychologically, that of the collective unconscious. Adoniram listens to Tubal-Cain, the "instructor of every artificer in brass and iron" (Gen. 4:22), as he speaks of his ancestors, of his own suffering. As Adoniram listens, he feels himself advancing into a deep area of silence and of night, into some infinite space, and he experiences a strange affinity with this mysterious man who is guiding him through these unknown, cold, damp regions. He hears the dull, regular beat of the earth's heart and begins to see a white point in the distance, a world of people living in the shadows of these immense inner realms. Cain had lived here. The emerald stone that marked the center of Mount Kaf, Adam's burial place, gleams before him. In Mount Kaf's gallery hang the pictures of seventy emperors who had reigned for seventy thousand years before the creation of man, when the earth was inhabited by four giant races. These people, according to the Koran, had been formed "of noble, subtle, and luminous matter"[20] from a very hot fire and were called the Divas, the Djinns, the Afrites, and the Peris. These original races had warred with each other for twelve thousand years, and tired of observing their brutal ways, God fashioned man, a race blended from spirit and matter, which the Koran defined more precisely as lime and sandy earth. Tubal-Cain and his ancestors were descendants of these fire people and not from God's second creation— man. Adonai's tyranny, Tubal-Cain explained, ends in these regions. The fire people living under the earth are fed from the fruits of the Tree of Science.

No sooner does Adoniram hear this statement than he feels life breaking through all about him. The heat in this central region of the earth— this sanctuary of fire—was the normal temperature for these souls made from the element of fire. Although the people here were deprived of the sun, warmth was given them by fire, infusing them with life. They had been walled up within the earth by God who had become envious of their power and forbade them to communicate with men, fearing they might teach them the meaning of eternal happiness. But those who lived on the earth, Tubal-Cain states, had been made out of mud, had limited mental faculties, and were subject to death.

Adoniram's stay in the underworld, as described by Nerval, takes on the grandeur of an illusion, an apocalyptic vision. The gigantic people in these cavernous realms, who had lived on the earth in the early days of creation, converse with Adoniram. He studies their art: the fluid vegetation made out of metals, like "arborescent" trees, plants, and flowers, forever giving off a variety of aromas; the winged lions, griffons, sphinxes, androgynes; the infinite number of creatures standing about mysteriously as though animated by some arcane force.

Adoniram meets Cain, the "tiller of the ground" (Gen. 4:2), the vagabond whom God would neither destroy nor have destroyed. His beauty, Adoniram judges is "superhuman." His eyes are sad, his lips are pale, his forehead is full of concern, and upon his brow is outlined the form of a coiled golden serpent. He speaks to Adoniram, revealing the secret of his origins and his pain. Cain is a descendant of the fire people, an industrious and yet oppressed race. It is because of him Adoniram suffers, for all of Cain's progeny are doomed to pain as a result of his murder of Abel. Cain seeks to justify his act; he had, he claims, been unjustly treated by God. He, Cain, had sacrificed and worked hard to bring agriculture to the world; he had taught man how to plant wheat, how to

turn the arid land into arable and fertile fields. His brother Abel, meanwhile, had merely kept the cattle—had rested under a tree. Moreover,
Adam and Eve and God Himself had loved Abel more than him. Cain
had introduced murder into the world to rectify an injustice, but only
after ingratitude had embittered him. Those who work hard in the
world, he continued, are not rewarded but oppressed. After the murder,
Cain had experienced guilt, and to make up for his crime he had helped
Adam's children by teaching them the superior arts: industry and science. But God, angered with him, never forgave Cain for revealing certain secrets to man.

Adam's voice calls forth to Cain: "What did you do with your brother
Abel?" And Cain's heart beat, the weight of his act forces him to sink
to the ground. Cain's son Enoch now speaks to Adoniram, enumerating
the things he has done for man: namely, that he had taught them the
art of stone cutting, of building houses, of grouping these into citylike
formation. He "revealed" to them the manner in which societies are
built. Man was but a brutish beast before nations began building cities
based on Enochia.

Tubal-Cain resumes his narration. While man was being destroyed by
the Flood, the descendants of the fire people still living on earth were
saved. Tubal-Cain and his ancestors sent flames to cut the rocks in two,
to dig long galleries beneath the earth where man could hide; they built
the plain of Gizeh, the pyramids. And after the Flood, when he walked
upon the earth, he saw the change that had been wrought: the people
were small now and thin, the climate was cold, and he withdrew to the
inner domain, the land of his fathers. Ham's wife, the woman who had
married Noah's second son, found Tubal-Cain's son handsomer than
any earth man. From their union, Nimrod's father, Cush, was born. He
taught his brothers the art of the hunt, he founded Babylon and undertook the building of the tower of Babel. When God realized that
Cain's blood was the cause of such marvels, He dispersed His people.

Adoniram is unable to see the soul of Tubal-Cain's son. He had died
after the Flood and belonged to the earth, as did his descendants; they
all remained invisible to the fire people. But Adoniram hears him say
that in a moment of despair God had appeared to him and said:

—Hope . . .
Without any experience, isolated in a world
unknown to me, I answered timidly.
—I am afraid, Lord . . .
He resumed:—This fear will be your salvation.[21]

Then God informed Tubal-Cain's son that his name would remain unknown, as would his great deeds; that from him weaker beings would

be born and would die (only their souls would remain eternal, thereby retaining that "precious spark" which made for both their suffering and their genius). His descendants would be superior people but would be honored only after death. They would have to accept their fate—an earthly existence in which they were doomed to suffer, to be rejected, to know poverty and despair. Adoniram realizes that as the heir of these fire people, he too will have to submit to his destiny.

Adoniram returns to the surface of the earth as mysteriously as he had entered its depths. With the knowledge he has gained, he makes his molten sea and astounds the multitude, the ten thousand workers, Soliman, and the Queen of Sheba. As he wins his acclaim, Sheba's bird Hud-Hud, recognizes his master and alights on Adoniram's hand. Sheba knows then that Adoniram is to be her lord. And he calls her Balkis. He recognizes her as the Spirit of Light. He realizes also that she too is made of fire and that she is of the same lineage as he, a descendant of Tubal-Cain, and in direct line with Nimrod's brother, Saba. But this secret, he informs her, must be kept from man. Sheba becomes Adoniram's bride and carries his son within her. They decide to leave Jerusalem separately, as this would be the wiser course.

The three companions who had betrayed Adoniram the first time he had attempted to create his sea of molten metal find him in the temple. They try to extract from him the secret of his art, the secret of the master artist, which may be learned through a password that only he knows. When Adoniram refuses, one of the men takes his scissors and plunges them into Adoniram's thigh, and the other grasps the point of his compass and digs it into Adoniram's heart. They bury him and plant a young acacia branch on that spot.

Adoniram is no longer seen in Jerusalem, and rumors of his death flood the city. The people demand retribution. Soliman orders nine masters to find the artist's body. When they come upon a freshly planted acacia branch on top of which a strange bird has lit, they dig into the ground. They decide that the first word anyone of them is to utter when they discover Adoniram's body is to be the password, *Makbenach,* meaning "The flesh is leaving the body." Soliman and the people are informed of Adoniram's demise.

After Sheba's departure, Soliman tries to find solace with other women but is unable to do so. He builds a temple to Moloch and has another castle constructed for himself on Mount Kaf. There he casts his spell: he commands all the animals, elements, and substances to remain immobile—not even to decompose. He mounts his throne and dies. But Soliman has forgotten to include the little worm in his spell, and after two thousand years it has eaten away the pillars that had supported his throne. When the throne falls, the spell is broken and the world is released from its immobility. According to the Koran, life begins anew:

And when he had decreed his death, they did not know that he was dead until they saw a worn eating away his staff. And when his corpse fell down, the djinn realized that had they had knowledge of what was hidden, they would not have continued in their abject servitude. (Sourate 34)

Nerval's version of the Soliman-Sheba-Adoniram myth had special significance for the Masons. In fact, every detail and event depicted is replete with Masonic symbolism.

Adoniram (or Hiram) for the Mason is a seminal force, a master builder, a generative power. He is a doer, an actor. His strength lies in the consciousness of his creative instinct and his desire to make his labor manifest. His great work consists in building a soul—in transmuting himself, a creature of matter, into a purer, higher, and more spiritually oriented being. His trails and turmoils are a series of initiations: the word "initiation" comes from the Latin *in ire*, meaning "to go within" or to reconstruct one's knowledge of life. For the Mason, the real world is the inner one; the exterior realm is merely a façade, a mask. When Socrates said, "Know thyself," he meant discover the inner man, the real being. To gain such knowledge requires inner probing, a sounding out of the force or being inside.[22]

Adoniram had to discover his spiritual self, the fire that burned within him, his own creative element. To search out this "spark" he had to shed all "base metals," all superficial forms of material existence—the world of mere appearances, the impurities in which he was embedded.

Adoniram's ordeal has become the essential part of the ceremony of reception to the Grade of Master in the Masonic Order. Each initiate is compelled to go through the test of the four elements (earth, fire, water, and air) in order to find the inner core, the focal point from which all creative spirit emerges. Man's life task also centers upon finding his core, bringing forth and developing the "celestial" force that lives within him. For the Mason, Christ offered himself as the supreme symbol of such work.[23]

In the Masonic initiation ceremony, as in the ancient mysteries, the acolyte experiences the death of the "profane" self and the "birth" of the new spiritual being. The object of the initiation is to lead the neophyte into the experience of an inner illumination, the transcendental light or the center of Self. Since Masonic initiation is mostly intuitive, it proceeds through universal symbols, signs or analogies, which bring the neophyte into closer contact with the invisible, the infinite world, creating unity out of diversity.[24]

Because the inner experience the initiate undergoes cannot be expressed verbally (an emotion cannot be articulated), it must, of necessity, remain secret. As the neophyte proceeds he may at some point know what is termed "efficacious grace," or the divine state preceding man's fall. According to some eighteenth-century Masons, namely Martinès de Pasqually, the initiation is supposed to help man reintegrate back into the universal pleroma. When this occurs, the neophyte is imbued with a type of "nostalgic desire for a rhythmic Light and Harmony," which he had once known and longs to experience again.[25]

Solomon's temple is also an important symbol for the Masons. It represents the rebuilt human body, the one that the neophyte has reworked after his successful initiation—a body renewed, the most perfect of all possible earthly bodies.[26] According to Claude de Saint-Martin, religious philosopher and Mason, the temple stands for the mind, the abode of the spirit, divine essence. Since man is God's priest, it is his duty to spread His word by enlarging the godly area, by seeking to enlighten His living corpus within man.

At the outset of Nerval's tale, Adoniram had already built the temple, and, therefore, had completed a certain stage in his initiation. He had revealed both his power and wisdom when making the Tau sign, thus calling his thousands of workers together in split seconds. According to Masonic belief, the Tau sign indicates "rectitude in action"; the square in the Tau sign implies that all lines are put in "right relation to each other and are united with each other."[27] But Adoniram's power was evidently not complete: he was a victim of treachery, the implication being that he had not yet sufficiently sounded out his own depths. The deceit meted out to him by three workers was a manifestation of his own weakness, perhaps his vanity, his inability to see himself in the proper perspective. He had not yet mastered his own creative impulses. More tests were needed; greater depths had to be known.

Adoniram's stay in Cain's realm may be looked upon as a withdrawal from the outside world into man's inner domain. It permitted him further reflection and increased knowledge, a period of meditation that is indispensable if truth and reality are to be experienced. The Buddhist, for example, has made meditation central to his religion. The Mason is also intent upon the indwelling process so that all facets of external reality may be examined from within, in greater harmony. The Masonic credo is: *"Visita Interiora terrae, rectificandoque, invenies occultum."*

Adoniram's inner probings permit him to come into contact with the divine spark that lives within him—the creative principle that permits him to perform his miracle of the molten sea. In the arcane realm of his ancestors, Adoniram takes stock of himself, converses with Cain, Tubal-Cain, Adam—the forces they represent within him as experienced through projection. They had been dormant until stimulated or provoked into action during Adoniram's inner meanderings. The indwelling, the meditation paved the way for his discovery: that he was the descendent of fire people. Once he has contacted these elements, once he has dipped into the realm of the infinite, he returns to the upper world resurrected or reborn. Now he can become the crator of immortal works that had lived only *in potentia* within his fantasy world. Had Adoniram not experienced the first great failure and pain, he might not have felt impelled to meditate, to turn inward, to communicate with the transcendental forces within himself. He would not have labored to express what lived within him and so would not have achieved his monumental work.

When Adoniram left the inner world of contemplation, Tubal-Cain told him he needed a hammer (or mallet) for his work. This instrument, basic to the Masonic cult, represents the will needed to accomplish one's work and to achieve one's goal. It is an instrument used to transform crude matter into perfect shapes—a tool capable of building a temple (body-mind). Before performing the miracle of the molten sea, Adoniram dons his white wool apron, which symbolizes constant toil for the Mason. Then, by an incredible extension of will, he begins his task.

Adoniram is slain by workmen for not revealing the secret word, which stands for the creative process, the secret that Masons are not supposed to disclose. So he is stricken first with a scissors which, according to Masonic tradition, indicate "discernment in investigation," then with a compass symbolizing "moderation in the search," passion controlled and measured by reason.[28] A clap of thunder was heard when Adoniram died. Such cosmic manifestations always occur when traumatic events take place: Christ's death, Charlemagne's battle with the Saracens, Moses' reception of the Ten Commandments on Mount Sinai.

In terms of ancient solar beliefs, the acacia branch that the murderers had placed on Adoniram's tomb indicates new vegetation that came into being as a result of the sun's force: a visualization of Adoniram's own creative powers. In this respect, Adoniram has been compared to Osiris, who had been dismembered and whose wife-sister, Isis, had rebuilt him, after which he withdrew into the underworld. According to Egyptian mythology, when the sun descended into Osiris' tomb, he was reborn into a new phase of existence. His widow Isis then gave birth to their son Horus, just as Sheba gave birth to her son after Adoniram's demise. Masons are called the "Children of the Widow"; and with the birth or reappearance of the god—understood as a purification of the self—the Masons take on the name "Children of Light."[29] In like manner, Horus became associated with the sun and Sheba's offspring was to follow his mother's tradition and become a fire- or sun-worshipper.

The fact that Adoniram was buried under the altar in the temple that he had himself constructed indicated that he had succeeded in his endeavors: his body had been rebuilt and rested in the holiest of central points.[30] Adoniram's death and resurrection in the son Sheba bore him made him eternal—able to participate in cosmic life, in divine knowledge. The reborn Adoniram is considered omnipresent in each initiate. Only his flesh had left his bones—*Makbenach;* his soul had attained immortality.

Nerval's version of the Soliman-Sheba-Adoniram legend may also be interpreted alchemically.

Alchemists believe the world is one, a vast organism that is alive and animated and, thereby, possesses a soul. All is linked and connected within the universe, like the rungs of a ladder, from the tiniest particle of sand up to God.[31]

From primordial unity there arises duality: woman and man, solid and liquid, life and death. To assure some semblance of balance within the universe, a third force—manifestation—comes into being. These three forces are present in the cosmos (God, nature, man) and are manifested in three principles: sulfur, salt, and mercury. In the human being they are referred to as spirit, body, and soul. Everything contained in this trinity becomes an analogy of the other since all in the universe is, as we have stated, linked. The star of Solomon (David), for example—which is not only a Jewish, but a Masonic and Alchemical symbol—is composed of two interlocking triangles indicating the union of duality.

The alchemist's scientific goal of extracting the "gold" or "philosopher's stone" from base metals requires seven stages of purification: separation, calcination, sublimation, dissolution, distillation, coagulation, coction, also expressed as black, white, yellow, red. The alchemist cooks the various elements he seeks to transmute in what has been called a kind of "philosophical egg," a receptacle formed like a uterus. In this receptacle, the elements are blended by means of fire and pass from chaos to purity. Such a mixing process has an inner philosophical meaning. In Adoniram's case, the mixture had been faulty the first time he attempted to create his molten sea. Therefore, the substance in the philosophical egg had not yet been sufficiently purified. Only after his visit to the inner world and his confrontation with all the substances within the earth could he reach the state of purity necessary to create his gold or, symbolically, his great work.

In the underworld, Adoniram saw the base metals in a state of ebullition, that is, both solid and liquid as they poured out of each other. And he exposed his "naked human spirit"[32] to these elements in the raw: earth, air, water, and fire, thus gaining the secret of how he must proceed in the various stages of distillation, or the creation of his molten sea. Adoniram actually had to experience, physically, the turmoil and the chaos necessary to undergo the distillation, coagulation, and coction that would lead him to the perfect creation.

Nerval details Adoniram's evolution in terms of color. Black (chaos) represents putrefaction, the chaotic period when Adoniram had failed in his mission and had been instrumental in causing Benoni's death along with the hundreds of others who were burned and drowned during the uncontrollable flow of molten metal. Blackness, for the alchemist, symbolizes the demise of the profane, uninitiated human being, the one who lacks vision, maturity and thus, discernment. As the cooking

process is pursued, the black is transformed into white, which represents
the resurrection of the elements: a change in attitude, form, and substance. Sheba, when she first met Adoniram, is dressed in a white gauze-
like garment. Though Adoniram has failed in his molten-sea experiment, Sheba does not repudiate him; she is perplexed. She does not
know what course to follow. She marvels that he had been able to control
thousands of workmen, but is still unaware that Adoniram is to become
her god of fire, that he will attain enlightenment.

In the underworld, Adoniram is exposed to intense heat: red is the
most important tonality. Here he is transformed into a young king, and
relives the spiritual and physical suffering (he dies, so far as the earth
people are concerned) and is reborn as the *"spiritus mundi,"* aware of his
powers and his art. The miracle of the molten sea is performed, but it
was within the bowels of the earth that he learned the secret of creativity
or how to make the philosopher's stone, which the great alchemist Paracelsus described as being a composite of opposites: fluid, liquid, like
mercury able to penetrate all hard bodies, transforming them all into
gold.

In the last phase—that of *rubedo* or redness—fire became the most important of all principles, or vehicles of transformation. It is the first sign
of divine emanation, a fecundating entity able to engender all beings,
a vital force that makes for the very composition of the universe itself.[33]
Fire is fluid. It gives light and warmth, electricity, movement and energy; it illuminates, it permits vegetation to grow (man, animal, vegetable, mineral). It also destroys, as it did during Adoniram's first attempt
at the molten sea, when he lacked the necessary insight and had not yet
been able to create the proper chemical balance. He was blind and unaware of his betrayal because he was too interested in his own aggrandizement to be a true master. His perspective was so limited that he
unwittingly sacrificed the child, Benoni, his only friend and helper, having concluded unwisely that he had betrayed him.

Creation occurs only when power (fire) is transformed into the act in
a well-channelled and orderly manner, when the various possibilities in
life are reduced to one. Adoniram had not yet reached this stage.

For the alchemist, as we have seen, there are three forces present in
the cosmos (God, nature, man), and these are manifested in three principles (sulfur, salt, and mercury).[34]

Because Adoniram is the energetic, creative element in the drama, he
may be associated with sulfur. Astrologists have likened sulfur to the
sun principle, which may also be used to define Adoniram's role in this
tale. He stands, as does the sun, for life, creativity, a power-driven force,
universal strength and form. Since all astral bodies are endowed with
sexes in alchemy, he would be identified with the father principle. In-
sofar as he is likened with sulfur, he would represent the masculine,

active element, hot and powerful enough to attack other metals. Because he is so powerful a principle, he is also a complex of opposites and is, when considered in terms of sulfur, unchangeable, fixed in his intentions and having only one goal in mind—creating.

The alchemist classifies sulfur, mercury, and salt in terms of the four elements (earth, water, fire, air). In Adoniram's visible and solid state (sulfur-sun), he would represent the earth principle, that is, the fecundating force, the physical, strong, truly masculine man whom Sheba calls a "real" man. In that he is also a fire principle (the sun); as the descendant of Cain, Tubal-Cain, he stands for passion and creativity. Like the sun, Adoniram disappears from view and pursues his existence in an occult or subtle state. His withdrawal is proof of his ability to live in two realms: that of sunlight or reality and the hidden underworld—the domain of occult and subliminal forces.

Metals are considered living entities by the alchemists, endowed with souls. So the molten sea, which is made of brass is also equipped with body and soul. The soul is the vaporous element that emanates from metals as they are being distilled. The body, or matter, is that part of the metal which remains visible. When metal is heated and flows, both body and soul are united into one. Adoniram's initial failure shows that his initiation or the work in progress had not yet been perfected. He had not been able to fuse body and spirit into a harmonious whole.

Sheba is associated, alchemically, with mercury, and, astrologically, with the moon. As the moon, she reflects the sun's strength; that is, she is fertilized by the sun and cannot act or function independently. Her moods also vacillate. Because Nerval refers to her as the "Morning Star," she possesses some of the sun's characteristics and in this respect is frequently mistress of herself; her thinking function predominates under certain circumstances (a rather uncommon phenomenon in most women). When she talks with Soliman about poetry and artistic creativity, and argues in favor of her god, of her people, she is always opposed to him. Her manner of discourse is reasonable and rational (in former times, male-oriented), though she argues in favor of the heart and accuses Soliman of being overly cerebral in poetry and too materialistic. To add to her conflicting nature, the caravans she brought with her to Jerusalem are piled high with matter: precious stones, ivories, myrrh, aromatic perfumes, those very things she claims to detest.[35] Because she represents mercury and the moon, as well as the sun principle, her attitude is ambiguous and enigmatic.

When likened to mercury, she may be considered passive, cold and, at the same time, volatile. Like mercury, she is malleable and changes as each new situation arises; she acts and reacts accordingly and not to a set pattern. She can "fuse" (as does mercury) and also sparkle and burst forth, as she does when meeting Adoniram for the first time. Here, because of her ability to insinuate herself into various events, she may be compared to a liquid. Like mercury, she is an occult force with magic powers and an ability to rule over the bird world.

Adoniram, according to alchemical tradition, is considered the active principle. Sheba, by definition, would be the relatively passive element. Each is constantly attracted by the other. During their earthly life they are separated from one another (man and woman); they combine under the influence of fire (passion). By means of the alchemical fire, Sheba is able to know Adoniram. Her feelings guide her, not her cold, rational mind. Through these feelings—where neither the eye nor the body can penetrate—the inner fire causes her to seek her mate.[36]

Soliman stands for the alchemist's salt, the astrologer's Ether. He is a mediating element, a modality or state of matter that brings things together. By contrasting Soliman's materialism, Sheba learns to appreciate creativity and spirituality. Soliman's sage and "passionless" brow enables her to become interested in Adoniram's youth, beauty and energy. Soliman's wisdom (or in Nerval's rendition, his senility) makes Adoniram's creative force stand out all the more compellingly; Soliman's hypocrisy, dishonesty, jealousy and pettiness underscore Adoniram's sincerity, honesty and originality. As associated with salt, it is he who makes the union of Sheba and Adoniram possible; without his presence or blending power, without his intervention, they might never have met. In this respect, Soliman is comparable to the "vital spirit" of the alchemist which makes for unity, brings matter of all types and forms together.

In order for the three elements (mercury, sulfur, salt) to operate, activity must occur, thus enabling an alteration in their consistency. Adoniram's molten-metal experience, or the alchemist's heat, enabled him to create his great work. The meaning of this miracle has been compared to the great creation myths in the world religions.

The union of Sheba and Adoniram, or the discovery of the philosopher's stone, paves the way for ecstasy, or the soul's liberation from the body, the birth of the child (the artistic creation), and the immortality of man. The original substance from which the new and creative elements are born must, of necessity, die—or the hero becomes incorporated into the status quo. The alchemist believes, however, that he (or what he represents) lives on in his child (his creation) and will, as such, regenerate once again in nature's cyclical process: darkness of night, whiteness of dawn, redness of the resplendent days.

The three assassins who murdered Adoniram represented the forces of nature: spirit, soul, and body. They were, alchemically, responsible for bringing out his dissolution, putrefaction, and rebirth. Once union had taken place between Sheba and Adoniram (mercury and sulfur), a condition of stasis would have developed had the murder not taken place. Since all in nature is in a perpetual state of flux, it follows that the metamorphosis would take place and with it, perpetual renewal, reassessment and reevaluation. The child born from the union of Sheba and Adoniram would, it is presumed, go through his own initiation and life process, seek his own purity, potential and evolve in his own way.

The Ars Magna of alchemy is the science that permits man to reconstruct the very processes of life and earth in his laboratory, to purify the substances with which he is working by ridding them of all base elements. This allows absolute beauty, truth, and goodness to emerge. Nature's processes are eternal. Gold is a state of mind and it, too, is subject to change, evolution, and spiritualization.

Nerval's drama of Soliman-Sheba-Adoniram is equally fascinating from a psychological point of view. It demonstrates, perhaps more readily than any other of his works, the need to overthrow the old, repressive, conventional attitude that the author held and to fructify his personality with the addition of that foreign element.

Sheba represents the Eternal Feminine. The fact that she came from a sun-drenched land and adored the solar disc indicated her need for illumination (consciousness) and a longing for the spiritual or wise attitude she thought Soliman would bring to her. She came with gifts from the distant land of Yemen. She spoke of the fecundity of her native country, the riches her earth yielded now that it had been brought under cultivation. Sheba therefore brings certain values to Soliman: beauty, work, also aggressiveness and pride. In Nerval's tale she is an independent figure, a composite of masculine (sun) and feminine (moon) traits: passionate and cerebral, active and passive.

The riddles she poses to Soliman activate her masculine side, that is, the thinking principle within her and not her affective tendencies. Since the word "question" may be translated from the Hebrew as "test" or "tempt," her questioning becomes comparable to the Sphinx' riddle in the Oedipus myth and may signify a test for power. Will Sheba's way predominate, or Soliman's? That is, will patriarchy or matriarchy win out? Since Soliman's patriarchal society has already regressed to a luxury-loving, sensual, and almost pagan community, it can be only a matter of time before it disintegrates completely. In this court, everything is corruption. Soliman even answers the riddles deceitfully. There is no tension, no struggle, no heroism. When a land (or personality) is in a regressive situation, it no longer experiences the strain, the sacrifice, necessary to build and evolve. Nothing, therefore, can readily come from Sheba's relationship with Soliman. It is based on artifice and mistrust. We know from the outset that another hero must and will be found—another force able to fructify, to bring about the renewal needed to pave the way for rebirth.[37]

Sheba is Adoniram's anima figure—goddess, queen, mother, sister, and wife. She is as positive a force in his life as she is a destructive one in Soliman's. She is not only seductive (in that she seeks to attract Adoniram), but as a goddess, as a sibyl of sorts, she wields magic powers. She is subtle when resorting to deceit (she gives Soliman a sleeping potion when he tries to make advances toward her); strong when she must maintain her independence, sacrificing her magic ring and yielding her power over birds.

In Nerval's tale, the Hoopoe bird belongs to her. In the Biblical legend, it is Soliman's. The bird is frequently looked upon as "an intuitive thought" because it is believed to have the ability to experience inner feeling before it emerges into consciousness. The bird also has spiritual attributes; it acts as a guide for Sheba's own feelings: it points the way, and more important, it confirms externally what she feels inwardly, her love for Adoniram. Through this bird she is led to fulfillment, and her gentle, feminine, loving aspects come into being. She experiences Eros (relatedness) with Adoniram who, in this story, represents not only the artist-creator, but a higher form of spirituality.[38]

Soliman, the father image, the patriarch, stands for the old order. He lacks initiative and spirituality and is carried along by the court's corruption. To maintain his power, he resorts to trickery, bribery, and lies. Captivated by the beautiful, winsome Sheba, he would offer her anything in his kingdom, his entire being if need be, to win her affections. She remains uninterested because he lacks the one element she longs for, the masculine or higher spirituality. Her rejection of this monarch is another example of the ritual slaying of the old kings: the ruling attitude has become sterile and must die.[39]

Adoniram, though a fire principle, as is Sheba, differs from her considerably. He is a rebellious and creative spirit of mysterious origin. He represents a personality unaware of its potential, unfulfilled, untried, unredeemed. His imagination, his desire to create, his dissatisfaction with himself compel him to experience inner torment. The failure of his molten sea, or of his outward or external attitude, leads to profound introversion. Afraid of life, he withdraws from the world and concentrates on his inner development. He is living, therefore, a one-sided existence. Unwittingly, he had sacrificed his only friend, Benoni, really a projection of himself: the child artist, who has not yet developed the strength necessary to perform a heroic work. The child in Adoniram had to be sacrificed in order to bring about inner development. If he would have knowledge, his isolation had to be complete.

Adoniram withdraws into his inner world, a cleft in the mountain. Mountains where gods dwelt (Olympus, Parnassus), or where their words were heard (Mt. Sinai), or where punishment was experienced (Prometheus' immolation on Mt. Caucasus); as ethereal areas (Christ on the Hill of Calvary); as sanctuaries for mysteries (Holy Grail built on Mt. Salvatch in the Pyrénées). Mountains may be looked upon as vehicles for mystical or spiritual ascension, for psychological growth.[40]

During his underworld visit, Adoniram confronts his collective unconscious and experiences its riches. Tubal-Cain, Cain, Adam and the superhuman metallic forms or phantoms that he sees in this realm, permit him to bring these aspects of his personality into consciousness. Each being, each figure represents an inner quality: fear, guilt, suffering, nobility, obsessions of various sorts, phobias, longings, hatreds. His rejection at the hands of society has been transformed into feelings of hatred for Soliman and his god. He seeks to destroy these negative father images as represented by the patriarchal society in which he grew up. Adoniram along with his ancestors, Adam, Cain and the rest—was willing to sin by destroying the values these negative father images stood for, and in so doing, bring into the world the unnameable, the unimaginable.

To consider oneself the harbinger of extraordinary ideas or fresh approaches to art or life in general, is to suffer from hubris, or an inflated ego. Such an imbalance does not go unchecked. The first time Adoniram felt himself capable of great things, he was betrayed by his workmen (as Christ and Osiris had been in their time). Such an outcome indicates that no man or god has the answer to life—that the cosmos, always subject to constant changes and upheavals, is forever evolving. Answers may only be temporary at best. The new element that Adoniram introduced into Soliman's empire—the molten-sea experiment—was the product of his life experience and not that of another. The secret it contained could not be divulged.

Man can neither rest on his laurels nor state his artistic mastership in a given work. Man is not eternal. Just as the cosmos lives and breathes, changes in form and shape, so the personality responds in a variety of ways to each new event and fresh coincidence. It is the individual who must learn to cope with the ever-changing forces and evolve accordingly.

For Nerval, the urge for the new, the harmonious to come into being through alliance with the positive aspects of the Great Mother archetype that Sheba represented, was a necessity for his well-being and evolution as an artist. He needed to experience the harmony that such a *coniunctio* would bring about because of the destructive way the external world had reacted to his fantasies. The humiliation his own father had brought upon him was projected on both Soliman and his patriarchal religion.

Because Nerval believed so strongly in renewal, he could not help but be attracted to the distant and the new. Such an outward attitude might represent an example of exogamous psychic energy or a countertendency within man that would prevent inbreeding and stagnation. Because of the incest taboo inherent in certain civilizations, marriages were usually exogamous. Symbolically, the Sheba-Adoniram relationship becomes just this, though both Sheba and Adoniram come from different lands. They are fire principles and in this sense descendants of the same person—Cain. An endogamous urge compels them to fuse. For Nerval, such an association might represent a need to consolidate the disparate psychic forces tearing him apart, the desire to experience a coalescing of the component parts of his personality. Only through the Great Mother could he experience the masculine side of his own being. Once he became aware of his own masculinity, he might be able to work in harmony with the feeling function and experience fulfillment both as man and artist.

Nerval's trip to the Middle East was coming to an end. He had been to Damietta, Beirut, Jaffa, Saint-Jean d'Acre, and Saïd. Students of Nerval's life have not been able to determine when he arrived at the capital of Lebanon or what his activities were during his stay in Syria. In his writings, Nerval indicates that he lived among the Marionites for a month and took excursions into Lebanon, and that he did not go to Damascus because of an outbreak of the plague, or to Balbeck because the road had been cut off by the Druses. At the end of July, Nerval and the archeologist who had accompanied him during his sojourn, Fonfrède, went to Cyprus and Rhodes, and then arrived in Constantinople, a land of "pleasure" and sheer "delight." Nerval was happy to see the bright lights, the excitement in the cafés, the theaters, and most of all, the French newspapers. He felt a twinge of nostalgia. He longed to return to Paris.

On October 28, 1843, Nerval was en route to France. He sailed via Malta, to Naples, Marseilles, then traveled on to Arles, Nîmes—stopping for visits in various cities. He arrived in Paris on January 2, 1844. Though his trip lasted a little more than a year, it had encompassed a lifetime.

14 CHAOS BLACKENS, DAWN WHITENS, THE RESPLENDENT FLAME PURIFIES

> *The struggle to apprehend the supernal loveliness*
> *—this struggle, on the part of souls fittingly*
> *constituted—has given to the world all that*
> *which it [the world] has ever been enabled at once*
> *to understand and to feel as poetic.*
>
> Edgar Allan Poe, *The Poetic Principle.*

Back in Paris, Nerval pursued his career as a journalist. He also undertook the translation of Heinrich Heine's *Lieder,* the *Zeitgedichte,* and the *Intermezzo.* Both these men seemed doomed to great suffering, and perhaps this is why Nerval referred to Heine as his "spiritual twin." In his spare time—that he had much of it seems almost inconceivable—Nerval continued writing short stories.

One of Nerval's finest, *The Marquis de Fayolle,* is no ordinary piece of fiction. Once façades are shorn, the narrative takes on the depth and prismatic ramifications of an alchemical drama. The protagonists, who appear to be drawn in childlike and naïve strokes, with simplistic gestures and a forthright vocabulary, are, in reality, tightly etched entities, symbols, visualizations; behind them lies a mysterious world peopled with transpersonal beings. Also, the spiritual and psychological growth and decay that Nerval's protagonists undergo follow specific alchemical modes, each of which contributes in molding the *prima materia* within the characters' subjective world. Finally, the scenes adhere to certain tempi and color tonalities that may be described in alchemical terms: the early or cold phase is relatively free of motion, but with the intervention of the catalyst (fire), energy accelerates, gestures and ideations are transformed into a series of chaotic masses, setting off sparks, scintillae until blackened; a new calm or serenity comes into existence, dawn whitens and distillation takes place; in the last cycle, the flame used for purification brings the philosopher's stone (gold) into existence—that perfect entity with its godlike powers.

Nerval's tale evolves in accordance with the three main transformatory phases alchemists have depicted in terms of color: chaos blackens, dawn whitens, the resplendent flame purifies.

Part one of *The Marquis de Fayolle* takes place in June, 1770, in a small town in Brittany. Helen, a twenty-two-year-old, convent-educated girl, is depicted as beautiful but naïve in worldly affairs. Her marriage of convenience to the comte de Maurepas had made her life in the Château d'Epinay dull and routine. One day, her husband is unexpectedly sent on a political mission to Paris and takes Helen with him. No sooner do they arrive than he is imprisoned in the Bastille. Alone, Helen solicits the aid of one of her husband's relatives, a lady in high society at whose home she meets the marquis de Fayolle. He is handsome, charming, adventurous and well-versed in the fashionable esoteric and occult teachings of the day; a rapport is soon established between the two.[1] After the release of Helen's husband from prison, the couple return to Brittany. One evening, the count returns unexpectedly from a hunting trip to find his wife packed and ready to leave with the marquis de Fayolle. Pistols are drawn, the count is killed, and the marquis leaves for America. Helen remains at the Château d'Epinay and dismisses her servants except for Yvonne. Months pass. A priest is seen leaving her home with a bundle. Yvonne is then married to Jean le Chouan and is given a farm as a wedding gift. Helen retires to a Benedictine convent.

The first alchemical phase—"chaos blackens," or *nigredo*—represents undifferentiated, inactive, or dead *prima materia*. A catalyzing agent (fire) is then used to attack the base metals; it burns and dissolves them, reducing their component parts to different forms. With the changes in their chemistries, a rearrangement of their material states occurs—an attempt, on the alchemist's part, to "correct nature."

The alchemist's fire is an energizing force (an emotion, for example) capable of dissolving the component conscious or unconscious factors within the human personality. The passion may be potent or lukewarm, depending upon its hold on the individual. The chaotic, affective situation arising from the introduction of the catalyzing agent colors ideations, blots lucidity, blurs notions. During this tumultuous period, the unconscious domain invades, in effect, the conscious outlook; or the conscious attitude has been driven into subliminal, shadowy, or black areas.

Metaphysically, the alchemical fire alters the individual's obsessive attachment to terrestrial matters. The blending or melting process that metals or alloys undergo brings about a concomitant disorientation in man's spiritual attitude. It provokes him to question his worldly ways, shatters the status quo, and offers him a *rite de passage* into a new world.

As Nerval's story opens, the reader is confronted with a stagnant situation. Feelings of inertia and stasis overcome every facet of the protagonists' lives. Yet beneath the façade of stability, a world *in potentia* is about to bubble forth. The setting of Nerval's story attests to this dual aspect. The small Breton town, with its castle, its paved roads, its bell tower, has "conserved its physiognomy of the Middle Ages,"[2] and gives the impression of stability. The disclosure of the political situation foreshadows impending violence, as though outer events were encroaching or imposing their energy on an inner drama. The royalist insurrection that preceded the war of the Vendée and continued throughout the

Consulat—the Chouannerie—is described in detail in mounting crescendo.

Nerval's images of the protagonists—Helen and her husband—is alchemical in quality, revelatory of an arcane substance existing within the psyche's subjective world. Helen is pictured in juxtaposition to "fiery" and "black" elements—symbols used frequently by alchemists to express certain stages in the firing of metals.

> The fire is dying in the hearth; the light from two copper candlesticks lit, rather dimly, one of the rooms in the Epinay castle, leaving the family portraits, the furniture and the black and white checked wall tapestry in the shadows . . .
>
> The countess was a small woman, barely twenty, white and pink with beautiful light chestnut hair and without powder, frail, thin, like a child.
>
> From time to time her large blue eyes, closed half way, bathed in sleep, would look up to the hands of the clock, then fall back fatigued on the pages of the novel.[3]

The image of fire, with all of its emotional and metaphysical ramifications, was frequently alluded to by the alchemist as the sun. Such an entity may be experienced in the warmth of companionship, in fertility, in spirituality, in consciousness through illumination. For example, when the sun shines brightly on a field, it helps fecundation and growth; when light penetrates into man's inner world, it paves the way for discernment and consciousness. When darkness prevails, or when unconscious forces flood the psyche, chaos ensues.

We learn that "the fire is dying in the hearth," that the light given off by the candles is too feeble to illuminate all but a small area of the ground floor. Clearly, the fire or very life principle of Helen's existence was about to die out; her naïve state had created a vacuum within her world. If such a situation were to continue, stagnation ond eventual disintegration would take place.

The "shadow" or darkness that covered the "family portraits, the furniture" in this image, defined in terms of an absence of color, reveals an empty marital relationship. The material world that her husband represents could no longer stir Helen's interest. On the contrary, the encroaching shadows paved the way for an invasion of a cold, dismal, deadly, unproductive—even destructive—element.

Other colors are introduced in this same picture: pink, blue, light brown. These "angelic" tones and "virginal" hues imply purity. Reminiscent of childhood, of some paradisiac state, these pastel shadows conjure forth a realm of fantasy, one far removed from the world of actuality.

Helen is endowed with the colors and the personality that alchemists have attributed to the moon. She is passive, reflective, really unformed unless the sun's rays shine upon her, thereby endowing her with life and substance. Thus far she is a person whose existence is strictly peripheral, one who has not yet become conscious of her own identity nor of her role in life.

Nerval later declares, "she would remain in her room alone, and would be bored to death reading pious books."[4] Purity, beauty, piety enshroud her life. Just as she is psychologically undeveloped, so her spiritual attitude is equally immature. She has never been taught to think, to question the notion of divinity, her relationship to it, its place in the world. She follows church regulations, the dictates of her father confessor, and believes in all the beautiful and harrowing stories she has learned in convent school. Her whole world is circumscribed and because of her inexperience and naïveté, she is particularly vulnerable to any kind of "fire"—passion.

The image of the Count Maurepas, the crudeness of his ways, the brevity of his words, establishes from the outset the dichotomy that separates husband and wife. Neither hatred nor love exists between them, neither admiration nor disdain; no kind of living substance could bind them; only the empty, shell-like words of matrimony compel them to remain together. Had even feelings of anger or enmity existed between the two, rather than those of sublime indifference, their relationship might have developed further.

When the count announces their impending visit to Paris, Nerval again describes, in terms of light and darkness, what could be interpreted as banal, romantic visualizations of a situation, but which is far from that. "In one word, for her it was the sun suddenly rising, brilliant and radiant in the midst of the night. . . ."[5] The juxtaposition of fire and blackness here implies turbulence and conflict. Indeed, Helen reacts to the trip as a moth stirs and tingles with excitement at the sight of light.

The sun symbol is complex and must be examined in some detail. For the alchemist, as we have seen, the sun principle represented a primal force, a source of life and creation, an energizer, an activator, a transformer of *prima materia*. The ancients adored the sun because they recognized it as a visible expression of a universal or divine force within the heavens. Though positive, the sun could also bring destruction, as such ancient myths as those of Icarus and Phaeton tell us. The sun, if approached too quickly and too closely, may burn and destroy. Psychologically, such a situation may be looked upon as follows: an illumination may create an overly active condition in the unconscious, with a concomitant lowering of the rational function. When the subliminal realm becomes hyperactive or overly traumatized, the conscious outlook is bruised or vanishes entirely. At this point, a lucid frame of reference or view of life, an ability to cope with situations in daily existence is nearly impossible. Spiritually, a veritable eclipse or unawareness of the terrestrial situation occurs, and, at the same time, an invasion of divine force within the person's inner realm.

Helen's arrival in Paris and her husband's subsequent imprisonment leaves her in a most precarious position. Ignorant of the ways of the world, of her ideations, unaccustomed to questioning, to assessing situations, she is an easy prey for any "firebrand" who might present himself.

The marquis de Fayolle becomes the catalyzing agent. The alchemist has now introduced "fire" to the alembics, retorts and crucibles; their concoctions are heating up, their metals are almost aglow, paving the way for new blendings, new combinations of alloys. The life-giving force, this sun principle that Helen meets in Paris, is described by Nerval in dynamic, volatile, passionate color tones as well as in terms of a highly accelerated series of gestures.

> . . . his black, ardent eyes shone with feverish brightness; his straight and well furnished eyebrows, his long and pointed nose, his broad mouth, his pale and swarthy face, his violent, jerky and impetuous movements, revealed at a glance a type of character which was neither capable of controlling outbursts of love or hate.[6]

Elsewhere, the marquis is alluded to as a "shining" force among the guests, an "ardent interpreter" of mystical notions. Indeed, he spoke freely and easily about illuminism, hypnotism, and other occult sciences that were so much à la mode. He enthralled the most sophisticated; certainly it would be relatively simple for him to captivate and seduce the provincial, not yet defined, Helen.

The metaphysical notions upon which the marquis elaborated, and which succeeded in transforming the calm and composed Helen into the chaotic and tenebrous mass she becomes, were those of Dom Pernety, Saint-Germain, and Swedenborg. Dom Pernety, at once a Benedictine monk and a Freemason, was also the founder of what was to become, in 1784, the well-known Illuminist sect. Pernety claimed to have been inspired by God, who ordered him to found a hermetic society for the purpose of encouraging His people to flourish and to enable them to ascend the ladder into more spiritual spheres. It was because of God's intervention, it was said, that Dom Pernety had attempted to create the elixir of life.

Swedenborg was a man for whom the invisible world was merely an extension of the visible domain; he believed in the transmigration of souls, that death was not an end to life but a long sleep after which the individual awakened to an eternal realm. All within the cosmos, he affirmed, was linked; life as we know it is merely a reflection of a perfect world existing in the divine realm. By means of a system based on self-discipline (including fasting, prayers, and breathing exercises) Swedenborg claimed to have ascended into divine spheres and to have contacted interplanetary beings, even heaven itself. His conversations with angels, his perceptions and insights into outer-worldly domains were recorded in an eight-volume work, *Arcana Caelestia*.

As for Count Saint-Germain, he was perhaps the most fascinating of them all. His influence upon Louis XV and Frederick the Great was said to have been very powerful. Brilliant, erudite, an alchemist capable of transforming anything and everything into gold; a man whose talents on the piano and clavichord amazed even the famous Rameau; a man who painted in a manner that astonished La Tour and Van Loo; a linguist who spoke nearly all tongues fluently; a man over two thousand years old who never ate and who had known the Queen of Sheba and Christ, to mention just a couple of his personal acquaintances—Count Saint-Germain was understandably the talk of European society.

The more the marquis de Fayolle spoke of Dom Pernety, Swedenborg, and Count Saint-Germain to Helen, the more she was attracted to him— the harbinger of such "extraordinary" values. The marquis de Fayolle became a Lucifer, or light bringer, who was capable of transforming the "ideal" or "supernatural" world into the "real" one.[7] Helen's world, formerly a realm *in potentia*, was concretized into the act. Her altered chemistry was expressed alchemically in terms of heat; the sparks that first set her ablaze—burned her, scorched her, leaving only charred remains.

The goal of alchemy is the union of opposites—Sol and Luna—which then, it is hoped, pave the way for the birth of a new creation. Such a *coniunctio* indicates a new orientation and view of life. In Helen's case the passive moon figure that she was has been too suddenly, too dramatically, exposed to the blinding light of the marquis' personality. Instead of integrating the life-giving force he offers, she is overwhelmed by it. What had hitherto been dormant and inactive—her Eros or instinctual qualities as measured by every woman's need for affection and warmth—has been transformed into jarring emotions. Unable to understand what has occurred to her, she simmers down only to become a type of receptacle, experiencing the marquis as a fertilizing force but never as a companion. Her rational function has been totally eclipsed during the melée. As a result, she does not attempt to assess her situation. She plays the part of an agent within which a seminal force could be nurtured, but without her help or knowledge.

The trauma that her pregnancy and her husband's death cause her is never assimilated within her psyche. It does not, to use alchemical terminology, transform chaos into cosmos. Because of the transformation, she is divested of her lethargy, at least for a brief period, but the rest of her days would be spent in seeking redemption and forgiveness for the criminal act she had caused, a type of modern version of the original sin myth.

Helen fell into sin as Adam fell into matter. She became the victim of the Devil's grasp, that is, of her own instinctuality or sensuality, which had always lived within her but which she had repressed. According to

Christian dogma, to earn redemption is to destroy or to sacrifice what is natural to man—his physical realm—to become a saint. In so doing, man's divine attributes are encouraged to expand, with a concomitant rejection of anything that smacks of the flesh. Such an overevaluation of man's spiritual, intellectual, or divine side creates a dangerous imbalance. The "inflation" of the concept of good—an outcome of the Platonic, Neoplatonic, and Stoic philosophies—places the onus of earthly misery on man and on nature. God, in this context, becomes the representative of absolute good and works in direct opposition to man and nature, forcing his creation to experience a *privatio boni*. The blame that then falls inevitably upon the human being is not only difficult to bear but may also result, as in Helen's case, in a completely negative outcome.

Helen seeks to expiate her crime by punishing herself—by rejecting her life and motherhood—causing the needless suffering of an innocent child. She is at fault because she was unconscious (unaware of life's forces) of her own instincts. To sin against nature is to earn the wrath of the transpersonal factor with which each individual must contend during the course of his existence. Sheltered in her childhood by convent existence, Helen once again withdraws from the world, its conflicts, and its exigencies—a type of suicide. Helen, like her ancient counterpart (who brought misery to Troy and Greece), became a destructive force in Nerval's story in that she refused to give her son a name that would enable him to assume a place in society.

Helen's change was too sudden; the alchemist's fire had been too extreme; the metals had been unevenly and improperly heated, their vital parts overly activated, causing alembics and retorts to split. Once the flame—the marquis—had been removed, inertia returned and all regenerative forces simmered and then vanished. Helen had withered. Because she remained uninvolved in the growth and future of her child, she stayed outside of the problem. Such a lack of engagement symbolizes a rejection of newborn forces. The union between Sol and Luna, so sought for by alchemists, had materialized. The product was real, but the relationship that brought it about remained undeveloped. For all intents and purposes, Helen was dead, burned to a crisp—vegetating in chaos that blackens.

In the second alchemical phase, dawn whitens, eighteen years have elapsed. Because the comte de Maurepas had left no heirs, the Château d'Epinay, by some strange coincidence, was bequeathed to the marquis de Fayolle's brother, the comte de Fayolle, a widower with a sixteen-year-old daughter, Gabrielle. Two priests, frequent guests of the comte de Fayolle, figure in this episode. Father Huguet, spouting liberal political and economic views, believes in equality on earth as in heaven and is accused of being a deist. Father Pechard, limited in his views, a believer in the division of classes, accepts without question the totality of church dogma. Huguet, for some strange reason, is accompanied by an eighteen-year-old lad, Georges, who, according to hearsay, was found when an infant on the church steps. As is to be expected, Georges and Gabrielle fall in love. They take their vows in secret and, as a token of her affection, Gabrielle gives Georges a ring that had belonged to her parents. Vague rumors concerning their relationship reach the priest. Huguet, dismayed over the situation, sends Georges to Rennes to study medicine; Gabrielle is urged to accept another suitor. Meanwhile, the revolutionary spirit pervading in France gains momentum. Georges, now affiliated with a militant group, is shot in the shoulder by one of Gabrielle's suitors. She faints after witnessing the scene. Her father now insists she ask for the return of the ring and for a release from her vows. Gabrielle complies and visits Georges who is recovering from his wound. Though he returns the ring, he asks her to wait two more years before retracting her promise. She accepts. When the marquis de Fayolle returns unexpectedly from America, he learns, coincidentally, of the existence of Helen's child—which could have been his. He visits her at the convent, where she has become abbess, and there she reveals the existence of a boy child but refuses to name him. The scene changes. Georges, now captain of the revolutionary guards, has been ordered to see to the evacuation of the convents; they harbored, it was claimed, royalist prisoners. Georges confronts the abbess—his unknown mother— and experiences an eruption of some strange emotions. Meanwhile, the marquis who has taken part in the royalist plot—the Chouannerie—to overthrow the Republicans has been imprisoned along with his cohorts.

The alchemist's work in this second phase may be described as a type of neutralization or balancing of chemicals and their component parts. It is a period of assessment, a return from disorder to order, darkness to light, a kind of resurrection or reshuffling of metals and chemical agents.

In psychological terminology, the immense stillness and silence—or inactivity—that comes over the individual after the preceding stormy incidents permit the energies within the unconscious to recede, thereby paving the way for broader, clearer vision: the coming of dawn and a new day.

Metaphysically, after battling with unknown forces of doubt, pain, misery, and evil, the neophyte withdraws from the terrestrial and material world into a serene frame of reference, prior to attempting his ascension into higher, purer spheres.

In this second phase the protagonists come to terms with life and intend to cope with its antagonistic forces. We learn of the existence of two children: Gabrielle and Georges; two priests, Huguet and Pechard; two brothers, the comte and the marquis de Fayolle. The dualism existing between these principles: male and female, spirit and matter, the two syzygies[8] is a potent factor preliminary to a new state of awareness on the part of the protagonist.

The name Gabriel (Gabrielle in the story) means "force of God" and was, according to Biblical tradition, the archangel who appeared to Daniel with good tidings (8:9) and to the Virgin to announce the birth of Jesus (Luke I:26). Gabrielle, whose name may be associated with her Biblical counterpart, represents the transforming feminine influence in Georges' life.

At the outset of this second section of Nerval's story, Gabrielle's personality has not yet coalesced; she is uncertain of her life's attitude and of her own essence. Such ambivalence is understandable. Deprived of a mother's love and guidance, she has been thrust into a patriarchal realm in which ideational divisions are blatant. Huguet, a father image, speaks of social equality, liberalism and a kind of deism, as opposed to Pechard (another father image), who is bigoted and spiteful. Her real father, reiterating Huguet's broad views when it is a question of abstract situations, is just as materialistic and as narrow in his ideas as Pechard is when his daughter's future is involved. Gabrielle, therefore, has no clear image of what society expects of her.

Georges, whose name may be associated with the fourth-century Christian soldier who was put to death under Diocletian's reign, is a martyr figure. He has no family that he knows about and, therefore, has never experienced the warmth of acceptance or unselfish parental love. His abandonment arouses feelings of rejection fostering timidity. On the other hand, Huguet's benevolence toward Georges and his liberal ideas, nurture within him a spirit of hope for the future. Nerval's image of Georges encompasses both sides of his own nature: active and passive.

> ... this young man's timidity disappeared little by little, his eyes shown and his traits were imbued with an expression of pride, audacity, energy, and savage passions.[9]

In Gabrielle's presence, Georges' male-oriented and patriarchal upbringing vanishes. The world of feeling, sensation, nostalgia, totally absent from his entourage, comes to the fore. Because of this, he reacts to Gabrielle intensely and completely, comparing her warmth and kindness to Jean-Jacques Rousseau's pastoral heroine, Julie.[10] The exquisite love scenes Nerval sprinkles into this section of his tale are marked with extreme depth of feeling, yet with great delicacy and reserve. We are not in the presence of an uncontrollable fiery principle, an all-consuming passion, but rather the distilled, purified, and spiritualized force of two people deeply in love. Georges' solitude, the richness of his pain, the joy he feels when in Gabrielle's presence, is expressed in the following image:

> Both kept that very tender silence which comes when a heart is filled with ineffable sentiments . . .
> The young girl smiled as angels must, when they are in love.[11]

The transformation of Gabrielle and Georges' "ideal" love into an overt relationship occurred when vows were exchanged and she gives him the ring. The ensuing conflict was caused, in reality, by the contrasting views of their elders: the difference between their abstract notions and those practiced in the everyday world.

Huguet's egalitarian, utopistic, optimistic ideas, which had been shared by the comte de Fayolle, had caused him to declare that his daughter could marry "an honest man . . . if he has an honorable position."[12] When Gabrielle and Georges hear these words, they look at each other "triumphantly." Georges' course now seems clear. He speaks up with self-assurance. "Monsieur the Count said before . . . that he would give his daughter to a man of the people. . . . And what am I, then?"[13] Father Pechard counters in negative terms: "You? My poor boy! You're not even a man of the people. . . . You're a foundling."[14]

Georges, suddenly divested of past and future, is cut to the quick. The credo of equality instilled in him since childhood has suddenly become meaningless. The application of Huguet's beautiful notions excluded present company. But the shock provokes Georges' coming to consciousness, his coping with his existential situation and the creation of his identity.

At Rennes, where Huguet had sent him to study medicine, Georges came into contact with revolutionaries, philosophers, metaphysicians. Unlike his unknown father, the marquis de Fayolle, who had been so well-versed in various occult ideologies, Georges listened, absorbed the views he heard at the cafés. Constantin-François de Chasseboeuf, comte de Volney (1757–1802) believed that classes retained certain characteristics despite intermarriages and when he looked at Georges' hands and face, he assured him of his noble lineage. It was during this period of growth, away from his immediate environment, that Georges became associated with a militant group that seemed to assuage the pain of his rejection. In effect, he was transforming a battle he had experienced on an individual level and giving it collective dimensions. The passive, timid country boy was to become the harbinger of energy, the propagator of a new life—of a new way.

Georges represents a world in transition: a fire principle that burns bridges but then builds them anew. He is not a negative force as was his father—egotistical, adventuresome, Don Juanesque, considering life merely in terms of himself and a series of exciting escapades. Now that Georges had become affiliated with a political group, he had a message; his life had taken on meaning and point. Georges was no longer a martyr, an orphan boy to be sent here and there—wallowing in despair. He had become, because of circumstances, a positive hero type, aware of what he was doing, acting consciously and fully cognizant of the possible consequences of his acts.

Heroism, whether rash or reflective, is dangerous. He knew he was risking his life daily, but fought for his credo even so. The desire to establish a new, productive social order in which he could carve out a future was uppermost in his mind.[15]

Associated with a patriarchal group—revolutionary students—Georges did not come into contact with any female company in this phase of his development. On this level, he knew he was still more deprived of the feeling principle. Therefore, when he saw Gabrielle once again, he promised himself—intellectually—not to permit his emotions to run havoc with him. At first, he was overwhelmed with joy, but then came despair. Slowly, he simmered down, finding the strength to return the ring, which represented a material translation of their relationship, but retained the vow, symbolizing the spiritual bond.

It was difficult for Georges not to be overwhelmed. A reaction was forthcoming when he was ordered to evacuate the Benedictine convent. When he saw the abbess kneeling before him, begging him to leave the nuns in their house of worship, he "felt a strange and until now unknown feeling surge up within him."[16] It was as if some primitive transpersonal, instinctive force had entered his life; some contents within his psyche, dormant until now, had suddenly erupted into his conscious life and altered the chemistry of his body. When Father Pechard, present at the scene, informed him that the abbess was his mother, Georges could not undertand how his feelings could have informed him of something about which his mind was still unaware.[17] He expected some sign of recognition from his mother as she left the convent, but none was forthcoming. Troubled as she was, she was abandoning him for a second time.

Georges came through his difficult situation. Now that he had a definite goal—the pursuit of revolution—the strength of his ideations helped him pursue daily tasks and relate to his companions and to himself, at least on a functional level.

Gabrielle also went through a transformative process, an illumination so to speak, or a dawning of consciousness. After the marquis de Fayolle returned from America he gave a ball to celebrate the event. Gabrielle was invited and, in Nerval's words, "a young girl at a ball is like an angel thrust in the Philistine camp."[18] She attracted young men to her orbit and the beautiful gowns, the excitement, the compliments, the lights and the dancing aroused agitation within her—the birth of a host of fresh emotions.

> The brilliance of the candles illuminated them in terms of certain unknown things; ensconced now in their high collared dresses, they are growing jealous of the young ladies who lay bare their throats; . . . they study each other, ways of tightening their corsets about their waists, of bending, standing, walking, talking on graceful and teasible poses; the heat of the ball mollifies their soul, their innocence vanishes; their dis-

quieted imagination wanders off in their search for an unknown realm.
New sensations which they cannot understand, make them shiver, and
strange dreams torment their solitary beds.[19]

This picture indicates Gabrielle's withdrawal from the adolescent
stage and her entrance into the active phase of life. Her world would
now include conflict and entanglements with which she would have to
learn to cope. She would no longer remain a passive repository for
emotion. She wanted to participate in the drama of life. But to be initiated into womanhood requires certain *rites de passage,* a series of tests
or initiations to be successfully completed.

Gabrielle's first test occurred when Georges was wounded by her
suitor, the young man her father had destined for her. When Georges
fell to the ground, Gabrielle, watching from a balcony, fainted; she was
unable to come to terms with the reality of her situation. Her workaday
world was blotted out. This momentary eclipse of consciousness drove
inward the psychic energy used in her rapport with external events, giving her unconscious time to rearrange and deal with the onslaught of
emotions. The possibility of life without Georges—a life without simplicity, tenderness, and sincerity—was not acceptable to Gabrielle; nor
was a world to be shared with a husband her father had chosen for her,
a man who stood for wealth, position, and sophistication.

The second test occurred when Gabrielle's father and Pechard prevailed upon her to seek the return of the ring and the vow. At first,
upon seeing Georges, she was in control of the situation. But when he
revived segments of their young love, stirring primitive emotions within
her, the past erupted and Gabrielle was filled with nostalgia for what
had been. Aglow with sentiment, she yielded to Georges' request that
they keep their vow for two more years.

During this scene, Georges saw Gabrielle in a new light. No longer
was she simply the naïve, demure, beautiful country girl. She took on
woman's positive and negative aspects. He had previously seen her only
in an idyllic way, as a kind of Virgin Mary, as a totally spiritual force in
his life. Now that she had come to ask for his love to be returned, she
became Eve-like—hurtful to him, a reincarnation to some extent of Ishtar and Venus.

> I could have loved the timid young girl, the angel about whom I dreamed;
> but I have nothing but disdain now for the woman who so coldly leaned
> on the balcony while men were being killed.[20]

The consciousness of the dangers involved protected Georges from sub-
mitting completely to her demands. His mind compelled him to redress
the balance; his emotions suffused him with the energy to give back the
ring but not the vow.

The marquis de Fayolle's return to France indicated his attempt to confront his situation, to right a wrong. In alchemical terms he was ordering or stabilizing his metals or chemical concoctions. His desire to transform his immature, unstable, and irresponsible youthful ways not only indicated his ability to cope with life, but to redirect it, indicating both psychological and spiritual growth.

The marquis attempted to repair the damages he had incurred by visiting Helen. Though she revealed the existence of a boy child, he could not compel her to tell him his name. When she spoke to him, her attitude was, in Nerval's words, "glacial" and "coldness" marked all of her features; she had taken on the insensibility of a statue." Yet beneath her masklike glare, one saw traces of excruciating suffering—part of a dormant past.[21]

Helen was "dead." No amount of "fire" could ever warm her again. She was the product of a decadent spiritual and political society, neither developing with the time nor willing even to partake of it. She stood for stagnation, regression, and unproductive sacrifice. It is no wonder that Nerval's image of her took on the bleak colors of death: "She was a phantom who slid, noiselessly, on the black and white diamond-shaped cloister floor."[22]

The marquis de Fayolle, Georges, and Gabrielle, all evolved in this second phase of Nerval's tale. The marquis attempted to redress an unbalanced situation, to give both name and fortune to the son he had so "unconsciously" abandoned. Georges sought to change the status quo, thereby earning a place for himself in society and expressing his love to Gabrielle. As for Gabrielle, she passed her first two tests. They did not disorient her; she was capable of assessing her feelings, her position, of expressing the warmth she felt for Georges and, at the same time, in a spirit of compromise, of accepting the society for which her father stood.

Gabrielle's father asks her to use her influence with Georges so that the marquis and his group may be released. Georges and Gabrielle meet again: reminiscences are exchanged, emotions are revived, but no conclusion is forthcoming. Nerval's story ends here.

During this last alchemical phase, the resplendent flame purifies (red or *rubedo*), and coloration, distillation, purification takes place. The inferior or base metals have undergone new blendings, making for a better melange and the creation, therefore, of more perfect and noble materials. According to the great Paracelsus it was during the *rubedo* phase that the philosopher's stone emerged: an entity capable of all things, of healing the sick, of transforming negative into positive faculties, unifying what was divided, relating man to God.[23]

Psychologically, the immature man has been transformed by experience; by passing rigorous and frequently painful tests and initiations, he approaches the creation of an observant and understanding being. Acquainted with the laws of life, with the position he occupies in nature and in society, he has gained insight into the world at large and is able, therefore, to function on both an individual and on a collective level.

Metaphysically man at this juncture does not look upon his fall into matter or the traumas resulting from guilt as a paralyzing force. Because of his toil, pain, agony and also the joys of involvement, he has earned redemption and regeneration. He has experienced, in this respect, the quintessence of worldly and spiritual existence.

Three years have passed since the marquis returned from America and tried unsuccessfully to discover his son's identity. He has not only met personal failure but was also imprisoned for his antirepublican activities, his associations with the Chouannerie. The fact that his brother and Gabrielle have been called upon to see to his release is an indication that he was still a positive force in Nerval's narrative.

> Seeing Gabrielle again, he had promised himself not to lend an ear to her sweet words . . . to close his soul entirely to an impassive love, and there he was, suddenly, after listening to some words of magic, the evocation of some childhood souvenirs, touched and in a state of agitation.[24]

Georges knows, however, and perhaps this accounts for the stability of his present ways and reactions—the fact that he has a mission in life; he is no longer an individual acting for himself alone, but *un homme engagé* who represents a new order. He understands the full impact of Gabrielle's words when she states her "grave and important" mission, which could bring both "happiness and misfortune" to their lives. Gabrielle, in this instance, has also taken her individual problem out of context, and has rephrased it on a transpersonal level. World-shaking events are at issue: "blood" may come between them, she declares, "bloodshed."

Blood represents for the alchemist the culmination of his efforts. Like fire, blood indicated passions, a life-giving force without which earthly existence could not continue. Blood also had numinous qualities. In ancient times animal and human sacrifices were made to the gods to earn redemption or health, and to appease their anger. Today, it is used symbolically in communion services for similar reasons. Psychologically, blood is an automonous and powerful force that, if used in a primitive way (that is, unconsciously or unchanneled) may have severe repercussions. Undirected, such a powerful force could destroy a person's orientation and rapport with the outside world as well as with his inner realm. Used productively it serves to enrich the conscious personality, bringing new ideations and fresh emotions to light.

Nerval ends his narrative at this important point, unable to unravel the various integuments at stake. We do not know whether blood will be used by Georges and Gabrielle as an instrument of salvation or destruction. Nerval's narrative ends as Georges "looked at her fixedly, trying to read the depth of her thoughts."[25] Like his protagonists, Nerval also attempted to reach into his depths, to increase his awareness, to enrich his conscious existence by means of an inward march *ab extra ad intra*.

Nerval was unable to finish *The Marquis de Fayolle*. He could not resolve, either psychologically or spiritually, the entangled mass that functioned almost autonomously in his subliminal world. Archetypical images of all sorts encroached upon his consciousness during the months to come. Frequently, Nerval did not know whether he was living a real situation or whether his fantasies were running wild. Still tormented by the visions of Jenny Colon, he came more and more to believe that she returned to him in the form of spirits and that she could hear what he said. One day, according to Eugène de Mirecourt, one of his friends, some person had begun talking about Jenny. "Be silent," Nerval interrupted. "She's dead; and I am convinced that the souls of the dead are around us and listen to us."[26]

Spiritually, he was confused. A student of many religions, he tried in vain to discover one that would satisfy his needs, one that would offer him the peace and calm he so longed for. It was to no avail. There were too many points of view, none of which could fill the void in his life.

Hope was rekindled when *The Montenegrins* opened at the Opéra-Comique on March 31, 1849. It closed shortly thereafter, however, the critics having been almost unanimous in their condemnation of it. The plot was uninteresting and far from original; the music composed by Limnander was prosaic, banal, and utterly "mediocre."[27]

It is strange how little perception Nerval displayed in assessing his literary abilities. In the short story, few could surpass his gift for delineating character, for creating subtle and intriguing plots, for increasing suspense in a subdued manner, for depicting visually human emotions and ideations. In the drama, however, his plot lines were awkward and far too complicated, and his presentation was prosaic.

Just as Nerval was frequently unable to understand where his talents really lay, so he could not comprehend the failure of his last theatrical endeavor. It dealt him another powerful blow. For days and weeks during the months of April and May 1849, Nerval felt debilitated, as if nothing were worth salvaging from this world, as if life itself had ceased to have meaning. At the instigation of his friends, he consulted Dr. Ley, whose office was conveniently located near the Champs-Elysées, and also a friend of Gautier's and his, Dr. Amédé Aussandon.

Nerval's latest nervous crisis lasted only about a month. With more theatrical failures in the offing, his depression worsened. His play *The Child's Chariot* opened on May 13, 1850 at the Odéon—and ran for just seventeen performances.[28] *The Printmaker of Haarlem* based on the life of Laurent Coster (1370–1440), the inventor of movable type before

Gutenberg, opened on December 11, 1851, at the Porte Saint-Martin, and it was also not well received. Jules Janin called it "an awkward imitation" of "Shakespearian form."[29]

Three days before the opening, as if Fate had willed it, Nerval fell down some stairs. His knee was twisted out of shape and his chest struck against a sharp corner. The following day, he developed a bluish looking tumorlike growth on his chest. He took his accident seriously—as an ill-omen. His physical condition worsened, and early in January, 1852, his doctors diagnosed his ailment as erysipelas. His discomfort was great; his fever ran high and the pain was almost continuous. But Nerval did not lack friends. Eugène de Stadler, the young playwright whom Nerval had helped a few years back, nursed him almost continuously through the difficult days to come. The photographer Nadar, another friend, who had taken such a stunning photo of Nerval, came to relieve Stadler of his burden every now and then. The doctors advised hospitalization. The recuperation was slow.

15   THE ILLUMINISTS

*Clearly we must go back into the history of the
idea of our being—and thus into the realm
of the unconscious being—if we want to find the
primary cause for our individuality.*
                    C. G. Carus, *Psyche.*

Nerval became progressively engrossed in matters he considered to be
of eternal value—the mystical and metaphysical notions connected with
man's earthly and celestial evolution. Nerval was a holist; he believed
that everything in the cosmos was related to everything else and participated in a total cosmic drama. He experienced the particular in terms
of the general, which accounted in part for the impact certain myths
made upon him.

Myths divest man of his ephemerality. They permit a person to look
upon himself as part of a continuous process and give him a sense of
eternity.[1] Myths integrate past into present, allowing one to participate
in the whole, in the universal flow of things, and thus lose one's particular or individual status.

The myth enabled Nerval to create a bridge between himself and the
world about him; through the myth he avoided the abyss that saved him
moments of such dread isolation. It is understandable that he would
respond potently to myths concerning heroes with whom he could identify, whose lot—in general or symbolic terms—could mirror his own.
Cain, Tubal-Cain, Adoniram were all artist-creators who suffered and
had been rejected by society—even by God; the had known a similar
fate, the excoriating void implicit in the pariah's psyche. Nerval also had
his Faustian side, which filled him with an intense desire to investigate
the infinite realms and to discover nature's secrets so as to be able to
master her.

Man has always sought to expand his knowledge, to discern what was
hidden, to extract what was amorphous, to create what existed before
only *in potentia*. In the nineteenth century an increasing interest in the
psyche's participation in the universal mystery was felt not only by poets
but also by scientists and medical men. C.G. Carus, the Dresden-born
court physician to the king of Saxony, held that the human psyche was
comparable to "a great, continuously circling river which is illuminated
only in one small area by the light of the sun."[2] He divided the psyche
into three distinct parts, each related to and working upon the others.
The conscious (or rational) function can comprehend only the limited
and temporal realm. The unconscious is divided into the relative (individual) unconscious and the absolute (collective) unconscious.[3] Whereas

the relative unconscious may become or has been conscious at one time and belongs to the individual (personal) and is subjectively experienced, the absolute (or collective) unconscious remains "inaccessible to the light of consciousness" except when it reveals itself in flashes of intuition or dreams; it is a limitless, atemporal realm. As such, it is a "reservoir of our energies" and thus constitutes humanity's past. It lives eternally within the individual and by manifesting itself in his present actions and thoughts plays a part in his future. "The key to an understanding of the nature of the conscious life of the soul lies in the sphere of the unconscious."[4] Because the conscious is connected to both the absolute unconscious and the relative unconscious, each is dependent upon the other and affects the other through the individual's actions vis-à-vis himself and society at large. According to Carus,

> we must realize that our unconscious life is affected by all humanity by the life of the earth and by the universe, for it is definitely an integral part of this totality. The number of ways the unconscious is affected is infinite. The movement of the planets, other than the sun and the moon, affect our inner sentience, but to such a small degree that we may compare it to the earth's attraction to a falling stone. . . . Changes in the atmosphere and in our planet's electric and magnetic currents, however, affect our unconscious life as deeply as do changes in the lives of human beings who are much closer to us. Indeed, the correlations in this sphere are most essential. At first, they are all unconscious, although under certain conditions there may be communication from this dark realm to consciousness. Presentiments in dreams, empathy with the events on the earth and in the heavens or in the fate of men, the astonishing magnetic rapport between distant persons, and other riddles whose solution normal psychology cannot provide may be fully explained only by these observations.[5]

The unconscious, then, is forever being tapped by the conscious and is thereby brought into cognition. Plato referred to the act of "cognition" as "remembrance" and defined it as a "finding within," that is, a going back to the absolute world of the unconscious.[6]

Nerval had gone to the Middle East in response to some inner urge, some compulsive desire to revive feelings that had lain dormant within him. He had felt a need to understand and to write about the world of the Illuminists, those eighteenth-century visionaries who claimed to have seen "the light." What secrets or mysteries had Dom Pernety, Martinès de Pasqually, Claude de Saint-Martin, Restif de la Bretonne, Cazotte, the Abbé Bucquoy, Cagliostro discovered? What had their entry into arcane areas signified? Were their flights into outer-realms—even heavenly spheres—a sign of madness? Or had such journeys brought them in touch with a profounder reality? Were coincidences, precognitive dreams, the world of magic and metempsychosis the outcome of an acausal factor in the universe?[7]

The founding father of illuminism was a Benedictine monk, Dom Pernety, who claimed to have been inspired by God, whose word he had heard in 1784. God had ordered him to found a secret society which would teach man how to ascend the ladder from material to spiritual life.

Dom Pernety's ideas were based for the most part on those of Emmanuel Swedenborg. For Swedenborg the invisible world was merely an extension of the visible domain. Interplanetary space, therefore, was peopled with angels who lived in a variety of spheres, according to their degree of perfection; the soul was eternal and reincarnated. Swedenborg had discovered secret correspondences between himself and the universe at large that enabled him to come into contact with divine spirits and to record his conversations with angels—his revelation of God.

The theosophist Martinès de Pasqually, who was also an Illuminist who had been influenced by Swedenborg, founded the Masonic Lodge of Montpellier in 1754. His *Treatise of the Reintegration of Beings into Their First Properties, Spiritual and Divine Powers and Virtues* taught man how to expiate the crime of Original Sin. Prior to his separation from God, resulting from Adam's and Eve's evil ways, man was devoid of arrogance and corruption. Because of the schism between himself and God, man revealed his desire for infinite knowledge, his intention to become a Creator, a Demiurge—God's rival. But despite man's evil ways, Pasqually affirmed that all was not lost. Man's salvation was a possibility because of God's infinite goodness. To contact cosmic forces and, in so doing, God and the dead who now inhabit other regions, man must go through a rigorous initiatory period. The neophyte must learn to overcome temptation, take an oath of secrecy, learn certain magic formulae and secret words, and prostrate himself on the ground. Only then can he recover his essential dignity and so increase his spiritual knowledge. Some members of Pasqually's sect experienced union with Christ, a reintegration in Him, and thus became part of what Pasqually called an "elect" group.

Claude de Saint-Martin, Pasqually's disciple, felt that his master had been overly immersed with theurgy and not sufficiently involved with deity. In *The Unknown Philosopher,* Saint-Martin stressed a return to Biblical texts, to the Gospels, to the Book of Revelation in particular. The neophyte, he suggested, must build himself up—must construct *himself* as Solomon's Temple had been built: from individual pieces of stone to the completed monument. Only then could inner growth, unification, and illumination occur. Such a building process could be accomplished through self-discipline, a tension of the will: one had to break carnal and terrestrial bonds, thereby strengthening the inner man. Initiations based on individual tests (including those associated with the four elements) followed and could lead to rebirth. Saint-Martin quoted from the Gospel of St. John: "Jesus answered, and said unto him, Verily, verily,

I say unto thee, Except a man be born again, he cannot see the kingdom of God" (3:3).

Man's innate desire to evolve, to grow, to ascend into higher realms was manifested in both the physical and spiritual world as attested to in the story of the Abbé Bucquoy, which Nerval included in *The Illuminists*. Jean-Albert d'Archambaud (1660–1740), known as the Abbé Bucquoy, had been falsely accused of certain crimes that he had not committed but had, for some unknown reason, witnessed. On circumstantial evidence, he had been found guilty of theft on many occasions and was forever being incarcerated in prisons throughout France, from the Conciergerie to the Bastille. Each time, however, he succeeded—in some spectacular, even miraculous, manner—in freeing himself—even from the Bastille, from which no one had ever escaped. When not in jail he roamed through France, adhering to a variety of philosophical and ideological groups. For a while he joined the austere Trappist order. Then he decided to preach the teachings of St. Paul. He founded a seminary in Rouen that he called "The Dead." He joined the Jesuits. He was imprisoned again, escaped, fled to Switzerland, Holland, and perhaps even to Germany.[8]

The Abbé Bucquoy's spiritual views intrigued Nerval. As the author of *Anti-Machiavelism, Metaphysical Reflections on General Authority, Arbitrary Power in Particular,* the abbé decried the extreme monarchy existing in France and argued for a more liberal monarchy to be headed by a "wise" man able to lead people to greater understanding of themselves and the beauties and joys inherent in life. Perhaps even more alluring than Bucquoy's political notion were the symbolical ramifications of his escapes from prison.

The abbé's escapes could be looked upon as miracles, as feats of magic, as examples of the transformatory element within the universe itself. Like the neophyte, he seemed to be preparing for an initiatory ritual and succeeded each time in liberating himself from whatever enchained him, whether physically or ideologically. His mind and his body were alike permitted to roam the world and the universe. Society, with its limited and simplistic attitude toward life and death, was forever enchaining the creative individuals who, like the prisoners in Plato's "Allegory of the Cave," were unaware of their predicament.

The abbé's feats transcended rational explanation; they verged on the occult and had analogies with a situation that arose much later in Warsaw in 1939. At that time the mystic Wolf Messing had been put in jail for having predicted (among other things) Hitler's death, and he wrote the following statement describing his "miraculous" escape from prison.

"At the police station I realized either I leave Poland instantly, or I die," says Messing. Using all his phenomenal powers of mind, he says he compelled all the police who were in the station at that moment to assemble in one room. All, including the chief and the sentry guarding the exit, began to feel a strange urge to go to that particular room in the station. "When, responding to my will, the police had all gathered in that room, I lay entirely motionless, as if dead. Then, quickly, I ran into the corridor. Instantly, before they could come to, I slid the iron bolt on the door. Now I had to hurry."[9]

Methods of escape, whether on a physical or spiritual level, always struck a responsive chord with Nerval, who was himself so victimized and imprisoned by his own emotional turmoil. How did the Abbé Bucquoy accomplish his feats? Nerval gives us no answer. He was still searching, trying to uncover some way to solve the mystery of freedom.

Of even greater interest to Nerval were the life and works of the eighteenth-century theosophist, sensualist, and pantheist Restif de la Bretonne.[10] Restif (1734–1806), one of the most paradoxical figures to emerge from the so-called Age of Enlightenment, baffles scholars and psychologists alike, who have attempted to unravel the imbroglio that was his life. Brought up in a household in which morality, virtue, and edifying lectures were *de rigueur,* in an environment that caused two of his brothers to become "fanatical" priests, Restif rejected the notion of sin (which he felt was destructive) and founded a "religion of voluptuousness." Because of his erotic ways, he was labeled (with tongue in cheek) "the Rousseau des ruisseaux" and the "Voltaire of the chamber maids."[11]

As have other mystics, Restif believed in a monistic cosmos. All things were, for him, interconnected, and all people were fundamentally alike. The deeper one delved into one's own soul, the greater was one's understanding of humanity, of God who was present in all individuals. "I judge God through me. To study Him, I study myself, and I reach Him through analogies." The sun was the generative and divine principle in the universe that created the earth, all other planets, and the galaxies; it was the center of everything, "embracing all, animating all, absorbing all, reproducing all and giving each thing the intelligence suited to it, whether one calls this instinct or reason!"[12] The sun was not distant, but something with which he was personally involved, with whom he could talk: "Unique being, how much I love you."[13] Restif believed in reincarnation and that the earth would be reabsorbed into the sun, itself part of a Sovereign Principle—God—another world would be created; man, therefore, would again be born, live, die, and be re-created ad infinitum. In this re-creation process, however, man would conserve his identity or his own soul even after a dissolution of his physical being took place, because his soul was indestructible. When, therefore, the soul returned to God, and was absorbed into Him and was re-created by Him, it would retain its individual general traits and feelings.

Whereas the Illuminists and Theosophists spiritualized Divinity, Restif materialized God, defining Him in terms of man. God, Restif stated categorically, is the "source of all intelligence and all matter"; He excretes these entities by means of a type of "crystallization" or "densification" of His own "essentially activo-volatile" substance. Restif endowed God with man's anatomy: "The Sun is that Great Animal's Mind, the Moons are his testicles; in the planets repose his intestines. . . . The tail of the comets is the Great Animal's urine. Now, God calls for the comet as frequently as he has to piss; he pisses at irrevocably fixed times."[14] Because life's goal, according to Restif, "is the production and conservation of life," and because life could be maintained only through copulation—each being bears part of divinity with him—physical union must be looked upon as an expression of godliness: a union between man and God.[15] God created his solar world in the same way that man brings forth his progeny. Religious rituals must therefore be planned for the worship of God in a satisfactory manner: on a mountain summit where the sun and the earth—the sacred parents of all beings—may be worshipped.[16]

What earned Nerval's deepest sympathy was Restif's theory of resemblances. Man falls in love with only one woman in a lifetime, Restif believed; all the others he meets or with whom he has liaisons are merely avatars of the first. It is understandable that Nerval should share such a view: he still constantly worshipped Jenny Colon in the guise of Isis, Astarte, the Virgin Mary, and other feminine archetypes. "Love alone occupied his thoughts," Nerval wrote of Restif, but whereas Restif was most preoccupied with the sensual side of his relationship with women and created a philosophical credo that would justify his acts, Nerval centered his thoughts on the spirit.

Nerval identified with Restif's innumerable disappointments in love, his high hopes, his despair when these were not realized. When Restif's passion for an actress was not reciprocated, Nerval sympathized only too keenly with his feelings: the hypocrisy of women who are always in the process of acting in "the false light of stage illumination." Nerval analyzed the sentiments and characters of the man he considered in this respect to be his mirror image: "Nothing is more dangerous for those who are naturally inclined to dream than a serious love for a person connected with the theater; it is a perpetual love, the dream of a sick person, the illusion of a madman. Life attaches itself completely to an unrealizable chimera, which one would be happy to preserve in its state as a desire and aspiration, but which vanishes as soon as one wants to touch the idol."[17]

Illusions, dreams, fantasies? What were they? Where did such phenomena come from? Why was it that by admiring a woman from afar, one saw only the mystery, the magic, the "celestial beauty," while the moment one approached this vision her many faults became obvious, intruded upon the perfection, and compelled the rapprochement, the idealization to vanish? Why was it that Restif saw the same woman in all those he loved? "She resembled you, she had many of your features, your smile, and nothing can console me from such a loss except to be able to admire you."[18]

What was love? Why was one forever disappointed when involved in such emotional ties. Before forty, unrequited love is bearable, Nerval wrote; after that age it causes excruciating suffering. "Each pain in the present awakens the pains of the past; the man who has reached full development, suffers doubly from these affections and from his outraged dignity."[19] And Gérard de Nerval was one to know: he was forty-six years of age. For Nerval, love could only be negative, a vicious circle. Each time a passion is declared, it is doomed; illusion can never be equated with the flesh-and-blood woman; the torment of disappointment ensues and awakens all past love experiences and their implicit sadness. Such love, based on experiences already known, could never lead to fulfillment.[20]

The most exquisite sections of Nerval's essay on Restif deal with the love episodes drawn in eighteenth-century Watteau-colors, with the delicacy of miniatures. The women he delineates are like paintings— ethereal, delicate, with velvety skin tones, nuances ranging from pinks to mauves; gentle contours, smiling countenances; slim bodies that joyously frolic about in enchanting country scenes: ". . . a fleeting vision, like a dream, and that I didn't even think of ever realizing for one of those impossibilities that I pursued my entire life."[21]

Nerval and Restif had other characteristics in common:[22] both were introspective, both were philosophers and theoreticians: and the word "theory" (from the Greek *theatai,* implying "behold, see") indicates an outlook on life that lacks involvement. Nerval and Restif were people who observed, analyzed, but who did not partake in the world: "We do not live! we analyze life! The other creatures are our eternal toys."[23]

The dream factor and what is now called "extrasensory perception" accounted for Nerval's interest in the Illuminist Jacques Cazotte, who had been Nodier's friend and had influenced Gautier, Balzac, and countless others.

"All this appears to me in a dream," Cazotte said when talking about the secret rituals he had described in his novel *The Devil in Love,* "but is human life more than this? I dream in a more extraordinary manner than another, and that's all."[24] Prophetic dreams and clairvoyance are not unknown to the artist or the poet: in Latin, another word for poet is *vates,* meaning visionary or prophet. In ancient times the creative artist was the seer, a being who observed life beyond the world of appearances, who saw its eternal aspects and who could, therefore, envision it as a unit, not merely in its ephemeral or differentiated phases.

Cazotte not only believed in precognitive dreams but in living spirits with whom he could communicate whenever he so desired. When spirits made their presences known to him at various times, they stirred his thoughts into certain channels. Just as bodily motion destroys the "column of air . . . we support," so everything in the universe is alive and moves and is transformed into something else with each breath or thought-wave. The void, Cazotte maintained, does not exist. He even distinguished between the opacity of certain souls. Those who want to remain earth-bound retain a type of thickness and resemble the living being for a long time. Others, who want to withdraw into the heavenly realms, become more and more transparent.[25]

What Cazotte sensed (and what physicists have since proven) is the fact that all living things (plants, animals, humans) possess a type of "energy matrix," that is, they are endowed both with a physical body (atoms, molecules) and with another corpus, made up of energy and referred to as "The Biological Plasma Body." (In physics, plasma is considered "the fourth state of matter—streams of masses of ionized particles.")[26]

Cazotte, more sensitive and introverted than most people, might have felt the flow of this energy, or the pulsating of the magnetic fields of which the atmosphere is replete; he might have entered into another time dimension in which past, present, and future no longer exist as separate entities.[27]

With age, Cazotte became more and more immersed in his visions[28] and made it a practice to predict the day's happenings every morning though these might have taken place five-hundred leagues away. He also talked frequently with dead friends and relatives and spent long hours trying to rid the world of what he called its Evil ways, by confronting and fighting the Satanic soul, demons and elementary spirits that hovered about in the air.[29]

One evening in 1778, Cazotte was at a dinner party and prophesied that Condorcet would take poison, that Chamfort would commit suicide by cutting his veins with a razor, that Louis XVI would be guillotined and that thousands would die in a similar manner, and that women as well as men would be brought to their death in open carts. As for himself, in a long poem entitled *Olivier* he had described his end thirty years before the French Revolution: "I saw my head lined up on the tiers, next to eight hundred other heads of both sexes, of all ages and colors."[30] The predictions all came true. Cazotte was guillotined after a trial that lasted twenty-seven hours. When the time came for his end, he stared at his prosecutor, his eyes never expressing a trace of anxiety or of concern; he spoke gently and firmly to both his wife and daughter, then looked toward heaven, lowered his eyes to express his thanks to the people who had imposed this death sentence upon him, and then shouted to the multitude: "I die as I have lived, faithful to my God and to my King."[31]

Prophetic dreams, coincidences, mantic procedures have usually been relegated to the domain of superstition, ignorance, nonsense, or magic. Albertus Magnus, the great medieval magician, felt that coincidences and supernatural happenings, which he described in his *Mirabilis Mundi*, belonged to the kingdom of miracles and were an attempt by man to capture outer forces in order to understand and cope with them. The Bible, the Koran, the *Book of the Dead*, the *I Ching* also include atemporal happenings and present them as manifestations of Divinity. Goethe, attempting to pin a scientific label on supernatural happenings, declared in his *Conversations with Eckermann*, "we all have certain electric and magnetic powers within us and ourselves exercise an attractive and repelling force, according as we come in touch with something like or unlike."[32]

Mesmerism and magic also entered into Nerval's field of interest and so he included, in *The Illuminists*, Peter Balsamo (1743–1795), otherwise known as Cagliostro.[33]

Cagliostro has been called charlatan, hypnotist, magician, alchemist, intriguer, blackguard. He held an entire generation enthralled, from Queen Marie Antoinette to the humblest peasant of Lombardy. The son of a bankrupt Italian merchant, Balsamo's childhood consisted of a series of adventures: running away from a seminary, playing in the back streets of Palermo, working as an apothecary, traveling to the Middle East with Althotas—a magician able to "dematerialize himself," a theosophist who had discovered the secrets of the Egyptian pyramids; a medium who had already visited paradise and communicated with the dead; a visionary able to predict the future. After Althotas' death, Cagliostro wandered through Portugal, London, Germany, Italy, France, and Russia, displaying his talents wherever he went: turning hemp into silk, enlarging small diamonds, transforming base metals into gold, curing the sick. To attract the devout, he founded his own "Egyptian Order of Freemasonry" and stated that only those initiated into his sect could communicate with Deity. He set down special rules for the neophytes: they must retire to the country in the middle of May for thirty-three days, they must pray for three hours a day, and they must take five drops of primitive matter on the seventeenth day. Cagliostro had learned crystallomancy in Egypt and made particular use of this art both in France and England, gathering children to practice this new method of sorcery or science. He asked the children to look into a pitcher of water or into sand crystals or ink spots and to reveal the visions that emerged. He also mixed magical herbs and prepared the much-wanted elixir of life.[34]

At times, when Cagliostro's knowledge of the supernatural seemed to him to be inadequate, he consulted the greatest "visionary" or "miracle worker" or "charlatan" of them all, Count Saint-Germain. The count told his followers that he was two thousand years old, that he never ate, that he had known the Queen of Sheba, Christ, and many other illustrious figures. It was said that he spoke almost all languages. When he received Cagliostro in a room called the "Storehouse of Wandering Souls," he was dressed like a Madonna and sat on an altar. While incense burned, his followers, sitting on either side of him, welcomed Cagliostro. Then the count—so the legend goes—imparted occult knowledge to Cagliostro: regeneration, purification of the soul and the body, rituals that permitted communication with Deity and the ability to know perpetual youth.[35]

Quintus Aucler also figures in *The Illuminists* owing to his interest in the mysteries of antiquity, particularly those practiced in Samothrace. An adherent of the Pythagorean system, and to Martinès de Pasqually's doctrine, Quintus Aucler was convinced of the fundamental unity of all things, that the earth was an inferior presentation of celestial sphere, and that a universal being who transcended all things guided man along his course. Unlike other Illuminists, but in common with Restif de la Bretonne, he rejected Christianity as well as all existing religions, believing them to be repressive, constricting, and dogmatic forces that kept man from fulfilling his destiny. Christianity did not take into consideration what Pythagoras had called the "intelligent" planetary bodies that so deeply affected man's course in life. Nor did it accept the "natural" way of life implicit in ancient beliefs—the positive attributes of the "animal" in man.[36] Ancient religions and the ancient mysteries, which Aucler described in his *Threicie*, permitted man to understand himself and therefore others—and in so doing, Divinity.

What did all of these metaphysical philosophers have in common? For the Illuminists included in Nerval's volume, there was little difference between the material or realistic world and the nonmaterial or atemporal. They could hop through centuries, wander into outer space, commune with souls, demons, cover spatial areas, transcend the differentiated world. What did such an ability mean for the psyche? Did the powers given them, in precognitive dreams or predictions of events as in Cazotte's case, imply that the psychic function exists outside the "spatio-temporal law of causality?"[37]

Ever since Newton established his theory of causality man has been led to believe that everything within the universe has a causal explanation. If Newton's law was valid, then it might be postulated that chance itself could be the result of a causality that had not yet come into existence. Then how could one know about something that had not yet taken place? How could one explain telepathy? Coincidences? Synchronicity? Swedenborg's vision of Stockholm burning at the very instant that the fire was raging did not take spatial distances into account; his vision and the event occurred simultaneously.[38]

Causality is a philosophical principle that came into existence as a result of natural law. Modern physicists, whose conclusions are based upon statistical truths, consider the causal principle to be relative to other factors that are unfamiliar to man. An acausal event is virtually impossible to imagine. Since it is unthinkable to believe in anything that is not based on what we already know, we must conclude that acausal events do not appear in nature. Though the world of chance (or coincidence, precognitive dreams, telepathy) may seem frequently to be causally connected, in reality they are not: you buy a theater ticket with the same number as your house number or your telephone number, or you dream of receiving a letter and it arrives the following day. Coincidences sometimes run in series: the cycles of the gambler, his good and bad days. Albert Einstein, impressed with Paul Kammerer's experiments along these lines (described in *Das Gesetz der Serie*), found himself unable to relegate synchronistic events to the realm of superstition or magic.[39]

Telepathy and precognitive dreams cannot be explained by the time-and-space factor since each breaches distances. The psyche travels in a "variable space-time concept" or in another dimension governed by laws and an order foreign to us. One may posit the belief that acausal phenomena (as in ESP) is an energy relationship.[40] But if the event has not yet occurred, how can energy apply? Man's rational space-time concept is an abstract intellectual notion, a hypothesis, as is his belief in causality.[41] The psyche functions in another dimension and according to laws of its own. Certain "patterns of behavior" may be deduced or "archetypal patterns" from the psyche's, each giving off effects or a "specific charge,"[42] but they cannot yet be explained. When someone dreams or experiences certain coincidences (synchronistic events), emotional aftermaths occur. One is affected by certain "unconscious instinctual impulses and contents"; when the unconscious flows into consciousness it brings certain subliminal intuitions or perceptions ("forgotten memory—images"). The images that emerge may be acausal. That is, the person experiencing them cannot think of any connection between what happened in reality and the occurrence in the dream. The images that came into consciousness seem to have no rational or causal relationship with the objective situation the person has just experienced—at least, not so far as he knows.[43]

According to Carl Jung, some mantic or prophetic processes may be explained in terms of emotions. By arousing someone's fears, hopes, or interests one stimulates some content within the unconscious that manifests itself in one or more archetypal dream motifs. Perhaps, such was the case with Cazotte's precognitive dreams. The archetypal images that come to him and that he either transferred into poetical images in his writings or expressed vocally to his friends throughout his life emerged from his collective unconscious (an atemporal frame of reference). Many archetypal dreams nourished in the collective unconscious, include a collective past and present, implying an abolition of what rational man alludes to as time and space. Jung describes such happenings in the following manner:

> The deeper "layers" of the psyche lose their individual uniqueness as they retreat farther and farther into darkness, "lower down" that is to say as they approach the autonomous functional systems, they become increasingly collective until they are universalized and extinguished in the body's materiality, i.e. in chemical substance. The body's carbon is simply carbon. Hence "at bottom" the psyche is simply "world."[44]

This "bottom" level lives within each of us. By tapping such resources, lowering the threshold of consciousness (which comes automatically with *un abissement du niveau mental*) a person may experience the effects that open the door to "absolute knowledge." As far as one knows, no mechanistic laws exist that relate causal to acausal processes. An acausal phenomenon is "the precondition of law, the chance substrata on which law is based."[45]

How else except through the acausal factor theory, which permits the unconscious to exist and live beyond the physical space-time delineations, can one explain Cazotte's vision of his own death, the fact that he saw his own head cut off thirty years before the event; that he described the death of others as they also occurred after the vision? How else can one explain the Abbé Bucquoy's miraculous escapes? Restif de la Bretonne's theory of resemblances? Cagliostro's feats of magic? Jung writes:

> the meaningful coincidence or equivalence of a psychic and physical state or event which have no causal relationship to one another. Such synchronistic phenomena occur, for instance, when an inwardly perceived event (dream, vision, premonition, etc.) is seen to have correspondence in external reality: the inner image of premonition has "come true" similar or identical thoughts, dreams, etc. occurring at the same time in different places. Neither the one nor the other coincidence can be explained by causality, but seems to be connected primarily with activated archetypal processes in the unconscious.[46]

The creative act, like the dream, draws upon unknown factors and therefore belongs to the field of acausal phenomena. The artist or the visionary extracts "the contingent partly as a universal factor existing from all eternity, and partly as the sum of countless individual acts of creation occurring in time" and reduces this material to his own frame of reference.[47] Wagner, Mozart, and Rachmaninoff described inspiration as a burst or upsurge of productivity. Rachmaninoff said that when he walked in the country his head seemed to burst into music and that all the notes flowed into existence right before him. "All the voices at once. Not a bit here, a bit there. The whole grows. When it came, how it began, how can I say? It came up within me, was entertained, written down."[48] Certainly something within the unconscious had been triggered by some unknown acausal factor.

The more scientists investigate the extratemporal, or what has been alluded to today as the "subatomic" and the "supergalactic" spheres, the more they become aware of nature's diversity and man's longing to understand and regain a sense of its primordial unity—and the more *"science parallels mysticism."*[49]

Mystics such as Nerval, Restif, Aucler, and Cazotte believed in a realm beyond the rational or clock time, in a world peopled with invisible entities. Democritus maintained that the universe was filled with atoms. Pythagoras, Plato, Nicolas de Cusa, and Pico della Mirandola were convinced that the cosmos was a living and breathing entity. Kepler affirmed in his *Stella Nova* that to experience reality one must go beyond the world of appearances:

> Nothing exists nor happens in the visible sky that is not sensed in some hidden manner by the faculties of Earth and Nature: (so that) these faculties of the spirit here on earth are as much affected as the sky itself. . . .
> The natural soul of man is not larger in size than a single point, and on this point the form and character of the entire sky is potentially engraved, as if it were a hundred times larger.[50]

Leibniz believed in the monad, the smallest entity of all.[51] As science advanced, certain "elementary particles" (electrons, protons, neutrons, etc.), made up of matter, were found to be making their way around space, imposing their force in what looked like a series of pathlike "rows of tiny bubbles in a liquid."[52] Because of the energy aroused by these particles, physicists are able to examine "the transformation of mass into energy and of energy into mass."[53]

Increasingly, quantum physicists are drawn to a realm that had previously only seriously interested the mystic—that of acausal phenomena. That such a working rapport may become even more popular in the future is not unthinkable. Let us recall that in 1956 the Atomic Energy Commission succeeded in isolating neutrinos, "the most ghost-like or elementary particles." They were alluded to as ghostlike because they have, it seems, "no physical properties: no mass, no electric charge and no magnetic field."[54] Yet they exist.

Equally fascinating is Adrian Dobbs' theory, which postulates "a second time dimension in which the objective probabilities of future outcome are contained as compresent dispositional factors, which incline or predispose the future to occur in certain specific ways."[55] According to this theory, a physical explanation for telepathy and precognitive dreams and hallucinations could be forwarded.

Dobbs employs the word "pre-cast" rather than "pre-cognitive,"[56] indicating certain factors that could be perceived and would predispose a happening "toward a given future state." But such precasts are not merely haphazard, nor do they follow any known rational system. Man can discover something about these factors only through a "hypothetical messenger," which Dobbs labels "psitrons" and which function in a second time dimension. The psitrons have "imaginary mass (in the mathematical sense) and thus, according to the theory of relativity, can travel faster than light and indefinitely, without loss of (imaginary) momentum." Professor Margenau writes of imaginary mass as follows:

> At the forefront of current physical research, we find it necessary to invoke the existence of "virtual processes" confined to extremely short durations. For a very short time, every physical process can proceed in ways which defy the laws of nature known today, always hiding itself under the cloak of the principle of uncertainty. When any physical process first starts, it sends out "feelers" in all directions, feelers in which time may be reversed, normal rules are violated, and unexpected things may happen. These virtual processes then die out and after a certain time matters settle down again.[57]

Other theories concerning "will influence" and "mind influence" were posited by Sir John Eccles, who believed that certain entities or substances act upon neurons in the brain and frequently influence brain activity in a startling manner.[58] Certain factors within the brain may increase or decrease its awareness, expand its consciousness, thereby making telepathy, clairvoyance, and other acausal situations possible.[59]

The manner in which energy is transformed into consciousness is still a mystery. That such questions have invaded the scientist's world is particularly revealing about the course of today's research.

Artists, who are perhaps more sensitive than the average person, sense their way into other dimensions, into magnetic fields that remain shut to the "normal" individual. When Cazotte, Aucler, Cagliostro, Restif, Pasqually, Saint-Martin and other such visionaries described their hallucinations or dream images, as incredible as these may seem—there were some, Nodier, Gautier, Balzac, and others—who took them seriously. They sensed the validity of the acausal-factor theory long before physicists began to focus their attention on these matters.[60] And Nerval not only sensed them—he was *living* them.

16 THE INTERNMENT

*It is very painful not to be at peace
with oneself.*
Gérard de Nerval, *Oeuvres complètes,* I.

Despite the publication of *The Illuminists* and *October Nights*[1] and con-
tracts for such future works as *Small Castles of Bohemia,* Nerval was still
plagued with financial problems. His growing lack of confidence caused
him to experience a crippling sense of disillusionment.

Nerval's depression was so intense that he was taken, on February 6,
1853 to the Maison Dubois at 11 Faubourg Saint-Denis, where he remained until March 27. Always acutely sensitive to his physical and mental well-being, he attributed this last illness to a "nervous disorder," to
extreme worry over his financial situation. In a letter to Franz Liszt, he
mentions his anxieties and also his tremendous disappointment over the
failure of *The Printmaker of Harlem.*[2]

Nerval ate little and spent most of his time taking long walks. Walking,
he believed, was beneficial to his condition: that the physical fatigue
dulled his senses and permitted him to sleep free of the painful nightmares that had become so common of late. Sometimes he walked
throughout Paris. On other occasions he went to the Valois region,
where he had spent such happy years during his childhood. There his
mind wandered back to Uncle Boucher, to Mortefontaine and to that
wonderful attic with all those marvelous books, to the pretty little country girls dressed in their white dresses on feast days. And yet, no matter
where he was, one singularly searing question came to him again and
again: was he still capable of writing? He had noticed that it took him
longer to collect his thoughts and to put them down on paper. Was
something happening to him?

Nerval knew that he was losing ground. In letters to friends he mentioned that he was easily distracted while writing, that he had difficulty
following a train of thought, that he felt his creative powers diminishing,
that his memory was failing him.[3]

Some of Nerval's contemporaries attributed his deterioration to an
overindulgence in alcohol. Others maintained that Nerval drank very
little, but that he reacted strongly even to a tiny glass of red wine.[4]

For whatever reason, writing had become a chore. Ideas were scarce.
Visions predominated. The rational function, whose job it was to sort
out archetypal images when they burst forth from the unconscious, was
growing increasingly weak. Nerval had to expend great effort to write
a simple short story, a brief article, a poem—and a dread sense of doom
accompanied each effort of the pen.[5]

When ideas did surge forth, no sooner did Nerval try to set them down on paper than they would vanish. And if they remained with him, as they occasionally did, Nerval was usually dissatisfied with the results: he had not succeeded in concretizing the thought in the "perfect" manner in which he had first envisaged it. He was frustrated every step of the way. "I'm not able. It's deplorable. Perhaps it's due to the fact that I am trying for perfection. Because I erase almost everything as I write."[6]

After Nerval's release from the rest home he resumed his former life as best he could. He grabbed at straws; he wrote articles, reworked old stories, and, when he felt incapable of writing at all, he became a nomad of sorts: he walked endlessly, ceaselessly, throughout Paris and its environs. He haunted all types of dives and in the most grimy and sordid neighborhoods, hobnobbing with alcoholics, derelicts, bums, prostitutes. He ate less and less; he slept anywhere and everywhere, and with the refuse of humanity, in the slime of Paris, attempting always to forget, to rid his mind of excoriating thoughts, visions, hallucinations .[7] Perhaps he was trying to assuage guilt feelings by resorting to such physical hardships, trying to rid himself of what he considered unacceptable in him; perhaps he simply didn't care.

Surprisingly, it was during this poignantly distressing period that Nerval wrote one of his literary gems, *Sylvie*.[8] No one knows whether the excitement connected with the publication of this most remarkable work was instrumental in bringing on another mental crisis or not, but shortly thereafter, on August 27, 1853, Nerval was once again taken to Dr. Blanche's rest home at Passy, where he remained until the end of September when Dr. Blanche, yielding to Nerval's intense desire to leave the rest home, released him prematurely. Nerval was interned again at the end of the month, this time in a state of extreme delirium (*délire furieux*). And this time it would be for a long stay. Nerval's condition was very serious.

Just as Dr. Esprit Blanche had shown Nerval great kindness during his first internment in 1841, so his son, Dr. Emile-Antoine Blanche, who had replaced his father as head of the rest home, adopted a similar attitude of gentleness and understanding. But there had been changes during the twelve years between Nerval's lengthy incarcerations. Dr. Esprit Blanche's rest home had been located in Montmartre and was moved only in 1846 to Passy—with its fine houses and large gardens. Once this abode had been owned by the duchesse of Lauzun, then by Duke Albert de Luynes and other well-known members of the French royalty and aristocracy. After Dr. Emile-Antoine graduated from medical school, he seconded his father in his work. Just as perceptive as his father, he too enjoyed the confidence of his patients and their affection. When a heart ailment forced Dr. Esprit Blanche to rest a good deal of the time, Emile took over his father's duties. Dr. Esprit Blanche died on November 5, 1852; he was mourned by many, particularly those in the art and literary worlds.[9]

When Nerval was brought to Passy, Dr. Emile Blanche offered him his friendship and his medical acumen. He never inquired about payment, but Nerval, during his moments of lucidity, felt deeply troubled by his inability to pay. He did not want to accept charity, though he knew that many in the rest home were unable to pay but were treated in the same way as those who were wealthy. Eugène de Stadler, Georges Bell, Théophile Gautier, and Alexandre Dumas helped as best they could. They also solicited the government for financial aid and were granted a pension for Nerval for a hundred and sixty francs to be paid to Dr. Blanche. Certainly this amount did not cover the care involved, but it was a sign of the government's interest in the case.

Nerval's disease was serious. At times he lost all lucidity and spoke at a very rapid pace, uttering only the last syllables of words. On certain days, he would suffer an entire personality change. He who had always been so kind and gentle, so considerate would rant and rave until his actions were considered dangerous both to himself and others. For hours he would hallucinate, a victim of his own inner world. No one could understand what he thought or felt—perhaps not even he. He remained apathetic, withdrawn, unable to read, to write, or even to talk as he lived out some cruel destiny.

During periods of remission, which were few and far between at first, Nerval always returned to his writing—his all-consuming passion. Uppermost in his mind was his desire to collect some of his short stories, essays, and poems and put them in volume form so as to be able to sell them to a publisher and be able to pay, at least partially, for his stay at Passy. He contracted for the publication of *Tales and Facetiae* and *The Daughters of Fire*. The funds received were minimal and Nerval himself had no concept of the value of money. As soon as he had gathered a few sous, he gave some to Dr. Blanche; the rest would be spent in no time. It was not uncommon for him to give his last centimes or bits of clothing to a poverty-stricken family or to a beggar he met on the street. In a letter to Mme. Solms, the daughter of the British minister to Athens and of Laetitia Bonaparte, Nerval asked that she not give him the beautiful books she had promised for his birthday, but to use this money more positively—to send it to a family in desperate need, whose children were on the verge of starvation. On his last visit to this family (he told Mme. Solms) he was so disturbed by their wretchedness that he not only gave them his coat but the forty centimes he had left. And to cheer them up, he continued, he told them that one day a beautiful and great lady— a fairy queen—would visit their home and give them all the gold pieces they needed. The children's mother began to laugh and then to cry:

"I think," Nerval continued, "that I really promised them rubies and diamonds." He added with a tone of pain: "There is someone poorer than I—in this world!"[10]

To give up a gift of books was indeed a sacrifice for Nerval, who had always taken immense pleasure in beautiful bindings, engravings, and prints, in the whiteness of the paper, its shadings, the various watermarks. But these loves were secondary to his great love and compassion for humanity.

When Dr. Blanche informed Nerval that his case was serious and that he would be obliged to live at Passy for quite some time, he suggested that Nerval bring his furniture and all of his possessions to the rest home. Eugène de Stadler saw to all the details of the move, made certain sums of money available to him, and devoted much of his time to settling Nerval's financial problems.

Nerval looked upon this altruism as a gesture with outerworldly ramifications. In his view, every act that takes place on this earth was of eternal significance: "It is impossible for one creature to be more grateful to another than I am to you: but everything will be accounted for elsewhere; to inform you of this is all I can do."[11] Like Boehme, Nerval believed that all events and ideas enacted and expressed on earth would be inscribed in a type of "ether" surrounding the world, an area with an "eternal memory" known as the Akasic Record. Today, psychologists would equate this mystical notion with the collective unconscious; no thought or action is ever lost or obliterated but lives on in a variety of forms for generations and in all mankind.[12]

Nerval's condition was far from stable. There were days, even weeks, when he suffered from extreme depression: a sense of isolation, a feeling of being cut off from everyone, even from God. Later, when he felt better, he referred to these moments as *"papillons noirs."*[13] But even during his periods of remission, some of his actions seemed rather bizarre to his friends. While strolling in the Palais Royal, Gautier reported, Nerval dragged a lobster he had attached to a blue ribbon. When questioned about this, Nerval replied:

> Why is a lobster more ridiculous than a dog, a cat, a gazelle, a lion or any other animal one has following behind one. I like lobsters because they are calm, serious, and know the secrets of the sea, they do not bark and do not swallow the peoples' monads as do dogs; who were so repugnant to Goethe who was, nevertheless, not crazy.[14]

One afternoon Nerval strolled through the Tuilleries Gardens and passed a large pond with goldfish in it. That their heads rose out of the water every now and then seemed to Nerval a sign of recognition. He began talking with them and relayed their massages to his friend, Champfleury, who was with him at the time. "The Queen of Sheba is

waiting for you," the fish told Nerval, who was "flattered" by the attention being paid him by the emissaries of so awe-inspiring a figure. Nerval
did not accept the invitation, however, because, as he told Champfleury,
he "did not want to hurt Solomon's vanity."[15]

On other occasions, Nerval appeared totally normal. He visited his
friends, recited poetry, talked about his dreams, his concepts of life with
the depth, charm, and delicacy that had always endeared him to those
he knew.[16]

His disease seemed to run in cyclical patterns. Periods of normality
would be accompanied by feelings of doubt concerning his literary ca-
pabilities, anguish over his financial situation. His only escape was to
walk or to distract himself in some way. Dr. Blanche, who was well aware
of Nerval's need to roam about and to be free, permitted him to travel
about Paris, either alone, when in good spirits, or accompanied by a
friend. He even agreed to let Nerval travel to London to attend to some
details concerning the publication of a translation of one of his works.
On August 25, the night of his scheduled departure, Nerval suddenly
became deeply troubled and moments later was in a state of acute delirium and raving. The trip was cancelled. For the next few days, Nerval
was submerged in another world. He had become violent. His hallucinations were unremitting; his mind, a confused mass; his field of awareness was flooded by his unconscious. The focus of his disturbance, as
had been the case during his other bouts with schizophrenia, had been
the collapse of the ego. He could no longer relate to reality at all. In
these acute psychotic states, Nerval became hyperactive and walked in-
cessantly; he even danced, chanting some primitive melody, some in-
cantation that had once attracted him. But no sooner had his crisis subsided then he considered himself cured and able to cope with worldly
problems. Then he would beg, cajole, and even demand to be released,
or at least be permitted to walk about Paris.

Usually, after the acute phases of his sickness had subsided, Nerval
experienced states of extreme elation. He felt free, as if released from
some terrible weight. During such times, he planned a brilliant future
for himself, with specific projects in mind. He would write a story based
on the *Hypnerotomachia*—the passion of Francesco Colonna for Polia. He
planned another libretto, to be written this time with Hippolyte Lucas,
for one of his favorite works, Mozart's *The Magic Flute*.[17] He envisioned
a play, *The Death of Rousseau*, in which he would reveal the true story of
Rousseau's end—that, because this poet had been rejected by both society and friends, he had committed suicide, first by taking hemlock and
then by shooting himself.[18]

During Nerval's lapses, his ideas came in swift succession. Feelings of
well-being were uppermost. Hope reigned high. He minimized his sickness, rarely spoke in detail of his symptoms and rather overlooked the
entire episode. To Stadler, he spoke of a relapse, "another little acci-

dent—still in the head—but I am learning little by little how to overcome this sickness."[19] To Georges Bell, equally solicitous of his well-being, Nerval declared: "Five or six days ago I was suddenly seized with a mental condition; I did crazy things. Now, my mind is healthier and I am writing you to find out. . . ."[20] To Gautier, he said that his stay at Dr. Blanche's rest home had been very beneficial and that he would be "completely cured."[21] To Ludovic Picard, his sickness was a type of "nervous fever" that came over him every now and then but that he could easily overcome.[22] Nerval told his aunt, Madame A. Labrunie, not to worry about his relapse; it had been due to the fact that he had been prematurely released from Dr. Blanche's clinic. It was not a "serious illness," he claimed; his financial problems had simply gotten the better of him, that was all. Now that he was cured, both morally and physically, things would be better.[23]

Though Nerval attempted to minimize his sickness, his friends had become more and more distressed over his behavior. Nerval was only in the prime of life, but he was a man transformed. His memory, once so "prodigious," his "gaiety," so endearing to others, his ability to regale listeners with tales from foreign lands, with anecdotes from past eras, with exotic and metaphysical notions—all had deteriorated.[24] Nerval's mind wandered. His conversation was sometimes incoherent. His eyes took on the glazed look of a man staring into the distance—into some other dimension.

When in a relatively lucid state he maintained a façade and hid his fears concerning his sickness, but his anguish was betrayed in his letters. Perhaps the most poignant ones were those to his father, a man who had always instilled in him a deep sense of guilt, inadvertently or not. Nerval sensed that his father did not respect him, that he treated him with pity and frequently with coldness. Dr. Labrunie admired only the realistic and strong types who faced matters squarely and dealt with them accordingly. He had always tried to steer his son along the right course, and his son was a living example of his failure. Yet Nerval loved his father, the very person who had caused him such pain. Because of his attachment he experienced guilt in an even more poignant manner than usual—and he suffered the further destruction of his own self-image.

Despite Nerval's frequently irrational behavior, there were times when his friends were amazed by the logic of his arguments. He could make even the strangest statement sound reasonable. Champfleury was convinced that the German doctor, the inventor of phrenology, Franz-Joseph Gall, was right when he maintained that the mind is two-sided and that when someone became insane only one side of the head was affected, the other remaining perfectly free and clear. How else could one account for such lucidity in Nerval's case?[25]

During Nerval's manic phases, his metaphysical ideations sometimes, changed. Schizophrenics frequently create their own rituals—prayers, spells, incantations, anything they feel will ward off what either terrifies them or what they want to capture in some area in outer space.[26] Nerval began drawing all sorts of prayers, occult verses, signs, and figures over the walls of his room. He wrote to his father that he was the son of a Mason and that certain secrets had been revealed to him, certain mysteries that he had set down on the walls for posterity.

> Son of a *mason* or a simple *wolf cub,* I amused myself by covering the walls of my room with kabbalistic figures and pronouncing or singing certain things which are forbidden to the profane; but they are unaware here that I am an Egyptian companion (*refik*). Well, I finally succeeded and I hope that no one has to go through the same tests.[27]

Some patients, in certain manic phases, are convinced they are undergoing mystical experiences. They actually feel, they say, a unity with the cosmic pleroma. Their sense of reality is heightened, their visual impressions are intensified, and they are sure they see beyond the phenomenological realm. There are moments when they feel themselves to be in direct rapport with supernatural powers, in possession of some mystery, the recipient of some arcane ritual.[28] Nerval was no exception.

In his letters to Alexander Dumas and George Sand, Nerval wrote in alchemical, kabbalistic, astrological, and Masonic terms and symbols. He filled his letters with allusions to Venus, the sun, the tarot, the Devil's Map, the Gemini twins. Man is merely the plaything of immutable forces, of planets whose designs are fixed and unalterable, he observed. He drew the crux ansata, signed his letters Ammon-Ra, Duke of Egypt. Perhaps he associated the word *amour* with Ammon-Ra—and also Aramis, one of The Three Musketeers. All of these, in a cryptic way, spell what Nerval considered his secret name, Roma.[29]

To Dumas he signed his letter Gaston Phoebus d'Aquitaine, alluding to the sun hero, to Phoebus Apollo, the fire principle. He considered himself one of those beings who suffered from the passion of love, which Venus had aroused within them. Sometimes Nerval signed his letters Sultan Chera-Cherai, Count of Abyssinia, Duke of Egypt or Baron of Smyrne. Dumas, heartlessly perhaps, went so far as to publish an article in the newspaper *Le Mousquetaire* in which he stated that Nerval had alluded to him as his suzerain and had asked permission to declare war on Emperor Nicolas.[30]

In Nerval's letter to George Sand occult notions and signs are intermingled with perfectly lucid statements. The startling recurrence of the number two in this letter may be looked upon as a symbol of the duality that resides not only in the cosmos but within Nerval himself, accounting for the growing tension between his outer and inner worlds. To stress even further the sense of duality, Nerval writes on two sheets of paper pinned together with an acacia thorn. The acacia, as we know, is a particularly important symbol in the Masonic initiation ritual. When the neophyte says, "Acacia is known to me," this indicates his knowledge of the superior or higher realms. Scholars have shown that *acacia* is also a pun on the Sanskrit word *Akasha,* meaning ether or quintessence. George Sand was a Mason, and perhaps for this reason the symbolism takes on an even greater meaning than one might at first suspect. The mention of the legendary brothers, the Gemini twins, further underlines the duality implicit in the letter to Sand.

In this letter Nerval compares his internment in Dr. Blanche's clinic to an "exile of the soul," to the same type of rejection that Ovid had suffered during the reign of Augustus after the publication of his "immoral work," the *Ars Amandi.* According to Pythagorean, Platonic, and Gnostic traditions, those living on earth have been exiled from heavenly spheres. Nerval divides the names George Sand into two parts: Geo ^{R} Sand; *Geo* or *Ge,* meaning earth, is united with Sand. An affinity also exists between the first letters of *Ge*orge and *Gé*rard.

Other interesting allusions are also present in Nerval's letters to George Sand, for instance, the words *"Pervigilium Veneris"* or "Nocturnal Cult of Venus," lines from the poem of an unknown author. The refrain of this poem may be translated as "Love tomorrow, you who never have loved; you who have loved, love again."[31] This may be an allusion to the Celestial Venus in all her avatars—the same Venus with whom Nerval had always been preoccupied and under whose dominion he had fallen victim early in life. A letter Nerval wrote to Dr. Blanche may confirm this interpretation: "She will return the one I love in another life. Here, I do not listen to the voice of a dream, but to the sacred promise of God."[32] Nerval was still convinced that, in the life to come, Jenny Colon would be his.

Dr. Blanche encouraged Nerval to write letters to him, to tell him anything and everything. In one such missive Nerval compared his internment to an Egyptian initiation rite and stated that his "ordeal had come to an end." And he continued:

"I placed Osiris' key on the altar of Wisdom." I feel myself delivered from a great responsibility and since I am not Cinna, that is a traitor, I do not feel unduly embarrassed playing the role of Ovid. If my feelings result in my exile to Sarmates, I see nothing unpleasant in this. Until then, I am content and I like everyone, especially the ladies, and especially you, who know how to be a doctor for the soul as well as the body.[33]

There were days when Nerval's allusions to remote deities were even more obscure. When Philibert Audebrand listened to him discussing certain initiation ceremonies in Egypt, particularly those involved with

Cheops' (Khufu's) pyramid, he could see how intent Nerval was—how annoyed if Audebrand should smile. "Why do you mock sacred things?" Nerval questioned. "Are you a *mopse?*" Audebrand asked him what a mopse was. "A scion of the angel Eblis," Nerval replied.[34]

Nerval's immediate reaction to what he looked upon as mockery of himself and his beliefs is common among schizophrenics. Their loss of object-relation increases their distrust of the world at large. Contradiction becomes unbearable and can even result in violence.

Everything touching upon the occult, whether it was related to the ideas of Claude de Saint-Martin, Martinès de Pasqually, to the great kabbalists, or to Boehme or Swedenborg—Nerval considered as revelatory of certain arcane messages. He was certainly receptive to Swedenborg's world of fairies, saints, and God—a domain which he could enter at will. Swedenborg's world had become reality for Nerval. In fact, Nerval saw himself as a type of vehicle, a transforming agent through which or by which the outer world could become manifest. The signs he had drawn on the walls of his room were transpositions of certain mysteries that had been revealed to him by outer-worldly forces. Ordinary people, with their impaired vision, their limited frames of reference, could not decipher the signs of divinity—of heavenly spheres. But Nerval was a descendant—so he believed—of the Roman emperor Nerva and, as such, he had been given second sight in some previous incarnation; he was privileged to see directly beyond the world of appearance into the cosmic pleroma. Owing to some rash act on his part— perhaps he had revealed, like Prometheus and Cain, esoteric secrets to mankind—he too was doomed to punishment. Shunned by the masses, his work would remain unacceptable to the reading public, and he was destined to remain incarcerated in Dr. Blanche's rest home. Nerval was so convinced of his martyrdom, of his guilt, that on certain occasions he was able to take his situation in stride, knowing as he did that he would be forgiven eventually, and that he would attain a superior sphere—but only after the ordeal of life had ended.

In such moods, Nerval informed Dr. Blanche and his friends that he had come into direct contact with the sacred—with the universal life principle. Such communion seemed to instill in him momentary feelings of security, as if his *tête à tête* with powerful forces had aided him in some way. The stronger his attachment to these mystical filaments, the less terrifying was his anguish—and the greater his belief that, someplace in the universe, there was always some gentle, maternal force to protect him.

Nerval's ability to record his visions was amazing. He did so with the accuracy and detail of a photograph. It is not uncommon for schizophrenics to describe their insights in minute detail: genealogical relationships, mystical notions—whatever. Nerval described people, objects, and sensations with precision, but his descriptions were often disassociated and lacking in perspective. Judgment and synthetic values were nowhere to be found. It was not that Nerval's intelligence had withered; his ego (which normally sifts the sensorial messages received by the brain) had become virtually powerless.

Mystics of many lands and periods have frequently experienced an egoless world. So long as they are able to sink into themselves—to enter their archetypal domain at will and draw from it images that aid in expanding their consciousness—they are enriched by such forays. But when such indwelling is at the mercy of the will, when rational function has no power over actions or thoughts, loss of sanity may result.

Fearful dangers confront the mystic. In his Faustian attempt to experience more than his soul can comprehend (or his ego cope with), he may be overwhelmed by cosmic forces (or his unconscious) and eventually be destroyed—that is, he may lose his ability to return to the world of reality at will (or in psychological terms, to handle the archetypal images that his unconscious is forever thrusting into consciousness). The light viewed by the mystic when approaching Deity is so dazzling that it may shatter or blind the person who peers at it too steadily. His universe may become so enlarged—this was the case with Balzac's *Louis Lambert*—that he may remain forever an exile from terrestrial life. When man attempts to play God—and this is pointed out in all the myths of all cosmogonies—he must always be punished for his hubris. Man cannot know both worlds. Because he is man, he is finite and mortal, limited and incomplete.

Like many schizophrenics, there were times when Nerval developed extreme astuteness in handling people whom he considered his persecutors. Some patients create ingenious systems and build up façades so as to appear to be "normal." Of Dr. Blanche, for whom Nerval came to feel an increasing antagonism, Nerval wrote, "I thought we no longer understood each other . . . ," and yet at other moments, "I love you like a relative, like a brother."[35] There were days when he could not hide his antagonism. He blamed Dr. Blanche for imprisoning him unjustly and for the withering of his talents. He lacked outside stimulation—intellectual commerce with his friends; Nerval was, he felt, stagnating at Passy, an arid wasteland. His faculties were deteriorating; his ideas ran in circles. "I am working a lot, but it's going around in the same circle."[36]

Dr. Blanche, though aware of Nerval's frustrations, was also aware of the dangers involved in releasing him. He asked Nerval to transcribe his dream-vision and to entrust the pages to him for safe keeping. Nerval did just that. On December 2, 1853, he wrote Dr. Blanche: "I am sending you some pages which should be added to the others I gave you yesterday. I shall continue this series of dreams if you wish me to."[37]

Nerval was entering a new phase in his writing career—the great period. He was finally finding himself, as an artist if not as a man.

PART III
THE DAUGHTERS OF FIRE

O sages standing in God's holy fire
As in the gold mosaic of a wall,
Come from the holy fire, perne in a gyre,
And be the singling masters of my soul.
Consume my heart away; sick with desire
And fastened to a dying animal
It knows not what it is; and gather me
Into the artifice of eternity.
      W.B. Yeats, *Sailing to Byzantium*

17 ANGÉLIQUE

Love that moves the sun and the
other stars . . .
Dante, *Divine Comedy, Paradise.*

The Daughters of Fire,[1] a remarkable work, includes a veritable metaphysics of fire, which takes on mythical and philosophical ramifications.
The heroines of the tales in this volume—Angélique, Sylvie, Octavie,
Isis, Corilla, Emilie—are all fire spirits, descendants of "that cursed
race."

Fire is associated with solar symbolism and heroes: Helios or Phoebus
Apollo; the worshippers of Mithra who looked upon the Sun as a conqueror: *Sol Invictus.* Because of the sun's daily rise and fall, it came to
represent death and resurrection of the hero—the eternal repetition of
life. The sun is a heroic force, synonymous with vital heat, creative energy, and a guide to man in his daily ventures. Heraclitus considered it
a "mediator" between the created and the uncreated.[2] Its energy (both
spiritual and animal) makes it a catalyzing force capable of "transmuting" people and things, melting metals and chemicals. Paracelsus drew
an analogy between fire and life, both of them elements being necessary
for growth and production.

Being so powerful and aggressive, and an illuminating principle connected with intelligence, the sun has been endowed with masculine qualities. Its positive attributes include growth, fecundation, vital heat, and
the like. But it can also burn, blind, scorch, and cause sterility. Empedocles felt this dichotomy so acutely that he could no longer bear the
conflict and threw himself into Mt. Etna.

For Nerval, fire meant heroism and suffering. Prometheus, Cain,
Adoniram, Tubal-Cain—all had helped mankind bring in new attitudes,
and all, therefore, had been compelled to suffer the fate of the hero
who acts against the status quo, against God. Such creative types are so
blinded by the fire within them that they overlook the dangers involved
in accomplishing their goals; they are determined to brave the rigid circumscribed world. But in so doing, they earn the wrath of the forces
they seek to annihilate and are tormented. Their reward, if any, will
come to them only in some remote future.

The suffering heroes with whom Nerval identified may be looked
upon as fallen angels. Eblis, according to Mohammedan tradition, represents evil; he is a fallen angel who refused to adore Adam as God had
commanded. Eblis argued that since he and his friends had been formed
from fire and not from a lesser material, earth, as Adam was, they would
not be subservient to him. The Persian poet Esfahani expressed the idea

as follows: "Fire, which is the origin of nature and of Ibba's pride, will be the instrument of his punishment."[3]

Prometheus, Cain, Tubal-Cain, Adoniram, Sheba, Eblis, Lucifer[4]—all belonged to the "red race" and were doomed to eternal martyrdom for having been "light bringers"—for having refused to adhere to certain fixed and immutable laws promulgated by God in his attempt, they believed, to enslave man.

The Illuminists, such as Martinès de Pasqually, had written at length about these fire beings, that is, those responsible for the discovery of the molten metals that saved man from virtual annihilation after the flood. Romantic poets such as Byron, de Vigny, and Hugo identified with Cain and Prometheus and viewed themselves as Messiah types, as inventors of new literary credoes and techniques—and as victims of society's callous attitudes. Nerval, more than the others, bore the mark of Cain because his suffering had been more intense than theirs: he had been incarcerated and they had not; he had not won the admiration nor achieved their popularity. Nerval, like Cain, was prepared to endure his agony. He was truly of the "red race," and to prove his lineage he merely had to point to his name: "Labrunie," which means "the one who seizes thunder," and the word *"brunnir," "brennen,"* to burn, indicating the presence of the dynamic fire principle.[5]

Angélique

Nerval chose the name Angélique for the heroine of his story very deliberately.[6] The semidivine "angels," composed of fire, water, or both, and "divinely harmonized," were looked upon as agents capable of encompassing both celestial and earthly spheres—messengers (as the word *"angelos"* in Greek and *"malakh,"* the Hebrew word, indicate). Angels are of all types: destroyers (II Samuel, 24, 16); interpreters of God's message (Job, 32, 23), protectors as in Exodus, prognosticators as described in the Gospels. Angels may assume any form, according to their particular function.[7]

Angélique is a messenger, the harbinger of a new way. Like her illustrious predecessors, the fire-people, she braves conventions and, because of her rebellious spirit, must suffer the punishment meted out to transgressors. Because she is pure in heart and irreproachably honest, Angélique may be used by the others to their advantage—bringing destruction both upon herself and those surrounding her.

Nerval's *Angélique* is a quest, an odyssey wih mythic grandeur. It is a search for the treasure hard to attain—a symbolical expression of an inner drama, a numinous or sacred experience. Nerval may have chosen the mythic form because, in a sense, it "takes" man back to past times, which then become part of present reality. Fabulous and miraculous adventures may be integrated into the world of actuality. The teller of the myth divests himself of chronological time and lives in a "trans-figured" realm, surrounded by supernatural beings or peoples. Myths may also "solidify" beliefs previously considered incredible, or they may justify new situations.[8]

Nerval declared in his preface that he had "seized the series of all of his anterior existences"; that "it was no more difficult for me to consider myself to have been a prince, a king, a magus, a genie and even God."[9] *Angélique* might thus be the vehicle that permitted him to fuse a mythological and limitless past with his mortal existence. In so doing, he became part of an eternal life cycle.

Because a myth narrates an original or religious experience—because, that is, it "relates back to the past" or to some nebulous precognitive realm—Nerval could use such a literary device as a stepping-stone toward the discovery of what he considered to be his own fabulous origins. Was he not the descendant of Nerva? Was his secret name not Roma?

A longing to establish oneself in some time long past reveals an intense dissatisfaction with present conditions. Yet a return (or a regression) into a spaceless and timeless mythical past may constellate new ideas and principles, and may even pave the way for a new orientation *if* such a retreat is fully understood. Nerval's *regressus ad uterum,* as delineated in *Angélique,* so autobiographical a tale, may be looked upon as a symptom of his urgent need to reimmerse himself in the "waters of life," in the "earth's womb," and so to free himself from guilt and sin.

Nerval's myth takes us on a quest for a book. He is looking for a volume that describes the exploits of a historical figure, the abbé Bucquoy. He first explores the libraries in Frankfurt and then pursues his labors in the libraries and book shops of Paris and the Valois region. Clues appear in each episode; digressions and asides associated with the abbé are inserted at regular intervals, enlarging the story's dimensions. Finally, Nerval discovers a volume in the Compiègne library describing the life of one Angélique de Longueval, the abbé's grandaunt, and he sets out for Paris coincidentally on the day that this town commemorates the dead. Nerval looks upon this solemn occasion with awe, and upon his walk with the village folk as a pilgrimage in respect to the memory of Angélique, whose life he now begins to narrate.

Myths are filled with special objects, even sacred ones—*hierophanies,* that their heroes are forever retrieving either from the hands of enemies or from loss: the Chalice in the Grail Legend, the word that must be recovered in Masonic mysteries, the philosopher's stone in alchemy. The volume relating the life of the abbé Bucquoy is a hierophany; it enables Nerval to make forays into the past, to revive a world long since dead—and to write a work of art.

Secrecy is usually attendant upon a quest. As Goethe wrote: "A very deep meaning lies in that notion, that a man in search of buried treasure must work in utter silence; [that he] must speak not a word, whatever appearance, either terrific or delightful, may present itself."[10] For philosophical reasons, Nerval made excellent use of secrecy in his narration, but secrecy also served to enhance the literary values, to intensify the suspense, and to increase the pace and excitement of his tale.

Nerval's quest begins in a world he knows well: the cerebral realm of the library, the written world—specifically, the Arsenal in Paris, with all its wonderful memories for Nerval. This had been the home of one of the finest story tellers of them all, Charles Nodier, and here Nerval had often met his friends Gautier, Balzac, Dumas, Lamartine, Musset, and others. Now, like so many phantoms from the past, these figures would intrude upon his present: in *Angélique,* each time Nerval describes a library he visits, or its entourage, he associates his friends with historical or literary figures, linking specific incidents to objective situations—and thus making use of another myth-making device.

Nerval surely identified with Angélique, the daughter of a wealthy nobleman. Her character coincided with his in so many ways. She was angelic, pure in heart, a victim of injustice; she was also a dreamer who dwelled in another world, frequently in the dominion of death.

> Ever since the age of thirteen, Angélique de Longueval, whose character was sad and dreamy, neither enjoyed, as she said, costly precious stones, beautiful tapestries, nor beautiful clothes; she aspired only for death to cure her spirit.[11]

As the story progresses, Nerval's identification grows more intense. When he tells of the love the young man bore for Angélique (and who because of his passion had been so cruelly murdered by her father's orders), he talks of the excoriating pain experienced by the one left behind: "The tearing apart which she experienced with this death revealed her love."[12] Angélique first knew love in relation to a loss.[13] Before his death she had been unaware of the meaning of affection and, like Adam and Eve, had been living in a paradisiac state; after his demise, which we may equate with Adam and Eve's fall into matter, she began her worldly existence.

The letter Angélique's suitor wrote her before being killed was premonitory—a warning such as that found in many myths. He described his passion for her in terms of contrasting colors: dawn, light, circle of darkness, shadow—always underscoring an essential duality, the great separation in store for them. The color symbolism also implied that he would be the victim of some overpowering force—some black and evil principle—that would make him incapable of breaking out of the circle of doom into the clarity of celestial spheres. Other dichotomies are also implicit in the letter: the impact of a spiritual and ethereal love based on illumination (golden hues) and the dark forces of his instinctual self (the more sombre and lugubrious tonalities).[14]

Angélique, like Nerval, associated her love with death. Unlike Nerval, after two years of mourning, she found a substitute to "take the place of this eternally dead being."[15] Another young man in her father's employ, La Corbinière, develops a passion for her. After innumerable trysts, Angélique flees with him, but not without taking some of her parents' silverware to ensure their immediate financial security. The couple goes to Italy, where La Corbinière joins the army, on to Germany, and then back to Italy. In the course of all this, La Corbinière begins leading a dissolute life. The silverware money is soon spent and both he and Angélique are reduced to penury. After much suffering, he dies. Angélique returns to France to live out her life in solitude and poverty.

Some authors, Nerval wrote, "cannot invent without identifying with their imaginary characters" to such an extent that their lives are sometimes fashioned upon one's own; their "ambitions" and "loves" become the author's.[16] The same can be said of Nerval in his Angélique tale— not the actual events that were experienced, but the manner in which they were lived, and the make-up of the protagonist's personality and temperament.

More important, perhaps, were the autobiographical events that Nerval wove into this subjective tale. To commemorate the pain that Angélique had experienced during her lifetime (and, by association, Nerval's own pain), he set out on a pilgrimage, together with the people on the day reserved to commemorate the dead. As he began, he felt as if he were entering consecrated territory, penetrating a mystery, a secret *rite de passage*. Each person, tree, lake, house, event, the scenery itself, took on a mystical aura and was transformed into a series of hierophanies.[17]

Pilgrimages link one's own past with that of another. Both Nerval and Angélique would be merged in the fluidity of time, and Nerval would succeed in abolishing the present temporal reality.

To enter an atemporal (or mythological) realm is to lose one's own individuality, at least temporarily. Such a journey can be accomplished through a double-memory technique (objective and subjective), which Nerval uses with felicity. The objective memory, when recounting Angélique's life, is used to recall or examine specific historical dates and personal reminiscences. The subjective memory filters through the subliminal realms, recreating anterior existences and, concomitantly, the feelings, sensations, and ideations appropriate to the eras involved. To be capable of reentering the past, as Nerval had done in this tale, is to master a formidable weapon. It gives one the ability to reshape one's life, divest oneself of the negative Karma that had predominated until this moment.[18] Nerval had always felt himself to be the victim of some negative astral or divine force that was bent upon destroying him, and he longed, therefore, to reenter time and to recast his life.

Nerval's return to the past via the double-memory technique required a sacrifice: the loss of his identity. According to Plato, waters from the fountain of Lethe were given to each person before he was reborn and returned to earth. Proper use of one's memory implies the recollection of ideas that have been forgotten—of transpersonal and eternal truths that were lost through "forgetfulness" before one's birth.[19] One's subjective memory was designed to restore, as best it could, the experiences of past existences that had been washed away before one's "return" to earth. To discover one's past, Plato intimated, was to experience one's previous life. Accordingly, Nerval questioned the meaning of "imagination" at the very outset of his story. "To invent, really is to remember," Nerval wrote, quoting both Plato and Pythagoras.

Nerval achieved his goal. He recaptured the use of his subjective memory when walking through the melancholy autumnal landscape, which he continually personified and termed "the most beautiful and the saddest."[20] He was again in the land of his ancestors. In this almost transparent atmosphere of foggy climes, reddish hues, and denuded trees, which he compared to the colors that the Flemish painters splashed onto their canvases, he felt a certain *reverie*. Through his return to the past, to his ancestors, he gathered new strength. "I feel strengthened on this maternal soil."[21]

Through *Angélique* Nerval was able to create a veritable cult out of *reverie* or *souvenir*.

> Whatever one may have to say philosophically speaking, we are bound to the earth by many bonds. One does not carry the ashes of one's ancestors on the soles of one's shoes, and the poorest guardian recalls a sacred souvenir which brings to mind those who loved him. Religion or philosophy, everything proves to man the importance of the eternal cult of souvenir.[22]

As Nerval walked further into the country, other associations came to mind with an ever-increasing circular effect. The countryside echoed the Watteau painting *The Embarkation for Cythera,* with its fragile delineations, its medley of delicate harmonies. As peasants came into view, Nerval stopped and listened to their chatter. He was receptive to the musicality of their language, their rhythms and intonations. They spoke, he observed, as their ancestors had spoken centuries earlier. Their language had remained untouched by outside influences and each word was uncontaminated and "rose to heaven as does the song of a skylark."[23] It was as if time had stopped and Nerval were entering still further the remote regions of the myth.

It is no wonder that Nerval was moved by this visual and aural spectacle. Scholars such as Richer have pointed out that *Angélique* was constructed in the manner of a concerto with its prelude, its main and secondary themes, each winding in and out of the piece, a first movement.[24]

Nerval had always loved ancient ballads, the lyrical stanzas that the bards and troubadours of France had sung in medieval times and during the Renaissance—songs commemorating a variety of occasions: a wife complaining of her husband's infidelities, a beautiful shepherdess fending off a nobleman, a nun lamenting her vocation, a knight riding to meet his lady love—political songs, weaving songs, satirical verse.[25] Nerval knew the songs of William of Poitiers (1071–1127), Jaufre Rudel (1147), Bernard de Ventadour (1150–1170). He had made a study of certain songs of the Valois region, which he published in magazines and included in *The Daughters of Fire.*

Music not only had a hypnotic effect upon Nerval, but acted as a stimulant to his subjective memory. When he listened to the peasant boys and girls singing their village songs, sections of his past were reintegrated into the present; "a melody with which I had been cradled" emerged before him.[26] More than ever, he realized how precious his childhood had been—the few days spent with his Uncle Boucher at Mortefontaine before his father had intruded upon his existence and taken him back to Paris. And there were the wonderful but all-too-short summer vacations. Now, all those he had loved were dead—as was his youth. "The souvenirs of childhood revivify when one has reached the half-way mark in life. It's like a palimpsest the lines of which one is able to bring to view with certain chemical procedures."[27]

The visual image came into sharper focus now. Nerval saw the little peasant girls dancing about so merrily and it was as if he were witnessing a magical ritual—like Shiva creating the world through his dancing; like some divine spirits emanating from the world beyond. The girls were like hieroglyphics weaving arabesques in outer space. They became potent factors in his mind—constellating sacred powers, forces that succeeded in conjuring up time past. They were no longer individual little girls, but had taken on mythical proportions; they had been depersonalized, transformed into archetypal figures.

Like Angélique these maidens must have been made of both water and fire—they too had the power of angels, of restoring chunks of past life into present reality. Their dance, like those of the Greek girls Nerval had seen on one of his trips, took on circular patterns, created serpentine effects, encouraged a hypnotic reverie—enabling him to wander still further back into the past.[28]

Nerval's associations grew firmer, more detailed. They centered around a mystery play he had seen as a child. He recalled a particular scene: Christ's descent into hell. A beautiful blond girl had starred in the play. She was dressed in white, with pearls interwoven in her hair, a nimbus surrounding her head; she held a golden sword.[29]

Nerval's objective memory had aroused his subjective faculty of recall by moving from the immediate object (the young girls) to an incident he had experienced before (the mystery play). In unifying these dual memory functions, he encouraged an even more remote past to emerge; the historical time in which the medieval mystery play had been written and Christ's era.[30] To these two epochs was added the image of the ideal female principle: the blond girl dressed in white, associated with the Virgin Mary or with Sophia (the representative of divine wisdom).

Christ's descent into hell is of particular interest in these scenes as it may be equated with two other journeys into the underworld: that of Orpheus when he tried to claim his beautiful Eurydice, and that of Osiris when he retired to the underworld after his dismemberment.

By associating Christ and Orpheus (and Osiris) with his own descent into the past, Nerval was in effect experiencing an *imitatio dei,* a desire to return to the primordial unity, the center of the "Earth's Umbilicus," the self or the beginning. To reenter the *axis mundi,* where opposites no longer exist, a timeless and spaceless area, is to identify with the eternal and universal principle—with God. Aristotle called this central point that of the "unmoved mover" because it is at the center that creation starts and extends outward, frequently in circular fashion. In most mythologies, the cardinal points emerge or are born from the center. (In many cathedrals and temples, the altars are placed in the center.) Nerval's desire to reach the focal point, the center of his problem, indicates an obsessive desire to relive his life. To experience the center necessitates a *rite de passage* that enables the initiate to go from the transitory to the eternal, from the profane to the sacred, from life to death.

Nerval's fusion wih his personal (subjective reminiscences) and collective (historical, Angélique) past, using the Abbé Bucquoy as the vehicle for his quest, lends further credence to his own need to escape from his present condition, to his desire to regress into some past existence or anterior world.

Angélique has been considered Nerval's double. She slipped through life from misfortune to misfortune, always buoyed by her dreams and reveries. While she represents the negative, shadowy side of Nerval, the little girls with their freshness, vigor and spontaneity, stand for his positive attributes. They also represent the collective image of life as it bursts into song and dance—as it burgeons each spring and fecundates the earth, when all avenues are open, all possibilities still available.

Angélique, an archetypal image, represents a fire principle—that of the young girl who loves too naïvely, too blindly, and whose life is consumed by these very forces. Because she lacked wisdom and insight—that burning force within her, which scorched rather than illuminated—she was forced to suffer and live in exile until her husband's death, and then in penury in her own land. Yet, because of the beauty of her passion, she succeeded in living life thoroughly, fully, totally, not as a superficial joyride but as a *rite de passage,* enabling her eventually to earn rebirth in another domain—that of the myth.

18   SYLVIE

He is not disquieted by the moon that he sees
every night, till it comes bodily to him, sleeping or waking,
draws near and charms him with silent movements, or
fascinates him with the evil or sweetness of its touch.
He does not retain from this the visual representation, say,
of the wandering orb of light, or of a demonic being that
somehow belongs to it, but at first he has in him only the
dynamic, stirring image of the moon's effect, streaming
through his body. Out of this the image of the moon personally
achieving the effect only gradually emerges. Only now, that
is to say, does the memory of the unknown that is nightly
taken into his being begin to kindle and take shape as
the doer and bringer of the effect. Thus it makes possible
the transformation of the unknown into an object, a He or a She
out of a Thou that could not originally be experienced, but
simply suffered.

Martin Buber, I and Thou.

Sylvie, one of the most exquisite prose works in French literature, is considered by men of letters a superb example of French "clarity of expression." Paradoxically, it was written at a time when Nerval was a victim of schizophrenia.[1] Its language is limpid, musical, and delicate; its images, which serve to delineate individual protagonists and situate events, also encourage Nerval's optical meanderings, which frequently take on circular or cyclical contours.

Sylvie is a myth because the experiences revealed in it are both personal (they depict events experienced by Nerval during the walking trips he had been permitted to take to the Valois region while in and out of rest homes) and transcendental because they are associated with events and people in his own "fabulous" and remote past—when he was a child in Ermenonville, Loisy, Châalis, and Senlis. In the early years of primitive times, life seemed beautiful and was filled with infinite possibilities; each time he returned to it—either through the dream or reveries—he felt refreshed, renewed, cleansed. It was as if he had undergone a baptism, a purification ceremony.

Because the narrator felt reborn with each foray into the past—particularly the early ones—*Sylvie* may be looked upon as a creation myth. When dwelling upon his youth, he experienced an obliteration of chronological time and a resurgence of cyclical or sacred time. Past events became contemporaneous, lending a sense of eternity to the narrative. The entire scene assumes extratemporal dimensions, since it is no longer subject to the ravages of chronological time. The protagonists who make up the narrator's world, endowed with almost prehuman or superhuman personality traits, assume mythical grandeur and enjoy divine powers: the ability to appear and disappear in the story, as had the goddesses of old. Because they are such fleeting forces, they remain mysterious, evanescent, intangible, and abstract. Their power over the narrator is immeasurable.

At the outset of the tale, the narrator lives in Paris and goes to the theatre nightly to admire from afar his beloved stage star Aurélie, whom he has not yet met. One evening, after a performance, the narrator thumbs through a newspaper and notices an article concerning a celebration to be held at Loisy, a district not far from Paris where he had spent his childhood. A whole series of impressions invades his conscious mind: his entire life passes in review before him. The creation myth takes root as he plunges back to the past: he is a young lad at Loisy and in love with Sylvie, a beautiful country girl with black eyes, regular features, and a most ingratiating and outgoing personality. He sees himself dancing a round on a beautiful lawn in front of a castle dating from the time of Henri IV of France. The rules of the dance oblige him to kiss Adrienne, the girl who finds herself in the inner circle with him. As her "golden hair brushed against his cheek,"[2] he is overcome with feelings of a "strange uneasiness." He listens to Adrienne sing an old French romance, then places a crown of laurel leaves on her head and kisses her, while Sylvie's eyes brim with tears.

Some years later, the narrator returns to Loisy for the celebration of another national holiday. He renews his friendship with Sylvie and with her brother, and learns that Adrienne has become a nun. As they walk in the woods, chatting and reminiscing, they experience a revival of times past.

On another occasion, the narrator and Sylvie visit her Aunt Othys. They disguise themselves (as children often do) in the aunt's wedding dress and her husband's uniform—a visualization of their unconscious desires.

Now older, the narrator experiences conflicting sensations. He ponders his relationship with Sylvie. She is good for him, he reasons; she represents earthiness, health, and life. But he cannot forget that celestial vision of Adrienne, which returns to haunt him. Nor can he obliterate the image of Aurélie, the actress. The three female images blur in his mind, and he wishes desperately that they were one. Conflict and indecisiveness have entered his life. He is no longer living in a carefree child's world—in an Eden-like paradise.

In Paris, he meets Aurélie, writes a play for her, then tours with her and her troupe in the Valois region. When he tells her of his feelings for Adrienne, she realizes that he is not in love with her. She marries the manager of her troupe, who offers her love with a workable relationship. When the narrator sees Sylvie again he knows now that for her own well-being she must live in the world of reality, even though he cannot. She marries a hard-working young man, Le Grand Frisé. The narrator learns that Adrienne had died many years earlier, in 1832, when in the convent.

The narrator, who had attempted to recreate himself by returning to his origins, is aware of his failure to achieve his goal, but he cannot adjust to the world of reality in which he is forced to live. He opts for escape in travel.

The three female protagonists around whom Nerval's tale focuses—Aurélie, Sylvie, and Adrienne—are all archetypal figures, aspects of the Eternal Feminine or the Great Mother. The narrator's goal is to unify what is divided, to create one person out of the three, to incorporate the characteristics and qualities of each in the others, thus creating a complete or total being who for him represents the ideal.

If such a *coniunctio* were possible, the narrator could render the infinite finite, the abstract concrete. In his perpetual attempt to create unity, he is bringing forth a prismatic world, forever seeing aspects of Adrienne in Sylvie, Adrienne in Aurélie, differentiating still further what he seeks to bind together. Only in a state of reverie or dream can he reshuffle his emotions and coalesce the three women.

Aurélie, Sylvie, and Adrienne—three deities—are not fecundating forces for the narrator because he experiences their powers as an observer: he is a sterile receiver, not an activator. The forces these deities arouse within his psyche serve only to stir his feelings, but never sufficiently to make him act overtly; so he slips in and out of their lives as he does his own reverie. Nothing has changed in his situation—except that at the end he realizes the impossibility of changing three into one and thus of changing his own life's course.

Because the three female figures are archetypal they take on eternal significance—enter the realm of the divine. Aurélie, Adrienne, and Sylvie are representatives of the triunal aspects of the Magna Mater as viewed in Venus in her celestial, terrestrial and infernal manifestations; in the Moon goddess called Selene during the full moon; Artemis with the waxing moon and Hecate when the moon is dark; in the Virgin Mary as saint (the mother of Christ), in her earthly guise as the mother of the other children she had by Joseph; as sinner in Mary the Harlot.

1. Aurélie
Venus (Infernal): Hecate (Dark Moon): Mary the Harlot (Sinner)

Because Aurélie is an actress and represents the world of illusion, which glows only when artificially lit, she stands for Venus in her infer-

nal aspects. Like Venus, she has the power to lure men to her fold, to
compel them to fall victim to her power, to incorporate them into her
since she is a deity, a transpersonal force. She is an infernal Venus such
as had been worshipped in ancient Assyria and Babylonia: goddesses of
sensual love and immorality. In Eastern lands such women became sacred prostitutes, consecrating their bodies to the earthly representatives
of certain deities.[3]

The narrator is obsessed with his vision of Aurélie and "indifferent"
to everything except for this "one well known apparition which illuminated the empty space, infused life with one breath and one word, into
those faces which surrounded me."[4] She embodies his ideal and because
she injects life into him, he believes her to be a creative force in his life.
In reality, he responds passively to her—as a votary before a goddess.
He worships her from afar.

> I felt myself living in her and she lived for me alone. Her smile filled me
> with infinite beatitude; the vibration of her voice, so tender and yet whose
> timber was strong, made me shudder with joy and love. She possessed, for
> me, all the perfections, she answered all my bursts of enthusiasm, all my
> caprices, beautiful like the day when illuminated by the stage lights which
> shone on her from below, pale like the night, when the stage lights were
> dimmed, letting the rays from the chandelier above shine on her, showing
> her in a more natural manner, glittering in the shadow from her beauty
> alone, like the Divine Hours, with a star on their forehead, sculptured on
> the brown background of the frescoes at Herculaneum![5]

The Divine Hours to which Nerval referred were goddesses, in the
service of Venus, representing time: years, hours, minutes, seconds—all
united and linking all generations together. By associating Aurélie with
these Divine Hours, he infuses her with an eternal quality (cyclical time)
and since they are in Venus' employ, with love. By adding the city of
Herculaneum to the image, he gives historical credence to what was
merely a fantasy before and, by the same token, endows Aurélie with
a real, ideal, and eternal existence—thereby fixing time. But Herculaneum has its negative side. It was destroyed by volcanic eruption—and
the narrator's vision of perfection in Aurélie could also be shattered. To
prevent such an outcome, he refrains from approaching her, and signs
the notes he hides in the bouquets he sends her, "from a stranger."

Ideals—such as his vision of Aurélie—cannot remain potent forces in
terrestrial relationships; they cannot be nurtured on earthly contact.
Since Nerval's ideals are anima figures, they feed in unconscious and
dark realms; the light of consciousness causes them to vanish, to shrivel:
"It's an image that I am pursuing, nothing more."[6] The narrator stays
aloof. He avoids coming into contact with Aurélie, rationalizing "that

actresses were not women," that "nature had forgotten to give them a heart," that they were cold, elusive, beautiful, unfeeling, hypnotic in their ways. Unconsciously, he must feel that familiarity breeds contempt.

> Love, alas! vague forms, rose and blue hues, metaphysical phantoms! Seen from close, the real woman would revolt our ingenuity; she had to appear as queen or goddess, and under no circumstances should one approach her.[7]

To contact Aurélie would be to demythify her by humanizing her. Distance is essential for worship. Perfection incarnate exists only as an abstraction, a creation of the mind; it can be kept alive only when experienced in some remote realm—illuminated on stage by an artificial light, functioning as an illusion, wearing a mask. Yet the fear of losing or destroying the image he has of her comes into sharper focus: "I was afraid of troubling the magic mirror which reflected her image."[8] To stare as he had at Aurélie or at a "magic mirror" (or any mirror at all) is to become narcissistic, and this limits any kind of development and leads to death. Gazing into one's own reflection is comparable to an incarceration; it is a fixing, immobilizing agent. If his idealization of Aurélie is not in some way altered, it will not only remain unproductive but will become an agent of self-destruction.

Because of the way Aurélie is illuminated on stage and comes to life only at night in the creation of a world of illusion, she is comparable to the moon goddess Hecate in her blackened phase.

By worshipping the moon, as the narrator does through Aurélie, he is returning to a matriarchal social structure, to even more remote periods in the world, antedating patriarchal sun worship. The "unseen powers of the spirit world," as manifested in the moon's "mysterious qualities," held the narrator spellbound, lulled him into unconsciousness and perhaps even death.[9] So long as he remained in the theatre, he stated, he was happy; the minute he left and his image vanished, he was invaded with melancholy, "the bitter sadness which remains after the disappearance of a dream."[10]

Only at night, in the darkened realms, did the narrator come to life. The Hecate aspect of the night deity, the goddess of the darkened moon who reigned over the lower world, tantalizes the narrator. In ancient times she was worshipped as a goddess of ghosts and magic; she haunted crossways and graves, accompanied the dogs of the Styx and the shadow of departed specters. Aurélie, in her "glorious" and "terrible" aspects— her "nonhuman" way of life—mesmerized the narrator,[11] and engendered beauty, mystery, and excitement within his psyche.

Because she is a representative of infernal love, the passion she inspires is dark, Hecate-like, mysterious, frightening, and perhaps even fatal. Like Hecate, Aurélie causes confusion, chaos.[12] The epithet *phosphorous* has been associated with Hecate, who is frequently pictured as carrying a torch. She is a "light bringer," not of purification but of consciousness.[13]

The light illuminating her on stage brings out her sensuality, her volatile nature; it shimmers, underlining an erotic and passionate side. In this respect, Aurélie may be likened to Mary the Harlot (or Mary the Egyptian) before her redemption.

Mary the Harlot represented the infernal side of this triunal figure, the debauched individual who remained so until her conversion. This "infernal" Mary prostituted her way to the Holy Land, and then lived as an anchorite in the desert. Along with Mary Magdalene, this infernal Virgin is frequently depicted in sculptures and paintings as black. In Einsiedeln, Switzerland, the black Virgin "stands on the moon" and works miracles for cripples and invalids. In Chartres, the statue of the Black Virgin bears a dark face. At Notre Dame de la Recourance (Orléans), the statue of the Black Virgin, highly prized, is supposed to possess great powers.[14] Aurélie also shines "in the shadow of her beauty alone"—and returns to darkness, as does the moon, when not lighted by some external force.

When the narrator listens to her recite Schiller's verses, he is enraptured by the "sublime" manner in which she brings them to life. He sends her a note, then leaves for Germany. He wants this image to remain with him eternally: "That's something fixed for the future." To alter his relationship with her would be to personalize it and to bring it down to earth, to debase his love by putting her on a footing with other "vulgar ones."[15]

When the narrator returns to Paris, she agrees to act in his play; then he goes on tour with Aurélie and her troupe, and the ideals begin to slip as the world of reality takes possession of him. The narrator invites her to lunch at the castle of the "white queen," and as she rides over the fields in her riding habit, her blond hair floats in the wind, reminding him of "a queen of yesteryear," a goddess. Even the peasants stop, astounded, and look at her. He takes her to the place where he had first seen Adrienne, and tells her of his love for this beautiful girl. Aurélie understands, and says, "You don't love me! You are waiting for me to tell you that the actress is the same person as the nun; you are searching for a drama and the ending escapes you . . ."[16] Dismayed, he questions: "Then it wasn't love after all?"

The illusion has vanished. The attempted fusion of Aurélie (the symbol of all that is infernal, dark, and sinful) and Adrienne (the world of the spirit) cannot take place in the domain of reality. Now Aurélie flows out of narrator's life back to some remote past, some fabulous era—a fantasmagoria.

2. Adrienne
Venus (Celestial), Moon Goddess Selene (Full Moon),
Virgin Mary (Saint)

Adrienne is the most elusive and haunting figure in *Sylvie*. She may be linked to Venus in her celestial aspects and called "the Heavenly" one who represented pure and idealistic love. Many temples to honor her were built on mountains and citadels in Greece and Asia Minor. As a goddess and celestial figure, she inspired mystery and awe, which rendered her even more captivating than Aurélie with whom he could come into contact at will.

Adrienne is first described dancing around with the little girls from the ancient province of Valois. The reddened stone façade, the pointed slate-covered roof, the varied carvings on the castle that stood at the far side of the lawn—all injected an outer-worldly atmosphere onto the scene. Adrienne began singing as "the setting sun pierced through the leaves with its flaming rays" and he heard an ancient French romance which filled him with "melancholia and love."[17]

The coloring and hues used by Nerval to describe Adrienne attest to her spirituality and purity: "heavenly" blends of pastel tones, blond curls, the whiteness of her skin and countenance. All these stand in sharp contrast wih the surrounding tonalities. And because of these hues, she is associated with one of the triunal aspects of the moon goddess, Selene, who was worshipped in East Asia and Syria, as a celestial figure depicted in subdued light. She was a beautiful woman with long wings who wore a golden diadem. When her great love, Endymion, died, Zeus bestowed on him eternal youth, which could only be experienced in a sleeping state. It was believed that Selene came down from the heavens nightly to embrace her beloved in his grotto.

Adrienne also possessed spiritual and reflective qualities. As she began her song, the moon became visible in the distance, its diaphanous and ethereal hues invaded the entire scene, "the shadow descended along the great trees and the moon light thus being born shed itself on her alone, isolated from our circle. . . ." It was as if her "divine" essence were being illuminated, all blending so exquisitely with the beauty of her song, the stillness of the evening, and the intensity of the emotion she had aroused in the narrator. The narrator, believing himself to be "in paradise," kissed Adrienne, as was the custom, and she became a "sacred" object for him.[18]

Adrienne was the same type of evanescent human being as the Vestal Virgins of old who performed their religious rituals in natural surroundings, exuding spirituality and implanted in a diaphanous setting: the grass "was covered with condensation which gave off feeble vapors which unrolled their white flakes on the tips of the grass. . . ." It was as if all the elements—the universe united—had come into play in this image: water, fire, earth, air.

As the image comes into sharper focus, Adrienne represents the celestial aspects of the Virgin Mary: the mother of Christ, the heavenly, saintly, immaculate and perfect side of the triunal great mother archetype. She is surrounded with "the shining leaves on her blond hair dazzling when illuminated by the pale rays of the moon. . . ."[19] Like many statues, paintings, and descriptions of the celestial Venus, Selene and the Virgin Mary, Adrienne's face was bathed in an ethereal and spiritual light. A halo encircled her head—not brilliant or brash, but "pale," representing the internal or reflective qualities in a human being. Because of the dreamy atmosphere, the narrator considers her to be semidivine—like Dante's Beatrice—a soul in all of its beauty and purity.

The fusion of Adrienne as a moon deity and as the celestial Virgin Mary is even more apparent when recalling the sculptures in medieval art, when the Virgin Mary was featured "enthroned" on the moon and called by Catholic church fathers "The Moon of the Church, or Moon, the Spiritual Moon, the Perfect and Eternal Moon."[20] As Adrienne stood on the lawn singing her ancient romance, the rays of the moon filtered through the surrounding trees and shrubs, lighting up her countenance, infusing it wih a mysterious power.

In antiquity the moon goddess, believed to be the "actual fire of the moon," was depicted carrying a torch and wearing a moon crescent. The festival of candles (or torches), celebrated in her honor in pagan times on August 15, was carried into Christian tradition to mark the day the Virgin Mary ascended to heaven, "when the course of her earthly life was run" and she "assumed in body and in soul to heavenly glory." (This belief became doctrine by papal decree in 1950.)

Some years later the narrator returns to Valois region and learns that Adrienne had become a nun. He goes to Châalis, a town with monuments dating from the Renaissance. With Sylvie's brother, he enters an ancient abbey and watches a medieval mystery play that depicts Christ's descent into Hell. Adrienne suddenly appears to him in the role of the Virgin Mary.

> A spirit was rising from the abyss, holding a flaming sword in its hand calling the others to come and admire the glory of Christ vanquisher of Hades. This spirit was Adrienne transfigured by her costume, as she already had been by her vocation. The golden colored cardboard nimbus which surrounded her angelic head appeared to us quite naturally a circle of light: her voice had increased in force and in dimension.[21]

After the performance, the narrator and Sylvie's brother go to the guardhouse where they see an ancient coat of arms on the door: a swan with outspread wings.[22] The swan, an animal close to the narrator's heart, is known to sing out his beautiful song just before he is to die.[23] An ominous tone seems to be injected into the narrative at this juncture—a premonition of death.

But Adrienne was already dead to him; she had become a nun and departed from the world of the living to enter the realm of God. His image of her singing on the lawn as a young girl had not grown dim; on the contrary, it became more powerful in his mind's eye in an idealized and divine form. Her portrayal of the Virgin Mary seemed, therefore, to corroborate his own inner feelings: she had really entered the world of the divine—as a swan she had eclipsed herself from his life.

The narrator is told only at the end of the tale that Adrienne had died in 1832 at the convent of Saint S. . . .[24] Death, however, was not an end to life for the narrator and was considered merely as a temporary change. According to certain ancient sects, including the Pythagoreans, the dead went to the moon for three nights (when the moon was not visible). On the fourth night, when the moon could again be seen, it was believed that the individuals who had departed from the earth had been reborn in light and in joy. Pythagoras spoke of the "Isle of the Blessed," a celestial plane located on the sun, the moon and the Milky Way. Plutarch believed that after death the spirit went to the sun; the body remained in the earth and the soul was purified in the moon. It is understandable that the narrator associate the divine Adrienne with the celestial aspects of the moon.

Throughout the tale the narrator attempted to unify what had been severed, to fuse the celestial and infernal aspects—Adrienne, Aurélie. Aurélie, who held the narrator's attention nightly was a theatrical performer: an entertainer, a seductress, a sinner, a Mary the Harlot type, an incarnation of the sensual Venus (infernal) of the Hecate Moon figure. Men succumbed to this type of woman, to her wiles; Zagreus, Pentheus, Orpheus had all, passively, bowed to her ways.

Yet the memory of the celestial Adrienne invaded his very being— "the flower of night as it emerges, pink and rose phantom slipping onto the green grass half bathed in white vapors.[25] He could think only of her.

Unable to capture what was evanescent, to unite what was divided, the narrator's feelings forever oscillate. Aurélie incorporates his being. "I felt myself live in her."[26] Then he recalls Adrienne as she sang, as she entertained, and perhaps, they were one and the same person: saint and sinner. "To love a nun under the guise of an actress. . . . It's enough to drive one insane!"[27]

Mythologically, the narrator's desire to incorporate the differentiated aspects of the Magna Mater archetype is perfectly valid but can only happen in a nondifferentiated realm—either in the unconscious, in the cosmic pleroma, in death, or in the religious cult. During these moments, each aspect inhabits the other; just as the maiden becomes the future woman and the woman once again the maiden, the two become one. In the Eleusinian mysteries, the initiate celebrated and worshipped Demeter as both girl and woman—and in this very unification the mystery was buried.[28] It was neither unusual nor contradictory to unite opposites in ancient religious and philosophical thought. The moon goddess promoted fertility but she also destroyed life. In Christian tradition, God in Christ cannot be both good and evil, fertile and destructive. He is one or the other. The other then is either the Devil or the Anti-Christ. Moon worshippers expressed the duality of their divinity in terms of the brightness or darkness of the moon: the full or celestial moon was interpreted as spreading goodness; the smaller the crescent, the greater the dimness and darkness in the heavens and, therefore, the possiblity of evil.[29]

As the narrator attempts to fuse the saint and sinner in his tale, his visualizations grow increasingly mysterious, blurred. What he seeks cannot exist in the clear, rational, differentiated world of reality. Only in his dream could the memories of Adrienne and Aurélie coalesce; then, engulfed by their presences, he sensed "a fatal attraction toward the unknown, like the firefly escaping into the rushes on stagnant waters. . . ."[30]

3. Sylvie
Venus (Earthly), Moon Goddess Artemis (Waxing Moon), Virgin Mary (Terrestrial).

Sylvie is the only feminine figure with whom the narrator establishes a direct and relatively continuous relationship. She represents all that is normal, healthy, beautiful, fresh, pleasant, and natural.

Sylvie stands for the earthly Venus, as manifested in ancient times in her appearance in groves, gardens, spring time; she is fructifying and creative. Sylvie belongs to the country; she is in harmony with nature and featured always in pastoral scenes.

Because Sylvie is described as the most "beautiful" girl at Loisy, "good and pure in heart," she may be likened to Artemis and to the Virgin Mary. Artemis was a fertilizing force; she helped seeds to germinate, plants to grow, affected tides, and was instrumental in the evolution of plants and animals. She was also looked upon as the luminous god of the day. She is portrayed as a huntress chasing wild animals; a joyful maiden dancing, bathing with her friends; she is revered as a virgin goddess, instrumental in the healthy development of childbirth, though not necessarily marriage. Like the terrestrial Virgin Mary—the mother who gave birth to her other children with Joseph—Sylvie too will become a mother and wife at the end of the tale. That Sylvie may be associated with the virgin goddess Artemis as well as with the Virgin Mary becomes clear when analyzing the word *parthenos* associated with the great moon goddesses of antiquity. *Parthenos,* in ancient times, meant "unmarried," but not necessarily chaste as it came to mean with regard to Mary. When Isaiah wrote "and a virgin shall be with child" he meant simply that an unmarried woman would give birth.[31] The virgin goddesses of antiquity differed from the Christian Mary in that the latter had been chaste when giving birth to her firstborn; the other children she bore with Joseph in a natural manner.[31]

Because she is an earth principle and represents the human side of Venus, the moon, and the Virgin Mary, Sylvie stands for balance and relatedness—the wife, maiden, and mother archetype all in one. She was a positive force for the narrator because she brought him down to earth, focusing, orienting and stabilizing him as best she could. She possessed everything he lacked.[32]

Sylvie also comes to represent chronological, irreversible time. When the narrator focuses his attention on Loisy and Sylvie, he asks himself: "What time is it?"[33] and wonders what she is doing at this very moment. Though he has no watch, he looks at a rococo clock wih the figures of time encrusted on it and with "the historical Diana" leaning on her stag and "depicted in bas relief under the face of the clock."[34] By associating mythological time (Diana-Artemis) with chronological time (the clock), he injects eternity as well as earth-bound aspects into his image.

Time plays an important part in this tale with respect to Sylvie, as it had with Aurélie (when he noticed the Divine Hours depicted on the frescoes of Herculaneum).[35] When young and enjoying Sylvie's company at Loisy, he had no notion of time; it was as meaningless as it had been for primitive man. Youth stands for activity, growth, and futurity; it cannot be viewed objectively. Only with age, when distinctions came into existence (past, present, future) does the narrator become aware of the destructive nature of time and equate it with loss of youth and death. When the narrator looks back at his adolescent years, he realizes that time is his arch enemy, propelling the days, seasons, years. Only by plunging back into his youth (through the dream or reverie) can he avoid the negative time factor.

Both cosmic and historical time are brought in during the national holiday celebrated in the "land of old families," in "castles lost in the forest," domains hidden from civilization. In part, the festivities consist in crossing a small pond that takes the guests onto a tiny island on which an unfinished temple stands, once dedicated to Urania, the muse of astronomy represented with a globe and compass. As a representative of the cosmic world (astronomy, astrology) she gives orientation and focus to her ideations by means of the globe and compass, making order out of chaos. The maidens, as they frolicked on this tiny island, reminded the narrator of beautiful Greek girls celebrating their festivities centuries back. The entire scene is likened to Watteau's painting *Embarking for Cythera,* the island on which Venus had once been worshipped and where Francesco Colonna experienced beatitude with his love. The image is not flawless: modern times intrude in the form of the up-to-date clothes worn by the guests. Once again he realizes that he is unable to experience either complete reimmersion in the past or perfection in reality.

Before and during the feast, "toward the last rays of the sun,"[36] the narrator notices a change in Sylvie: she is more seductive, more irresistible than his last image of her. Her smile has transformed her into a Greek statue: the symmetry of her features has become exquisite, her hands, delicate and white, "worthy of antique art" and "during the night hour" she becomes even more captivating and enchanting.[37] The narrator and Sylvie chat of their "childhood souvenirs," which, with the lapse of time, have become sacred to them; the past has been transformed into a hierophany. As their reverie deepens, so nature descriptions acquire new dimensions, uniting in their imagination both celestial and earthly spheres: images of trees that reach up toward heaven and bury their roots deeply into the ground follow; "their shadows are cast" on the waters, and such seemingly disparate forces as sky and earth are linked.[38]

During the festivities, a wild swan, hidden in a basket under the garlands and crowns of flowers, flies forth toward the "dying sun" and in its flight displaces the garlands that the guests grab for themselves. The narrator avails himself of one, places it on Sylvie's head, kisses her as he had Adrienne so many years before, obliterating in her mind the pain he had caused her as a child.

In Adrienne's case, the swan image had been associated with death. With Sylvie, it represents womanliness—and a union of opposites or, for the alchemist, the hermaphrodite. The swan's body is female in its rounded contours but its elongated neck, associated with the phallus, symbolizes the male. The fact that Nerval's swan flies toward the sun, dropping the garlands of flowers on it way, stresses the dual aspect of the image—man (earth) and spirit (as it rises upward and drops the floral or female components that fall to earth, thereby returning them to mother nature).

In Wagner's *Lohengrin* (1846–48), the knight of the Holy Grail is led by a swan to rescue the Princess Elsa of Brabant, whom he marries. Upon learning of her violation of a pledge (she was not supposed to ask him his name or details of his life) he departs on the back of the swan to the Grail castle forever. The implication of the Wagnerian motif is that it is best to remain aloof from others, best to refrain from delving too deeply into relationships, because if one does so, love vanishes. To become intimate is to kill love, an emotion that is enhanced by distance and imagination.

The image of the swan as a composite of opposites and as used in *Lohengrin* may be a visualization of the course of the narrator's relationship with Sylvie.

Because of the narrator's desperate need to unite what is disparate, Adrienne's image intrudes upon certain scenes. When he walks through the country drenched in Rousseau-like atmosphere, he approaches a convent where he thinks Adrienne may have lived: "the moon hid from time to time behind the clouds, hardly lighting the dark grey rocks." These rocks, dating from Roman times, lend a sense of mystery to the atmosphere; they are also mirrorlike, reflecting a vague, clouded vision of ancient periods. As the narrator walks, his conscious mind is focused on Sylvie, yet he is invaded with Adrienne's presence. Both Sylvie and Adrienne seem to come to life in the spectacle of nature before him. He lies down on the grass, attempts to take in the entire cosmos in his embrace, falls asleep and reawakens the following morning to the sound of church bells. He is tempted to climb the convent wall before his departure but refrains from doing so because he feels it would be a "profanation" of Adrienne's image. The word *profanation* implies that Adrienne is a goddess; to approach divinity would be to demythify her and render her powerless.

Sylvie's earth-bound nature becomes all the more evident with the passing of years. Yet some quality remaining within her infuses her with extratemporal characteristics. She is a maker of fine lace now, and as she worked with agility a "divine smile" seemed to radiate from her face, elevating her; she is not a remote deity but an earthly and breathtakingly beautiful goddess. Later, as the two walk through the forests and meadows, listening to the birds, the sound of the flowing water, the entire vision is impregnated with flowers, trees and grass—a fitting background for this maiden, who draws her real strength from the ground.

Water images, used throughout the tale, link and unify what is disparate. The water is always "calm," describing most succinctly the soothing nature of Sylvie's attitude toward life; when walking, "the reflections of heaven cast their shadows on the waters," indicating the narrator's desire to encapsulate the world through her. He says: "I saw the distant ponds etched out like mirrors on a foggy plain." This suggests the muddiness and ambiguity of the narrator's attitude toward life, his constant dissatisfaction with the world of reality in its differentiated form. A puddle "formed a little lake in the middle of gladiolas and irises"—underscoring the fluid, mysterious and dreamy aspect of his relationship with Sylvie, as well as its terrestrial side.[39]

Without water, life could not exist. It is a creative element, just as Botticelli's painting *The Birth of Venus Emerging from the Waters* depicted it. The flowing, calm and serene waters in the early sections of *Sylvie* are transformed little by little into dead or stagnant waters, or coexist, as in the following image.

> The Thève flowed to our left, leaving at its bends eddies of stagnant water where yellow and white lilies grew, where, daisies like the frail embroidery

of starfish burst forth. The fields were covered with bundles and stacks of hay, the odor of which went to my head without making me drunk, as the fresh odor of the woods and thickets with flowery thorns had formerly.[40]

The stagnant waters in which the lilies grow symbolize the narrator's narcissism, his desire to fix things and to prevent any kind of change, his longing to live permanently in a world of beauty, idealism, abstraction. The immobility of this image is present in the very motility of waters: its continuous metamorphosis, its ceaseless activity. Its transitory nature is endless and, therefore, eternal. The lilies that have grown from the depths of these waters represent a fertile and positive force, but they also usher in moods of melancholia because they are rooted in dead waters—notions that have never evolved.[41] Yet even narcissistic meditation and obsessions may have their positive results: they may produce a work of art (flowers)—in the narrator's case, the story itself. The piles of wheat in the distance also have value: they nourish and activate, and they indicate life's desire to cope with the forces that may hamper it. Wheat, as the "staff of life," encourages earth-bound nature to grow and pursue its course. Wheat suggests Sylvie, the earth-being; the stagnant waters, the narrator or poet. They are poles apart at this juncture, and it is fitting that he now realize Sylvie no longer loves him.

Sylvie, who has entered womanhood, is no longer satisfied with the tenuous, imaginative, poetic world that the narrator offers her. She must have more tangible things: a husband, children. She affirms life. When he realizes that he has been rejected from her world, he throws himself at her feet. "I confessed while weeping." He promises to change his ways. Just "Save me" he pleads. But both know that for Sylvie to enter the narrator's domain would be as fatal as for him to become part of her world.[42]

When the narrator learns that Sylvie is to marry another childhood friend, the hard-working down-to-earth Grand Frisé, who is to become a baker, the Sylvie he had once idealized as Artemis, as the earthly Venus, as the sublime Virgin, is transformed into the prosaic country bourgeoise. "Illusions fall, one after another, like the skin from fruit and the fruit, is experience. Its taste is bitter, yet there is a bitterness about it which strengthens."[43]

The narrator's pain is lessened when he remembers that her husband-to-be was his *frère de lait;* in a remote way they are related, so he is still bound to Sylvie. More important, Le Grand Frisé, who once saved him from drowning when he was a young boy, represents the steady, heroic force in life: the swimmer, the conqueror of the elements. By marrying Sylvie, he prevents another death—hers, which would have been inevitable if she had married the narrator.

Later, the narrator understands the meaning of his "lost star" of the loves he had experienced when a youth "which glistened with double power . . . two halves of a single love." Adrienne was the "sublime ideal," and Sylvie, the "tender reality."[44]

The love the narrator felt for the three feminine deities in their triunal aspects—Adrienne, Aurélie, Sylvie—is a deep-seated death wish. By projecting onto them so continuously he had become completely passive, seldom reacting overtly in any way—rarely, except in the case of Sylvie, establishing any relationship with them. He experienced their force as a votary, a sacrificial agent. Unlike the aggressive heroes he so admired—Prometheus, Cain, Tubal-Cain, Adoniram—the narrator's sacrifice was in vain. He found no true love and could never concretize his ideal vision because he was himself incapable of loving either of the three protagonists as they were, on their terms. He could only love those characteristics he projected on to them, those aspects of himself or those he saw in them at certain periods in his life. As such, "they became a function of his own psyche,"[45] and when they could not conform to his standard, he experienced dejection and alienation. He was forever imprisoning Adrienne, Sylvie, and Aurélie in his own limited vision of them, viewing them always in terms of himself.[46] Because he was unaware of what was happening to him, he was incapable of judging, analyzing, or assessing their personalities objectively. He was dominated by his own inner world and what it saw in the three archetypal figures involved. No mediating function between the image he had of the three young girls and reality ever emerged. Only further disparity between the ideal and the real could possibly ensue—and with it, increased tendencies toward self-destruction or emotional castration.[47]

19 ISIS
THE CULT OF THE MADONNA

*I am that which was, is or will be and no
mortal yet has raised my veil.*
          Inscription on the Temple to Isis
          at Saïs.

Nerval's narrative *Isis* (1845) is an expression of his synchretistic approach to religion and, in particular, an example of the immense role played by the feminine principle in his cosmology.

Isis takes place in Herculaneum and Pompeii, cities destroyed by the eruption of Mt. Vesuvius A.D. 79. It is night. The moon shines brilliantly and the illusion of the past grandeur of these cities is complete. Nerval tells us that an ambassador in Naples had given a costume ball a few years earlier and in so doing had revived all the ancient Roman customs for the festivities: the dance, the chariot races, the temples with their vestal virgins, the stores and merchants with their wares. This "palingensian attempt," wrote Nerval, was interesting, but the most fascinating ceremony of them all took place at sundown in the "admirable" temple to Isis.[1]

The physical features of this house of worship are then described: the two altars in the temple, the statues of Isis, and the two vases containing holy water on either side of the entrance, which he compares with the fonts in Catholic churches. Nerval then outlines the rituals involved in the secret cult of Isis while underscoring the similarities existing between the Egyptian and Christian rites. The high priest, together with his deacons, recite special prayers and litanies, burn incense on the altar while flutes play softly in the background; sistrums are sounded by the devout and the life story of Isis is enacted before the congregation in pantomime or in symbolic dances. The most awe-inspiring part of the entire ceremony, according to Nerval, took place when the high priest, with his deacons standing on either side of him, covered his hands with the fine linen of his robe and elevated the holy water, which contained the living presence of Osiris, before the worshippers. The devout then raised their hands heavenward and expressed "the miracle of divine mercy" and cried out: "We have found it and we—all of us—are joyous!"

Nerval then focuses his attention upon Lucius Apuleius and his initiation into the Isis mysteries, as recorded in *The Golden Ass*. Nerval underscores the affinities existing between the ancient Egyptian Isis cult of the Madonna and the worship of the Virgin Mary in the Christian religion.

For Nerval, Isis was a positive manifestation of the Great Mother archetype. He viewed her as he did the Virgin Mary, as a figure with outstretched arms, always ready to comfort and hold him in her embrace. Nerval pointed out many similarities between Isis and the Virgin Mary. Not only are there "a thousand analogous details in the ceremonies" involved in their worship, but in the many concrete depictions of them. Both Isis and the Virgin Mary held their child-god in their arms;[2] both held a cross, gave milk, were born under the same sign of the zodiac, were featured with a moon placed either below their thrones or in the background, wore a glowing nimbus around their head.[3] Isis was a *mediatrix* between man and the divine; Mary, between the sinner and God. And, Nerval adds, "the adoration by man of a Celestial Mother whose child is the hope of the world" is not only understandable, it is a necessity."[4]

The worship of the eternal feminine (the Great Mother, Mother Nature or the Madonna) dates back not only to Egyptian mystery cults but to the very dawn of history. In China and Japan, for example, the mother goddess Kuan-yin was most frequently depicted with her child in her arms or lap and she was considered a savior and a symbol of mercy and gentleness. In India, Sakti or Kali Durga, the Great Mother was equally beneficial in her relationships with men. In the ancient world, along the Tigris, Euphrates, and Nile rivers and in Asia Minor, she was worshipped under many names: Ishtar, Isis, Atargatis, Rhea, Cybele, Artemis, among others. During the last years of paganism there was an attempt to unify worship throughout the ancient world. Isis became this composite figure known as "The Divine Mother, The Blessed Queen of Heaven."[5] The cult of the Virgin Mary was a continuation of this tradition.

Nerval lists the various names under which Isis was worshipped in antiquity: Venus, Ceres, Persephone.

CELESTIAL VENUS: (Aphrodite): In this manifestation she acted through her son Eros (Cupid), enabling all of mankind to unite, to come together. Eros, the god of relatedness, enacted his mother's wishes.

TERRESTRIAL CERES: (Demeter): The corn goddess, the origin and source of all that grows on earth. When her daughter Persephone was taken from her, she became barren. She was productive only during the six months of the year when her daughter was returned to her: summer-winter.

INFERNAL PERSEPHONE (Hecate): Ruler of the dead, of the ghosts. She watched over the living as well.

Together, these three goddesses, as embodied in Isis, represent a totality. The three have their psychological equivalents. Venus, for example, represents man's need to unite, to relate to others, to strive for spiritual values. Ceres stands for his earthly aspects, his desire to reproduce, his conscious and daily activities. Persephone symbolizes man's unconscious, that tremulous realm where fears, rancor, as well as secret positive forces rumble.[6]

During the early centuries of Christianity, when the ancient world was declining and new ways were taking hold, a struggle between matriarchal and patriarchal traditions was widespread. Isis worship was a powerful force at this time. As the bearer of a divine child under mysterious circumstances, as a wife who bore her husband's death with strength and who brought about his renewal in her son—all possibilities and mysteries lived within her.[7] Because she remained one of the most important factors in Egyptian religion, she posed a severe threat to early Christians and repeated attempts were made by them (following Hebrew tradition), to wipe out the Madonna cult. St. Paul, the harbinger of patriarchal Christianity, did his best to unseat matriarchal worship as witnessed by his attitude toward Diana. We read in Acts:

> Demetrius, a silversmith, which made silver shrines for
> Diana, brought no small gain unto craftsman . . . (19:24)
> . . . but almost throughout all Asia, this Paul hath persuaded
> and turned away much people, saying that they be no gods,
> which are made with hands; (19:26)
> So that not only this our craft is in danger to be set at
> nought; but also that the temple of the great goddess Diana
> should be despised, and her magnificence should be destroyed,
> whom all Asia and the world worshippeth. (19:27)
> And when they heard these sayings, they were full of wrath
> and cried out, saying, Great is Diana of the Ephesians. (19:28)

As a result of the suppression of matriarchal deities, certain strange Christian sects developed during the early Christian centuries. The Collyridians, in the fifth century, worshipped the Virgin Mary in the same manner as the ancient Egyptians and Greeks had adored Isis and Diana. The orthodox Epiphanius halted such rites and declared: "Let Mary be held in honour, and let the Father and the Son and the Holy Ghost be adored, but let no one adore Mary."[8]

At Ephesus, the center of the Artemis-Diana Madonna cult,[9] a council of Christian bishops gave Mary the title of "Theotokos," "Mother of God," an appellation that took on the power of dogma. It was "she who gave birth to God," who became the "vessel that was found worthy to contain Him whom heaven and earth cannot contain because of the vastness of His glory." The Virgin Mary became the transmitter of the divine "mystery."[10]

In early Christianity the cult of the Virgin, therefore, had not yet been strongly integrated into church doctrine. The miracles of the Virgin in the Middle Ages and in later history (Lourdes and Fatima, for example) were individual expressions of an immense need among the people.[11] In the western church, the ancient cult of the Virgin was "replaced by the institution of the Church."[12] Priests remained celibate, monks were tonsured, just as Isis worshippers had also always remained chaste. All these deprivations were signs of an inner sacrifice. The union between the physical priest and the spiritual female principle in Roman Catholicism is represented by the celebration of the first Mass read by the priest. This is his most solemn moment. The priest is the bridegroom who is marrying the church (Mary) and is giving up the human woman for complete union with her spiritual manifestation. He is in effect becoming the "bride of God" and the "bride of Christ" and in this sense, he "is feminine."[13] The extreme need Christians felt for the female principle became manifest in the twentieth century with the proclamation of the Assumption of the Virgin Mary as dogma. Her Assumption was a "prototype of man's bodily resurrection. As Bride of God and Queen of Heaven. . . ."[14]

For Nerval, Isis and the Virgin Mary filled an aching void in his heart and soul.

While describing Lucius' deep immersion in the Isis mysteries, Nerval was in effect projecting his own inner contents onto Isis. She became for him a composite figure: the Egyptian goddess Isis and the hyperdulian Virgin Mary.

Lucius was born in North Africa (A.D. 155), studied in Carthage and Athens, and spent several years traveling and learning the mysteries implicit in a variety of occult arts. In his novel *The Golden Ass* he relates the tale of his transformation from man to donkey. Because he had attempted to learn certain secrets in the art of magic from a slave girl, with whom he was having a love affair, he had violated certain religious laws. He was punished for his transgressions by Isis, who felt he was unprepared to comprehend fully the occult arts whose secrets he had not merited but had tried to win through deceit. The rest of the volume deals with Lucius' adventures as an ass, the suffering and humiliations he endured, his final initiation into the Isis mysteries, his transformation back to man, and his departure for Rome, where he became an eminent lawyer—always working, thereafter, in complete harmony with his deity, Isis.

Why should Lucius have been drawn to Isis worship and not to Mithraism or Christianity? In a growing patriarchal society, Lucius, who suffered from a mother complex, could not relate to the prevailing form of worship. He needed a *mediatrix* who would help him express his feelings and give him the experience necessary to handle people and situations. Only through the positive aspects of the Great Mother, the bearer of the feeling principle, could he come to know and experience a sense of belonging. Once such feelings of warmth could be enjoyed, he would be able to go one step further and know redemption which, in psychological terms, means fulfillment.

Nerval suffered from similar problems. Like Lucius, he could not adapt to his times. He suffered intensely because of an inability to relate to or understand women. He had never been given the kind of maternal love so necessary to a child during his early years. Whenever he did fall in love, therefore, he divinized, adulated and worshipped the object of his projections. Because of this naïve view of women, he neglected to take into consideration their negative side and, as such, not only became vulnerable but was the recipient of their destructive aspects.[15] The more powerful his hurt after loving such women as Jenny Colon and Marie Pleyel, the more isolated he felt and the greater was his despair. The agony of life became almost unbearable. As a way of release, he began fantasizing about women. Rather than worshipping living beings, as he had done in the past, he resorted to spiritualized women, divinities: Isis, the Virgin Mary, or some celestial force—a star. In so doing, he felt safe. He could not be rejected. He would never experience alienation. But he was withdrawing from life, slowly withering away.

The fact that Isis first appeared to Lucius in a dream is significant in our study of Nerval. Real life at this juncture in Nerval's earthly sojourn was experienced only on an unconscious level. Everyday existence was peripheral. His dream world had become the most intense and exciting part of his experience. Nerval does not merely translate Lucius' description of Isis in his narrative; he paraphrases it, incorporating his own subjective feelings in the picture.

> Her long thick hair fell in tapering ringlets on her divine neck, and was crowned with an intricate chaplet in which was woven every kind of flower. Just above her brow shown a "silvery moon"; vipers rising on either side of the blond partings of her hair. Her robe, with its myriad reflections, changing with the folds, from the purest white to saffron-colored yellow, from which its flame red seems to be borrowed; her mantle, deep black, is bordered with a luminous fringe; her right hand holds the bronze sistrum, which sings out clearly; in her left hand, is the golden vase in the form of a gondola.[16]

Isis is associated with the "silvery moon." Let us recall that moon worship was the product of a matriarchal society that antedated patriarchal sun worship in Egypt. Since the moon reflects color, it symbolizes the unconscious, as opposed to the sun, which is linked to thinking or consciousness. Because the moon at its fullest has the greatest power over all things (vegetative, animal, mineral) it is believed to govern life and death. Likewise, the moon, as incorporated in the Isis deity in the above description, may be said to have ruled over the psyches of both Apuleius and Nerval.

When Nerval writes, "Just above her brow shown a silvery moon," this image recalls Plato's third eye: it paves the way for inner vision. The "silvery" part of the moon image takes on the value of a mirror; it shines, reflects, and projects whatever comes into its range. When looking at the "silvery moon" one sees oneself as an object outside of oneself or in projection. Accustomed to a subjective evaluation of oneself, one is frequently unable to recognize or accept such an image.[17] Confrontation with this other self is meaningful. It forces another attitude into focus, engendering new insights, as does the dream, that unconscious depiction of conscious events. Through the "silvery moon" Lucius (and hopefully Nerval) first understands his need for Isis. Only she can replenish what had been drained, fecundate what had been stunted: his capacity to express his feelings openly, to relate to others.

The crown of multiformed and multityped flowers on her "divine neck" not only stands for the goddess's beauty, freshness, and fertility, but injects the notion of spring, seasonal change and, therefore, of death and rebirth—the transitory nature of creation. It is interesting to note that Egyptians frequently brought all types of flowers to their feasts to underscore the reality of death and to encourage people to enjoy life. Flowers had always been associated with Greek and Roman goddesses, and the celestial flower with the Virgin Mary. Because of their shape, flowers have come to symbolize the world and its center. As such, they are considered archetypes of the soul. Such an act expressed an unconscious desire to penetrate the very heart of creation, the dawn of their own beings. Psychologically, it expressed a desire and need to return to their past, to experience a rebirth on a higher level—the goal of all initiations and mystery cults.

The vipers "rising on either side of the blond partings of her hair" also indicate an intense need for transformation. Vipers, snakes, and serpents stand for a most primitive strata within the unconscious and are associated with energy. They are catalyzing forces. Didn't the snake inspire Eve to pick the forbidden fruit from the Tree of Knowledge, thereby disobeying God and disrupting the smooth-running patriarchal order? In *The Book of the Dead* (XVII) the reptile was the first living creature to believe in the sun god Ra and to greet him as he emerged from the waters. Because the snake sheds its skin, it represents the eternal force of renewal, regeneration, and resurrection. Since the snake is strong, and fights fearlessly, it is given the tasks, in myths and legends, of guarding springs, caves, and hidden treasures. The psychological implications of snake symbolism are vast. If not properly understood or handled, the snake (as energy) may become destructive, shedding evil and poison, as in the Perseus-Medusa tale. But if the "snake" energy is properly channeled and accepted as part of life's active process existence can be enriched. Within Isis, then, there live both positive and negative forces, but neither Lucius nor Nerval had yet learned to cope with this dynamic entity. Lucius had violated her secret. His rash act indicates his inexperience with the negative side of the female principle and an inability to cope with it. He suffered Isis' wrath. Nerval, who had always overlooked the negative side of the feminine principle, was forever confronted with its destructive force.[18]

The four colors mentioned in the description of Isis (black, white, yellow, red) may be interpreted alchemically as an expression of a need for initiation. Initiation requires confrontation with pain, fear, and anguish, self-discipline and control. Completing such a trial successfully may lead to a fuller and more wholesome existence.

The black in Isis' "black mantle" represents the first phase in the alchemical transformative process. During this period all matter coalesces, churns. Black, for the alchemist, does not necessarily represent evil, but rather the "world beyond" or the "inner world." In Genesis we read:

> . . . and the earth was without form, and void: and
> darkness was upon the face of the deep.(I:2)

Chaos and turbulence exist in the void—but also the creative element. In darkness, germination takes place. Richard Wagner and Victor Hugo considered black, when surrounded by light, a maternal and fecundating principle. Psychologically, only through a descent into the unconscious can illumination be experienced and former attitudes transformed. Orpheus' journey into Hades (grottoes, caves) is a quest to reach the darkest point within, the center, after which inner development or germination may occur. Christ also descended into Hell for three days, after which his soul was redeemed and resurrected. A descent into self or a withdrawal from the world is an outer expression of an inner process.[19] Isis' black mantle indicates that within her lives a world *in potentia,* burgeoning forces of all sorts—spiritual and physical.

White and yellow ("white to saffron-colored yellow") are associated in alchemical terminology with purity, gold, and the sun. They represent the coming to consciousness of an idea or attitude, the emerging of the rational thinking functions, the ordering of heretofore turbulent forces. In Sparta, China, and certain African countries, white is associated with death. Such death can be the end of a previously held philosophical or psychological attitude. In Lucius' case, through his initiation into the Isis mysteries his transformation back to man occurred—from black to gold. Not so for Nerval, who could only experience his initiation into the Isis (Mary) cult vicariously (cerebrally) and, therefore, not authentically.

"Flame red" (or blood) is the alchemical color that imitates the creation of life or the philosopher's stone. Red stands for the very essence of life, the vital force without which nothing could exist. In Egyptian tombs (and in prehistory), corpses, as well as the inside of many coffins, were painted red, indicating that life was eternal and existed after death, though in a different form. In that Isis wore red, she represented both the living and the dead: celestial, earthly, and underworld attitudes.[20]

Lucius was now ready to experience her as a totality, as a living incarnation of the philosopher's stone, a means through which purification and the individuating process could be achieved. But Nerval could only long for such an experience. As a nineteenth-century Christian he could not revert back to Isis worship, nor, as a student of religion in general, could he find fulfillment in the "perfect" image of the Virgin Mary. Because she represented only one aspect of human nature, she could not help him cope with the evils and difficulties of life. To worship her meant further withdrawal from life.

Isis carried "the bronze sistrum" in her right hand. The sistrum was an instrument sounded during the religious ceremony to ward off any evil ghosts or destructive forces. The bell sounded during Catholic mass, which calls attention to the solemn moment at hand and drives away all that is unholy in the Isis ceremony.[21] The fact that Isis holds the sistrum in her right hand—always associated with consciousness—indicates that she stands for a rational way of life and is in the process of relegating all chaotic and tenebrous thoughts and emotions to another sphere. Lucius and Nerval, in their attempts to experience Isis as a totality, are given the means to bring order out of turbulence, accord out of discord.

"In her left hand is the golden vase in the form of a gondola." The left hand ("sinistra") is the dreamer, or so the saying goes. It represents the forces of the unconscious, the underworld—man's shadowy, mysterious, secretive, and arcane regions, the source of his creativity. The fact that the vase is made of gold, the most precious and the purest of metals, implies the immense value placed upon it and its contents. It is shaped like a gondola to indiciate Isis' power over sea-faring vessels. Isis was the goddess of navigators, a function inherited by the Virgin Mary.[22] But the water contained within the vessels is of great import.

The elevation of the holy water to honor Isis was the most solemn moment in the service. The water from the Nile was placed in the golden vessel, symbolizing the body and essence of Osiris, the world fertilizer. Osiris, who represented the father spirit of the living and the dead, came to life during the morning and evening services, each time the high priest showed the people the *hydria,* the golden vessel that was then adored.[23] The water, as the carrier of the divine essence, power, or mana, was capable of bringing about rebirth, healing, miracles, and cures of all sorts, like the waters of Lourdes for the Catholic. The part played by the holy water for the Egyptian is comparable to the transsubstantiation in the Catholic service.[24] The fact that the holy water is contained in a vessel (a female symbol because of its containing quality) implies the blending of the masculine (water) and the feminine forces (vase) or the uterus in which the foetus is born and grows. The female "receptacle" is then a *mediatrix* between the uncreated and the created. In the Isis mysteries, water symbolizes an eternally mobile world and as a result Osiris is in the process of being reborn in his son Horus and bequeathing his powers to him. Isis, in that she holds the vessel in her hand, becomes the vehicle through which the mystery occurs, the rebirth of the living God. Only through the woman, as represented by Isis, may Lucius and Nerval experience rebirth—that is, the renaissance of the Eros or feeling principle within them.

Lucius prayed most fervently to Isis to transform him back to a man and in so doing experienced the greatest of all turmoils. When an animal acts like an animal "he is in harmony with himself," but when a man acts like one, it is an indication of inner chaos.[25]

> You see me here, Lucius, in answer to your prayer. I am Nature, the universal Mother, mistress of all the elements, primordial child of time, sovereign of all things spiritual, queen of the dead, queen also of the immortals, the single manifestation of all gods and goddesses that are. My god governs the shining heights of Heaven, the wholesome sea-breezes, the lamentable silence of the world below. Though I am worshipped in many aspects, known by countless names, and propitiated with all manner of different rites, yet the whole round earth venerates me . . . call me by my true name, namely, queen Isis.[26]

Why did Isis transform Lucius into an ass? Why not into some other animal? The ass was considered by Isis to be the most "hateful" of all animals. The ass was the animal of Osiris' murderer, Set. But the ass also had positive features: he was the sacred animal to such youthful savior gods as Dionysus, Attis, and Tammuz; and the ass carried Christ around Jerusalem and was present at his birth in Bethlehem. Saturn is associated with the ass and, therefore, is endowed with such characteristics as helplessness, creativity, suffering, depression.[27]

As an ass, Lucius was in a state of despair. A composite of destructive and evil forces (Set), of gentleness (Christ carrier), of helplessness (Saturn), he suffered from the conflicts raging between his various traits (his animal form and his human soul). The intensity of his pain brought him to his senses. Turmoil and suffering are part and parcel of all initiations; they brought illumination or light, making him worthy of bearing his name, Lucius—*lucere,* "light."

Light came to Lucius only when he looked at his situation objectively, when he became aware—through Isis—of his inadequate life attitude. The ancient religions (alchemy, masonry, and other occult sects have continued this tradition) believed that the "eternal personality is established in this life and not projected into a postmortal sphere."[28] One must therefore try to experience inner evolution within his mortal state so as to build both body and soul to as high a level as possible. Christianity, on the contrary, stresses an afterlife in which there is hope of redemption—hope of immortality after the last judgment. It was to Lucius's advantage to experience the anguish of initiation on earth. As a Christian, the choice was open to Nerval. He was not driven by that inner compulsion for perfection, and he knew that no matter what the fault or sin, he could or would eventually be pardoned in the hereafter.

Thus, Nerval was not concerned with Lucius's peregrinations as an ass. He could not identify with these aspects of Lucius's mystery. He projected only on Lucius's adoration of Isis and her divine intervention on his behalf. Though he did not quote Lucius's prayer to Isis, "O Blessed Queen of Heaven,"[29] which was later used by the Catholic Church in worship of the Virgin Mary, did look upon her as an eternal and universal principle, as a living corpus, an all-embracing and comforting power.

Lucius' actual initiation was kept a secret. Isis had wisely counseled him to do so.

> Only remember, and keep these words of mine locked tight in your heart, that from now onwards until the very last day of your life you are devoted to my service. It is only right that you should devote your whole life to the goddess who makes you a man again. Under my protection you will be happy and famous, and when at the destined time of your life, you descend to the land of the ghosts, there too in the subterranean hemisphere you shall have frequent occasion to adore me. . . . Further, if you are found to deserve my divine protection by careful obedience to ordinance of my religion by perfect chastity, you will become aware that I, and I alone, have power to prolong your life beyond the limits of appointed destiny.[30]

Initiation can never be revealed since it is a subjective experience. An inner transformation must be lived out on an individual basis, as are birth and death. If the secrets of initiation are related to another, the entire experience loses point and power. The ancients were well aware of the importance of such secrecy. Herodotus never reveals the essence of the mysteries he witnessed in honor of Osiris in front of the Temple of Athens, at Saïs in the Delta.

> It is on this lake that the Egyptians act by night in what they call their Mysteries, the Passion of that being whose name I will not speak. All the details of these performances are known to me, but—I will say no more.[31]

Nor did Christ reveal any facts concerning his initiation, his descent into Hell.

When Nerval visited the Temple of Isis at Pompeii, he underwent a numinous experience that permitted him to understand—though only cerebrally—the complexities of his own problems, problems that face many sensitive people today who find it difficult to exteriorize their feelings. Nerval was incapable of relating to those about him. He needed a *mediatrix,* an intercessor, some force to temper life's cruel ways. Isis, the Queen of Heaven, the Mother of God, the World Principle, the Redeemer, as Nerval called her, understood and loved mankind. She would react and become a helping force to those who took both her positive and negative sides into consideration. If one aspect of her personality was accorded more respect than the other, imbalance resulted within the votary's psyche, making him vulnerable to her power.

Just as Isis had helped Lucius in his battle with life, so Nerval looked toward her and the Virgin Mary, to succor him.

> O nature! O eternal mother! Have mortals come to the point of rejecting all hope and all prestige. O Goddess of Saïs! Has the most brazen of your followers, while raising your sacred veil, come face to face with death?[32]

We know nothing of Nerval's descent into self, into darkness. To penetrate one's inner realm is to undergo the greatest mystery of all!

20 THE CHIMERAS

*The divine spark which guides us upon earth is in us;
it becomes a flame in the temple, a star in the sky. Thus
the light of truth grows brighter. Listen to the Lyre of
seven strings vibrate, the Lyre of God. . . . It causes
worlds to move! Listen well! May the sound penetrate you,
and may the depth of the heavens open!*
                    Edouard Schuré, *The Great Initiates.*

Nerval's twelve sonnets, which he grouped under the title *The Chimeras,*
are among the most beautiful poems in the French language. They may
be sung or recited for the exquisite joy experienced in the musicality
and engaging rhythms of their lines. But it is as a synthesis or quintessence of Nerval's metaphysical and aesthetic principles that *The Chimeras*
will be analyzed in this chapter.

That every word in Nerval's verse is linked to the next in some mysterious manner is not merely due to an aesthetic concern but bears out
his metaphysical concepts, as well. For Nerval, a monist, the world is
one, a living and vibrant organism; the material or visible world is
merely an aspect of or a reflection of a precreation or primordial unity.
To bring forth the feeling of diversity that arose with each creation and
the ensuing tensions, Nerval endows each word with hermetic value, injecting each with multiple possibilities of meanings, rhythms, tonalities,
colors. In so doing, he sets up a series of reverberations, associations
within the body of the sonnet itself. The "correspondences" of ideations,
feelings, and sensations are not necessarily experienced passively, but
frequently force to the surface a series of repelling, colliding motions
within the stanza itself, disturbing the flow of vibrations until they are
reabsorbed into a harmonious whole at the end of the sonnet.

Nerval's approach to religion is also monistic or synchretistic, that is,
he combines "differing beliefs in religion, philosophy"[1] thereby making
them one. Because the world of appearances is differentiated, so each
civilization, each group considers its own beliefs to be unique, infallible,
and perfect, though these are merely avatars of God's original world.
For example, the belief in the death and resurrection of Christ is compared and linked by Nerval to more ancient views, such as the death
and resurrection of Osiris, Dionysus-Zagreus, and Iacchus; the Virgin
Mary is an avatar of Isis, Aphrodite, Artemis, and other goddesses of
antiquity. Because man lives in a state of diversity, he suffers the pain
of antagonism and longs to return to or be reintegrated into the primordial oneness—into God—where he can be lulled into a state of *participation mystique.*

Nerval's metaphysical concepts are based on those forwarded by many ancient sects: the Orphics, the Pythagoreans, the Platonists, the Gnostics, the kabbalists, the alchemists, the astrologists and those who adapted these mystical notions—Swedenborg, the Illuminists, and others. In order to penetrate Nerval's abstruse cosmological realm, a brief résumé of the most basic ideas of Orphism, Pythagoreanism, and Boehmism will be offered.

The Orphici, a mystical sect, claimed Orpheus as their founder and began celebrating his mystery about the sixth century B.C. Orpheus, considered to be the greatest poet and musician of all time, possessor of a seven-stringed lyre capable of mesmerizing peoples, animals, and rocks, was, according to some legends, the son of Oeagrus and the Muse Calliope—according to others, the son of Apollo. Orpheus was credited with having accompanied the Argonauts on their expedition, and with saving their lives by playing music more beautiful and hypnotic than that of the Sirens. He married the nymph Eurydice, who later died from a serpent bite. Orpheus descended into Hades to claim his beloved, played on his lyre and so moved Persephone, the goddess of the underworld, that she allowed Eurydice to return to earth with one proviso: Orpheus could not look back at her as he led her out of Hades. When he did, Eurydice had to return to the underworld forever. Orpheus' bitterness was so great that, once back on earth, he rejected all women and condemned the orgies of the Thracian Maenads. Angered at such rejection, the Maenads, in one of their mad frenzies, dismembered him. His friends, the Muses, buried his limbs, but his heart and lyre floated down the river to Lesbos, the isle of the poets, where they were buried.

During his lifetime Orpheus spread the mystery involved in the death and resurrection of the god Dionysus-Zagreus, which became the focal point of Orphism. Dionysus, the son of Zeus and his daughter Persephone, was torn to pieces and then devoured by the Titans. Hera's jealousy had incited them to commit this act. After Dionysus' dismemberment, he was named Zagreus, "Torn to Pieces." Athene, grieved by such cruelty, stole Dionysus' heart and gave it to Zeus who, with Semele's aid, swallowed it and reincarnated him into Dionysus—the "Divine Child." Thereafter, he was known as Dionysus-Zagreus. Angered by the Titans' destructive act, Zeus sent a thunderbolt and destroyed them all. Man, born from their ashes, is, therefore, a composite of opposites: divine elements (from Dionysus-Zagreus) and Titanic ones (evil, the parts inherited from the Titans).

Orpheus wandered throughout the ancient world singing the mystery of Dionysus-Zagreus—the one who died and was resurrected; he was himself looked upon as the great unifying principle in nature. As the son of Apollo, Orpheus represented light, consciousness, solar spirituality, order, and clarity—the divine aspects in man. When identified with Dionysus-Zagreus, whose doctrine he preached, he stood for the mysterious aspects within man—the darker, tenebrous, invisible inner realm, the domain of the beyond.

Orphic rites are based on the purification of human nature: an attempt to transform what is brute and crude in man's terrestrial nature (the elements imprisoned in his "titanic body") into its divine form. To transcend man's earthly and limited state through ascetic practices (purification rituals, prayers, expiation) not only facilitated his liberation from domination by the flesh but from the infinite reincarnations to which he had to submit before he could attain complete immersion in the divine universal force.

When celebrating the Orphic mysteries in the sanctuaries of Apollo, the priests wore crowns of myrtle and cypress and were clothed in white. They carried ebony scepters with ivory heads, wore golden belts embedded with crystals that shimmered like "multiple glowing stars." Orpheus counseled his followers, who sought to partake in the divine mystery of death and resurrection, to adhere to the following rules:

> Withdraw deep within yourself in order to lift yourself to the Principle of things, to the Great Triad which flames in the immaculate other. Consume your body with the fire of your thought; detach yourself from matter like the flame from the wood which it devours. Then your spirit will ascend into the pure ether of Eternal Causes as the eagle rises to Jupiter's throne.
>
> I shall reveal to you the secret of the worlds, the soul of nature, the essence of God. Hear first the great mystery; a single Being rules in the deep sky and in the abyss of earth, the thundering Zeus, the ethereal Zeus. His are profound counsel, powerful hate and delightful love. He rules in the depths of the earth and in the heights of the starry sky. He is the Breath of things, the untamed fire, eternal Male and Female, a King, a Power, a God, a Grand Master!
>
> Jupiter is divine Husband and Wife, Man and Woman, Father and Mother. From their sacred marriage, from their everlasting union, unceasingly come fire and water, earth and ether, night and day, the proud Titans, the changeless Gods and the floating seed of men.
>
> The loves of heaven and earth are not known to the uninitiated. . . . A little while ago the thunder shook these rocks; lightning fell like living fire and rolling flame, and the echoes of the mountains roared with joy. But you, you were trembling, not knowing whence this fire comes nor where it strikes. It is the male fire, the seed of Zeus, the creative fire . . .
>
> And now look at the firmament. See that shining circle of constellations over which the filmy veil of the Milky Way, the dust of suns and worlds, is thrown! That is the body of the divine wife, who is revolving in celestial harmony to the wrongs of the husbands. Look with the eyes of the spirit, and you will see her head inclined, her arms extended, and you will lift her veil, strewn with stars![2]

According to the Orphic initiatory process, each neophyte must pass into the land of the dead for seven nights and seven days, remaining in a dark, cavelike area where he will experience, both physically and emotionally, the terror connected with this event. In this manner, he enacts and identifies with the death and resurrection of Dionysus-Zagreus. After completing the initiation—and what has been referred to as the Orphic descent (a descent into Self)—the high priest appears with his lyre and speaks to the neophyte in the following terms.

> Hail to all of you who have come to be reborn after the sorrows of the earth, and who are being reborn at this moment! Come, drink of the light of the temple. You who appear out of the night—mystics, women, initiates! Come, rejoice, you have suffered; come, rest. You who have fought! The sun which I invoke above your heads and which will shine in your souls is not the sun of mortals; it is the pure light of Dionysus, the great Sun of the initiates. Through your past suffering, through the trial which brings you here, you will conquer, and if you believe in the divine words, you already have conquered. For after the long circuit of dark existences you will finally leave the painful circle of births, and all of you will find yourselves as a single body, a single soul, in the light of Dionysus![3]

The neophyte must experience the Orphic truths if his initiation is to be complete.

> God is One, and always resembles Himself. He reigns everywhere. But the gods are myriad and varied, for Divinity is eternal and infinite. The greatest are the souls of the stars. Suns, stars, earths and moons—each star has its own soul, and all have come out of the celestial fire of Zeus, the Primal Light. Semi-conscious, inaccessible, unchanging, they rule the Great Whole with their regular movements. And into its ethereal sphere each revolving star leads hosts of demigods or shining souls who once were men, and who having descended the ladder of the kingdoms, gloriously ascend through the cycles once again, finally to leave the circle of births. It is through these divine spirits that God breathes, moves, appears. They are the breath of His living Soul, the rays of His eternal consciousness.[4]

The neophyte, now purified and redeemed, is empowered with the capacity to break the cycles of reincarnation and enter into the Light of Deity.

Orpheus was considered the "master of sacerdotal Greece," and Pythagoras the "master of secular Greece."[5] Pythagoras codified, interpreted on a scientific, mathematical and metaphysical plane, Orpheus' teachings, then added his own powerful insights; the result was a complete cosmogonous set of principles.[6]

Pythagoras based his metaphysical arguments on astronomical, geometrical, and numerical calculations. He did not reject the Olympian gods, but incorporated them in his pantheon as symbols endowed with metaphysical qualities and so provided them with universal and mythical import.

Pythagoreanism was an "astral" religion. Its fundamentals were based on astronomy, geometry, and numbers. It was opposed to the numerical and conceptual beliefs of the Babylonians and Chaldeans; the former traced the path of astral bodies and divided them into twelve parts, endowing each with a sign of the zodiac. Stars and planets were considered immobile, their course was "disorderly," and they wandered about the heavens without any plan. The Chaldeans, however, noted a correlation between the planetary orbits and life on earth, which led to the founding of the science of astrology. Careful records were kept of the planets, their positions vis-à-vis fixed stars and earthly activity. Time was divided into a Great Year, at the end of which the sun, moon, and planets returned to their initial positions in terms of fixed stars.

The Pythagoreans "dilated" the universe. They proved that stars and planets existed on different planes—that the sphere was the perfect geometric figure and, coupled with circular movement, explained celestial motion. Pythagoras posited the assumption that the sun's motility was based on a "double movement, diurnal and annual, that is, going from the Orient to the Occident on the one hand, and from the Occident to the Orient, on the other."[7] Unlike the Chaldeans, the Pythagoreans held that the sun and the planets obeyed their own laws, that their "erratic" movement was merely an "optical" illusion.

Pythagoras and his disciples constructed a "heliocentric universe." Astral movement was circular and eternal—therefore, divine (eternity is an attribute of divinity). The Pythagoreans juxtaposed the "intelligent," "rational," "circular," and "uniform" movements of the heavenly bodies with the "irrational," "erratic," and "disorderly" paths of terrestrial entities. Terrestrial motion, they further observed, was rectilinear, and therefore limited (the object moves, rises, falls and then remains immobile). Because heavenly bodies function in a closed orbit, their course is immutable and eternal. Stars and planets, according to Pythagoreans, move in harmony with a heavenly plan, in perfect order, and are endowed with souls and intelligence. Celestial bodies are divine.

That part of the universe which stands between the sphere of the moon and the earth is dominated by chance; it is mortal and perishable, as opposed to the divine planets, which are immortal. The duality between the celestial and terrestrial domains creates a duality in substance. Celestial bodies, the Pythagoreans believed, are simple in formation, consisting of fire and ether; earthly bodies are complex, unstable, and impure since they are a mixture of the four elements.

The duality in earthly entities is also inherent in man. The divine spark in the body is part of the World-Soul, and is, therefore, eternal, mobile, rational, and pure. But because it is imprisoned in the body, it is subject to material and sensual influences, which it must fight off through ascetic practices. The duality implicit in man is described in Plato's *Phaedrus.*

> The soul is immortal, for that is immortal which is ever in motion; but that which moves and is moved by another, in ceasing to move ceases to live. Therefore, only that which is self-moving, never failing of self, never ceases to move, and is the fountain and beginning of motion to all that moves besides. . . . But if the self-moving is immortal, he who affirms that self-motion is the very idea and essence of the mortal soul will not be put to confusion. For the body which is moved from without is soulless; but that which is moved from within has a soul, and this is involved in the nature of the soul. But if the soul be truly affirmed to be the self-moving, then must she also be without beginning and immortal.[8]

The creation of man came about through a celestial fall of the soul caused by discord in the heavens that engendered the material universe. Man's goal is to return to the heavens, to the astral sphere from whence he came. Such an ascension is possible through a series of reincarnations in the planetary cycles and man may thus find himself reincarnated in humans or animals.[9] Since the soul is a "celestial principle" or a "parcel of light" it is an impersonal entity and has nothing to do with an individual's personality. When reincarnation does occur, therefore, the soul incarnated in the new being or animal does not take on the personal characteristics of previous incarnations.

Extreme rigor is required to escape the cycles of reincarnation. The rule of silence, which forbids any discussion concerning Pythagorean teachings, must be obeyed (along with many other rules), during the initiation process, which lasts from two to five years. The neophyte must also be totally submissive to his master's ideations; he must study numbers. The moral training exacted by the Pythagoreans was intended to develop what they believed to be the higher faculty—that of intuition— and thereby to create harmony between the initiate, the divinities, and the cosmos.[10]

The Pythagoreans believed that the secrets of everything existed in numbers. Each number was not only significant in itself but corresponded to all things in the universe. Some of the mystical relationships between the primal numbers are as follows:

Number one is the number of God, "the Source of universal Harmony . . . ,"[11] "the Great Monad, the essence of the Uncreated Being . . . composed of harmony, the Male Fire that passes through everything, the Spirit that moves itself, the invisible, great nonmanifest, whose creative thought the ephemeral worlds make manifest, the Unique, the Eternal, the Unchangeable hidden under many things which pass away and change.[12]

Number two ". . . the Great Monad acts as a creative Dyad." From the instant God becomes manifest He becomes double, divisible, active (masculine), passive (feminine). The Dyad stands for the union of the eternal masculine and the eternal feminine in God.[13]

Number three "the visible unfolding God in space and time" makes for the real world, which is threefold. "Man is composed of three elements, distinct yet blended: body, soul, and spirit." The universe is also divided into three "concentric spheres: the natural world, the human and the divine world. The Triad or the three-fold law . . . constitutes life."[14]

Number four "Human and divine three-foldedness, summed up in the Monad, constitutes the Sacred Tetrad."[15]

Other numbers are considered variants of the first four, though the numbers seven and ten are endowed with special significance. Seven is the compound of three and four, "a union of man and divinity," and ten is considered "the perfect number . . . formed by the addition of the first four which also contains the preceding one. . . ." It stands for "Divinity in an evolved unity."[16]

Man's task is to ascend the ladder to perfect unity by means of expanded consciousness: to recapture what he had lost—the "harmony of the spheres."[17] In Pythagoras' *Golden Verse*, we read:

> You will see that the evils which devour men
> Are the fruit of their choice; and that these unhappy ones
> Seek far from them the good whose source they bear.[18]

The ancient occult societies—the Egyptian mystery schools founded by Hermes Trismegistus, the Orphics, the Pythagoreans, and others—and the Christian-era societies that emerged from them (Alchemy, Astrology, Gnosticism, Masonry, Rosicrucian sect, Illuminism) have several points in common; they all believe in (1) reincarnation, (2) a process of initiation and purification, and (3) expiation and redemption:

1. The neophyte must pass from one stage to another: from an inferior frame of existence to a superior one. Such an ascension may be achieved through moral and physical discipline, fostering the death of the inferior being and encouraging the rebirth of the higher aspect of this same person.

2. The initiation process consists of a continuously growing inner awareness of self; an ability on the part of each being to fulfill his potentials. In order to realize this knowledge of self, he must complete a *rite de passage*, which must remain secret. Aristotle, describing the Eleusinian mysteries, justified this secrecy by explaining that initiation is not a question of learn-

ing, but rather of experience—it is not the cerebral exercise which is of import, but the influx of new feelings which emerge from his trial.

3. The actual test begins with a voyage into darkness, accompanied by frightening scenes of all types which compel the neophyte to be torn with fear, to sweat, to experience anguish. After the impression of death has been successfully understood, a sudden influx of light or illumination is then felt by the initiate. Plutarch describes this infiltration in the following manner: ". . . a marvelous light offers itself to the eyes, one passes into pure areas, prairies, where voices can be heard and dances are being conducted; sacred words, divine apparitions inspire religious respect.[19]

Jakob Boehme, a mystic whose goal was to experience the Godhead through a spiritual ascension, had a great influence on such philosophers and metaphysicians as Swedenborg, Saint-Martin, Hegel, Feuerbach, Newton—and Gérard de Nerval. Boehme's metaphysical view is complex and was constructed around the Gnostic concept of opposites: the *deus absconditus,* the hidden, unknowable, transmundane, nameless divinity who is not only alien to man's universe but who neither created it nor governs it—and the *Demiurge,* the creator of man's universe, a vengeful, destructive evil force.

The realm of the *deus absconditus,* or the alien god, is made up of light. It is remote. One may know this deity only through revelation or illumination. The Demiurge, the leader of the Archons (Plato's *Timaeus*), the "world artificer," is the creator and ruler of the holy powers; the earth is an area imprisoned in darkness, the lowest cave or cell within the universe. The Archons inhabit seven spheres and their "world rule" is called *heimarmene* (universal Fate). Each Archon seeks to keep man in his subservient position; each attempts to prevent the soul from ascending and reintegrating itself into the divine. Man's goal is to leave the earth, to make his way through the seven spheres into God's "divine substance." His voyage, however, is fraught with difficulties since it consists in fighting off the destructive Archons.[20]

Boehme distinguishes, as did the Gnostics, between deity and the manifested divinity. He calls Deity, the *Ungrund* or "the depth of the Divine being" who is neither the beginning nor the end, nor creator of the visible or material world. The *Ungrund* precedes the Creation and the Trinity. Though He is unknowable, absolute, He has a "potential Will," a type of "autorevelation" that compels him to know himself. Because of the *Ungrund's* desire "to understand Himself," he must become manifest and does so through his will. The will produces the "mirror image" by means of which the *Ungrund* sees a reflection of himself in the now-formed Trinity. The Father becomes the will of the *Ungrund;* the Son, the will endowed with the desire to know oneself; the Holy Ghost, the unifying principle of these two aspects. The "Virgin

Sophia" enters the picture as "the perfect image of the divine hidden splendors."[21]

The earth, according to Boehme, was not created *ex nihilo*. It evolved from the *Ungrund*'s desire to know himself and the duality that came into existence as a result of manifestation. A dynamic structure was created from the emergence of antagonistic principles: light and darkness, good and evil, love and hate. Because of the *Ungrund*'s will to know himself he became "divided against himself." The Trinity, as projected into Eternal Nature, caused further conflict, which Boehme expressed in the following manner: Astringency, Bitterness, Anguish, Tenderness, Light, Sound, and Essence (body). Each of these manifestations of divinity has analogies within the cosmos and may be discerned through astrology and alchemy.

Boehme believed in an orderly creation. First came the angels, then the material world. Angels were made up of two opposing principles: "obscure fire" and "light." Their luminous quality hid their fiery essence. "Angels possess free will and in this sense are detached from God." Lucifer, the "prince of the world," was a rebellious angel who used his free will badly by provoking an imbalance in the cosmos; this caused his fall. Because of this imbalance, a "tenebrous, formless, void" came into being as opposed to the "kingdom of light." It was at this juncture that time, as a destructive force, appeared—and with it, the first Adam, an androgynous creature endowed with a dual nature (igneous and luminescent). The first Adam succumbed to temptation because he used his free will badly; instead of bringing light and harmony into existence, he liberated the fire principle, bringing blackness and death upon himself. Christ was born from Adam and forced Lucifer to abdicate his powers, then accomplished the redemption of man. By uniting man's soul with that of Christ his free will is obliterated and the eternal and universal dominion of the luminous realm is restored, putting an end to the dark earthly domain.[22]

Nerval called his twelve sonnets, *The Chimeras,* perhaps after the Greek fire-breathing monster, the Chimaera, who was considered a plague to mankind, a symbol of volcanic turmoil, a mirror image of the poet's equally turbulent, and in many instances negative world.[23]

Nerval's sonnets are a composite of symbols, reflections, and analogies. Seemingly disparate images have been welded together on the deepest of levels within the stanzas, lines, and words, each an aspect of the other, each living out an infinite number of symbiotic relationships. Because of Nerval's Orphic descent or his two severe mental breakdowns (1841 and 1853), he was plunged into an area that few had penetrated—the collective unconscious. There he experienced the vigor and energy of the archetypal imagery erupting within him. That he returned from these forays into the light of consciousness was in itself incredible; that

he succeeded in concretizing his visions in his sonnets is still more spectacular. Not all of them were written at the time of publication; some
had been conceived and created long before that period, but retouched
for publication. Like Dante's *Divine Comedy,* Nerval's sonnets offer a
map of his inner domain, cut to his dimensions.

1. *EL DESDICHADO (1853)*
"fatal destiny" [24]

Je suis le Ténébreux,—le Veuf,—l'Inconsolé,
Le Prince d'Aquitaine à la Tour abolie:
Ma seule *Etoile* est morte,—et mon luth constellé
Porte le *Soleil noir* de la *Mélancolie.*

Dans la nuit du Tombeau, Toi qui m'as consolé,
Rends-moi le Pausilippe et la mer d'Italie,
La *fleur* qui plaisait tant à mon coeur désolé,
Et la treille où le Pampre à la Rose s'allie.

Suis-je Amour ou Phoebus? . . . Lusignan ou Biron?
Mon front est rouge encor du baiser de la Reine;
J'ai rêvé dans la Grotte où nage la Syrène . . .

Et j'ai deux fois vainqueur traversé l'Achéron:
Modulant tour à tour sur la lyre d'Orphée
Les soupirs de la Sainte et les cris de la Fée.

First Stanza
I am the Tenebrous one,–the Widower,–the Disconsolate,

The poet calls himself the "tenebrous one" because his realm is that
of darkness, comparable to Orpheus' during his descent, to Osiris' when
he became the passive underworld king. The poet dwells in this elemental domain of darkness and death, where all light and consciousness
have been eclipsed. Since "tenebrous" also means "taciturn," the poet is
not only somber but, like Heraclitus who always spoke in enigmas, is
incapable of uttering his turmoil save in half words, nuances, intimations.
    "Tenebrous" is an epithet used to describe the Devil (God's adversary),
a fallen angel, a rebellious type, a demon. Nerval had always sympathized with the downtrodden, the rejected, the alienated, the pariahs
such as Lucifer, Cain, Faust, and Prometheus. Desiring to transcend
their limitations, these beings fought whatever force made for their enslavement—including God.
    The poet is the "Widower": he has lost Jenny Colon, his spiritual
bride, his ideal, who has taken on mythical dimensions as the woman of

his dreams, even his mother. The poet looks upon himself as a mourner. Half his being lives in the underworld (tenebrous), and the other half longs for union with the divine or ideal being.

Nerval, a devotée of astrology, might have alluded to Saturn, who was also called a "Widower." To identify with Saturn, a planet boding misfortune, is to be a victim, as the title of the poem suggests, of a fatal destiny; planets dictate from birth one's course in life.

Saturn was also the god of time. As such, he devoured all life, including that of his own children. Nerval had always looked upon time as a destructive force, as something irreversible that ate up his past and forever led to implacable doom.

In alchemy, Saturn has been associated with *Mercurius senex,* the one with androgynous and ambiguous sexual proclivities. Because mercury is a transformatory principle for the alchemist, the entire frame of reference may indicate a state of blackness or original chaos before any alteration has occurred.

The "Inconsolable one" or "Disconsolate" indicates a protracted melancholia, a life suspended in space, without focus, goal or orientation— a being who dwells in a somber domain, a condition of stasis.

The Prince of Aquitania whose tower has been torn down:

Genealogy had always fascinated Nerval, who had gone to great lengths to try to prove his descent from the German knights. "The Prince of Aquitania" refers to Gaston Phoebus of Aquitania, one of Emperor Otto's knights, who had owned a castle in the Dordogne. Three silver towers were depicted on the family's coat of arms. The "tower" suggests Nerval's ancient lineage, a mythical and exciting past of which he could be proud.

The "tower" image indicates the poet's propensity for heights: towers, pyramids, mountains, fortresses. It implies perception, as in the personification, the "far-seeing tower."[25] "Tower" also indicates an ascension, a place from where one looks out over the landscape, views distances, higher realms. Too great an attraction for high places has its dangers, as the Tower of Babel allegory in the Bible attests. To rise too high above the ground may bring confusion and cut an individual off from the workaday reality; it may also encourage a sense of isolation, which may act as a compensation for a lack of relatedness toward earthly matters.[26] In a similar vein, the Tarot card[27] (the sixteenth enigma) pictures a tower struck by lightning, implying that anyone attempting to rise to any great height risks being consumed by lightning and insanity. The fact that the prince of Aquitania's tower had been abolished might mean not only that his family's title had been destroyed by the ravages of time but that alienation and madness had also ensued.[28]

A tower resembles the shape of the alchemist's furnace (athanor), the oven through which he transmutes his material and, as such, may indicate the tower's transformatory power.

In the first line of "El Desdichado," we noted that the poet traveled to Orphic depths; in the second, that he was ensnared in precariously high spheres, without a top or head, without any orientation. This rapid change suggests the hyperemotional state of a profoundly disturbed individual.

My only Star *is dead,—and my constellated lute*

Jenny Colon, Nerval's theatrical "star," died in 1842. Thereafter, she became the planetary star that regulated Nerval's destiny. Because the "star" has always been considered a symbol of the spirit (light), and becomes visible only at night, in contrast with the surrounding darkness, it has even been thought of as spirit struggling to dispel or destroy the engulfing forces of darkness (evil). Mystics believe that because the star gives off rays it represents the last ages in human development—multiplicity, after which dissolution and death come to pass. Unity existed before creation, they believed; after the creation (mineral, vegetable, animal, human), diversity set in—followed by extreme differentiation, then dissolution and possibly reintegration into primordial unity, and then re-creation. There is, it seems, a correspondence between "my only *Star*" in Nerval's lines and the word *death*.

"And my constellated lute" may refer to Orpheus' lyre and "the music of the spheres" that he created. Lute also brings to mind the ancient musical instrument still used today by Arab poets. The word *lute*, meaning "wood," is, according to Pythagorean beliefs, a living substance, as is everything in nature. Though many things may appear inanimate, they are nevertheless alive and endowed with a divine essence. Originally, the lute had four chords (then six, eight, ten, twelve); in the seventeenth century, twenty. It had nine keys on the handle and a central rose encrusted on its face. Its body was pear-shaped, and because of this the instrument was associated with the feminine (its containerlike quality resembles a woman's uterus). The rose on the instrument's face (on its heart) is associated with transitoriness, and also brings to mind the spiritual flower or the soul. However, the word comes from *lutum*, meaning "clay" or "loam" (the substance from which Adam had been shaped by God), and this indicates the male characteristics associated with this instrument. The body (feminine) and the substance from which the instrument was made (male) make it androgynous.

Loam is a type of cement used in alchemy to keep tubes hermetically sealed. Since it is a protective device as well as a containing mechanism, it both imprisons and conserves. Now that the poet's "only *Star*" is dead, his "constellated lute" imprisons him; the poet cannot seem to forget his love, his past, and is enslaved by them in his own depths.

The word "constellate" implies constellation and, according to Pythagoreans[29] and Platonists, the earth is an imperfect mirror image of the world above. The poet's earthly sojourn is imperfect and his destiny impaired. The "constellated" heavens may refer to a coat studded with the stars worn both by Isis and the Virgin Mary or perhaps by Jenny Colon in one of her roles, endowing her also with divine attributes.

Bears the Black sun *of* Melancholia.

"Black Sun," a composite of black and red, indicates profound discord within the poet. The burning red of the alchemist's flame is another manifestation of the sun, a vital universal principle or the primordial fire mentioned by both Heraclitus and Pythagoras, which infiltrates into every aspect of the cosmos and thus injects life throughout. Blackness indicates the alchemical process of calcination; it represents iciness, coldness, and, for the Pythagorean, death. Oppositions such as height and depth, and now color, serve to increase tensions, creating an even more acute sensation of anxiety and turmoil.

The conflict of opposites engenders melancholia, a state of being depicted in Dürer's wood cut. The Greek word *melancholia* meant "black" and "bile" and was associated with the blackness of one's *inner* realm— an area devoid of light, warmth, and relatedness. Those—Nerval in particular—born under the sign of Saturn or identified with this planet must be prepared for a melancholy destiny, for feelings of dejection and desperation.[30] But according to such Neoplatonists as Marsilio Ficino, who suffered long bouts of depression, melancholia can be beneficial. During such periods a cleavage exists between the outer and inner world; a "spiritual effort" is required to bring about the healing process or wholeness that, according to modern psychiatrists, engenders introversion with positive results. When a creative person suffers from melancholia, the energy he would have consumed under ordinary circumstances in the conscious realm is drawn into the unconscious, thereby putting him in contact with the deepest parts of himself.[31] A corroboration of this view is attested to by the name given Pluto, the Greek ruler of the underworld, the "giver of wealth." Pluto was not only a negative figure; he was frequently depicted as the god of agriculture, carrying a cornucopia.

SECOND STANZA
In the night of the Tomb, You who consoled me,

"In the night of the Tomb" may refer to the blackness of the Orphic descent or to the alchemist's *nigredo*, the first step in the purification process. Tomb and love are united in an alchemical allegory: King Mausole (Mausoleum) married his sister (his double) Artemis. She was disconsolate when he died, and had a monument built for him that became one of the seven wonders of the world. But after his ashes were burned, instead of placing them in an urn and then in the monument, she swallowed them, incorporating her husband's essence into her own being, thereby becoming both king and queen, man and woman, that is, the "alchemical hermaphrodite." She was "her husband's tomb" and, as such, became an example of the Pythagorean concept of *soma-sema* (body-tomb): the body is the soul's tomb or prison; life, then, is death.

For many Greeks, death meant to be loved by the gods and so love and death were closely allied. In the story of Amor (Eros) and Psyche, as related by Apuleius in *The Golden Ass,* Psyche dressed in funeral robes to meet Amor for her wedding. Psychologically, she was experiencing the death of her maidenhood and had to live in the realm of darkness for a certain period. She knew that her husband's death would follow her attempt to discover his identity, and yet she attempted to discover that identity by looking at him with the help of a lighted candle. She did this because she sought the truth—illumination—and she was punished for her transgression.[32] She had to go through an ordeal, enter the realm of the dead or meet death face to face. Only by means of such a confrontation could she experience the light of consciousness and a final and fruitful union with Eros.[33]

Other stories from antiquity link love and death. One is the legend of King Admetus and his wife Alcestis, who volunteered to die for her husband so that he could be released from his fate. Persephone was so touched by her devotion that she sent Alcestis back to earth.

"You who consoled me . . . " may refer to Marie Pleyel or to other women that the poet may have met during his trips to Italy (1834) or elsewhere, or to some deities, avatars of the feminine principle: Isis, Aphrodite, Artemis, the hyperdulian Virgin Mary.

Give me back Posilipo and the Italian sea,

A different mood is now injected into the sonnet, a desire to recall happy moments in the poet's past: the warmth of Italy, its lush colors contrasting with the melancholia-drenched black tones of the first stanza.

The image of Posilipo,[34] a promontory on the bay of Naples, and the sea beneath it is another example of Nerval's attraction for opposites— heights and depths and the tensions engendered by such juxtapositions.

The flower *so dear to my disconsolate heart,*

The flower symbolizes transformation; it also represents the heart or the sun's earthly counterpart. Since the poet is no longer in Italy, his world now lacks this solar element, and its absence has led to emptiness and desolation. The flower alluded to by Nerval may have been the "ancolia," a flower representing sadness and frequently referred to by romantic poets to create a mood of distress. In the flower language, the "ancolia" means "folly" or "madness."[35]

> *And the arbor where the Vine Branch intertwines with the Rose.*

The poet thinks back to his past—to Italy, to Greece, to the joys he had once known. The vine arbors, with their grapes, the roses in all their lustrous beauty, emerge here as segments of former years and become part of his present reality. The allusions to grapes and vines, blended with the rose, indicate an association between pagan and Christian religious ritual. Wine and grapes were used to celebrate the death and resurrection of Dionysus-Zagreus (Iacchus) and are used today during the Mass, when the worshipper imbibes the blood of Christ, partaking in his mystery.

The fact that the vine arbors and branches are united with the rose suggests Dionysus's union with Ariadne. In Italy, Dionysus is identified with the god Liber; Ariadne, the wine-goddess, is known as Libera.

The rose, sacred to both Aphrodite and the Virgin Mary, symbolizes perfection, the heart and the mystic center, the loved one. In alchemical terminology, it refers to the red powder that comes into being during the process of chemical, mineral, and metallic sublimation into gold. But just as the rose attracts through its beauty and sweet odor, so it inflicts pain because of its thorns. Like a rough-cut diamond, it casts rays all about, enlightening but also blinding.

So the poet recalls the harmony and beauty of his existence as he had in the previous verse, the love-death motif—a verbal resurrection of his own past.

THIRD STANZA
> *Am I Amor or Phoebus? . . . Lusignan or Biron?*

"Amor" (or Eros), the "fairest" of the Greek deities, was given the task of subduing the hearts of mankind by pricking them with the arrows of love. Hesiod looked upon Amor as a philosophical principle, his task being to "unify" everything within the universe through love. The fact that Amor was the son of Aphrodite and Chaos (though some said that Ares was his father) would imbue him with the capacity to engender chaos (and, if he was Ares' son, to provoke war). Thus, Amor, is an energetic, dynamic, fiery principle, an igneous God associated rather remotely with the Pythagoreans' central fire. Since Amor is a unifying principle, he may cause subjugation (of the heart) in love and bring about a counterreaction, rebelling against such enslavement, engendering turbulence. Amor's mother being Aphrodite, he is associated with the matriarchal mysteries and may readily thrust men into either the most "wretched" or the most "sublime" amorous situations.

Though the story of Amor and Psyche ended (after an anguishing trial period) on a happy note, the plights of Phoebus, Count Lusignan, and Biron did not. Phoebus, another name for Apollo, originally looked upon as the god of light, reason, illumination, and purity, fell in love with the chaste nymph Daphne. One day, when he was chasing her, she begged the gods to let her escape; they complied, changing her into a bay tree, which became sacred to Apollo. Comte Raymond de Lusignan belonged to a well-known medieval feudal family. The fairy Melusine agreed to marry him if he promised that once a week, on Saturdays, he would refrain from looking at her. He agreed, but one day he surprised her in her bath and discovered that her bottom half was that of a snake. Flustered, she escaped through a window and never returned except when misfortune was about to strike the family—when she cried on one of the towers of the Lusignan castle that she had built for her husband.[36] The duc de Biron, the warrior, during the course of his adventures fell in love with the saintly Sylvie; later he was decapitated.

The poet identifies with the four couples involved. All these destinies might have been his—or were his in previous incarnations.

My forehead is still red from the Queen's kiss;

The redness fittingly depicts the poetic turmoil. The "red face" may also apply to the "fire beings" (Adoniram) with whom Nerval identified—those who had suffered rejection, lived in an alien world, and could only be understood by a queen. In *The Voyage in the Orient,* Nerval described Adoniram's sojourn in the depth of the earth, his meeting with his ancestors, the igneous people such as Cain and Tubal-Cain, the discovery of the secrets of metallurgy, his return to the upper spheres, and his union with the Queen of Sheba, also a fire being.[37]

The fact that in Nerval's poem the queen kisses the poet indicates a linking of a higher principle (the queen, a divine feminine principle) with a lower form (man), a *hieros gamos* for the alchemist, or a union of heaven and earth, a blending of opposites prior to a return to primordial unity. The queen, in alchemy, is dressed in white and the king in red; the poet's image indicates the reverse, implying that a powerful matriarchal force exists in his life.[38]

In alchemy, redness implies the last transformatory phase of matter, when perfection and purification of the elements have come into being, "the beginning and end of all things." That the poet unites with this principle enables him to experience a *participation mystique* with his ideal.

The fact that the queen (perfection) kissed the poet (with imperfections) is a rephrasing of the goddess' Selene's story: when she descended nightly to embrace her sleeping lover Endymion in his grotto. For some, death results from a kiss because it implies the surrender of one's soul to God; we read in Deuteronomy (34:5): "And Moses died . . . by the mouth of the Lord."

The queen's kiss may mean a *hieros gamos,* but also the great and all-consuming bond that leads to captivation, enslavement, and so death.[39]

I dreamed in the Grotto where the Siren swims . . .

The "Grotto" alluded to may refer to Vergil's legendary burial place in front of the cave at the foot of the Posilipo summit. The fact that the "G" in "Grotto" is capitalized increases its value and may refer to the grottoes inhabited by the Delphic and Dodona oracles in Greece, and to those caves in which the ancient resurrection mysteries had been experienced: of Osiris, Dionysus, Zagreus, Christ; and those, such as the one at Lourdes, that were propitious for miracles. The saints also withdrew to grottoes to meditate. Grottoes imply confinement, enclosure, secrecy, protection—and imprisonment.[40]

Grottoes being associated with darkness, they have been compared with the alchemists' *vas hermeticum,* in which the coction is prepared. Because of their containing quality, they have been looked upon as a female reproductive symbol (womb, uterus), vessels in which the various chemicals or metals (foetus) grow, evolve, and transform. The archetype of the grotto may also be associated with Jonah in the Whale's belly: obscure, protected, hidden and when compared with the *vas hermeticus,* standing for warmth, protection, and the soothing moments before one is lulled to sleep.[41]

A Siren swims in the poet's grotto—perhaps the one who loved Lusignan; or perhaps the Queen of Sheba since, with the passing of years, Nerval believed that she lived in the depths of the gold-fish pond in the Tuilleries Gardens. The Siren in these cases would be beneficial, desirous of expressing maternal and positive female attributes. If associated with Circe, the Siren mentioned by Odysseus, who lured men to her island with sweet songs and then to death, such alluring and hypnotic figures are incapacitating and castrating.[42]

The Grotto suggests the poet's need to be lulled to sleep, his desire to experience a semiconscious state, a stupor—perhaps even death.

FOURTH STANZA
And twice I crossed the Acheron, a victor:

The Acheron, known as the "River of Woe," is a symbol of death. Heroes and gods of old conquered this passage to Hades: Orpheus, Heracles, Castor, Persephone, Psyche, Christ. But even they crossed into death only once. That the poet should have succeeded in reentering the world of the living after his descent into his own underworld (his bouts with insanity, 1841, 1853) was due to superhuman strength and sheer perseverance.[43]

Intoning in turn on Orpheus' lyre

According to Pythagorean doctrine, there exists a correspondence between music and matter. Each of the seven-strings or Orpheus' lyre is analogous "to a mood of the human soul and contains the law of a science and an art." The seven "sacred modes built on the seven notes of the heptachord correspond to seven colors of light, seven planets and seven forms of existence." Only Orpheus knew how to render the music of the spheres, which brought the soul into harmony with the individual, the cosmos and truth.[44]

To ascend to such realms where the body was "more vaporous," the "faculties more spiritual," beauty, absolute, where one lives by "drinking in sounds, forms and light," one can "float from life to death, from death to life" required extreme discipline on the part of the initiate.[45]

The poet's ability to "intone on Orpheus' lyre" indicates that he can experience both aspects of existence, the underworld (dark) and the celestial spheres (light), consciousness and unconsciousness, flesh and spirit, good and evil.

The sighs of the Saint and the cries of the Fairy.

The "sighs of the Saint" may refer to the pain experienced by the Virgin Mary, the cries emitted by Saint Sylvie who loved Biron or the periods of agony known to Aphrodite, Isis, and all grieving feminine principles.

The Fairy may refer to Mélusine, who weeps when danger confronts the Lusignan family. She is animal (snake, dragon) in her cold, icy characteristics, but tries to hide this, is unable to face it and so flees; dual-faceted, she is *also* a fairy, like the Saint, possessing celestial, uplifting, guiding, and comforting faculties. All these characteristics live inchoate in both the Saint and Fairy—and in the poet who longs to be united with the ideal feminine vision.

El Desdichado is a poetization of a fantastic metaphysical voyage through time (ancient Greece, Christian antiquity, the Middle Ages, and modern times); through space (Valois, Aquitaine, France, Italy) via various symbols (mountains, grottoes, tombs, towers, water images) and divinities (Aphrodite) and the hyperdulian Mary, fairies and saints; and three cosmic domains: heaven, earth, and hell.

2. *MYRTHO (1854)*

Je pense à toi, Myrtho, divine enchanteresse,
Au Pausilippe altier, de mille feux brillant,
A ton front inondé des clartés d'Orient,
Aux raisins noirs mêlés avec l'or de ta tresse.

C'est dans ta coupe aussi que j'avais bu l'ivresse,
Et dans l'éclair furtif de ton oeil souriant,
Quand aux pieds d'Iacchus on me voyait priant,
Car la Muse m'a fait l'un des fils de la Grèce.

Je sais pourquoi là-bas le volcan s'est rouvert . . .
C'est qu'hier tu l'avais touché d'un pied agile,
Et des cendre soudain l'horizon s'est couvert.

Depuis qu'un duc normand brisa tes dieux d'argile,
Toujours, sous les rameaux du laurier de Virgile,
Le pâle Hortensia s'unit au Myrte vert!

Nerval's sonnet is an aspotrophe to Myrtho, the sibyl, a prophet of Apollo, endowed with the power to foretell the future and the abiliy to converse with the gods. She symbolizes the unattainable, the woman forever out of the poet's reach—the poet who looks at her longingly. But she is also a mediating principle between earth and heaven, human and divine.

FIRST STANZA
I am thinking of you, Myrtho, divine enchantress,
Of Myrtho, burning with a thousand fires,
Of your forehead inundated with Oriental clarities,
Of the black grapes intertwined wih your golden tresses.

The poet observes the landscape surrounding this divine maiden; he personifies Posilipo's summit and calls it "haughty" with its thousand brilliant fires. In ancient times, altars were frequently built on the summits of hills, but in later centuries they were placed within caves within mountains. This change in location may correspond, symbolically, to a progressive obscuration of the poet's thoughts and feelings, to his desire for secrecy and darkness.

The "thousand brilliant fires" may allude to the sun's rays as it inundates or permeates the entire area, bringing to mind the alchemical fire, a projection of the poet's inner flame. The "forehead" (the seat of

man's knowledge) is "inundated" with clarities (lights) associated with
the Orient, indicating that the illuminating capacity stems from the East.
Aphrodite worship began in the Middle East, spread throughout the
ancient world, and has now bedazzled the poet. Myrtho then represents
a unifying force (Oriental and Occidental) and, since she is bathed in
the rays of the sun, she stands for the Pythagorean (and Sabbean) astral
soul—that which has risen above the crude material world, that which
the poet longs to experience.

The "black grapes" blended with her "golden tresses" is an ambivalent
image: spiritual and physical. Grapes are used in the celebration of fertility rites in the Dionysian mysteries. Taken in excess, they led to in-
toxication and frenzy. In Christian rituals, wine made from grapes (considered the body of Christ), when imbibed, permits the worshipper to
partake of divinity, thereby making him immortal.

The "gold" of Myrtho's tresses is an allusion to solar (or astral) light
and to the sun, which according to the Pythagoreans, is the central force
in the cosmos, warming the entire universe. The alchemist Michael
Maier explained a similar image in alchemy: as the sun makes its millions
of journeys around the earth it spins threads of gold around the planets
and these represent the rational principle (divine intelligence) that links
the universe. God (or blood red) associated with the fourth and final
stage of purification brings about the creation of the supreme treasure,
the philosopher's stone—spiritual light or illumination.

In the first stanza Myrtho became a vehicle within which all disparate
elements within the universe were fused—fire, clarity, gold (godly, active, celestial colors)—and juxtaposed to such somber hues as the blackness of grapes, representing the realm of blood, passion, the irrational—
a withdrawal from light and life. The diamond, which had once been
black carbon, is transformed within the earth and becomes the most exquisite, shimmering, and glowing stone; so too the poet must descend
within his depths and experience his initiatory process, permitting his
ideas to germinate and to evolve in the light of consciousness.

SECOND STANZA

It was from your cup also that I imbibed drunkenness,
And in the furtive lightning of your smiling eye,
While I was seen praying at the feet of Iacchus,
For the Muse has made me one of Greece's sons.

The poet's entire being was permeated by Myrtho, the vision of such
beauty: his senses were dulled, leaving him in a stupor before her
powers.

Nerval pursues the themes of rapture, love, and poetic inspiration,
focusing on specific areas of Myrtho's body. Her "smiling eye" and its
"furtive lightning" nourish him. The Egyptians looked upon the eye as
something divine: as the "sun in the mouth" or the "word"; the circle

around the iris, with the pupil in the center, fed the sacred fire or "the intelligence of man." Plato considered the eye to be the "mirror of the soul," the illuminating factor within man. The eye, then, is the vehicle by means of which the poet's inner realm germinates. Light filters into the poet's inner realm, causing the seed (his thought or vision) to germinate. When this force erupts uncontrollably into consciousness, it can consume and destroy, as does the thunderbolt. But the eye may also be looked upon as a symbol of sacrifice. Horus gave his eye to his father Osiris to replace the one that Set had wrenched from him, and Oedipus gouged his own eyes out. The poet must sacrifice something—perhaps an eclipse of consciousness, which results from an overflow of inspiration—in order to complete his poetic vision.[46]

The poet kneels before the feet of Iacchus, now that "the Muse has made" him "one of Greece's sons." Iacchus, associated with Christ and with Dionysus-Iacchus (Zagreus) of the Eleusinian mysteries, was torn to pieces and then reborn. So the poet, now reverting to ancient times, celebrates the most sacred of all mysteries: the death and rebirth of divinity. During this ceremony the mystai used to reenact Persephone's descent into the underworld (accompanied by the earth's bareness), followed by her reemergence and her return to earth and to her mother Demeter (the earth's fruitfulness), representing both phases of life as an eternal process. During the enactment of these mysteries, the mystai was crowned with myrtle leaves, then marched in procession along the way to Eleusis, preceded always by the image of Dionysus-Iacchus. The rituals—consisting of purification and the singing of sacred hymns—were divided into two parts: moments of sorrow (the mother searching for her lost daughter) and periods of intense joy (as when Demeter found Persephone). The transition from sorrow to joy was sometimes sudden and was manifested as color: darkness when the mystai searched for Persephone in the underworld (experiencing fear, suspense, expectation of death in so doing), and a return to light, splendor and intense joy with the rebirth into the land of the living. The poet is wedded to these heights and depths of feeling: despair and solitude during his Orphic descent, and joy when he ascends with the vision of perfection in the form of Myrtho—which led to the creation of the poem.

THIRD STANZA

I know why the volcano over there reopened . . .
It is because yesterday you touched it with your agile foot,
And suddenly the horizon was covered with cinders,

The poet now realizes why the volcano erupted again, why his inner turmoil, and the chaos and turbulence imprisoned within it, flared up. Myrtho has touched the volcano with her foot, contacting volcanic forces within the poet and causing combustion. Divinity, in alchemical terms, is a living spirit—a catalyzing agent, fostering the heat and fire of his temperament into frenetic activity—with destruction likely to ensue. Such identification parallels the Pythagoreans' belief that a volcano in the process of eruption is endowed with a soul.

The fact that Myrtho placed her foot on the volcano indicates communication between the inner and outer worlds. In some Greek legends, the foot represents reality, equilibrium (since it keeps man balanced and upright); when contact occurs between foot and volcano, electric sparks are triggered, indicating a volatile relationship.

Lava and live coals flood the surface of the land like the stream of images from the poet's depths; riches, once heremetically sealed, break through, blotting the poet's vision and causing vertigo. The poet is symbolically reenacting the Eleusinian mystery, the search in darkness (or death) during his imprisonment in the volcano and the dazzling light that comes to him with his reentry into the world of reality.

Fourth Stanza
Since a Norman Duke shattered your gods of clay,
Still, beneath the branches of Vergil's laurel,
The pale hydrangea mingles with the green Myrtle!

The poet castigates the Norman duke who took Naples in 1139, who destroyed Greek and Roman statues of divinities, who iconoclastically pulverized monuments of beauty because they did not comply with Christian thought. Nerval may also be referring to the persecution of Hypatia, the Greek philosopher, daughter of the well-known Alexandrian mathematician, who was forced into a church, stripped of her clothing, and scraped to death with oyster shells by an hysterical mob incited by monks under the control of St. Cyril, the bishop of Alexandria.[47]

Laurel, hydrangea, and myrtle unite both pagan and Christian religious worlds.

Laurel covered the heads of the mystae at Eleusis when they celebrated their mysteries; poets in ancient times were also covered with laurel wreathes to celebrate a creative act. Petrarch, the humanist, sowed laurels on Vergil's tomb situated at the foot of the Posilipo promontory. All of antiquity lives and breathes laurel in a variety of manners as did the Christian writers.

The "pale Hydrangea," pastel-colored, is a sterile flower that gives off no perfume; it has been associated with the Virgin Mary because of its white (purity), blue (celestial), lilac (regal) hues. When Christianity became a living force in Italy and Greece, incorporating the ancient religions in its doctrine, it brought sterilization. Everything pales. All deities were divested of their vigor, to make way for the "immaculate"; and it was not a catalyzing interchange.

The myrtle, Aphrodite's flower, had a far-reaching odor and was known for its longevity (over one hundred years). Judging from Vergil's *Georgics*, the ancients had an intimate knowledge of agriculture and a loving sympathy for nature—all made possible by Aphrodite, the loving goddess of groves and tender plants. When vegetation perished it was said that she was grieving over the death of her beloved Adonis. (A similar association was made with Demeter searching for Persephone in the underworld.)

The poet's task (and the lover's!) is to unite the pale (Christian) ideations with the active (myrtle and laurel) nature of ancient civilization: the light with the dark, outer with inner. The poet must go beyond the cluster of words and images (hydrangeas grow in clusters), beyond externals; to remain on the surface causes sterility; light without reimmersion into darkness cannot germinate and renew.

Unless love and poetry can be united; unless man's sacred realms can be tapped (temporal and atemporal, mortal and immortal, divine and human, past and present), no great work of art can issue forth.

3. HORUS (1854)

Le dieu Kneph en tremblant ébranlait l'univers:
Isis, la mère, alors se leva sur sa couche,
Fit un geste de haine à son époux farouche,
Et l'ardeur d'autrefois brilla dans ses yeux verts.

"Le voyez-vous, dit-elle, il meurt, ce vieux pervers,
Tous les frimas du monde ont passé par sa bouche,
Attachez son pied tors, éteignez son oeil louche,
C'est le dieu des volcans et le roi des hivers!

"L'aigle a déjà passé, l'esprit nouveau m'appelle,
J'ai revêtu pour lui la robe de Cybèle . . .
C'est l'enfant bien-aimé d'Hermès et d'Osiris!"

La déesse avait fui sur sa conque dorée,
La mer nous renvoyait son image adorée,
Et les cieux rayonnaient sous l'écharpe d'Iris.

In the Egyptian pantheon, Kneph was considered the most ancient god, the all or primal being, the "Alpha and Omega," the undifferentiated totality. Kneph represents the father principle, the patriarchal religious force in Egypt that, after it had spun its course, lost its productivity. When the old ways remain anchored, they crumble; they are subject to fear and trembling as the new ideations emerge.

FIRST STANZA
Trembling, God Kneph shuddered the universe:
Then Isis, the mother, lying on her bed, arose,

> *Made a gesture of hatred at her savage spouse,*
> *And the fire of old shone in her green eyes.*

Isis, the Great Mother, has given birth to Horus, thereby unseating the old king and destroying what is no longer productive. Mother, wife, and sister, Isis incorporates all the other deities: Cybele, Minerva, Venus, Diana, Juno, Hecate. As a mother figure she represents for the poet all that is positive, nourishing, fruitful, and kindly. From the father's point of view she is destructive, however, and does away with the reigning principle that precedes her emergence as mother.

After Horus' birth, Isis expressed hatred for her husband Kneph, whom some scholars have identified with Set, the promulgator of evil in Egyptian religion. Isis was intent upon bringing the new into existence by permitting the sun to glow radiantly on her son. Horus, represented as a falcon by the Egyptians, a bird that could soar to the heights, represented the rational solar principle in man and was called "Horus of the horizon." In later Egyptian mysteries he was featured as a child "holding his finger to his mouth," for within him was contained "the great secret of the Egyptian mysteries."[48] As a composite of the old (he was the product of his parents' union) and the new (his own personality), Horus restored wholeness to the universe. As the divine child, as the harbinger of the future, he stood for regeneration and resurrection. The new blending within Horus (old and new) was a ramification of Nerval's synchretistic point of view; he considered the Egyptian trinitarian concept (Osiris or Kneph as the father; Isis, the mother; Horus, the son) as a prototype of the Christian Trinity.[49]

Certain scholars believe that Horus also stands for the duc de Reichstadt, Napoléon's son, who died of tuberculosis at an early age, thereby destroying the illusions of many who had hoped he would again be France's leader. So Nerval, who considers himself related to Napoléon (his genealogical tree), also considers himself a disappointment to his father because he had failed to become a doctor.

That Isis despised her husband indicates her need to cut loose from decaying integuments, the sterile world that Kneph had by now come to represent. Through her son she participated in the new, the richness of life, its ardor and fire that Pythagoreans and Platonists looked upon as the heat of life. The green eyes of Isis stood for her fecundating elements, the eternal cycle of death and rebirth for which she was the transmuting agent.

SECOND STANZA

> *"Do you see him," she said, he is dying, the old pervert,*
> *All the frosts of the world have passed through his mouth,*
> *Attach his crooked foot, put out his shifty eye,*
> *He is the god of volcanoes and the king of winters!*

Isis watches Kneph wither, and associates him with winter, ice, the death state of the Pythagoreans. His crooked or twisted foot represents the crumbling nature of his realm, the imbalance within his reign.

In this stanza, the poet rephrases the perennial myth: the old king must die so that the new may evolve. If we liken Kneph to Set (the Greeks called him Typhon), he represents evil, the tempest, war, atmospheric disorder, and the murderer of Osiris. No fire remains within him; as the personification of winter, he represents dejection; because of his physical impairments, he is associated with ugliness. He is a cripple, both spiritually and physically, and has lost whatever relationship he had with the earth since all withers and ices up in his kingdom. Isis calls for the destruction of his eye (mirror of his soul) and the end of his power.

Some scholars believe Nerval was alluding to Dr. Blanche in his description of Kneph, and to the growing aversion he felt toward his imprisonment in his rest home and the sterility that ensued.

Third Stanza
"The eagle has already passed, the new spirit calls me,
I clothed myself for him in Cybele's dress . . .
He is the beloved infant of Hermes and Osiris!"

The eagle, an allusion to the solar force in Egypt, to Zeus (Jupiter), to Napoléon, represents life, activity, heroism. In Christian doctrine the eagle has been looked upon as a messenger and represents the spirit of prophecy, ascension, God. Horus compels Isis to view him as a falcon (or eagle) as a new heroic force. She dons Cybele's garments for him— she, the goddess of nature, the founder of cities and towns, symbolizing eternally reproductive powers.

The child she created, Horus, is the beloved infant of Hermes (Mercury), the messenger of the gods. Hermes is also identified with Thoth in Egypt, who had been recognized as the protector of Horus and who asked the tribunal of gods to recognize his legitimacy. Thoth-Hermes, representing the spirit of wisdom, was known as Hermes Trismegistus, the "thrice great," because he was considered the master of three worlds: heaven, earth, and the underworld. As the founder of the hermetic art of alchemy, he became known as the transmitter of tradition, the divinity who taught man how to regenerate himself, how to reject the profane in favor of the spiritual, the crude for the pure. As the son of Osiris, the king of the underworld, he possesses the secrets of both realms and stands for hope, eternity, and depth of perception.[50]

For Nerval, Horus represents the messiah-type that he associates with Christ and the new creed. Christianity has incorporated all theogonies, fused all beliefs; just as Isis represented man's need to "adore" a "celestial Mother whose child is the hope of the world," so the Virgin Mary gave birth to Christ, replacing the old with the new.

FOURTH STANZA
The goddess had fled on her gilded conch,
The sea reflected for us her adored image,
And the skies flamed under Iris' scarf.

Aphrodite (Venus) was born from the waters and emerged from her shell; her image was forever reflected in the waters—prismatic, radiating light and beauty throughout the world. Scholars believe that an analogy may also be made with Letizia, Napoléon's mother, who left Corsica on a boat (conch) to follow the works of her "divine" son.

Iris' scarf or sash refers to a rainbow, which links heaven and earth. Only gods may walk on the rainbow; man must make his way beneath this exquisite burst of light. The rainbow itself, named after the virgin Iris, whose wings were of gold and who ran as quickly as a breeze in her capacity of messenger of the gods, is the personification of beauty, perfection, purity—the cohesive force in nature.

Horus proposes that nature evolves and as it changes and makes way for the new, it destroys the old: this is as true of religion as it is of nature.

4. ANTEROS (1854)

Tu demandes pourquoi j'ai tant de rage au coeur
Et sur un col flexible une tête indomptée;
C'est que je suis issu de la race d'Antée,
Je retourne les dards contre le dieu vainqueur.

Oui, je suis de ceux-là qu'inspire le Vengeur,
Il m'a marqué le front de sa lèvre irritée,
Sous la pâleur d'Abel, hélas! ensanglantée,
J'ai parfois de Cain l'implacable rougeur!

Jéhovah! le dernier, vaincu par ton génie,
Qui, du fond des enfers, criait: "O tyrannie!"
C'est mon aïeul Bélus ou mon père Dagon . . .

Ils m'ont plongé trois fois dans les eaux du Cocyte,
Et, protégeant tout seul ma mère Amalécyte,
Je ressème à ses pieds les dents du vieux dragon.

Anteros, Eros' brother, the son of Aphrodite and Ares (Mars) came to be known as the god of unrequited love; his bitterness and anguish caused him to seek revenge, to become violent and aggressive toward people and life in general.

FIRST STANZA

You ask me why I have so much rage in my heart
And why I carry an unflinching head upon a flexible neck;
It's because I come from Antaeus' race,
I hurl back the darts against the conqueror god.

Anteros looks upon himself as a martyr, always wronged, ever down-trodden. The poet identifies with him as he does with the other fire beings: Cain, Faust, Lucifer, Prometheus. Anteros, who remains un-loved, suffers from solitude and, since he is proud of his lineage, bears his silence alone.

Because Eros was considered the god not only of sensual love but also of unity in nature, his brother may be looked upon as a discordant agent who breaks up harmony, dismembers what is unified. According to Pythagorean metaphysics, the world was born out of discord and imbalance. To wish for eternal equilibrium is to value what is static, unchangeable, unreproductive. Anteros, in this sense, may be looked upon as a positive as well as a negative being—both brothers are necessary in nature.

As a descendant of the giant Antaeus, the son of Poseidon, and the earth goddess Gea, he will fight for recognition, as had his father who wrestled with all strangers who came his way, winning battle after battle, always touching the earth, thereby enabling his mother (Gea, the earth goddess) to infuse him with energy and strength. Only Hercules raised Anteros' father from the earth, thus cutting him off from his mother's protection and strength, which led to his demise. Anteros represents fire, belligerence, and struggle in nature; he will return to his element.

SECOND STANZA

Yes, I am one of those whom the Avenger drives,
He has scarred my forehead with his angry lip,
Under Abel's pallor, alas! covered with blood,
I sometimes bear Cain's implacable redness!

Anteros, like Cain, was singled out by the Divine to suffer, to bear his mark. By comparison, Abel is "pale," a shade, a sterile force; he does not possess the energy, the ebullience of the "red race."

For Heraclitus, Pythagoras, and Nerval, fire (red) was the basic stuff out of which the universe was created—the vital element. The Sabbeans and the Zoroastrians (sun worshippers) looked upon fire as representing the forces of good. Nerval saw it as the vital élan. Anteros searches for the primal fire, though it implies pain and anguish.

Third Stanza
Jehovah! the last to be conquered by your genius,
Who, from the depths of hell, cried out: "O tyranny!"
Is my ancestor Belus or my father Dagon . . .

Jehovah depotentiated all ancient gods: Belus, the Canaanite Baal; Dagon, the fish god of the Philistines whose statue was smashed before the altar at Ashdod. These were Anteros' ancestors.

Fourth Stanza
Three times they plunged me in the waters of Cocytus,
And protecting alone my Amalekite mother,
I sow once again at her feet the old dragon's teeth.

Achilles' mother plunged her son into the Styx in order to render him invulnerable; the Christian sacrament of baptism purifies from sin and grants spiritual rebirth; the water within the mother's uterus also acts as a protective force during prenatal existence. All forms of initiation, whether baptismal or otherwise, are intended to strengthen the neophyte, increase his endurance, and ward off the suffering connected with the existential domain.[51]

The Amalekite mother may allude to a mythical figure (the Queen of Sheba, Lilith) or the warlike people who were enemies of Israel and whom David finally defeated (Samuel II:9,11).[52] The Amalek represent both violent and belligerent forces (Anteros), but since the Arabs called them a race of giants, they stand for the fabulous realm of this superhuman force. Anteros defends his mother and the tribe since he is a warring principle, always creating rebellion, movement, and dynamism so as to prevent stagnation.

The "teeth of the old dragon" that Anteros plants alludes to Cadmus, the king of Phoenicia, who planted the teeth of the dragon he had slain; when men rose from these, they fought and slew each other. These dragons' teeth suggest certain mythical couples: Harmonia, Cadmus' wife; Medea, who married Jason after she helped him harness the bulls of Ares. Both planted dragon teeth from which armed men also sprang forth and killed each other. Both legends end in violence; turmoil emerges from man's earth-bound attitudes.

In *Anteros,* the poet expels his anger, humiliation, and rage. Nerval was an exponent of tenderness and passivity, so this poem has been looked upon as an "ontology of struggle."[53]

5. *DELFICA (1845)*

La connais-tu, DAFNÉ, cette ancienne romance,
Au pied du sycomore, ou sous les lauriers blancs,
Sous l'olivier, le myrte, ou le saules tremblants,
Cette chanson d'amour . . . qui toujours recommence? . . .

Reconnais-tu le TEMPLE au péristyle immense,
Et les citrons amers où s'imprimaient tes dents,
Et la grotte, fatale aux hôtes imprudents,
Où du dragon vaincu dort l'antique semence . . .

Ils reviendront, ces Dieux que tu pleures toujours!
Le temps va ramener l'ordre des anciens jours;
La terre a tressailli d'un souffle prophétique . . .

Cependant la sibylle au visage latin
Est endormie encor sous l'arc de Constantin:
—Et rien n'a dérangé le sévère portique.

The poet looks back on antiquity, with its festivities, its sorrows and religious rituals to commemorate all within man's soul. These did not end with Christianity but were incorporated within it; though names have changed, man has not: he still longs for the same communion with the divine elements as did the people of old.

First Stanza
Do you know this ancient romance, Daphne,
At the foot of the sycamore or under the white laurels,
Beneath the olive tree, myrtle or quivering willows,
This song of love . . . which always begins again? . . .

Delfica refers to the Oracle at Delphi (or to sibyllae in general), a prophet in ancient days, generally a maiden able to reveal the gods' words to mortals, guiding them thereby in their daily existence. She also had the ability to heal the sick and to help mortal man ascend to the harmonies beyond, enabling him to hear the "music of the spheres."

The poet asks Daphne whether she had heard an old romance, a love song, the name repeated over and over again in nature's eternal course. Here, there is a personal reference, to the romance Adrienne had sung (described in *Sylvie*) representing a whole segment of his past that is restored to the present. Songs, one of the earliest forms of lyrical expression, are also equated with abstract inner harmonies that have not been imprisoned in the phenomenological world.[54] The poet is referring to Orpheus' music—the tonalities of pure thought, as ethereal as the spirit, as liquid as the water, and as luminescent as astral light: sounds that enrapture and capture man's essential need for love.

The trees mentioned in this stanza (the sycamore, laurel, olive, myrtle, willow) were instruments of self-destruction in ancient times; youthful lovers hanged or castrated themselves on these branches, or were killed when they attempted to cut them down.

The sycamore was connected with the Isis-Osiris myth: the two brothers, Anubis and Bata, slain by treachery but resurrected by his twin's kindness, came in the form of a bull to Egypt, where he was again slain and where, from his blood, grew the sycamore tree that was cut down by order of his wife. The tree in this case represents the young man, a victim of the terrible-mother principle.[55] The sycamore also represents resurrection; it was used in the early festivals celebrating Osiris' rebirth, and a wooden effigy of the god was placed in the bough of the sycamore tree.[56]

The laurel or bay trees, sacred to Apollo, were incorporated in the Orphic mystery rituals. Apollo, the cause of Daphne's transformation, had also committed other crimes: he slew Pythos, the dragon at Delphos, the protector of hermetic knowledge. To atone for his crimes, he had to complete a series of purification rituals in a sacred grove of bay trees. Because he was pardoned, mankind looked upon him as a healer of the spirit or guilt-ridden human beings.

The olive tree was sacred to Athens ("fate"). Halirrhothios, who had wanted to cut it down, was killed by his own axe.[57] In Christianity, the olive tree stands for asceticism, for symbolic castration of the priests who serve the church (the Great Mother).

The myrtle is associated with Adonis's death and resurrection, which Aphrodite celebrated annually. According to certain legends, Adonis was believed to have been enclosed in the trunk of the myrtle.[58]

Willows may refer to the romantic poet, the wounded lover who is forever shedding tears, suffering sorrow.

Trees in this stanza come to represent dismemberment and death. But since the poet talks of the continuous nature of romance, he injects an eternal quality into the suffering.

Second Stanza
Do you recognize the Temple with the immense peristyle,
And the bitter lemons where your teeth impressed themselves,
And the grotto, fatal to imprudent visitors,
Where the conquered dragon's ancient seed sleeps . . .

The temple, which is capitalized, may refer to St. Peter's basilica in Rome since it was built directly over a temple to Apollo; it may also allude to the temple at Delphi. In antiquity, men would yearly reenact Apollo's murder of the serpent Pythos (Gaia's son), guardian of the cave and dictator of prophetic pronouncements, and his atonement. Symbolically, the ritual slaying and punishment for this aggressive act was the manner in which a youth destroyed the "terrible mother," who either overtly or covertly prevented him from discovering the secrets of life and winning independence over his guardianship.

The poet may also look upon his art as destructive, as a "slayer" of all preceding forms: as the destroyer of all paternal and social dictates. Just as Apollo had to atone for his crimes, had to experience the guilt that follows ritual murder, so the poet must also fight to preserve his creation, thereby purifying what has grown sick within him.

The bitter lemons Delfica tasted may be compared to the sour taste left after bitter amorous experiences; the golden color is an analogy with the solar principle, a cleansing, purifying, and nutritive force.

The "fatal grottoes" and the "imprudent visitors" are those who do not understand or who have not sufficiently meditated upon the Delphic oracles' pronouncements, which were most often dictated in grottoes, whose blackness that increased the sense of awe and mystery. To tread in these cavernous areas without having completed one's initiation could be fatal. Because of the ambiguity of oracular pronouncements, they were often hastily interpreted and therefore misunderstood. The Oracles at Delphi used to appear in their sanctuaries wearing flowing robes and ornaments in their hair. They drank the waters of the fountain, tasted the fruits of the bay tree, and then murmured their ambiguous pronouncements. Only with great perception could the inner meanings be understood; only through periods of meditation could *gnosis* be revealed.

Even today an aura of fright and mystery hovers over such grottoes as those at Lourdes and Fatima.

Third Stanza

They will return, these Gods you will weep for!
Time will bring back the order of ancient days;
The earth trembled with a prophetic sigh . . .

The poet comforts Daphne, reassuring her that the gods of old will return: the harmony of beauty experienced in antiquity—known to Orpheus and Pythagoras and their followers—will once again emerge from the earth and the celestial spheres. Every now and then, the earth trembles, as man believes he has discovered the answer—and a new religion is born. Only with time does he recognize its deficiencies, whereupon another comes into being.

Fourth Stanza

Meanwhile the Sibyl with a Latin countenance
Sleeps under the arch of Constantine
—And nothing has disturbed the severe portico.

According to historians, the Cumaean sibyl—who prophesied to Aneas—lies in the crypts beneath the temple of Apollo. The sibyl may also allude to the Sibylline books, which were of Greek origin and were brought to Rome, sold to Tarquinius Superbus and kept in a vault beneath the Capitoline temple of Jupiter, where rulers consulted them.

The Constantine who built the victory arch was converted to Christianity in 232, after having had a vision of a luminous cross surrounded by the words, "By means of this sign you will conquer!" His name stands for the victory of Christianity over ancient cults; it also indicates the power that prophecy has over the individual, whether in pagan or Christian cults.

For Nerval, all religions are essentially the same: each incorporates the others into its fold, each fights for what it believes is right, each worships what answers its needs.

6. *ARTEMIS (1854)*

La Treizième revient . . . C'est encor la première;
Et c'est toujours la Seule,—ou c'est le seul moment:
Car es-tu Reine, ô Toi! la première ou dernière?
Es-tu Roi, toi le Seul ou le dernier amant? . . .

Aimez qui vous aima du berceau dans la bière;
Celle que j'aimai seul m'aime encor tendrement:
C'est la Mort—ou la Morte . . . O délice! ô tourment!
La rose qu'elle tient, c'est la *Rose trémière*.

Sainte napolitaine aux mains pleines de feux,
Rose au coeur violet, fleur de sainte Gudule:
As-tu trouvé ta Croix dans le désert des Cieux?

Roses blanches, tombez! vous insultez nos Dieux,
Tombez, fantômes blancs, de votre ciel qui brûle:
—La Sainte de l'Abîme est plus sainte à mes yeux!

Artemis[59] is one of the most ambiguous of Nerval's sonnets. It may be interpreted alchemically, astrologically (Tarot), and metaphysically.

FIRST STANZA
The Thirteenth returns . . . She is once more the first;
And she is still the Sole,—or is it the sole moment:
For are you Queen, o You! first or last?
Are you King, You the One or the last lover? . . .

The thirteen in the Tarot cards[60] represents a "mysterious horseman, Death." On his banner a mystic rose, representing life or the Virgin Mary, has been engraved. Death, in accordance with alchemical, Pythagorean, and Boehmean thought, is not an end to life, but merely of the old self; from its embers, a regeneration of the soul begins. In alchemy, the number thirteen refers to the concept of eternity: adding the first hour to the complete cycle of twelve makes the totality—a beginning and an end, plus a new beginning.

Number one ("Sole" or only) in the Tarot cards features a magician; above his head is the figure eight, representing eternal life or infinity, the cycle of death and rebirth; on his waist is engraved the uroborus snake (the snake biting his tail), or the endless circle, the *prima materia* or "perpetual becoming" of the alchemists. One of the magician's hands is raised toward heaven, the other lowered toward earth, indicating that his attitude toward celestial and terrestrial existence is equally important. On the table in front of him are the four elements: air, fire, water, earth. Roses and lilies are growing in the garden. This figure, representing will, mastery, wisdom, and power, has the capacity to unite disparate forces, to transcend the norms, because it has discovered many of nature's secrets and in this respect stands above the mundane individual.

The first two lines of *Artemis* usher in the notion of death and rebirth, the sensation of eternity and totality, the alpha and omega. Words such as "only" or "solely," "alone," "one," and "thirteen" symbolize feeling tones as well as numbers and bear out the sense of eternity. For Pythagoreans, numbers were of primordial importance. One represented the center, the heart, the supreme power—before multiplicity came into being. According to Islamic mystical tradition, however, one does not signify unity because it is not a complete number; one represents divinity, because the double emerged from the one and with it, conflict, chaos and creation.

Numbers have a numinous quality. They are man's way of attempting to bring order out of chaos; they are vehicles that enable man to catch something that already exists but is still unknown. In traumatic periods in one's existence, numbers appear frequently in dreams as compensation for inner conflicts.[61] In *Artemis,* a poem based to a great extent on numbers, Nerval seems to be trying to reduce his amorphous and tremulous world to some kind of order.

The mention of the words queen and king in the third and fourth lines may be a reference to the alchemical king who lives on a solar plane, since he inherited his power by divine right from God, his father. In Egypt, when Ra passed his power to his divine son, the Pharoah, the king was thought to possess these godlike characteristics. In Japan, the emperor, before the end of World War II, was endowed with the sun's power and was believed to have descended from this body. When king and queen are combined in alchemy they represent the perfect marriage of heaven and earth, sun and moon, gold and silver, sulfur and mercury—indicating a physical as well as a spiritual *coniunctio.*

The *coniunctio* is also associated with the belief in the hermaphrodite.

In Plato's *Symposium*, the hermaphrodite is looked upon as the most primitive creation—a combination of two spheres, two sexes, the double. The King Mausole in alchemy was united after death with his wife-sister Artemis, thus creating a hermaphroditic figure.[62] In psychology, the hermaphrodite represents totality, an integration of opposing forces.[63]

SECOND STANZA
Love the one who loved you from cradle to grave;
The one I alone loved still loves me tenderly:
It is Death—or the Dead One . . . O delight! oh torment!
The rose she holds is the Hollyhock.

The love-and-death motif is implicit in this stanza: cradle to grave which, in French, takes on greater force because of the alliteration "*berceau* and *bière*." In such allusions Nerval may be referring to both his mother and Jenny Colon. As a unifying principle, love is not broken after death: the feeling still remains. Reference may be made to *The Dream of Poliphilo,* a love that went beyond the grave, for eternity.

Death and love are equated with a descent into self, an Orphic descent, part of the initiatory process, as in *Faust* (part II), where Faust descends to the Realm of the Mothers, the infernal regions where man's unconscious is in a state of ebullition, a world of torment and delight, of infinite riches.

The rose she holds appears on the thirteenth number of the Tarot: death on horseback carries a banner on which the mystic rose is emblazoned; the rose she is holding is the hollyhock, a symbol of totality, perfection, the mystic center and the Oneness before Creation. In Dante's paradise, the rose stood for his beloved Beatrice and for the Virgin Mary. In Grecian times, it was Aphrodite's flower. The rose thus stands for the feminine nature of the unconscious or the *anima*—the ideal, the vision of perfection in heaven.[64]

The fact that the female figure personified as death is capable of bringing forth both delight and torment might indicate her triunal function and influence. In French, *trémière* includes the prefix *tre* (3,13), which may signify the three spheres (heaven, earth, underworld; God, nature, man; body, spirit, soul) where she holds sway.[65]

The flower, the symbol of beauty, represents the ephemeral aspects of life. A conflict is thus engendered between the first stanza and the notion of cyclical time and eternity—and the notion of mortality; between love and death, male and female.

THIRD STANZA
Neapolitan saint with hands filled with fires,
Rose with a violet heart, flower of Saint Gudule:
Did you find your Cross in the desert of the Skies?

The "Neapolitan saint" may refer to Jenny Colon in her role in *Robert the Devil,* which Nerval had seen in Brussels. The action was situated in Sicily and she played a Neapolitan girl.[66] The fires she holds in her hands allude to the love and warmth she is capable of dispensing, and also to the alchemist's fire, the fire of life, the Pythagoreans' warmth.

The "Rose with the violet heart," or the blue flower, frequently describes the romantic poet who suffers because of an unrequited love and longs to resurrect an imaginary or fantastic past. The violet was the flower of Attis, the beautiful youth who castrated himself to escape Cybele's domination;[67] this would imply the domination of women over the poet. It was also the flower of St. Gudule, a seventh-century girl who gave up earthly commerce to consecrate herself to God and became the patron saint of Brussels. Thus Nerval was reminded of the last time he had seen Jenny Colon, after her performance in *Piquillo* at a party given by Marie Pleyel. The incident dug deeply into Nerval's psyche.

The cross and the desert may refer to St. Rosalie (rose-rosalie), patron saint of Palermo, who at sixteen retired from the world into a grotto where she lived in solitude; after her demise a chapel was built in this spot. The rose and the cross visible in heaven may refer to the Rosicrucian (rose-cross) sect, mandala symbols which stand for eternity (circle and the number four in the cross). Such images, which have religious connotations, indicate the depth of the poet's vision, the need for divine intervention.

In the first two stanzas Nerval linked the notions of Love and Death. Is there a distinction made between life and death? Saint Gudule and Saint Rosalie both gave up their earthly existence (rejected life, then died) in order to experience the vaster universe of divinity. For the Pythagoreans, the Orphics, the Platonists, life on earth *is* death; it is a forced exile from the heavenly spheres. Death, therefore, means a liberation of the Soul and the reemergence of life.

FOURTH STANZA
White roses, fall! you insult our Gods,
Fall, white phantoms, from your burning heaven:
—The Saint of the Abyss is saintlier in my eyes!

The rose, born within the obscure recesses of the earth, "crystallises in its whiteness" as does the diamond.[68] It is a symbol for both aspects of life: dark and light. It is a personification for the inner and outer worlds, and for war and peace.[69] "Fall, white phantoms" being written in the imperative, the poet commands the purity to drop, the spirituality to descend. That the poet envisions the flower as a white phantom may allude to lunar associations—passive, silvery qualities that the goddess Artemis possessed.

To fall from a burning sky would indicate the sun's active, aggressive, golden ways—the masculine force within the cosmos, dictating to the feminine rose. The solar force burns the saintly and virginal rose.

The rose also has its infernal aspects, and these darker regions seem holier than the celestial ones in the poet's eyes, perhaps because they are experienced more profoundly.

In *Artemis,* Nerval indicates that all matter, whether spiritual or physical, must go through the stages of death and rebirth: the king and the queen, the cradle and the bier, the rose as a saintly symbol and the saint in her abysmal phase—all make for rebirth and transformation, in life as in the poetic process.

7. *LE CHRIST AUX OLIVIERS* (1844)
Christ on the Mount of Olives

First Sonnet

Quand le Seigneur, levant au ciel ses maigres bras
Sous les arbres sacrés, comme font les poëtes,
Se fut longtemps perdu dans ses douleurs muettes,
Et se jugea trahi par des amis ingrats;

Il se tourna vers ceux qui l'attendaient en bas
Rêvant d'être des rois, des sages, des prophètes . . .
Mais engourdis, perdus dans le sommeil des bêtes,
Et se prit à crier: "Non, Dieu n'existe pas!"

Ils dormaient. "Mes amis, savez-vous *la nouvelle?*
J'ai touché de mon front à la voûte éternelle;
Je suis sanglant, brisé, souffrant pour bien des jours!

"Frères, je vous trompais: Abîme! abîme! abîme!
Le dieu manque à l'autel où je suis victime . . .
Dieu n'est pas! Dieu n'est plus!" Mais ils dormaient toujours! . . .

Christ on the Mount of Olives rests on a complete misconception of Jean Paul's poem, *Dream,* as it appeared in Mme. de Staël's *De l'Allemagne* (part II). Nerval quoted the following lines as an epigraph to his poem.

> God is dead! the sky is empty!
> Cry! children, you have no more father!

Nerval's *Christ on the Mount of Olives,* consisting of five sonnets, dramatizes the suffering of Christ and his disciples who withdrew to the Mount of Olives after the Passover supper and there predicted his own passion and resurrection. In this drama Nerval sees himself, his own martyrdom, his own pain and eventual rebirth.

The poet, as the sacrificial agent for mankind, abandoned by society, is like Christ who was abandoned by God; like the gods of antiquity (Dionysus-Iacchus, Osiris, Orpheus). He too knew dismemberment in crucifixion in order to bring higher values into existence. Nerval's Christ, unlike that of Vigny or Lamartine, was not Christian he was a type of failure in life, a demiurge trying to upset the harmony in nature or God's dictates.

In the first stanza, in an almost hand-hewn manner, Nerval depicts a sculptured Christ: his arms raised to heaven, standing amid the "sacred trees," bearing his "muted pain" and surrounded by "ungrateful friends." Nerval juxtaposes the vision and intent of Christ (the poet) and the coarseness and baseness of his disciples. As earth men, they are preoccupied with personal gain, material values only. The "sacred trees" under which Christ stands imploring his Father for understanding may be associated with those sacred trees of antiquity under which the sacrificial gods either hanged themselves or were castrated. Christ, the symbol of long suffering, the man who lived before his time, who perceived what remained veiled, did not succeed in his undertaking. Yet he kept his pain mute.

Christ "turned toward those who awaited him below," toward those "dreaming of becoming kings, sages, prophets" who took advantage of his perception to raise their own worldly conditions. Earthly gratification is what the disciples sought; they were lost in their "animal sleep," unable to experience the depth of his (the poet's) perception. Man on earth, according to Pythagorean and Platonic tradition, is man fallen into matter, "asleep," lulled by the flesh. The disciples, like the French bourgeoisie, had no notion of the immensity of Christ-poet's sacrifice. "God does not exist!" Christ cried out in desperation. Help will not be forthcoming; pain, death, crucifixion is the fate of those who seek to change earthly ways, to alter the poet's vision.

The disciples sleep while Christ begs God; he touches "the eternal vault" with his forehead, but instead of receiving comfort and understanding he comes away "bloodied, broken, suffering." Christ's prayers (like the poet's) are for naught; supplications remain unanswered.

Christ confesses his mistake. "I deceived you," he tells his brothers. All is an "Abyss! abyss! abyss! God is no longer." The heavens are empty. Only limitless blackness, an eternal cavelike expanse exists. Christ-poet is alone among friends. He is a victim of man's callous nature, a martyr before a cold and silent God. A maw faces Christ-poet.

SECOND SONNET

Il reprit: "Tout est mort! J'ai parcouru les mondes;
Et j'ai perdu mon vol dans leurs chemins lactés,
Aussi loin que la vie, en ses veines fécondes,
Répand des sables d'or et des flots argentés:

"Partout le sol désert côtoyé par des ondes,
Des tourbillons confus d'océans agités . . .
Un souffle vague émeut les sphères vagabondes,
Mais nul esprit n'existe en ces immensités.

"En cherchant l'oeil de Dieu, je n'ai vu qu'un orbite
Vaste, noire et sans fond, d'où la nuit qui l'habite
Rayonne sur le monde et s'épaissit toujours;

"Un arc-en-ciel étrange entoure ce puits sombre
Seuil de l'ancien chaos dont le néant est l'ombre,
Spirale engloutissant les Mondes et les Jours!"

Christ-poet has traversed the worlds and "All is dead!" All is in vain,
lifeless; he finds emptiness wherever he looks, wherever he goes, whether
in the higher "starry skies" or the "golden sands" or the "silver waters."
Christ-poet loses his orientation; he can no longer converse with God;
he can no longer transform the material substance with which he is dealing into pure gold and silver—the catalyzing agent is missing.

Christ-poet, faced with endless bleakness, deserted by God, lives in a
state of chaos, turbulence, and agitated waters. The universe has regressed to a preformed state, a preconscious totality, as it existed before
the Creation; it is devoid of life. Yet "a vague breath moves the vagabond
spheres"; life emerges but only slightly, and when Christ-poet attempts
to observe it more closely he discovers "that no spirit exists in these
immensities."

The first stanza dealt with Christ-poet's ascension into the heavenly
spheres and his search throughout the universe. The second charts his
Orphic descent into the abyss, the water mass; during his circular flights,
he knows only pain, emptiness, and a feeling of annihilation that invades
the scene.

The eye Christ-poet searches for reveals only the orbit; the eye, considered earth's counterpart by the Egyptians, an active force capable of
penetrating and understanding all of life's mysteries, has vanished. This
window on life, for Pythagoreans and Platonists the mirror of the soul,
leaves Christ-poet without a vision of him.

Because Christ-poet could no longer see the center of the pupil and
only the orbit, the bony cavity containing the eye, he could no longer
tap the source of creation—the center for mystics, where all forces of
the cosmos converge. Christ-poet failed to draw sustenance from the
eye, which would have helped him to succeed in his endeavor.

The blackness around him, the *prima materia* for the alchemist, is represented visually as an abyss, a nothingness, a "black" night, a "black
which is blacker than black"—in alchemical terminology: *"Nigrum nigrius
nigro."* [70] The agitated oceans, the storms, the turbulent spheres and
waters, the high winds, all alchemical terms representing man's fluid

body before shape, texture, and individuality have been incised. Such images are part of the *aqua permanens,* the liquid that alchemists believe flows through nature, nourishing and fecundating everything with which it comes into contact.

Therefore, when Christ-poet looks about him at the emptiness and void, he does not believe it to be negative but like a carbon-become-diamond: it radiates and thickens, it solidifies into doctrine and poem.

"A strange rainbow surrounds this somber well," Christ-poet declares. The rainbow is a link between upper and lower spheres; according to the modern physicists, the "color spectrum of the rainbow is a dispersion of the white sunlight" and able to prove that "the sum of all colours in light is white."[71] Christ-poet's vision includes, then, all the principles of light, and it is, therefore, a unifying principle, a nourishing force. The "strange" quality of this particular rainbow stems from the fact that it permits the perceiver to enter into another domain—the Hades of the Greeks, where the dead are called "shades" and live on as essences or shadows in a vaporous, ethereal domain.

"Threshold of ancient chaos" would indicate the Judeo-Christian pre-Creation chaos—before chronological time was initiated, before suffering and knowledge came into existence, when there was no beginning or end, and no death. Time, for Nerval, now conceived as a destructive force, is an evil that destroys mankind, corroding his very being. Before the Creation no divisions existed. There were no superior or heavenly spheres, no earthly domains and lower depths; these were brought forth from antagonisms, difficulties, and with them the irreversibility of time.

The entire Creation spelled disaster; darkness, regressive forces came into being and with them the "Spiral which swallowed up the Worlds and the Days!"

Third Sonnet

"Immobile, Destin, muette sentinelle,
Froide Nécessité! . . . Hasard qui t'avançant
Parmi les mondes morts sous la neige éternelle,
Refroidis, par degrés l'univers pâlissant,

"Sais-tu ce que tu fais, puissance originelle,
De tes soleils éteints, l'un l'autre se froissant . . .
Es-tu sûr de transmettre une haleine immortelle,
Entre un monde qui meurt et l'autre renaissant? . . .

"O mon père! est-ce toi que je sens en moi-même?
As-tu pouvoir de vivre et de vaincre la mort?
Aurais-tu succombé sous un dernier effort

"De cet ange des nuits que frappa l'anathème? . . .
Car je me sens tout seul à pleurer et souffrir,
Hélas! et, si je meurs, c'est que tout va mourir!"

"Immobile Destiny" and "the mute sentinel" do not answer Christ-poet's cry of despair. "Cold necessity" begins a series of images that blend with the bleakness and blackness of previous stanzas; as the universe grows "Colder, by degrees" it also pales and a lifeless existence begins; everything is frozen, congealed, inactive. The Pythagorean fire essence, the vital force has ended. Just as chronological time is divided into months, weeks, days, hours, seconds, so temperature is likewise divided, reinforcing the theme of diversity.

Christ-poet questions God: "Do you know what you are doing?" Christ-poet wonders whether his message will be transmitted from one world to the next, from one incarnation to the next. The suns are "extinguished," which implies that the primordial fire has vanished and with it all activity; the void reigns, limitless and deserted; the vision of emptiness is everywhere.

"Oh my father! is it you whom I feel within me?" Christ-poet questions. Does God really have the power to conquer death? Or is He dead? Christ-poet's voice grows more anxious; his despair more complete. He isolates himself on the promontory, begs for an answer from the vacant sky and wonders whether his Father has "succumbed during His last effort."

Lucifer had also been "struck with an anathema," excommunicated by God and cast down to the underworld. No one understands or sympathizes with his woes, now that he has been deprived of heavenly light. Christ-poet weeps and suffers and knows that with his death "all will die!" and that the universe will never be reborn.

FOURTH SONNET

Nul n'entendait gémir l'éternelle victime,
Livrant au monde en vain tout son coeur épanché;
Mais prêt à défaillir et sans force penché,
Il appela le *seul*—éveillé dans Solyme:

"Judas! lui cria-t-il, tu sais ce qu'on m'estime,
Hâte-toi de me vendre, et finis ce marché:
Je suis souffrant, ami! sur la terre couché . . .
Viens! ô toi, qui, du moins, as la force du crime!"

Mais Judas s'en allait, mécontent et pensif,
Se trouvant mal payé, plein d'un remords si vif
Qu'il lisait ses noirceurs sur tous les murs écrites . . .

Enfin Pilate seul, qui veillait pour César,
Sentant quelque pitié, se tourna par hasard:
"Allez chercher ce fou!" dit-il aux satellites.

"No one heard the eternal victim groan"—Christ-poet as he falters, abandoned; he is ready to succumb, his strength withdrawing. He was ready to call "the only" person in Jerusalem who had "awakened," the only one who *knew* what he was doing, who could experience the turmoil of guilt, the only one, therefore, with deep-seated morality.

Christ-poet begs Judas to "sell" him, to "end his bargaining," to put an end to his suffering; he implored Judas to be strong enough to bear his crime. Judas, thus, is not looked upon as a destructive but rather as an heroic force. He helped the suffering Christ-poet, who no longer had the strength to continue his work, to end his life. Judas braved the dictates of the law to assuage Christ-poet's pain.

But Judas was not yet strong enough to sacrifice himself for Christ-poet; he had not yet received enough money. Money here indicates that he was not yet prepared to bear the pain of "such intense remorse"; his own initiation had not yet been completed. His sacrifice for Christ-poet would require superhuman effort: a plunge into blackness; he would have to accept the hatred of the multitude, the anger of generations to come.

Pontius Pilate felt "some pity" for this "madman," Christ-poet and sent him to end his suffering. That Christ was alluded to as a "madman" indicates an identification with Nerval, the poet, as the harbinger of new values in the world, on both religious and poetic levels.

FIFTH SONNET

C'était bien lui, ce fou, cet insensé sublime . . .
Cet Icare oublié qui remontait les cieux,
Ce Phaéton perdu sous la foudre des dieux,
Ce bel Atys meurtri que Cybèle ranime!

L'augure interrogeait le flanc de la victime,
La terre s'enivrait de ce sang précieux . . .
L'univers étourdi penchait sur ses essieux,
Et l'Olympe un instant chancela vers l'abîme.

"Réponds! criait César à Jupiter Ammon,
Quel est ce nouveau dieu qu'on impose à la terre?
Et si ce n'est un dieu, c'est au moins un démon . . ."

Mais l'oracle invoqué pour jamais dut se taire;
Un seul pouvait au monde expliquer ce mystère:
—Celui qui donna l'âme aux enfants du limon.

Nerval compares this "sublime madman," Christ, to Icarus who flew too close to the sun; to Phaeton who brought death and destruction upon himself and the earth because he drove the sun's chariot too close to the ground; to Attis, who emasculated himself in order to liberate himself from Cybele's love. The rites connected with the Cybele mystery last three days, after which Attis' body is found and resurrected.

Christ was crucified; the earth was intoxicated with his "precious blood"; it felt "dizzy" as it leaned over on its "axis" and "Olympus for an instant staggered toward the abyss."

Whenever the death of a god figure takes place (Osiris, Dionysus, Orpheus, Christ), it is always followed by cataclysmic events: earthquakes, storms, all types of natural disasters. Psychologically, such events are traumatic because they indicate a complete change of attitude, a killing of the old way. The "blood" that flows symbolizes the dramatic change; it represents life as it enriches the ground, the people all around. When blood is spilled, according to various cosmogonies, it becomes a fertilizing force. After Attis castrated himself, violets sprang from his blood; after Christ's crucifixion, Joseph of Arimathea gathered up His blood in the grail, endowing it with the power of redeeming Lucifer's sin. The notion of sacrifice and self-chastisement was always associated with the grail and all the Arthurian legends.

When blood is spilled, therefore, it dazzles and dazes the Earth Mother, who sucks it in. As it travels through the recesses of her realm, it nourishes her, gives her the strength to bring something new into the world.

Caesar asked Jupiter Ammon, the famous oracle in the Libyan desert, to reply to his question: "Who is this new God who is being imposed upon the earth?" and adds: "And if it is not a God, at least it's a demon." Nerval's vision of Christ-poet as a demon indicates his sympathy for other so-called demons: Lucifer, Prometheus, Judas, Cain . . . the fire beings.

The oracle could not answer, could not explain the meaning of this new figure; only the alien god, the *Deus absconditus,* who felt nothing except his own power, his own infinity, could have revealed the secret to man.

Christ on the Mount of Olives is an impassioned diatribe against the inalterable, implacable alien god of the Gnostics, experienced on both a transcendental and personal level. For Nerval such an alien god represented a father principle, the mythical prototype of his own father: unfeeling, insensitive, and distant. Neither Judaism nor Christianity could really answer Nerval's emotional needs. The former, because God, according to the science of numerology, is one and uneven numbers are considered masculine; the latter, based on the Trinity, is again masculine, and for the same reason. The mystery religions, celebrating the death and rebirth of such divinities as Demeter-Persephone and Dionysus-Zagreus, were essentially feminine in structure since everything expressing the principle of rebirth is considered to be linked to feminine psychology. Only in this respect could Nerval identify with Christianity—in terms of the resurrection as well as its emphasis on the cult of the Virgin Mary.

In *Christ on the Mount of Olives* Nerval juxtaposes the suffering Christ with the superior terrestrial man and the emptiness of the skies inhabited by an alien god. The variety of colors and tinctures (blood, gold, silver, black, pastel rainbow hues, night, fire, ice, shadows) are visual equivalents of the emotions. According to Goethe, colors have special energetic values that emanate from the deepest areas within the human being. Each color is imbued with its own inner dynamism, and when accompanied with other tones, may act as aggressive forces in transforming feeling. *"Die Farben sind Thaten des Lichts, Thaten und Leiden."*[72] Nerval's hues were in effect *dramatis personae,* a manner of transforming emotion, sensation, and feeling into concrete form. The colors explode, burn, sizzle, ice up, freeze, as they pave the way for a series of haptic illusions to come into being, each participating in the cosmic and personal drama unfolding within the poem.[73]

8. *GOLDEN VERSES* (1845)
"Eh quoi! tout est sensible!"
Pythagoras.

Homme! libre penseur—te crois-tu seul pensant
Dans ce monde où la vie éclate en toute chose:
Des forces que tu tiens ta liberté dispose,
Mais de tous tes conseils l'univers est absent.

Respecte dans la bête un esprit agissant: . . .
Chaque fleur est une âme à la Nature éclose;
Un mystère d'amour dans le métal repose:
"Tout est sensible!"—Et tout sur ton être est puissant!

Crains dans le mur aveugle un regard qui t'épie:
A la matière même un verbe est attaché . . .
Ne la fais pas servir à quelque usage impie!

Souvent dans l'être obscur habite un Dieu caché;
Et comme un oeil naissant couvert par ses paupières,
Un pur esprit s'accroît sous l'écorce des pierres!

Man, free thinker! Do you think you are the only one who thinks
In this world where life bursts forth in all things:
Of the forces that you hold your freedom may dispose,
But from all your counsels the universe is absent.

Respect an active spirit in the animal;
Each flower is a soul which blossoms in Nature;

A mystery of love dwells in metal:
"Everything is sensitive!" And everything acts upon your being!

Fear in the blind wall, a prying glance:
A Word is attached to matter itself . . .
Do not debase matter!

Often in an obscure being lives a hidden God;
And, like a newborn eye covered by its lid,
A pure spirit grows under the cover of stones!

The Pythagoreans believed that all in nature was alive and sentient; that everything, from the supreme deity down to gross matter, existed in an ascending order; that death was not an end but a transformation and development of life into its next phase of existence; that souls leave their habitat and seek others, pass into beings in a never-ending process of transmigration of souls—from lower to upper life.[74]

To these basic assumptions Nerval added the alchemical approach as posited by Hermes Trismegistus in his *Poimander,* and Jakob Boehme's credo as revealed in his *De Signatura.* The alchemists, as we have seen, were convinced that metals were living entities and, when pure and healthy, were in harmony with themselves and appeared in gold; when unhealthy, they were manifested in lead. According to Paracelsus, "Nature, which includes the Universe, is one and its origin can be nothing more but eternal Unity. It is a vast organism in which natural things harmonize and sympathize reciprocally."[75] Paracelsus's goal was to establish such harmony and equilibrium in the body, mind, and cosmos.

In the *Golden Verses,* Nerval calls upon man the freethinker not to adopt an inflated attitude toward the cosmos—not to believe that he alone feels or thinks. Everything breathes and bursts forth with life—everything possesses a soul.

Man should respect the animal and the vegetable because within each entity is an "acting principle"; the flower has a soul. All that is visible and invisible—whether material or not—is a dynamic force. "A mystery of love reposes in metal," which acts and reacts on other living entities. Man is but one of these forces within the universe; linked to others, he is affected by everything and in turn acts upon everything. Isolation is nonexistent.

Like the alchemist, Nerval also believed that within metals there lived "a hidden spirit," arcane force imprisoned within the mass that enables the blendings of substance in an eternal rhythm. The "hidden spirit" in matter may be considered, by the poet, as an "undefined dream." [76]

Since everything is alive, acting and reacting upon other things, successive incarnations are circular or spiral in formation, each perpetuating itself in another, going from the finite to the infinite and back again. What man considers to be a "blind wall" may be endowed with eyes "which are spying on him," which are observing him and divining his thoughts, expressions, and sensations. Heterotopic eyes[77] indicate the possibility of clairvoyance in all species—a super eye. Mountains, earth, stone may all be endowed with this type of eye; they are equally discerning if not more than man's field of vision. Let man, therefore, use nature well and for no "impious" purpose; let him not mistreat or outrage natural forces. He should never permit imbalance to take place; otherwise all of creation will be out of harmony and cataclysms will follow.

Like the ancients, the poet believes that all is sentient, however dormant or impervious it may appear to man's imperfect eye. Vision must be developed if man is to succeed in transcending the "hard shell" or the veil covering the inner realm or the living seed within each entity that makes for its grandeur, its evolution, and its participation in cosmic life. Orpheus succeeded in moving stones with his music for he knew they were endowed with the "spark" of life and responded to their inner harmonies.

No poet before Nerval succeeded in creating in words, rhythms, images, and ideations such a feeling of Becoming, Eternity, and Infinity in verse. Neither Lamartine nor Vigny nor Musset nor Hugo. By merging the visual, oral, tactile, and auditive in a series of mobile patterns as he did in *The Chimeras*, Nerval rendered what was divided unified—returning, thereby, to a precreative state, to a new beginning. He always nourished the hope that one day his own inner realm of iciness and death would be warmed with the fire of life.

21 AURÉLIA

*Do not trust too much the sun or the moon;
come down with me to the darkness of the
night.*
Emmanuel Schikaneder, *The Magic Flute.*

During his long months of internment in Dr. Blanche's rest home, Nerval was encouraged to write down his dreams, fantasies, and thoughts—everything that came into his mind. The result, Dr. Blanche believed, would be not only a positive step in the treatment of his illness—a type of catharsis—but also a unique literary work, a depiction of the inner journey of a soul.

There were times during his stay at Passy when Nerval could not work at all. He succumbed to extreme manic phases and had to be placed in a straitjacket. But during periods of relative calm he was able to note down his hallucinations.

Nerval met a number of people of interest at the rest home. Antony Deschamps, for example, a distinguished poet of the romantic school, had been struck with a severe neurosis when relatively young and had had to remain at Dr. Blanche's rest home ever since. He and Nerval had much in common: they both were lovers of music, and they both wrote and discussed poetry. As he felt better, however, Nerval began to feel restless; he felt caged, trapped. Finally, he insisted upon traveling. His old obsessions returned: he had to write to earn a living and to pay his debts to Dr. Blanche and his friends. But Dr. Blanche had serious reservations concerning Nerval's release.

In the spring of 1854, Nerval became more and more insistent, and he informed Dr. Blanche of his intention to travel to the Middle East, to Constantinople. He was certain that a change of atmosphere would help him. However, he lacked the money needed for such a project. His friend Francis Wey, president of the Société des Gens de Lettre, wrote to the minister for public instruction[1] and asked that six hundred francs be given Nerval to study the political, aesthetic, and economic situation in Constantinople. Georges Bell and Eugène de Stadler also worked to establish some kind of fund for Nerval. By March 14, much to Nerval's delight, confirmation of the funds requested was received. Dr. Blanche, however, convinced that such a long trip would be too taxing, vetoed the journey. Nerval returned the six hundred francs to the minister of education, though he was so poor he could not even afford to buy himself a winter coat. Nerval's friend chided him on his extreme integrity, and pointed to the activities of others, people in government service, who spent thousands of francs illicitly.

Dr. Blanche finally agreed that Nerval could take a shorter trip, to Germany, with the proviso that he write him frequently, reporting all his activities and thoughts. Nerval received funds from other sources for this venture: a fifteen hundred-franc advance from the Comédie-Française for an adaptation of Kotzebue's play *Misanthropy and Repentance,* and four hundred francs from the minister of state for articles to be written during his German trip.

Nerval kept his promise to Dr. Blanche. He wrote assiduously, not only to his doctor but also to his father and friends. In his letters to his father, in particular, one detects a growing concern for Dr. Labrunie's health and a continuing desire to spare him all unnecessary worry; Nerval sought to reassure him in every possible way. On May 31, from Baden Baden, he told his father that he was having a wonderful rest, and that the enforced solitude, the lack of stimulating company, had improved his health to such a point that he felt renewed and able to continue his writings. He added that he felt that the results would be quite wonderful this time. What he needed, was "the courage" and "power" to forge ahead. He mentioned his deep debt of gratitude to Dr. Labrunie for his many kindnesses throughout the years, particularly for having taught him German, which offered him the opportunity to translate such works as *Faust* and Heine's poetry. "It is you who taught me this language; I owe the little glory I earned from my translations to you."[2]

Nerval's relationship with Dr. Labrunie had not changed much through the years. Always anxious to be independent and to improve his image, now at the age of forty-six, he was still his father's child. The "little glory" and money that had come to him had been due to his father's efforts. Nerval remained overcome by feelings of guilt; over and over in his letters he mentions his father's unusual career and his own, a disappointment to the one man he so sought to impress. "My principal torments in all of my moments of solitude have always been the thought of my father . . . the evils I forced him to suffer burden my heart continuously." His guilt mounted in intensity. "I am suffering too much— morally, I mean."[3]

Other anxieties, also connected with his father, began intruding into his life. He feared he was forgetting his German, but after indicating this in his letter, he quickly tried to reassure his father by saying that this happens "rather frequently to those people whose imagination is stronger than their memory."[4]

Nerval's growing identification with Dr. Labrunie was striking. "The older I get," he wrote "the more I feel you in me. It's your youth which is returning, and the example of your youth sustains mine, which has passed."⁵ Though Dr. Labrunie had always instilled in his son a sense of worthlessness, Nerval still felt a strange desire to intertwine his life with that of his father. To live through Dr. Labrunie afforded Nerval great pleasure, but it was also a clear rejection of his own identity, a situation that became more pronounced during this trip to Germany.

From Leipzig, Nerval wrote that he was going to see a Polish princess who had given him news of a woman who had saved and befriended Dr. Labrunie when he had been wounded at Wilna,⁶ "and you can imagine the pleasure this will give me." In Leipzig, Nerval met an innkeeper, a former military man who gave him details of the famous battle in which twelve thousand Frenchmen had perished during the Napoleonic campaigns; his father had been associated with that battle. Nerval spoke of those "cherished events" in the past and seemed to be reliving them in their minutest detail. His father's "heroism" became *his* heroism; his mother's death near Leipzig, his agony.⁷

From Stuttgart he wrote Dr. Labrunie informing him that his morbid frame of mind had all but vanished; it had been caused by the depression he had suffered in Paris, but now he was cured. The purpose of his trip, he declared, was to prove to Dr. Labrunie that he could be happy, and that one day he would prove his worth to his father.⁸

Nerval's need to win his father's approval verged on the pathetic. "Don't think that when I am far, that I am not near you. I would still be close to you, even in the tomb. If I were to die before you, I would, until the very last moment, think of you, perhaps, you never really knew me well."⁹ In Cassel, Nerval began suffering from acute anxiety concerning his father's health. Since he had not heard from Dr. Labrunie, he feared the worst. He wrote Dr. Blanche asking him for news of his father: "It isn't the future which torments me, but the sad feeling of that which is connected with the past." He reproached himself for having added to his father's worries, he wrote in another letter: "I would like you to rest assured in terms of myself, but I reproach myself bitterly for the many times I caused you to worry on my account."¹⁰ And, in virtual despair over his father's health, he stated, "Even though I left you in good health, I always felt that my departures were unpleasant for you." He begged his father to have faith in him.

Nerval's conflicts mounted. The dichotomy between what he should have been and what he actually was became, at times, almost too painful to bear. He tried to be strong but he was feeble; courageous but he was pusillanimous; healthy, not sick; great . . . He barely had a reputation —certainly the "tout Paris" knew his short stories, his dramatic criticism, his translations, but they did not yet know him *plain*. If he could only relive his life, be given another chance, be permitted to wipe the slate clean. There were times when Nerval realized how negative such regressions into the past could be. "Well, I finally realize that one must break with the ideas of youth and try to make a future for oneself fitting to one's age and strength."¹¹

Nerval's letters to Dr. Blanche are of a different nature, though there are many points in common. He looked upon Dr. Blanche as a father figure, sometimes positive, sometimes negative. Nerval understood Dr. Blanche's devotion to him; he had faith in his talents as a man of science, but he resented the strict rules imposed upon him at Passy. Nevertheless, he obeyed Dr. Blanche's commandments and wrote assiduously, drank very little wine and beer, and took no stimulants. From Strasbourg, where Nerval fraternized with some students and drank too much, he confessed his actions to Dr. Blanche and told him that he had learned his lesson. No stimulants, henceforth—and few invitations would be accepted. On the positive side, he informed Dr. Blanche that, after months of relative intellectual inactivity, he was able to write again. He was buying books, he said, going to libraries and actually working on what scholars now believe was *Aurélia*.[12]

Nerval always added a personal note when writing to Dr. Blanche, expressing his gratitude for what he had done for him: "You helped my morale most particularly, and that's what was needed."[13] And, in an attempt to impress Dr. Blanche, as he had his own father, he suggested: "I don't have any doubts anymore about the fact that I will be able to show myself worthy of so much affection and care, which you dispensed upon me." He further assured Dr. Blanche of the salutary effects of his trip: he was writing, he felt fine, and he was satisfied with everything.[14]

Dr. Blanche's fears were confirmed in the letters to come, each filled with a growing sense of despair and anguish.[15] He used an invitation to his wedding to induce Nerval to return to Paris.

Nerval, seemingly, was paying increased attention to strange encounters, coincidences, and their symbolic overtones. On July 11, 1854, he wrote Dr. Blanche telling him that he had seen a beautiful child opposite the railroad station and that he had asked him his name. "Emile," the boy replied. This was Dr. Blanche's first name. Coincidences, Nerval believed, were manifestations of cosmic forces in everyday life. Dr. Blanche had always observed that whenever Nerval's condition began worsening, he believed more strongly in outer-worldly signs and presages. "Whether it is a prognostication—I must agree that many superstitious ideas remained with me during my trip."[16]

Though Nerval kept reassuring Dr. Blanche of his good health, his anxiety concerning his father's welfare kept increasing: "I am suffering a great deal for several days now thinking of him." He turned on Dr. Blanche for having been, what he considered, harsh with him: "you spoke to me curtly in your last letter relative to my father." He implored Dr. Blanche for news of his father "whatever you think of me, and there are very many stern words in your letters, send someone quickly to his house." Nerval then confessed to periods of weeping and of regret. If he did not suffer so much, he asked, to justify his state of mind, "how would I know if I were right or wrong, if I am good or bad?" Nerval's suffering reached such a serious stage that he wrote Dr. Blanche for advice: "Tell me what to do, because I am suffering a lot, in my heart. If there is a moment during which time one can repent, well, I repent, but I am still walking in darkness and I await your answer and your counsel!"[17]

Dr. Blanche's next letter, filled with understanding and sympathy, urged Nerval to return to Paris in time for his wedding. By July 15, 1854, Nerval was in Frankfurt, and confessed, "The pain I am suffering is greater than you think . . . yet I have done nothing for which people could reproach me, I have only hurt myself."[18] He told Dr. Blanche that he had asked the hotel guests whether any of his actions were bizarre or if he had disturbed any of them. He was relieved to learn, he wrote Dr. Blanche, that he had acted normally. "Perhaps what I felt to be bizarre, only seemed bizarre to me, whose brain has been so abundantly nourished with visions and that I have such difficulty trying to distinguish real life from the dream."

Nerval longed to experience peace and quietude "the calm of my intimate thought . . . peace within me, I still have the hope of finding it again."[19]

On July 19, Nerval wished Dr. Blanche and his wife the happiness they both deserved and told the doctor that though he would not be able to attend his wedding, his thoughts were with him. As to his personal disquietude, it was great. He spent "terrible days and nights; I feel reassured now that I am approaching you and our friends; what good would doubt and despair do me? . . . I shall fall asleep confident."[20]

Nerval also wrote to his friends in the same vein, though perhaps less openly—but with mounting concern. One letter, to Georges Bell, is of particular interest because in it Nerval comments on an engraving that E. Gervais had made of him when he was sick: "sickness made me look so ugly," Nerval wrote, "melancholia, so negligent."[21] All around the picture he wrote cryptic signs, but also a phrase that reveals much about Nerval's frame of mind: "I am the other . . . ," confirming his own profound belief in his dual personality—in his double—which had haunted him throughout the years. Did he recall that, according to Germanic and Islamic tradition, to see one's image (one's double), is a sign of oncoming death?[22]

By the time of Nerval's return to Paris, in August, his mental condition was so poor that he was no longer submissive or apathetic, but subject to fits of irritation against Dr. Blanche and everything he stood for. So great was his anger that he had to be put in a straitjacket again. The sickness ran its usual course: manic periods followed by days of withdrawal and submission. During periods of remission, Nerval worked on the manuscript he had begun much earlier *Aurélia*.

Aurélia is a record of a series of dreams Nerval transmuted into a work of art and which, nevertheless, has retained the urgency and the depth of the original fantasy. Scholars, among them Jean Richer, believe that

Aurélia was started in 1841, when Nerval suffered his first mental break-down and was interned at Mme. de Saint-Marcel's rest home on Rue de Picpus, and that he had worked on it in a desultory manner through the years, but not seriously until December, 1853.

Aurélia

"The dream is a second life," wrote Nerval at the outset of *Aurélia*, and it is the domain of the dream that he sets out to investigate. Yet *Aurélia* is not simply strict reportage of the images that he confronted in his subliminal realm; it is also a work of art and, as such, is a composite of distilled, refined material, devoid of all extraneous, peripheral material. Nerval offers the reader symbols of extreme density and complexity, images left from the inroads made on his psyche by the works of men like Boehme, Cazotte, Bosch, and Saint-Martin. Nerval's unconscious meanderings manifest themselves in archetypal material that, after having been churned and turned about within his own *prima materia*, emerges in *Aurélia* as an entity unto itself.

Patterns may be established in *Aurélia:* an oscillation between feelings of sin and a longing for expiation; the fear of losing loved ones and the desire for independence; the need to be pardoned and accepted and the compulsion to inflict self-punishment. But Nerval was not alone in experiencing such torment and guilt, such feelings of rejection and alienation. It was symptomatic of his age: Novalis, Hölderlin, Chateau-briand, Vigny, Musset, and so many more suffered from this kind of ennui. Emphasis on pain and suffering was not only prevalent in the nineteenth century; it was part and parcel of Christian ideology.[23] While heroic virtues such as bravery and aggressiveness had been idealized by the ancient Egyptians, Greeks, and Romans, the crucifixion of Christ became a symbol for human agony and an example of characteristics that Christians should admire. Rejection, a sense of failure, pain, feelings that elicited pity, tenderness, and understanding were lauded throughout the Christian world. Had not Christ, the "suffering deity," been shamefully degraded? Hadn't he been worshipped by millions after having accepted such degradation? A strange type of martyr complex took possession of many writers during the early nineteenth century; perhaps this masochistic attitude helped them bear the collective condemnation by society of their literary works. After all, the majority ignored their poems, novels, plays, and rejected what little they read. Nerval had always identified with the misunderstood, the alienated; his sense of rejection was so extreme it may have paved the way for what later could be called his own *imitatio Christi*.

Aurélia is divided into two sections; they could be labeled the "ordeal" and the "redemption," a drama that was to be lived out most forcefully in his dream world. Because his dreams were a second life, Nerval wrote: "I have never been able to penetrate without a shudder those ivory or horned gates which separate us from the invisible world. The first moments of sleep are an image of death; a hazy torpor grips our thoughts and it becomes impossible for us to determine the exact instant when the 'I', under another form, continues the task of existence. Little by little a vague underground cavern grows lighter and the pale gravel immobile shapes that live in limbo detach themselves from the shadows and the night. The the picture takes form, a new brightness illumines these strange apparitions and gives them movement. The world of the Spirits opens up before us."[24]

Before plunging into an explanation of his own dreams, Nerval presents background material on Swedenborg, Apuleius, Dante—precursors in the "study of the human soul." He uses them as prototypes for his own transcription, the "impressions experienced during a long sickness which took place in the mysterious domain of my own mind."[25]

Nerval tells of his love for a woman (probably Jenny Colon) who had died some time back and whom he calls Aurélia. He describes feeling that he had been "condemned" to suffer an unrequited love because of an earlier "fault" he had committed. Having been rejected, he tried to find solace with other women (in Italy at a carnival) and succeeded in ridding himself of his melancholy thoughts. In Brussels, where he again met his love, he felt her "sad" gaze aimed his way and construed it as a "pardon," as if "the divine accent of pity gave the simple words she spoke to him, inexpressible value, as if something religious had been mingled to what had been until this time a profane love upon which a feeling of eternity had been impressed."[26] His being obliged to return to Paris and leave his beloved caused him great anguish and led to his hospitalization. It was at this time, he declares, that he began having visions of all types. A synchronistic experience, he was convinced, had brought on the dreams, hallucinations, and the visions that follow.

Synchronistic Event: One evening, around midnight, when Nerval was on his way home, he suddenly raised his eyes and saw a house, the number of which corresponded to his age. He lowered his eyes and saw a woman "whose color was livid and whose eyes were cavernous," bearing Aurélia's features. "It is her death or mine which has been announced!," he thought.

First Dream: Nerval found himself in "a vast edifice composed of several rooms." He thought he recognized the people studying in one of the rooms as his former teachers and fellow students. In the other rooms, conversations on philosophical subjects were taking place. Greek and Latin could be heard—"the monotonous humming of their recitations" reminded Nerval of the goddess Mnemosyne. Nerval began to search for his own room and wandered about in what he considered to be a type of inn with immense stairs and bustling travelers. He lost his way several times, then saw something strange: an immense vermillion being (man or woman) with wings that shone like thousands of reflections. It was flying above but with great difficulty—struggling to catch its breath, which was coming in short gasps; its strength was failing and it fell into the dark court, hurting its wings on the roof of its descent. Dürer's engraving *Melancholia,* which featured an angel, came to Nerval's mind and so terrified him that he screamed with fright and awakened.

Hallucination: Nerval went to say goodbye to his friends in Paris. He talked to them of cosmogonies, strange colors, numerology, and felt that he "knew everything and that the mysteries of the world were being revealed" to him "during these supreme hours."[27] One of his friends wanted to take him home, but Nerval believed that this was his "fatal" night and told him he was going to walk "Toward the Orient!" and search for a *star* he was convinced had power over his destiny. He found the star and stopped walking. His friend suddenly seemed to have grown in size, as he had; he took "on the traits of an apostle." Both men looked like Biblical spirits fighting each other. "No," Nerval said, "I don't belong to your sky. Those who are awaiting me are in that star. They existed prior to the revelation you announced to me. Let me join them, for the one I love belongs to them, and this is where we will find each other!" Nerval left his friend, and continued walking in the direction of the star; he sang a mysterious hymn, which he thought he remembered from some previous existence; he was filled with joy and felt as if he were "shedding his terrestrial garments." The road seemed to rise before him and the star grew larger; Nerval extended his arms, awaiting the moment when his soul would leave his body—when it would be attracted, magnetically, into the star's rays. Suddenly, he felt a chill, as though he regretted his departure, and begged to remain on earth. He felt himself descending, but endowed with immense force, with strength enough to overcome anyone who approached him—as if he were filled with electric force. He had to walk carefully.[28]

Vision: Nerval found himself on a bed. The sky was opening up before him, and he could see his destiny, his soul rising. But again he felt regret and wanted to return to earth. Immense circles emerged within the infinite space before him, "like the orbs which are formed in water troubled by a body's fall." Each circle, and the area within it, seemed to be peopled with radiant and colorful faces "furtive masks" of the "various incarnations." Nerval was aware of the presence of soldiers standing about him who had come to arrest someone whose voice, strangely enough "resounded in my chest." Nerval felt that his soul had suddenly been divided, that he had become *double.* He remembered the meaning attributed to such an image—death. Nerval closed his eyes, reopened them, and saw someone else being taken out of the room. "But they're making a mistake," Nerval cried out. "It is I they have come to get and it's another who is leaving!" Nerval made so much noise that they put him into solitary confinement.[29]

At length, Nerval was freed and spent the evening with his friends. As the "fatal" hour approached (as it had on the previous evening), he asked his friend for the Oriental ring he was wearing, and which Nerval looked upon as a talisman. Nerval took a scarf and tied it around his neck, attaching the ring to the scarf with the turquoise stone pointing inward, "where the soul would probably leave the body when a certain ray would emerge from the star I had seen the previous evening." Nerval fell to the floor, as he had the night before, as if struck by lightning. He lost all sense of time, saw no relationship between events, people or thoughts. He was taken to a rest home, and during this period all objects and people were like shadows—fleeting impressions—their configurations being perpetually modified by the play of lights, the combinations of colors which composed and decomposed them.[30]

The synchronistic event focuses on an analogy between the number Nerval saw on a house (his age) and the woman (skeleton) he considered to be a premonition of death. Such comparisons may derive from Nerval's preoccupation with Pythagoreanism and theosophy in general, based so largely on number symbolism, and his own fear of death, connected with his mother's early demise.

Psychologically, death represents a disintegration or dissolution of the ego—an end to consciousness through insanity.

Symbolically, death suggests a termination of a previous attitude or era. Transformation into another frame of existence, whether on a realistic (a new job, a new political point of view) or a philosophical level, requires sacrifice, a *rite d'entrée* during which time the individual's courage and fortitude are tested (Siegfried, Achilles, Balder). That death came to Nerval in the form of a woman—a mediatrix—may reflect the fact that he identified with his mother and so felt doomed to an early demise. Moreover, he had frequently associated love and death in such sonnets as *Artemis*. To be in love (with Jenny Colon most probably) is tantamount to death because it prevents one from loving anyone else and, thereby, participating in life.

Metaphysically, death may be looked upon as the source of life. Saturn pruned a tree to strengthen it; Shiva destroyed the human form (but never its essence) to recreate it. Transformation and evolution require dematerialization. Since death is followed by a decomposition of matter, it ushers in the new. A certain period of melancholia—a nostalgia for what was—accompanies such transitions. Thus when Nerval saw the woman, his emotions were stirred and he felt his creative powers emerging.

Nerval intimated that he felt death as he slept. The Greeks believed that death was personified as the Daughter of Night and the Sister of Sleep.[31] Nerval's attraction to this new world—death—created a tension within him because he felt an equally strong pull toward earth. He was not yet ready to pass the initiation, which required the complete sacrifice of his physical being. He still felt too involved with physical existence.

In the first dream, Nerval mentions his lack of orientation, his sense of total alienation. As he walks through the various rooms that lead him to his past "intellectual world," he refers to Mnemosyne,[32] the goddess of memory and to the hermaphroditic angel he saw fluttering above him, two important factors in this dream.

The halls and the rooms are a type of labyrinth in which he loses his way—an allusion perhaps to his own studies; to the cerebral aspects of his life; to the esoteric cults in which he had delved, none of which seemed to satisfy his needs (alchemy, astrology, tarot, numerology, angelology, the Kabbala); to the mass of facts he had absorbed but never really integrated into his psyche. The result: he had gotten lost amid the many notions and ideas and had no sturdy structure upon which to set his foot. The droning sounds made by the students reminded him of Mnemosyne (the goddess of memory), indicating the tremendous importance the faculty of recollection played in his world. Plato states in *Phaedo* that learning is merely the recollection of knowledge, information known prenatally and then forgotten at birth. Dreams can reveal certain "archetypal forms of human experience are preexistent."[33] The déjà vu that Nerval experiences when he enters the classroom is unusual neither in dreams nor in reveries and may be looked upon as a recollection of events theosophists believe occurred in anterior existences. By means of memory (Mnemosyne) Nerval was able to understand his destiny, experience his life and death.

The angel (or birdlike hermaphrodite) is a mediating figure, a link between man and God. The angel that Nerval sees is empowered to live in celestial spheres and descends in the form of a messenger—to serve the helpless dreamer, to try to mend the break between earth and heaven (spirit and flesh), to settle the conflict. The alchemists (anticipating Nerval's thoughts on the subject) considered the angel a sublimation or spiritualization of earthly forces.

That Nerval's angel had fallen indicates its depotentiation: it was scarred, maimed, punished—perhaps—for its former transgressions. Strength and life had been wihdrawn from it. The vermilion wings and the glimmering wings, which shone like a thousand reflections, were reflections from astral bodies.[34] Since Nerval's angel fell, it suggests other fallen angels wih whom he had always identified: Prometheus, Lucifer, Cain, Tubal-Cain—and their deaths in remote spheres.

Nerval's identification with the angel, a transpersonal force, indicates a slow diminishing of his own existence, a deterioration of his ego. He can no longer function as an independent human being, but is linked to everything about him. His terror when the angel falls to the ground (when he catches his wings on the roof) is acute, because he feels that *he* is being smashed against factors that intrude upon *his* life. The angel's attempt to extricate his wings from entanglement in the room might indicate Nerval's effort to free himself from both financial and emotional bonds (with his father, friends, memories) and his failure to do so, which eventually led to his incarceration.

In the hallucination, Nerval deals with numbers, generations, and alienation. Nerval, entrenched in mysticism, sees himself separated from the rest of the world, dependent upon cosmic forces. He informs his friends of his intention to go to the Orient to unearth the secrets of his own existence, the secrets of his past (not only his personal chronological past) and his anterior existence, as had "the wise men from the East" (Matthew, 2:1) when they went to Jerusalem. Perhaps Nerval's past lives were experienced on another planet, on another astral body, as the Pythagoreans posited. To return (via Mnemosyne) to other lives, to former destinies, by following the star in front of him, was Nerval's goal. His fight with his friend, who took on enormous dimensions (that of a spirit), exemplified the conflict within him: his spiritual and terrestrial needs. Because he took on the form of a spirit, as had his friend, a loss of identity inevitably ensued; each became a type of symbol, a collective and outerworldly force devoid of human characteristics. Such a transformation was in effect a rejection of the human realm and, at the same time, an incomplete acceptance of the transpersonal domain.

Nerval's conflict with the spirit takes on even more significance if considered as a struggle between two religious concepts, two theogonies: the Judeo-Christian versus the Sabbean astral worship or the mystery religions as practised by the ancient Egyptians and Greeks—and Nerval's feeling for Islamic concepts, which included in their theogony a whole race of giants and a complete pre-Adamite civilization. Nerval feels most deeply tied to the latter religions. His destiny is enclosed in a star (and those who love him). As his identification increases, his terrestrial existence becomes sublimated, rising from its concrete preoccupations to abstract idealizations.

The star as a transpersonal force had always been of primordial importance to Nerval; its significance increased during the latter part of his life. He associated the star with the female principle: the Queen of Sheba, the Star of the Magi (Matthew 2:2–10), Venus-Astarte, Isis, the Flamboyant Star of the Masons, the Star of David, the falling star mentioned in the Apocalypse (Revelations 8:9–10); the Star of Arcane 17 of the tarot, which signifies "radiant cosmic energy" and is "surrounded by seven smaller stars"—all of which radiate solar energy. Intercommunication between terrestrial and cosmic spheres is implied in the tarot star, which features a girl kneeling in the center of the picture called "eternal youth and beauty."[35] It is as if Nerval had experienced a revitalization of celestial luminaries, and that new energy had made it possible for him to transfer elements from one sphere to another.

In ancient times, each individual linked his personal identity to that of a star. Christ's star was brilliant and measured up to his "superhuman" fate. Wordsworth described such an association in "Ode: Intimations of Immortality" from *Recollections of Early Childhood*.[36]

> The soul that rises with us, our life's star,
> Hath had elsewhere its setting,
> And cometh from afar;
> Not in entire forgetfulness,

Once Nerval had found his star, he was intent upon keeping it. Because of its shimmering nature, the star has been associated with multiplicity and disintegration and would, in this connection, be linked to the increasing dissolution of Nerval's own ego, his growing inability to cope with worldly matters. So long as conflict between spirit and earth continued, Nerval's tension would dominate his subliminal world.

In his visions, which he called "the beginning of . . . the flowing over of dream on reality,"[37] he had the feeling that henceforth eveything he did and thought was double. He described his excitement when he believed that the cosmos was opening up before him—the sensations of power and strength that invaded him, electrical vibrations that he felt were intimately connected with universal forces. It is interesting to note that Strindberg also described his feelings of great excitement in terms of electrical currents within him: "Then I feel, at first only faintly, something like an onrush of electric fluid . . . the tension increases; my heart beats violently."[38]

Nerval's feelings of being "connected" to the universe (as he had been to the star), closely resembled a type of animism inherent in African and other primitive tribal groups. A child experiences a similar identification before consciousness (self-awareness) separates him from his environs—until he stops projecting on to nature. People who are products of civilized nations live isolated existences; they are cut off from nature and are dependent on their own resources. Nerval's attachment to nature infused him with its power, and he felt that he was in a position to divine its mysteries. Feelings of hubris (or inflation) invaded his being and he felt able—like Faust or the ancient magicians—to control, even to tame, universal forces.

The ring, he feels, is a shaman capable of putting him into contact with sympathetic forces that he will then be able to exorcise. Such an attitude is present in ancient magic as practised by the Egyptians, Chaldeans, Babylonians, and Assyrians who believed they could tap vital rhythms and forces through words, hymns, prayers, and other ritualistic devices, and that they also could enslave or mesmerize specific spirits. Once such control had come into being, other cosmic principles could be reached, leading to increased power. Primitive man, mystics, and theurgists viewed the universe as an entity that could be influenced, as did Nerval in this vision.[39]

That Nerval had recourse to the ring, a common symbol in fairy tales, indicated a link or chain, uniting two disparate forces: active and passive, evolution and regression, universal and individual, mortal and immortal, death and rebirth. The circle of the ring stands for wholeness, eternity, continuity, self-fecundation as does the ouroborus snake of the Gnostics, the snake that encircles the created world. The turquoise stone on the ring—used extensively by the ancient Egyptians, Persians and Aztecs in their jewelry and sacred objects—is associated with December, eleventh month (1 plus 10) numerologically—one, the first number, the beginning, and ten, the composite of one and zero or the circle that stands for both infinity and the ring. One and ten imply diversity and unity. Nerval's longing for "peace" and "calm" show clearly how differentiated and dispersed his personality was.

But the ring as a talisman did not work for Nerval. Reality was again lost to him. Visions, hallucinations filled his unconscious, and with this extreme dynamism there entered the image of the double.

Nerval's double, associated with death and with further fragmentation of his personality, terrorized him. Dual human beings—Metatron-Samael, the Gemini twins, Eros and Anteros—are prevalent in religious credos. Duality usually indicates a severing of being, an elevation of one aspect of the personality and a descent of the other—from passivity to activity. Nerval expressed such a view when he wrote on E. Gervais' picture of him: "I am the other . . ."[40]

The double sequence was traumatic; he projected on this "other" being he saw in the room his own negative characteristics—those that he rejected and had tried to annihilate or relegate to a dead realm. But what had happened? These rejected facets of his own personality had split into a complexity, into an autonomous entity with its own energy and dynamism. The shock of confronting this shadowy self was a fearful experience. He felt that he was facing an enemy, an uncontrollable force ready to take advantage of him at any time.[41]

Nerval was powerless to make his feelings known. He felt extreme guilt when the soldiers took away "the other," preventing him from experiencing the punishment he needed for expiation. In certain types of schizophrenia, though patients cannot exteriorize or articulate their feelings or thoughts, they can hear and understand what is taking place around them. Such was Nerval's case as he experienced the world within him as a transcendental force—past, present, future, celestial, terrestrial, and infernal all at once. It was as if he were experiencing heightened reality: a series of sensations that flowed together, separated, collided. His sense of vision grew more acute as did his senses of touch and smell. Objects of all types passed before him at a rapid pace indeed.

Saints have had similar visions. St. Theresa d'Avila experienced intense sensations so dazzling, she wrote, that she seemed actually to relate to outer worldly phenomena as Nerval had. Lights were no longer vehicles for illumination, but took on the iridescent twinkling quality of stars, a series of patterns of flickering lights. Peoples' faces changed, contours seemed endowed with outer-worldly qualities either increasing or decreasing the power of individuals. Trees, flowers, clouds lost their normal contours as does everything with which the mystic comes into contact. As he progressively loses his individuality, he becomes part of the cosmic flow.[42] A Canadian psychiatrist, Dr. R. M. Bucke, quoted by William James in *The Varieties of Religious Experience,* described cosmic consciousness not as "simply an extension of the self-conscious mind with which we are all familiar, but the super-addition of a function as distinct from any possessed by the average man as self-consciousness is distinct from any function possessed by one of the higher animals." A being undergoing such a transpersonal experience becomes aware of a "sense of immortality, a consciousness of eternal life."[43]

The greater Nerval felt his intimation of immortality had become, the greater his friends considered his "association of ideas" to be abnormal. Always fearful of being rejected by friends and society in general, Nerval became less certain of how to function in the workaday world. He retreated still further into his inner domain, perhaps like Jakob Boehme, who held that the soul seeks to return to the heavenly sphere and to feed on celestial nourishment, which is why it must withdraw from worldly matters. Until the soul is reunited with God in the higher realms, it would experience an "aching desire" for something else.[44] According to Persian theology: "Heaven is the vision of fulfilled Desire and Hell, the shadow of a Soul on Fire."[45]

During Nerval's periods of projection with astral bodies or outer-worldly forces, he felt a sense of belonging; no sooner did he return to the earthly realm than he was invaded by sensations of imbalance and nostalgia. At the close of this series of dream visions he felt part and parcel of a cycle, a whirlwind, a giant force that both smothered him and carried him along.[46] Powerless to stay its progress, he viewed himself as the center of a world of perpetually exploding images.

The next series of dreams related in *Aurélia* deals with Nerval's return to the past and the manner in which he relives, on a personal level, the universal creation myth, followed by the primordial flood, cosmic battles, the apocalypse, and the restoration of peace and harmony in the celestial spheres.

As we have seen, the reliving of ancient mythical material had special significance for Nerval. Such regression into his personal childhood, blended with man's beginning on a collective level, permitted him the hope of reworking or reshaping his own destiny. But each time he regressed, he redeveloped along the same lines: similar visions, a similar deterioration of his self-image, repeated feelings of guilt, and a need for chastisement, expiation and redemption.[47]

Though the other societies relive the notion of renewal in celebrations such as New Year's—when people plan to reform themselves and to make a new slate of things—Nerval's regression into an archaic past succeeded only in activating his delusions, which were experienced as autonomous emotions. The psychic energy the archetypal images aroused within him was not integrated into his conscious life, but drawn within, where they were further increased and recharged by heteroclite images, breaking down still further "the central image of self" and increasing the loss of object relation. The myth permitted Nerval the luxury of being caught up in a chronic desire to escape. The result could lead only to the shattering of whatever little hold he might have developed on reality. The impact of his visions was so great as to cause him to suffer intense religious experience, not always pleasant, frequently terrorizing, similar to those of a man whose *soul was sick*. William James, again in his *Varieties of Religious Experience*, describes the state as follows: "Desperation absolute and complete, the whole universe coagulating about the sufferer into a material of overwhelming horror, surrounding him without opening or end. Not the conception of intellectual perception of evil, but the grisly, blood-freezing, heart-palsying sensation of it close upon one, and no other conception or sensation able to live for a moment in its presence."[48]

Nerval's first cosmogonous dream: One night Nerval felt himself transported to the banks of the Rhine, where "sinister"-looking rocks lay buried in shadows. He entered a "laughing house," as a ray from the setting sun crossed its green shutters. It was his maternal uncle's house, a painter dead for over a century. Marguerite, an old servant whom he had known since childhood, told him to rest because he had "come from far away." He lay down on the bed and saw a "rustic clock" hanging on the wall; on it was a bird that started to speak. Nerval believed his ancestor's soul was in this bird, which talked about various people who, though they had lived in past eras, seemed to exist "simultaneously." Night thickens. Sensations fuse. Areas, locations become confused. Nerval feels he is falling into an abyss that crosses the globe. He feels himself transported as if by a current of "molten metal" of different colors and chemical compounds. Everything flowed throughout the lobes of the earth as they did those of his head; these currents, Nerval believed, were made up of "living souls at the molecular state." A whitish clarity infiltrated the scene, a new vision came into being—"islands surrounded by luminous waves."[49]

Nerval, now on another coast, saw an old man cultivating the ground, the same man who had spoken to him through the bird. Ancestors were speaking through animals who had become "mute observers." This man, his uncle, accompanied him to a land that looked like Flanders, where his ancestors had been buried. Nerval goes to an unfamiliar house: he sees many familiar faces in a large room, people he had mourned and who now greeted him kindly. "It's really true . . . we are immortals and we conserve the images here of the world which we had inhabited. How happy

I am to think that everything we loved will always exist around us. . . . I was very tired of life!"[50]

The uncle tells him not to rejoice too soon; that even in the new world he longs to enter, there are struggles and dangers: the earth where we have lived is always the theater where our destinies are bound and unraveled; we are the rays "of a central fire which animates and which has already been weakened . . . the earth itself is a material body the sum of whose spirit is the soul." At this very moment, the world seemed to become infinite. Nerval saw a chain of beings before him, and within them, himself: it was as if "my faculties of attention had multiplied to such an extent as to become unified." All notions of time and space had altered. Though there were only seven people in the room, there was a relationship between the number of people and cosmic harmony.

All changed. Nerval was wandering about in a strange city; there were hills. The people were a strange, energetic race; his guide told him they had retained their original virtuous state—which they knew when first created. As he walked down the hill, it was as if his "feet were sinking into successive layers of edifices of different ages." Nerval descended into inner areas and saw a man bearing a weapon who wanted to "prevent him from penetrating the mystery of these retreats." Intuitively, Nerval realized he was seeing a primitive mountain people dressed in white; he was told the whiteness was the effect of the light falling into their sparkling souls. Moved by the gentleness and beauty of these people, Nerval felt he was lost in paradise. He wept. Moments later he shuddered at the thought of having to leave this world where people believed in God. Despite his imminent departure, he realized that those he had loved and had died were now signaling to him, informing him of their "external existences." Nerval no longer felt separated from those who had died.[51]

Nerval's description of the Rhine and of Flanders, both romantic, isolated, tenebrous areas, indicates an involuted frame of mind: rocks become both sinister and dismal, like cliffs. From time immemorial, rocks have denoted something hard, strong, and solid. In ancient religions, oracles and gods dwelled in rocks. Nerval looked upon them as exterior manifestations of divine elements—and as passageways into subliminal realms. They aroused some kind of fear within him, perhaps of the unknown;—terror of the unforeseen, the uncontrollable.

Nerval felt at home in the "laughing house," with the sun shining upon it and the familiar faces. His old servant treated him with solicitude; his maternal relatives were all positive figures: the mediatrix once again indicated that he was regressing into the happy part of his childhood.

The clock he sees is an expression of linear time, with a beginning and an end: an omen of the inexorable nature of time as a destructive agent. But the bird above the clock is able to penetrate mythical or cyclical time, a counteracting force, since it is a time endlessly reproduced, going back to primordial eras. The more Nerval regresses into an anterior time, the more archaic the evolution of his own psyche becomes. He therefore appropriates to himself the animal that best suits his purpose, just as the ancient Egyptians had done for their theriomorphic deities. Nerval must have chosen the bird because it is equated so frequently with spiritual, angelic, intuitive, or supernatural qualities. Alienated human beings frequently relate better to animals than they do to humans, another indication that they are cut off from instinctual life.[52]

The fact that Nerval's bird was placed above the clock indicated his relationship to time. He was a messenger, a link, between historical and mythological time—life and death, the concrete and abstract.

Nerval's feeling that he was falling into an abyss indicates a loss of object relation again. His field of awareness or consciousness had become even more troubled or flooded by an enormity of archaic symbolic material; he felt even greater confusion, dizziness. The downward movement indicated renewed contact with earth: its center, where molten metals were still gushing forth, where the eternal and central fire burned eternally—the mystic center. The light in this underground area seemed more intense. Abnormal associations of ideas occurred and reoccurred, as if they had been twirling about in a whirlpool: the increased communicability further broke down his ego. Nerval was experiencing on a human level what rocks, mountains, the earth and minerals had gone through during their formative period. He compares the formation within the earth to human arteries and veins in the brain: again the image of the microcosm and macrocosm come into view—man in his progressive transformatory process. Just as metals are vile and crude, so man too once existed on an archaic level; just as metals flow outward from the earth's central fire, so blood runs through the human brain, circulates about. But the individual, unlike the mineral, reconstitutes himself, restores the purity he had known before Adam's fall. Nerval's sense of falling into an abyss is the prelude to what he alluded to previously as his "Orphic descent," his regression into primitive times.

Nerval's meeting with his uncle is a positive experience. This old man assures him of the eternity of the soul—more important, of being able to see his loved ones in the next world. Nerval is now enveloped in quietude, as if he had finally succeeded in reintegrating himself into the mythical era of his choice. His uncle warned him not to rejoice too soon, implying that his ordeal had not yet come to a close. Struggles also awaited him in afterlife: one should perfect oneself as fully as possible in this world, his uncle warned, enunciating the Masonic and Rosicrucian credo.

The uncle, a father figure, is a positive archetypal figure representing age-old wisdom on an impersonal as well as a personal level. Many of the old men who figure in religious literature are both active and constructive forces: the Old Man of the Kabbala, the Patriarchs; they possess "mana" personalities, they fructify, nourish and feed others, and act as a link with semidivine ancestors.

Such links between generations usually come into consciousness after severe alienation. It is the way the unconscious had of overcoming a person's horror of being cut off, disoriented or lost. Such family chains or genealogical trees are present in Genesis, in the Sacred Japanese Seven Sky Generations, the Theogony of Herios, the Gnostic Autopater, the Egyptian Pharoahs who possess fourteen kas (ancestral souls), Jesus' heredity, which goes back to David.[53] The genealogical tree that Nerval had built up for himself throughout the years also gave him a sense of historical continuity; now he saw his ancestors both physically and spiritually, giving credence to his supposition. Feelings of continuity are extremely important to those who feel rootless. Primitive people disintegrate or go to pieces when cut off from their tribe. So Nerval felt himself to be cut off, as he had been as a child, after losing his mother and father. To establish roots with one's ancestors, or with one's primitive past, gives one stability and a feeling of continuity and pride.

Small wonder Nerval felt elated when he contacted his grandfather and ancestors, when he assessed the situation and counted the number of people in the room—seven. This number is of great significance to the mystic: Noah's family counted seven; the Creation took seven days, the Orphic harp had seven strings, which expressed the universal harmonies of the soul; there are seven basic series of musical notes; the Mirkabah mystics believed in the seven planetary spheres; there are seven capital sins. Just as chains of generations give people, tribes, and nations a sense of continuity, so numbers are also used for mantic or divinatory purposes—and for the same reasons. The Kabbalists use numbers (by replacing letters with numbers) to divine the future; the *I Ching* employs a similar technique; African tribesmen throw bones. The Pythagoreans, as we have already seen, believed that numbers constituted the universe. Psychologists maintain that numbers possess numinosity because they indicate a desire for order, a way of "apprehending an already existing, but still unknown, regular arrangement or orderliness."[54]

After the number sequences, Nerval perceives the primitive mountain peoples—the archaic, virtuous, beautiful, paradisiac state before the onslaught of aggressive and evil generations. Throughout history mountain people have been considered sacred by many. They represent, it is believed, a link between heaven and earth (Jerusalem, Kaaba, Golgotha), and their remoteness infuses them with a sense of mystery and awe.[55]

When Nerval saw these pure and beautiful primitive beings he wept with joy. He felt as if he were in a Garden of Eden, that he was surrounded by people who believed in God, who felt the eternity of life; these people gave him the courage to go through with his ordeal. Nerval's vision is comparable to the heavenly Jerusalem described in St. John's revelation. That Nerval's beings were dressed in white indicated that they were no longer tied down to their material bodies, to those "dark frames." They had rid themselves of their burdens; they no longer had to drag their imperfect bodies around with them. Because they had entered the "sphere of reality," they could don their "glorified bodies."[56] To wear clothes is to "bring an unconscious content into consciousness or to materialize it." The qualities these primitive people represented (kindness, purity, sincerity, belief in God) were now coming into consciousness for Nerval. Earlier, this "calm" had been longed for but never experienced.

The positive aspects he had just encountered ushered in a dream featuring three women.

> *Dream:* Nerval was again at the home of his ancestors. The furniture was shining brilliantly. Three women were working in a room. Each woman possessed the traits of a woman he had known in his youth; their contours varied like flames, one feature passing on to the other in a perpetual interchange: smile, voice, color of the eyes, hair style, as though each had lived the life of the others and each was "a component of the others, similar to those painters imitate, taking on the best features of their models in order to realize a complete beauty."[57] Nerval felt like a child. He wore exquisite hand-woven costumes that had been in fashion in former times. The materials were soft, like a "spider web." One woman got up and went toward the garden. Nerval saw himself in the garden with white and black grapes; he walked through ancient alleys no longer cultivated, growing wild. Ancient poplars, acacias, pines, statues blackened with time rose in the distance. A woman walked toward him, her dress shimmering; she grew larger and larger as a ray of light focused on her. The garden took on her form, the roses and trees became part of her dress. ". . . she became transfigured because she seemed to disappear in her own grandeur." Nerval walked with difficulty through the thorns, then saw the bust of a woman whose features he recognized, who bore the "cherished traits" of the one he loved. Then he realized that the garden had taken on the features of a cemetery. Voices said to him: "The universe is in the night."[58]

These three women are avatars of protagonists Nerval had described in *Sylvie* and other works: three aspects of the feminine principle—celestial, terrestrial, and infernal. They have been called Isis, Artemis, Aphrodite, and the Virgin Mary and likened to the various phases of the moon. In the above dream, Nerval mentions that these three women had woven the fabric from which his clothes had been made.[59] The Greek Fates come to mind in this connection, for they too spun the thread of life and predicted man's destiny. Nerval is describing his own sacred mystery, his own fabulous myth, which is being woven by the Fates and which he is experiencing simultaneously.

Nerval now sees himself as a child. He is wearing the softest and sweetest smelling garments, which he associates with a spider's web. The goddess who invented the art of weaving, Athena, represents wisdom and by recapturing her epoch, Nerval integrates himself into an archaic past. His home, we have already mentioned, is an image of the cosmos and, as such, it is from the home that the three female figures arise. But the three, never really distinct from one another since each bore the other's features, have become one. The three are an idealization of womankind: another version of Goethe's eternal feminine. The woman who led Nerval had unusual features: she was evanescent, her dress shimmered, and she always kept her distance. The woman's mystery is maintained at all time; contact would merely render profane what was sacred. Her apparent growth in stature suggests her power over him, her divine essence. In many myths, aggrandizement indicates a growing sense of power, an indication of a transfiguration.[60]

That this divine figure leads him into the garden underlines her function as a *mediatrix*—an agent capable of taking him back to his childhood because she possesses kindliness, gentleness, understanding. Gardens usually represent an ordered, cultivated, subdued universe; but Nerval's garden is overgrown. Its lack of order stands for the primitive, archaic, instinctual aspect of the dreamer's subliminal world. It is Nerval's primeval past, his collective unconscious that emerges in a state of disarray.

The garden, Nerval further noted, took on the woman's configurations. Its containing aspect, the fact that it is limited and stands within clearly defined borders, suggests a receptacle, a uterus of sorts. Just as the Garden of Eden was associated with the dawn of mankind before Adam's fall, and the Garden of Gethsemane with Christ's sweat and agony, so Nerval's garden also seems to be a means to an end—an area through which he must pass. Like Theseus being led out of the labyrinth by Ariadne, Nerval is led out of the maze of thorns and shrubs by an exquisite human figure. He sees lying on the ground a statue bearing the features of his beloved. It is an intimation of death, he believes, a warning. If he follows the woman who is leading him, he will come into contact with death; all will become statuelike, immobile, stratified. Voices tell him that "the universe is night!", an understandable notion since the Greek Fates were known as the daughters of night and the sisters of the goddess of death.

We are later informed that Aurélia had died. Nerval mentions that he had given her an opal ring shaped like a heart. Since it was too large for her, he had the "fatal" idea of having it cut down to size; when this was done he saw "blood" flowing and realized with horror the implication of his act. The ring, which had symbolized continuity, had now been severed; the blood that flowed was life's force. His cutting the ring made Nerval responsible, he felt, for Aurélia's death. The opal, always a sign of bad luck, represented fire, the star, a vital force; it stood for differentiation since such elements (fire, star) gave off rays that are dispersed into the atmosphere. His burden of guilt was now so enormous it could no longer be contained. Disorder resulted, necessitating his internment in Dr. Blanche's clinic and a series of new visions that he drew on the walls of his room: "One figure dominated all the others: that of Aurélia." She became his divinity; everything he undertook would be for her. He now decided to write "a type of history of the world" in which he would blend his personal memories with those of the collective. While articulating his idea he felt himself "transported into an obscure planet where the first germs of creation were being discussed."

Nerval's cosmogonic revelations: Nerval saw gigantic palm trees, all types of venomous plants, arid land, rock formations that jutted out like a "skeleton from this rough outline of creation." Hideous reptiles came into view; the light from the stars had paled; everything seemed to turn bluish in a land with strange horizons. One star shown more brightly than the others in this atmosphere, where monsters were forever changing form, shedding their first skins. They began fighting with Nerval, who soon assumed their features. Suddenly, an "unusual harmony resounded." Screams, roars, confusion inherent in these primitive beings had been transformed into a "divine melody." The planet becomes lighter and lighter; greenery emerges; the monsters are transformed into men and women; the savage beasts, fish, birds are more compatible. "A radiant goddess" has brought about this miracle, guiding men through their rapid evolution.[61] Distinction of races comes into being; orders of semidivine creatures (Divas, Peris, Ondins, Salamanders) emerge. A fifth race now comes forth, born from the elements of the earth, created by the Eloims. Fighting ensues. Three Eloims, together with the "Spirits of their races were finally relegated to the south of the earth where they founded vast kingdoms."[62] They knew "the secrets of the divine Kabbala which link the world," are strengthened by their belief in astral worship, and keep their secret (the ability to be reborn in their children) to themselves. Each individual lives a thousand years and is then enclosed in a tomb; just before death each is nourished with the elixir of long life; they then sleep for forty days and are reborn in the form of a child. This race gathered their treasure unto themselves and hid it in underground vaults beneath the pyramids. The earth was exhausting itself by nourishing these families. The strange religious mysteries inherent to these people took place in central Africa, beyond "the mountains of the Moon, and ancient Ethiopia." Nerval, who had lived with these people, groaned over his captivity. The older this race grew, the more static and arid became their society.[63] The constellation Orion opened the cataracts and the great Flood ensued: for forty days the earth was rejuvenated. The mysterious arch came into being; the three Eloims fought each other on top of a mountain in Africa. At this point, Nerval's memory troubled him: he saw a woman on the mountain top abandoned, fighting against death. Her groans blended with the sound of water. He did not know whether or not she was safe. Above her head shown the evening star "from whose forehead spilled flaming rays." Meanwhile, Noah and his descendants worked on earth; necromancers in their underworld caves continued to gather more and more wealth unto themselves. They sometimes emerged from their hiding places, frightened the living, taught them certain scientific secrets, and then returned to the recesses of the earth. This "damned race" bore "hideous traits." Whenever Nerval turned he saw the suffering image of the eternal mother: in Africa, in Asia. . . . Fighting ensued in all lands: Grenada where Christians were fighting the Moors. Nerval wondered for how many centuries such fighting would continue. . . . "Until the sections of the snake surrounding the earth" and separated by iron will have again been "joined in a hideous kiss cemented by human blood."[64]

In this cosmogonic myth, Nerval is not playing a passive role, but recreating his own formation. As both an individual and part of the collective he has lost his pain and anguish in the process of becoming universal and eternal. Nerval's turmoil was so great when writing *Aurélia* that the psychic energy projected outward (to people, events, activities) was drawn inward, activating the imagery in his subliminal realm. Like the primitive, he felt connected with the universe; his inner world tingled with animistic forces.[65]

Nerval not only described the very beginnings of life (animals made of clay, mother earth, their growth and evolution) but what alchemists allude to as the original chaos, the *prima materia*—from the mass of molecules to its highest formal manifestation in man. Nerval's archaic domain is marked by brutal fighting and turmoil of all types; yet there are oases of calm, centers where spiritual pursuits take precedence, where *renovatio* becomes possible.

The energetic people who kept the secret of life within their community, and who had been banished by the other Eloims for their novel ideas, symbolized Nerval's own earthly situation. Their secrets resembled Nerval's own unconscious, with all its treasures. Since this ancient race had not perished, but became self-procreating, so Nerval, too, would pursue his dynamic struggle, though cut off from the outer world, at times. Yet after a while, aridity set in; stagnation ensued. They had drawn and sucked up everything from the land; the earth could give no more. Likewise, Nerval was cut off from the external world, and the images that grew in his unconscious also reproduced themselves ad infinitum. Unless some kind of link could be established with the outside world, stasis might result. Worse, his energy, his imagination would be drained. It is, after all, the external world that fructifies the unconscious.

Nerval's beliefs have their source in Masonic literature, the mysteries surrounding the building of the Egyptian pyramids, Kabbalistic writings, the works of Boehme, the *Bibliothèque Orientale* by Héberlot de Molainville, and many more volumes. From the last-named source Nerval had learned that the practitioners of Sabbeanism, the oldest known religion on earth, considered themselves descendants of Set, and that

Sheba was the grandson of Enoch; that the third pyramid in Egypt was Sheba's tomb.[66]

Nerval was fascinated that this enormously creative ancient race from the South lived under the pyramids and in the center of the earth. That center was of the greatest interest for him since its discovery indicated man's entrée into the world of absolute reality, the realm from where the veil of illusion had been removed. It is for this reason that religious edifices are usually placed in the center of a city: Mecca, Jerusalem, Rome. Psychologically, the center (or the Self) "is the ordering and unifying center of the total psyche (conscious and unconscious)"[67] and requires infinite fortitude to experience productively. For Nerval, the center is a focal point for his origins, and also gives his entire life perspective and orientation.

Nerval mentions "a goddess" who guided the new races on this earth in their evolution. The first time this female figure is mentioned, she is positive and dynamic. The second time she is brought into the peripetaia, she is looked upon as a suffering, sacrificial agent. Her brothers, the gods, have condemned her. No one knows whether or not she was saved. Above her head, Nerval saw the evening star, an indication that she is connected with the earth since she emerged from it; she is linked to the infernal realms, since she helped man evolve, and to the spiritual world in that she was associated with the star.[68] But what she represented (order, harmony, and a positive attitude) was virtually destroyed. Nerval considered her to be the holder of magic and religious powers, a regulator of destiny, an evening star able to guide.

Until the fifth race was created by the Eloims, all went well. Then conflict ensued, destroying the prior state of harmony. Numbers are significant in this section: the forty days of flood. The number four, according to Pythagoreans, Platonists, Kabbalists, and most mystics stand for completeness, totality, and harmony. It is equated with the rational and ordered principles and terrestrial life—the four seasons, the four corners of the earth, the cross (or man with arms outstretched), the four points of the compass, the four elements, the mandala, the four Evangelists. Just as the concept of the ternary is connected with action (in Hegel's thesis, antithesis, and synthesis are on an ever-ascending plane), so the quaternity is considered a complete and ordered spatial concept. Thus, when a member of the energetic race dies and is reborn after forty days, this time encompasses a complete cycle. Since four is an inactive number, an additional number (making five) becomes an irritant that brings growth into being again. The Afrites were created: evil demons, according to Arab mythology, who, because of their rebellious spirit, caused tumult, but not growth. This race of pariahs, banned from society, came to earth every now and then to frighten or to teach man the "fatal destiny of their sciences . . . ,"[69] and in this regard they were positive forces for mankind, if not themselves.

The flood, which was supposed to cleanse the atmosphere and lead to man's regeneration, did in part achieve this end. Water symbolizes regression into a preformal state, a world where the potential is infinite; it also represents subliminal depths, with its infinite riches. To be reborn from water, or from these depths, requires a constant, almost brutal struggle.

As for the female principle: "Everywhere the eternal suffering image of the mother was dying, was crying and was languishing."[70] War was rampant; her creatures failed to achieve harmony, or if they did, it was only for a short duration. The Gnostic image of the serpent surrounding the earth that concludes Nerval's vision, "cemented together from man's blood," may be looked upon as unregenerate matter; it represents the most primitive elements within the world upon whom light has never been shed and whose life, because it is turbulent, has not yet taken on meaning. The only hope lies in the woman as the guiding star—then as the sacrificial agent.

Nerval now describes the severe fall he had had, which had required his hospitalization. He considered it an evil omen, a brush with death, a sign of fate, a punishment for the facile loves that "had outraged her memory." As Nerval's guilt increased, so his dreams become bloodier, and more terrifying.[71]

Dream: he felt menaced by the various races who wanted to annihilate him and began to see his double again, and this terrified him. A man, dressed in an Oriental costume, turned out to have his face, but his body was larger and it was idealized. Nerval now had the sensation of living with two beings, two souls within him: actor and spectator, good and evil. He did not know which one he was and became terrified at the thought that Aurélia might no longer be his. Nerval heard a ceremony taking place in some other area: a mystic marriage—Aurélia with his "other" self. Nerval struggled against this usurper, this "other" self.

Horrendous dreams began and Nerval felt himself "slipping like an extended string whose length was infinite." Again he saw an image of the earth, in terms of "colored veins of metal fusing with one another," ranging from white to cherry color; then enormous pools of water became visible, but it was unlike the earth fluid we know; its consistency was like that of flakes.[72] Nerval arrived at a rather arid, beachlike area, greenish in color, yellowed at the extremities by the sun, dried out and parched. A castle dominated the coast, and he started to climb toward it, crossing a mountain; darkness invaded the scene, and on the other side a city became visible. He descended darkened stairs into the streets. Stores, buildings, workshops where clay was being modeled in the form of animals; llamas with large wings. These monsters seemed to "cross a jet of fire," with veins, arteries "fecundating in this manner inert matter"; artisans had very nearly discovered the "secrets of divine creation," and Nerval was told that "here they possessed the primitive fire which animated the first

beings." Nerval saw metal work of a nature unknown on earth, beyond
description: ornaments that might have emerged directly from metal
plants, the result of some metal or chemical concoction.[73] In a large room
draped in velvet, with a sofa in the form of a throne, people were talking
about a marriage. Nerval became violent. A worker carrying a large bar
with a ball of fire at one end wanted to lunge at him. As he heard a
woman's cry filled with pain and recognized Aurélia's voice, Nerval
awakened.[74]

After the dream, Nerval looked out of the window. All was quiet when
he realized that a link existed between the earthly and the invisible worlds,
that he had "troubled the harmony of the universe" because he wanted
to unravel a mystery that was close to him. He felt he would be damned
for doing so, that he had "offended divine law." Now "the irritated shadows fled as their screams pierced the atmosphere and tracing fatal circles
in the air as birds do when a storm is approaching."[75]

The entire dream sequence is infused wih a sense of despair, guilt,
fatality, and turmoil. Every element, race, situation, chemical, metal is
bent upon destroying him, he feels, and he finds his own damnation fit
punishment for the sins committed. Such excruciating guilt was felt by
other men of letters, other philosophers. John Bunyan's autobiography,
for example, is replete with semihallucinatory experiences in which he
too was overcome with despair, guilt, and self-contempt, a longing for
some kind of expiation,

> But my original and inward pollution, that was my plague and my af-
> fliction. By reason of that, I was more loathsome in my own eyes than was
> a toad: and I thought I was so in God's eyes too. Sin and corruption, I
> said, would as naturally bubble out of my heart as water would bubble out
> of a fountain. I could have changed heart with anybody. I thought none
> but the Devil himself could equal me for inward wickedness and pollution
> of mind. Sure, thought I, I am forsaken of God.[76]

Such negative feelings are also implicit in the writings of the Quietists,
such as Mme. Guyon: "everything seemed to me full of faults; my char-
ities, my alms, my prayers, my penance; one and all they rose against
me. Either by you, O my God, or by myself, or by all creatures, I felt
myself universally condemned."[77] St. Theresa of Avila also experienced
an overpowering sense of guilt: "All the favours ever granted me were
swept out of my memory. My mind was so greatly obscured that I stum-
bled from doubt to doubt, from fear to fear. I believed myself so wicked
that I regarded my sins as the cause of all the evils, and all the wicked-
ness that afflicted the world."[78]

At the outset of this sequence of dreams, Nerval felt that he was being
punished for his sexual adventures, the "sin" of the flesh. Such an attitude is not extraordinary in view of the stress placed on the flesh and

its supposed evils in Christianity. Because Nerval had not given up his corporeal existence, he felt that he was unworthy of "the Immaculate One." His body had been sullied and it was to be reviled. But to deny the flesh, which is part of mankind's essential equipment, is to reject life and to destroy human nature. It is an act *contra naturam*. Dr. Sebillotte believed that Nerval's impotence, which the poet refused to face, led him to justify his inability to function sexually by building up a whole spiritual edifice, a whole set of rituals, thereby hiding the truth not only from the world but from himself as well.

We learn that Nerval wanted to go through with his "mystic marriage" to Aurélia and that his torment arose when his double became the groom and not he. The double, now a hostile force, prevented Nerval from acting overtly. If the double is to be considered a shadow principle (a composite of what Nerval believed to be negative characteristics within himself), one understands why such a figure grows larger and larger and why his strength increases by leaps and bounds. Whenever anyone tries to dissimulate something, it always looms larger and presents itself as an ominous force. Such was the present situation. The shadow, now an Oriental prince, increased in size and, as Aurélia's husband, could be wedded to divinity. Only one means of salvation remained open to Nerval; he had only one way of depotentiating the strength of this enormous force: confrontation.

Such was not the outcome. Nerval's guilt increased, as did the split within his personality. He was unable to accept what he considered the evil within his personality. Such an acceptance would have been tantamount to a rejection of the Christian principle of *privatio boni*, that is, that evil exists only as an absence of good, not as an autonomous principle in God's world. Nerval continued to mask what remained unacceptable to him. The leading process, understandably, was impaired.

Nerval experienced his unworthiness (his double) not as a fact of nature but as a punishment. Since he never resolved the issue, he continued to experience a corroding sense of guilt and an increasing dissatisfaction with himself. Adding to this unfortunate situation was the fact that Nerval was convinced he merited God's punishment for having tried to divine the deity's secrets. An overidentification with Prometheus, Cain, and Lucifer as "fallen angels" made him feel that he too had fallen from divine grace. Certain mystics and saints when experiencing the godhead, reacted quite differently from Nerval, with feelings of joy. Ignatius Loyola's reactions have been described in the following manner:

> One day in orison, on the steps of the choir of the Dominican church, he saw in a distinct manner the plan of divine wisdom in the creation of the world. On another occasion . . . his spirit was ravished in God, and it was given him to contemplate, in a form and images fitted to weak understanding of the dweller on the earth, the deep mystery of the holy Trinity.

This last vision flooded his heart with such sweetness, that the mere memory of it in after times made him shed abundant tears.[79]

Jakob Boehme was filled with an inward light and convinced he could see into the essence of things when, at twenty-five, he walked in the fields at Gorlitz. After other such experiences he wrote:

> I saw and knew the being of all things, the Byss and the Abyss, and the eternal generation of the holy Trinity, the descent and origin of the world and of all creatures through the divine wisdom. I knew and saw in myself all the three worlds, the external and visible world being of a procreation of external birth from both the internal and spiritual worlds; and I saw and knew the whole working essence, in the evil and in the good, and the mutual origin and existence; and likewise how the fruitful bearing womb of eternity brought forth.[80]

George Fox also had cosmogonic visions: "I was come up to the state of Adam in which he was before he fell. The creation was opened to me; and it was showed me, how all things had their names given to them, according to their nature and virtue."[81]

The difference between Nerval's visions and those of Loyola, Boehme, Fox, and others lies in their relationship with external matters. Loyola, for example, was strengthened by his visions and hallucinations, his intercourse with the spiritual world. St. Theresa d'Avila was likewise energized. John Bunyan overcame his negativism to a great extent later on in life. Boehme pursued his existence with forays into subliminal depths but almost always emerged from these experiences enriched and renewed.[82] But Nerval's world—with its fatalism, its troubled and colliding harmonies, its storms and tumults, its overriding sense of guilt, its unworthiness—blocked his psychic energies. What he called his "electric power" burst forth from him effectively and violently every now and then—it could no longer be contained in his subliminal depths.

The more Nerval's self-image declined, the less he was able to communicate with the outer world, the more turmoil and blockage he experienced. At the end of part I of *Aurélia*, Nerval mentions a relationship that exists between his visible and invisible world and intimates that what he has experienced externally affects his inner world and would be experienced by his senses. Plato believed in a similar inner reality, which the rational mind could not order, control or view, but which the senses alone could experience. Kant likewise suggests that entities or things exist within man which the thinking principle cannot comprehend. The dfference between Nerval's "invisible" world and those of Plato and Kant is that his amorphous inner realm took precedence over external reality, guiding and dominating it.

The second section of *Aurélia*—or Nerval's second descent—begins with the epigraph: "Eurydice! Eurydice!"[83] Nerval is certain now that "all is finished, all is passed!" and that he is soon to die. But if death is nothingness, he questions, then it must be an end. He is terrified at such a possibility. He thinks of Aurélia and the name Jesus that crosses her lips. He weeps and unburdens himself, noting the following: "When the soul floats uncertainly between life and the dream, between mental disorder and the cold return to the thinking process, one must search for help in religious thought."[84] As Nerval wonders why he should feel such pangs of fright, he decides to visit a friend who believes in the omnipotence and immanence of God and feels even greater solitude and isolation because "God is within him, I cried out . . . but no longer with me!"[85]

Dream sequence: Nerval, who believed he had chased God away, castigated himself for everything he had done and said; he had "preferred God's creature to the Creator." Yet if God is kind he should pardon everyone. Nerval wanders about the streets, follows a convoy toward a cemetery. The dead hear and see the living, and so Nerval believes this man will be grateful for his company. In the cemetery he sees the tombs of his maternal relatives and feels something sacred taking place within him. He searches in vain for Aurélia's tomb. His forgetfulness, he believes, is a punishment inflicted upon him for his flightiness. He rushes home and takes out a little box that had belonged to Aurélia, in which he had kept her last letters. In the box is a series of hierophanies: a rose, crystals, mosaics. He finds the paper indicating the direction of her tomb, then changes his mind. Rather than return to the cemetery, he walks outside of Paris where he had spent many days in his youth.[86] The owner of the inn where he goes to sleep, whom he had known for years, tells him of a friend who has just committed suicide because of reversals of fortune. That night Nerval has a nightmare.

Aurélia emerges from a mirror. She seems sad and pensive, walks toward him, extends her hand and says: "We will see each other later . . . at your friend's home." He then sees himself in a deserted area filled with rocks, thorns, ivy, shrubs, but continues to do so because "I am expected over there![87] A clock rings out. "It is too late!" He hears voices. "She is lost!" He is surrounded by darkness. When he returns home he tears up the paper on which the directions to Aurélia's tomb had been written. It is too late.

The following night he has another dream. A woman he knew in his youth appears to him, reproaches him for a serious mistake: he had not sufficiently mourned his old parents, not as deeply as he had this woman. How could he have hoped to be pardoned? he thought. A series of confused images emerge. He now believes that all the religions, fables, saints' lives he had studied had been placed in his path in order to teach him "the secret of life." He had badly interpreted these religions. Now it was too late. "It's my last day!" A span of ten years had elapsed between the time he had been given the knowledge of the many religious notions and the present moment. Nerval had failed to rectify his judgment.[88]

Because Nerval had begun section two of *Aurélia* with a reference to Orpheus, one may deduce the following: just as the ancient Greek poet and musician had been unable to bring Eurydice back from the dead, so Nerval had failed to bring Aurélia to life. Aurélia, the vision of perfection that lived within his depths, had never really entered or functioned in the domain of reality: she had never been concretized, she had never become a flesh-and-blood woman. She had and would always remain only a fantasy, a remote divinity to be idolized and worshipped.

The dream sequence, beginning with the hearse that Nerval follows to the cemetery, is indicative of this obsession with death. Not remembering the location of Aurélia's tomb is strange for someone who thinks of her night and day, but if we interpret his inability to recollect from a Platonic point of view, one might say that just as infants before birth must be submerged in the river Lethe (forgetfulness), so Nerval experiences a similar oblivion and, therefore, would soon be ready for his rebirth.[89]

His relationship to Aurélia is surely that of a votary to its divinity: he kept all the little souvenirs linked to her memory, including her last letter, in a box. These hierophanies permitted him access to her world—the celestial spheres. Through profane and simple objects one can enter the domain of the sacred because objects and the associations they arouse have constellating powers and hence lose their normal value and function. Nerval himself stated that he had built a whole series of rites and superstitions around Aurélia. Indeed, the notion of rituals and magic centers upon man's ability to order and control natural forces—to earn God's pity. Unlike Faust, who also tampered with the realm of the occult, and went through his tasks to the bitter end, Nerval did not return to the cemetery to find Aurélia's tomb; instead he withdrew to his own past. Perhaps he was afraid to confront her and justified his inaction by stating his unworthiness. Once again, Nerval could not confront reality—either in his dreams or in the external world.

The mirror through which Aurélia steps in his dream reflects the concrete world of consciousness. Man contemplates himself in mirrors. Because the mirror is able to reflect an image it has been linked to water: it is ambiguous since it both reflects and distorts, contains and absorbs the viewer. Nerval's mirror enabled his divinity to come close to him, to give him the comfort he was missing: maternal love and affection. It served also as a door through which the soul could pass—an entrance between life and death, the inanimate and animate. Though Aurélia does not remain with Nerval, she declares that she will return. Nerval is not yet ready to experience a total eclipse from the external sphere; he is not prepared to become her soul mate and reject his bodily existence; nor can he sacrifice his earthly state, as communion with Aurélia would require.

Aurélia departs. Nerval finds himself in a forest filled with brambles, representing all types of difficulties that impede his march toward his goal. To be lost in a thickly wooded area implies, psychologically, utter disorientation. In *The Dream of Poliphilo,* Francesco Colonna was also lost in a bramble forest with gigantic animals and faced his surroundings with feeling of tremulous emptiness. Hölderlin's *To Nature* expresses a similar feeling of alienation. Dante vividly shows such a loss of perspective in this passage from *The Divine Comedy.*

> Midway upon the journey of our life
> I found that I was in a dusky wood;
> For the right path, whence I had strayed, was lost,
> Ah me! How hard a thing it is to tell
> The wildness of that rough and savage place,
> The very thought of which brings back my fear!
> So bitter was it, death is little more so.

Nerval hears the sound of a clock: chronological (rational) time intrudes upon his vision. Time, which devours life, has stopped him from reaching his goal; the rational or logical world has rejected his visions, and considers it a fantasy, not the reality that Nerval believes it to be. He is in a quandary. If he locates Aurélia's tomb, he would be forced to cope with the reality of the situation, but in so doing he would have to forsake communion with her, a union that can take place only in his subliminal world.

Even in Nerval's unconscious domain he loses Aurélia! She escapes his grasp and eludes him. What had he done to merit such punishment? Nerval verges on despair. He can experience no pleasure at all in reading or writing; he is unable to concentrate on anything. Melancholia invades his entire being. Nerval's state is comparable to what Tolstoi suffered during his depression and described in *My Confession.*

> I felt that something had broken within me on which my life had always rested, that I had nothing left to hold on to, and that morally, my life had stopped. An invincible force impelled me to get rid of my existence, in one way or another. It cannot be said exactly that I wished to kill myself, for the force which drew me away from life was fuller, more powerful, more general than any mere desire. It was a force like my old aspiration to live, only it impelled me in the opposite direction. It was an aspiration of my whole being to get out of life.[90]

Nerval feels that only expiation can assuage his guilt. He is certain that he is being punished for having studied and opted for pagan philosophies rather than for Christian ideas. Henceforth, he would rectify his ways and return to the "true way . . . via the beloved souvenir of a dead person."[91] It is Aurélia, the female principle—divinity and mother, beloved wife and sister all in one—who can guide him through his ordeal. What Nerval was now to experience was a veritable theophany—but rather than God revealed to man, it was goddess revealed to him. The Virgin Mary—a composite of Aphrodite, Isis, Artemis—came to Nerval in her most perfect image.

To rectify his ways would be his credo; to help others would be his raison d'être, his way toward redemption!

Hallucination: Nerval went to his father's house and told him he would fetch some logs for him in the attic; his father refused his aid.[92] Nerval felt great consternation. Outside, he saw two people fighting. A worker passes by carrying a child on his shoulders and reminds Nerval of Saint Christopher carrying the Christ child. Nerval felt useless because he had failed to break up the fight. Despair sets in. He sees a priest and wants to confess himself, but the priest says he is too busy and tells him to return the following morning. Instead, Nerval goes to Notre Dame de Lorette, throws himself at the foot of the altar of the Virgin, and begs her pardon. Something within him said: "The Virgin is dead and your priests are useless." He kneels down and slips a silver ring from his finger, the one engraved with: Allah! Mohammed! Ali![93] Religious services begin. Nerval cannot remember his prayers. Later, on the Place de la Concorde, he thinks of doing away with himself, but something prevents him from doing so: "the stars shone in the firmament." Suddenly, he thinks the stars have died and the Apocalypse is going to take place. "The eternal night commences and it is going to be terrible." No more sun. Clouds rush by rapidly. Several moons become visible. The earth is falling out of its orbit. Disorders in the heavens: stars are lighter, darker, smaller. At home he hears a mysterious chorus singing: "Christ! Christ! Christ!" Then he thinks: "But Christ is no longer!," and no one knows it. He goes to the home of a German poet and tells him: "I am lost."[94]

Nerval is taken to a mental institution. Released a month later, he wanders about the church of Saint-Eustache; he enters and kneels before the altar of the Virgin. He thinks of his mother and weeps. He leaves the church, buys a silver ring, then goes to his father's house with a bouquet of marguerites, then to a zoo, to look at the animals, which resemble antedeluvian monsters. He leaves the zoo; a rain drenches everything. He is certain the flood had started and went to sleep at a friend's house.

Vision: A goddess appears to him and says: "I am the same as Mary, the same as the mother, the same one under all the forms you have ever loved. After each successive test I remove the mask which veils my features and soon you will see me as I am." Nerval thought he was in paradise. That night he goes out with his friend Georges; they talk of transmigration of the souls, and he tells Georges he believed himself to be possessed of Napoleon's soul.[95] His hallucinations begin once again and Nerval is taken to the hospital and put into a straitjacket. He thought he was God and that he could heal the sick and that the straitjacket and his internment were tests imposed upon him by Isis. Nerval attributed a mystic meaning to the conversations of the guards; they were spirits that had taken on human form and Nerval's function was to "reestablish universal harmony via the kabbalistic art and to discover a solution by evoking occult forces of diverse religions."[96] All in nature took on multiple aspects: language was mysterious, odors and sounds were transformed. "All is alive, all is active, all corresponds: the magnetic rays which emanate from me and from others cross, without impediments, the infinite chain of created things." Destinies are regulated. The smallest atom can destroy everything and can save all. Nerval began dwelling on anterior existences and how he could prove his own worth. He thought of Isis, "the mother and the sacred wife; all my aspirations, all my prayers blended in this magic name, I felt as though I were living again in her, and at times she appeared to me under the guise of ancient Venus, sometimes also under the traits of the Virgin of the Christians."[97]

Nerval's doctor suggested he care for an autistic young soldier. He did so, considering this man to be the "ear of God," and when he uttered his first word, Nerval believed himself to be responsible for his return to health. Nerval had a wonderful dream that night. He was in a tower and was spending all of his time walking up and down. A door opened and a spirit, which looked like a sick man called Saturning said, "Come on brother." Both he and Nerval went to the country and saw the stars. The spirit extends his hands and places them on Nerval's forehead, just as Nerval had done to the young soldier. Suddenly a star begins to grow larger. Nerval's divinity appears to him in Indian costume: "The task to which you had been subjected has now come to an end." The stairs he had climbed and descended were his "former illusions which encumbered your thoughts." The day he feared the Virgin was dead he went insane. "Your vow had to be carried" to the Virgin "via a simple soul." It had to become detached from earthly things and succeeded in so doing via the autistic soldier that he had nursed back to health. When day dawned, Nerval wrote on his wall: "You visited me this night."[98]

Nerval had experienced what St. John of the Cross called "The Dark Night of the Soul."[99] He had gone through the most painful descent of them all. And in an attempt to extricate himself from his guilt, he had adopted an extroverted attitude. Acting in a manner foreign to his ways—fetching logs for his father, trying to stop a fight in the street— Nerval failed to be himself. The vision of St. Christopher carrying the Christ-child on his shoulder is a corroboration of Nerval's own burdens. Let us recall that St. Christopher, a giant, felt the Christ-child on his shoulders to be a tremendous weight. He was told, "thou has borne all the world upon thee, and its sins likewise." The ordeal was so enormous for St. Christopher that he died three days later. The giant, despite his size, had been associated with the symbol of sacrifice. The Christ-child represented the "sack of illusions" that so many people "carry" on their "backs into adult life," as well as the weight of guilt. Nerval, like St. Christopher, might also become submerged by the burden of his own problems.

That the priest, a symbol of patriarchal society, refused to confess Nerval, is understandable. Nerval, when he arrived at Notre Dame de Lorette, could not remember his prayers, and when he was told that the Virgin Mary was dead, he could not bear the pain. What could he do? Where should he go? He again thought of his guilt—this time for wearing a ring on which Mohammed's name had been engraved. He slipped it off his finger and was *still* unable to experience grace or even partake in the mass. He felt only extreme alienation from God and from himself.

To wish to be *absolutely* good, as Nerval had so desperately sought to be, indicated a childish and naïve attitude toward life. Man is a totality; both good and evil cohabit within him, each coming forth in different ever-changing situations. To want to rid oneself of evil is to divest oneself of what is basic to man—his duality. Moreover, to live one way is to increase one's sense of alienation. St. Augustine, in his *Sermones Suppositii,* encouraged an antihuman attitude: that of saintliness. Evil he wrote, is a *privatio boni.* It was not created by God and, therefore, did not exist and had no "substance." Corruption is the "desire or act of a misdirected will."[100] From where, then, did evil emanate, asked the early Christians? In order to answer such a question and to redress the balance that the concept of the all-Good Christ had brought forth, a counterpart, the Anti-Christ, came into being.

Nerval's desire to achieve goodness increased his sense of deficiency; his failures became all the more obvious. It also aroused an urgent desire for an *imitatio Christi.* Nerval's wish to be like Christ created another impasse in his life. It is impossible to concretize an abstract notion—the ideal. Moreover, even to desire to imitate perfection is an indication of extreme inflation. To seek perfection on the realistic sphere is to endeavor to change one's personality: in Nerval's case, this would be to transform his introverted personality to that of an extrovert. This was a dangerous attempt with fearsome results: it increased the chasm within himself and further blocked his emotions, which could then only emerge through violence. People who feel so imprisoned often have recourse to murder or suicide, the only difference between the two being the course the energy takes, outward or inward.[101]

When Nerval thought of committing suicide after being refused grace at Notre Dame de Lorette, he was prevented from doing so by the stars, or by the intrusion of the divine presence, the female principle, Aurélia. The positive, gentle, and understanding countenance of this composite image infused in him a sense of well being, thereby preventing such an aggressive act from occurring.

Nevertheless, the violence that Nerval felt building up within him and that might have led to imminent suicide or murder, was projected on to nature: the firmament in terms of cataclysmic events, the flood, the Apocalypse, the colliding stars, the multiple moons, the antedeiuvian monsters he saw in the zoo. According to the Book of Revelation, the ideal state or Heavenly Jerusalem would come to pass only after the Anti-Christ had dominated the world, bringing turmoil and destruction. Nerval was certain that the end of the world was at hand, that he would suffer from what has been called "the syndrome of the final catastrophe."[102] In Revelation we read:

> . . . and there were voices, and thunderings, and lightnings, and earthquakes. (8:5)
> . . . fire mingled with blood . . . and the third part of trees was burnt up, and all green grass was burnt up. (8:7)
> . . . and as it were a great mountain burning with fire was cast into the sea; and the third part of the sea became blood (8:8)
> . . . and there fell a great star from heaven, burning as it were a lamp, and it fell upon the third part of the rivers, and upon the fountain of waters . . . (8:10)
> . . . and the third part of the sun was smitten, and the third part of the moon, and the third part of the stars; so as the third part of them was darkened, and the day shone not for a third part of it, and the night likewise. (8:12)

According to Revelation, the reign of the Anti-Christ was to give way to the Second Coming, but only after inordinate suffering and turmoil. Such a conception had occurred to every group or civilization passing through particularly difficult times: in the eleventh century, for instance, when the end of the world was expected momentarily and cosmic cataclysms such as earthquakes and plagues, tidal waves and volcanoes, were experienced frequently. Millenarianism indicated the absence of hope in the real world on a collective level. Faith in the Second Coming and in the creation of the Heavenly Jerusalem gave people the strength to overcome their tragic condition on earth. Nerval also needed something to help him along his painful existential journey. The cataclysms (the earth flying out of its orbit, the flood) were visual descriptions of his own inner pain—preludes to his terrifying statement: "I am lost."

Just as Nerval had identified with St. Christopher, assuming the sins of the world upon himself and breaking from the strain, so he now identified with Christ, "who was no longer." The void within him, created by the emergence of an eternal abyss, left him floundering. Without faith, he could not find his way. When he prays at the church of Saint-Eustache to the Virgin Mary, he is "thinking of his mother," trying to live up to the image a mother has of her child; the hope of the world, in the future, resides in such an image. He discards his ring, which would have offended his mother's religious ideals; he runs to his father's house and buys him a bouquet of flowers. Everything he does at this point takes on an almost ritualistic meaning, as though each act were an attempt to conjure unknown and mysterious forces and put them in his power.

Nerval now oscillates between extreme powerlessness (his inability to experience grace) and inflation (*imitatio Christi*); whatever balance was left within him has been destroyed. When he sensed that Christ had vanished from the earth, it was as if the very basis of his existence had been destroyed, the "ordering principle" within him had been removed. Yet the dream he had at his friend's house seemed, at least momentarily, to redress the imbalance. The Virgin appeared and assured him that she would, at the right time, remove her veils one by one. The Virgin was the symbol of stability, order, strength, and hope.

When Nerval felt himself possessed with the "soul of Napoléon," he again experienced inflation—an identification of the ego ("the center of the conscious personality") with the Self ("the ordering and unifying center of the total psyche").[103] In periods of such inflation, Nerval lived in a state of unconscious wholeness and perfection, oblivious to everything that smacked of reality; he was, in effect, living in paradise. When identifying with such super human heroes he felt in tune with nature—as does the primitive: he felt no conflict, no reason for nostalgia, no desire to return to some previous state.[104]

Nerval's identification with St. Christopher, Christ, and Napoléon was so strong that all objective events (in his dreams or as experienced in reality) were related to him—either to test his strength, to encourage or discourage him from reaching his goal. Such feelings of ego-identification have been frequently accompanied by "messiah complexes" when, for example, an individual believes himself able to cure the world and its ills, and that he knows all answers.[105] When Nerval felt he had cured the autistic soldier, he considered himself a healer who was working in a mental institution. He believed himself to be superior to all the doctors in the rest home. Nerval was convinced that the patients were actually divine messengers sent to him to enable him to "reestablish universal harmony" in the world.[106] Nerval then was arrogating to himself what belonged to the realm of the gods—those transpersonal, omniscient, omnipotent beings. The "illusion of immortality" is the supreme notion of inflation. Most people, however, cannot accept any other alternative. Nerval's sense of continuity, his need to believe in the eternal life of the soul, in reincarnation, was an important factor in the last episode of *Aurélia*.

Nerval's positive inflation had been lived out negatively in Prometheus, Lucifer, and Cain. He oscillated, therefore, between two extremes of inflation, each arousing either elation or despair. When linked with nature, he was able to reestablish, he believed, broken harmonies, and to experience beatitude, joy in the infinite. But seconds later he felt him-

self alienated from the world, like the smallest atom capable of destroying the cosmos but incapable of action. He broke out into a sweat of
despair so full of fear and anguish that it was reminiscent of Christ's
sweat in the garden of Gethsemane as recounted by Luke.

> And being in an agony he prayed more earnestly: and his sweat was as it
> were great drops of blood falling down to the ground. (22:44)

It was after this traumatic experience, the "suffering of a soul,"[107] that
the vision of "the mother and sacred wife" appeared to him "with the
face of ancient Venus, sometimes also with the traits of the Virgin of
the Christians."[108] Equally important in reestablishing his relationship
with the cosmos and himself was his belief that he had healed the autistic
soldier. As Nerval placed his hands on the young man's forehead, he
tried to capture the rhythms of the universe, magnetize its forces.
Through this soldier Nerval succeeded in expressing his own feelings
of warmth, his own need for communication. He experienced a breakthrough when the soldier uttered his first word—as if Nerval had finally
been able to cut through the maze of his inner world.

The tower dream that followed the breakthrough led to the final image: his experience of salvation. The image of the stairs and his upward
and downward journeys indicate that all the religions he had studied
had offered him many illusions, all of which had led to sterility. He had
oscillated from one belief to another, one extreme to another: reality to
unconsciousness, terror to joy, life to death, good to evil. His inability
to regulate and order his life had exhausted him. Now he was ready to
receive the all-encompassing divinity who would take him into her arms,
cradle him, love him, and show him the *real* way.

The last visions in *Aurélia,* grouped under the title *Memorables,* included visions of Mary "queen of the heavens!", scenes of the Himalayan
mountains, a little flower (a forget-me-not), a star, silver pearls, divine
sighs, and finally the vision of the female principle and pardon.

> *Dreams:* "Courage, brother!" said the vision. "It's the last step." Her eyes
> seemed to "devour space," and her hair flowed in the giant expanse. It
> was "impregnated with perfumes from Yemen."[109] A blending of these
> dreams of female images takes place: Queen of Sheba, the Virgin Mary,
> Venus, and an *imitatio Christi:* "Heaven opened up in all of its glory, and
> I read the word *pardon* signed with the blood of Jesus-Christ. A star shone
> suddenly and revealed to me the secret of the world and the worlds." All
> those who worshipped other gods (Odin, Thor, Loki) were pardoned
> along with Nerval.
>
> Nerval admits that his "attempt to fix the dream" and to discover its
> secrets was "audacious." Since "sleep occupies one third of our life," Ner-
> val declared, he wanted to discover the meaning of this "new life" not

subject to the laws of time and space. There is a connection between sleep and death; between external and internal worlds. Nerval now was certain of the immortality of the soul and "the coexistence of all those people whom I had loved" and whom he now saw materially before him; he blessed them for having made him "reenter the luminous laws of religion."[110]

The joy Nerval now experienced with the heavenly pardon eradicated his suffering at the hands of his father, women, and society. With all his faults, and on his own terms, he had been accepted by Heaven. Christ's blood, with which his pardon had been signed, had a numinous quality for him. It was a living substance: an agent of sacrifice, and, when used in the mass, a link between worshipper and deity. As a symbol of Christ's sacrifice, it had a redeeming effect upon Nerval and humanity at large.

> For this is my blood of testament, which is shed for many for the remission of sins. (Matthew 26:28)

In a supreme *imitatio Christi,* Nerval felt that, just as Christ had sacrificed his blood, so Nerval would have to give of his own. The world of joy into which Nerval was now to be received was that of the Virgin and of Christ, her son—a domain of eternal bliss. The words of the Apocalypse seemed to have rung true for Nerval.

> And God shall wipe away all tears from their eyes; and there shall be no more death, neither sorrow, nor crying, neither shall there be any more pain: for the former things are passed away. (Revelation 21:4)

Nerval's ego had now almost completely identified with the collective, with mythical events as described in the various gospels and in Revelation. He was prepared to go through the supreme test—to experience concretely the destruction of the material realm so as to know resurrection in the divine spheres. Assured of the immortality of the soul, of reincarnation, of seeing his loved ones again, he knew the full implications of the words expressed in Revelation: "the time is at hand . . ." (22:10).

. . . she looked at her canvas; it was blurred.
With a sudden intensity, as if she saw it
clear for a second, she drew a line there, in
the centre. It was done; it was finished. Yes,
she thought, laying down her brush in extreme
fatigue, I have had my vision.
                    Virginia Woolf, *To the Lighthouse*

The longer Nerval was forced to remain in Dr. Blanche's clinic, the greater grew his resentment to both his incarceration and the man he considered responsible for his imprisonment. Dr. Blanche was not only aware of Nerval's change of attitude, but also of his need to be free—to roam the streets and country side, to fly about like the "apodal swallow" he was.

But Dr. Blanche also knew that, given Nerval's schizophrenia, his release could not be permitted. There were, to be sure, periods of remission, when hallucinations and visions took their rightful place in his unconscious, but these were infrequent. If Nerval were to be released, he would have to be under constant supervision.

Nerval had other plans. He prevailed upon his friends Godefroy, of the Société des Auteurs, and Jules Janin, editor of the *Journal des Débats,* to send Dr. Blanche a signed statement authorizing his release. Under such circumstances, the law would no longer be on Dr. Blanche's side and little could be done to force Nerval to remain at Passy. Though the doctor was unable to alter the situation, he imposed certain conditions before signing the release statement: someone, either a friend or a member of the family, had to be appointed to take charge of Nerval, and to provide him with sufficient food and a place he could call his own.[1]

Nerval's father, too old now, and probably unwilling to assume such a responsibility, did not take his son to live with him. Nor did Nerval's cousin, Dr. Evariste Labrunie, come forth. Finally a kind old aunt, the widow Labrunie, who lived with her son, offered her home and her affection. On October 19, 1854, at eleven in the morning, she came to Dr. Blanche's clinic and signed a statement that read: "I request that you commit my nephew, M. Gérard Labrunie de Nerval, to my care, and I undertake to receive him at my home until he finds lodgings of his own."[2]

The first few days following Nerval's release seemed euphoric. He spent much time visiting his old friends: Théophile Gautier, Arsène Houssaye, Eugène de Stadler, Maxime du Camp. They received him most cordially and with all the tenderness and affection he had always inspired in people. They were quite surprised, however, by his looks. He had changed. Though only forty-six, he looked seventy. His face had grown paunchy and was marked with deep furrows. His dress was slovenly, his speech dragged, and he could never sit still. Only his gentle smile remained the same. His eyes bore the look of despair. His friends noted a different quality in his conversation. It was marked by bitterness and filled, at times, with irony and sarcasm; it had been so optimistic before, so pleasantly humorous.

As the days passed, Nerval became more and more preoccupied. He felt guilty toward Dr. Blanche, who had befriended him for so many years, yet he also felt that he was justified in his departure from Passy. He wrote his friend Antony Deschamps, who was still under Dr. Blanche's care, and expressed his turmoil. He did not want Dr. Blanche to think him ungrateful, but he *knew* that he was cured and there was no reason for him to remain at Passy. He felt pained whenever he thought that he had "been excluded from *paradise*," or that he had earned Dr. Blanche's wrath over an incident, when in a letter he had written "You are young!," implying a type of *camaraderie* with him, rather than a doctor-patient relationship.[3] He asked Dr. Blanche not to take umbrage with him over such a remark and declared that "all will be explained" in due time. Nerval signed his letters "Initiate" and "Vestal."[4]

Nerval's religious notions had not changed. He still considered himself an initiate for whom his present life was a test, a *rite d'entrée,* for the next. He could accept neither his sickness nor the fact that he was not getting well. According to Maxime du Camp, Nerval's illness was getting worse. There was very little (if any) dividing line between fantasy and reality: spirits haunted his world, were with him always: Venus, Isis, Astarte, or the Virgin Mary—or evil demons such as Lilith, Lamiah, and the like.[5]

Nerval spent most of his days and nights walking about Paris—a nomadic existence. His aunt, who waited up for him nightly, cared for him with the warmth of a mother until she herself became ill. Nerval then moved to the Hotel Normandie on Rue des Bons-Enfants, but he spent little time there; no one really knew *where* he was. One night he might sleep at the Normandie; the next night, another cheap hotel—or he might even spend the night outside. Nerval had few clothes, and fewer material possessions. As he told a friend, he wore his wardrobe on his back. His pockets were filled with bits of paper, a small bottle of ink, and a pen. Frequently, he sat in a café and wrote; at other times, he found shelter in some hovel in Montmartre, amid the ragpickers, pimps, and prostitutes. For him, day and night were alike. If Nerval bought a glass of wine, he could spend long hours in a café, the warmth being a welcome relief from the iciness of the winter months.

Nerval's days and nights were not without incident. Sometimes disputes arose among the prostitutes, drunkards, and gangsters who haunted the dens he frequented. Once a by-stander, a policeman, asked what he was doing at a particular place. "I am thinking," Nerval answered. His interrogator was so surprised and annoyed by this answer, which he interpreted as mockery, that he took Nerval to the police station for the night.[6]

Despite the lack of physical comforts, the intense cold, the fatigue of such an existence, Nerval kept on writing. On December 30, 1854, a series of articles *Promenades et Souvenirs,* was published in the magazine *L'Illustration.* The pieces included descriptions of various parts of Paris such as the Butte Montmartre, situated at the outskirts of the city, and were detailed in a precise and poetic manner. Nerval had always been attracted to Montmartre, the breeding ground of clubs, dives, dens, cabarets—from the most spacious and elegant to the dingiest. There was a story to Montmartre—to the Butte, as it was commonly called by those who lived there—a story that reached far into the history of France. In the seventeenth century, Montmartre was known as Mons Mercurii; two centuries later, under the powerful King Charles the Bald, the name was changed to Mont de Mars; in the twelfth century, as a tribute to the Christian saints who shed their blood there, the Parisians baptized it the "sacred hill," Mons Martyrum. During the French Revolution, it was called Mont-Marat in honor of the Jacobin leader. Enthusiasm of such nature is of short duration, and a few years afterward the Butte once more became Mons Martyrum, or, as we know it, Montmartre.

It was the Montmartre of the Middle Ages that attracted Nerval. At that time it was the most picturesque part of Paris. At the foot of the hill, vast marshlands wended their way through the vine-stocks; fields, meadows, copses checkered the area. Henri IV used to go hunting in Montmartre, and then, after the day's shooting, he would live it up with his men and officers. It was this spirit of uninhibited enjoyment for which the region had become famous. In time, windmills dotted the hill, and from the distance one could see their wings slowly turning in the breeze; taverns, where masons, priests, and soldiers regaled themselves and the uninhibited spirit of Rabelais flourished. Residents of Montmartre were forbidden to enter these inns, and travelers and merchants passing through, in need of food and rest, took chances when they stayed there. On occasion, they never left: their money, their possessions were stolen by their hosts, after a skillfully dispatched murder. The nineteenth century saw the birth of the cabaret *artistique,* the *guinguettes,* the roadside inns, the *bastringues.*

Nerval described the windmills, the cabarets, the silent and tortuous streets, the rowdy night spots, always referring back to certain events in history in his descriptions, forever interweaving mysterious and dreamy qualities in his tales.

Baudelaire has described Nerval's wanderings as "his great joy,"[7] not only because Nerval was curious in spirit, but because he felt that walking was a curative agent, a healer. It fatigued him so that he would no longer be prone to his hallucinations, no longer victimized by them, but rather would sleep like a child from sheer exhaustion.

Nerval still kept in touch with Dr. Blanche, who had indicated his willingness to see Nerval when "all [his] false ideas will have given way to the right ones concerning the nature of [his] sickness and the care [that he had] received." Only then would Nerval be cured; only then would he understand who his real friends were, "those who had taken care" of him.

Dr. Blanche did not believe Nerval would ever be cured. He was well aware of the gravity of his patient's mental health: "for a long time, I felt he was not sound in mind." Dr. Blanche also knew, and this despite Nerval's optimism, that he would never write as he had before—assiduously, diligently—though he might spend long hours in the attempt. Something had corroded his mind; something had deteriorated.[8]

Yet Nerval, despite his nomadic existence, persisted in his literary endeavors. Every now and then, sometimes several times in one day, Nerval would drop in on his friends. His conversations seemed strange, reported Georges Bell. Frequently he spoke of his trip to Egypt, back in 1843, of his initiation into the mysteries of the Great Pyramid,[9] and other esoteric subjects.

On January 20, Maxime du Camp and Gautier saw him at the offices of the *Revue de Paris*. It was a particularly cold day; there was snow on the ground. Nerval entered with his worn black suit, no hat on his head and, worse, no coat. Gautier was concerned. He offered to lend him a coat. Nerval refused, claiming that he was wearing two shirts, which kept him warm. Besides, he said, "cold has a tonic effect; the Eskimos are never sick." He then walked on with the sturdiness of his ancestors, Foulques Nerra. He said that "the males in his family were recognizable because of a supernatural tetragram with which they were born, drawn on the left side of their chest, a little below the heart."[10] Claiming to have bought a very rare object, he took a piece of ecru-colored rope from his pocket: "This is what I have just bought . . . it's the belt which Mme. de Maintenon wore when she had *Esther* performed at Saint-Cyr."[11]

Gautier insisted that Nerval dine with him that evening. Maxime offered him lodgings. Nerval refused both invitations. He took a twenty franc piece from his pocket, implying that he could earn his living and support himself. "Thank you," he said. "I need nothing . . . I have enough for the week."[12]

On January 20 (or January 22), Nerval visited Charles Asselineau's home at ten in the morning. It was freezing outside and the snow had hardened into glazed ice. Nerval had neither an overcoat nor a hat, which he said he had lost. (Some of his friends believed he had pawned them.) He was in a state of agitation, like a trapped animal. He must have known, or so his friends felt, that his sickness was again encroaching upon him. His fear that he would be forced to return to Dr. Blanche's rest home was so great that he hid from all those who might have wanted to hospitalize him. Moreover, he was convinced he could overcome his ailment through exercise—walking. He had succeeded with this kind of treatment several times before, and he was persuaded he could do so again. Asselineau, aware of his frame of mind, asked him to remain at his home, to write there; he offered him food and money. Nerval refused, emphatically. He accepted five francs—and wandered off.[13]

Those who knew Nerval and saw him in this state of frenzy and disarray shuddered. They were fully aware that he needed to be cared for, that he was incapable of tending to his own needs. Arsène Houssaye told him that the treasury of the Théâtre-Français was open to him at any time. The editors of *L'Artiste* and *L'Illustration* printed whatever Nerval offered them. Gautier, du Camp, and other friends tried to prevail upon him to let them care for him. It was no use. Nerval refused all material as well as spiritual constrictions.

On January 24, Nerval's friend Paul Chenavard saw him briefly and was taken aback by some of Nerval's remarks. He talked of a "magnetic pilgrimage" that he had already begun. "Nothing, any more, can prevent its accomplishment," he insisted. "It has its stations, as does Calvary. I knock when passing at the doors of my friends, I salute the places which had given days of happiness for me in the past." He asked his friend to observe him closely. "Remember that today, you saw Christ . . . for it was the right hour. Remember."[14] Nerval and Chenavard wandered about Paris in a series of seemingly endless circles. They climbed the circular stairs of Notre Dame; then, half way up, Nerval saw something—ravens flying—that may have distracted his mind. They did not continue to the top, but walked down. Nerval said goodbye, and when Chenavard wanted to continue, he answered, "No my dear. Each one has his own path. Ours separate now, we must separate. Good bye."[15]

On that same evening Nerval went to a party at the home of the actress Mme. Béatrix Person, where he suddenly seemed charming, gentle, tender again. When he recited some of Ronsard's poetry, his speech was not garbled; his voice did not tremble or drag. On the contrary, when he began singing the old songs of France—those he had heard in his childhood in the Valois region, imitating the intonations and inflections of the various districts within which these tunes had originated—his musicality and artistry was obvious to all.[16] Heine had once described his diction as "pure" and "suave," as "inimitable," resembling the "incomparable tenderness of his soul."[17]

On the following day, January 25, Nerval wandered about Paris. Not wanting to worry his aunt, he sent her a note: "My good dear aunt, tell your son that he does not realize that you are the best of mothers and aunts. When I will have triumphed over everything, you will take your place in my Olympus, as I have my place in your house. Don't wait for me tonight, for the night will be black and white."[18]

It was 15° outside. Nerval was tired, perhaps frozen. He went into a cabaret; there, for the price of a drink, he could remain until closing time. But what could he do *then*? Where would he go? Nerval apparently knocked on the door of a rundown rooming house in which he had slept before; the hostess did not respond because all the beds were filled. He could not think of anywhere else to go to in the vicinity. He was probably exhausted and despondent. He wandered into the Rue de la Vieille-Lanterne. This street, dating back to the Middle Ages, about four feet by six feet wide, could be reached only by going down a few stairs. It was situated inbetween an intersection. Ravens made their home in and about this small impasse.

Hours passed. It was five or six o'clock on a bleak Paris morning. January 26—twice thirteen. A couple wandered down the street and saw something strange. "Look" the woman cried out. "What's that man doing over there? . . . He's frozen." Her partner walked toward the man, then jumped back. "No, this man has hanged himself."[19]

No sooner does horror become evident than crowds congregate—not to help, but to look on, to wonder. Nerval had committed suicide. He had hanged himself. An arm was still moving. Perhaps it was a reflex. No one wanted to take the body down. The body hung there, suspended from the iron bars above the stair case. An ecru-colored cord was tied around Nerval's neck—the one he had shown his friends and that supposedly had belonged to Mme. de Maintenon. Nerval was wearing the clothes that he donned for gala occasions: a high hat, a black suit, a shirt. No coat. A stone had been placed nearby so that when he stepped on it he could gain height. His legs were bent and hanging in the void. His death had been as meticulously planned as his works: with precision, dexterity—and thought.

The police arrived and cut the cord. Dr. Paul, in the vicinity, came quickly. He felt life return in Nerval's body. He bled him. He attempted artificial respiration. But it was all too late. Nerval was dead.

Dr. Labrunie did not want to claim the body. The emotion, he said, would kill him. His reaction to his son's death, according to some, was unfeeling, according to others, deeply felt. "Ah! the *young man* is dead . . . the poor boy! I miss him very much, he was a good lad. *Poor young man!* He used to come every now and then, at intervals. And tell me, Sir, what arrangements have been made for his funeral?"[20]

When told that Nerval's friends would attend to everything, Dr. Labrunie commented: "Well! it's for the best . . . at my age and the state of my health, it would be difficult for me to see to such a task. Ah! the *poor young man!*"[21]

Nerval's body was taken to the morgue. In his pocket were found a passport for the Orient, two hotel receipts, Asselineau's visiting card, the last pages of *Aurélia*, and two sous.

The funeral took place on January 30, 1855. Three hundred or more poets, writers, and artists followed Nerval's bier to the Père Lachaise cemetery. Francis Wey, speaking for the Society of Men of Letters, expressed everyone's grief at the passing of so great a writer, such a good friend, and a "noble intelligence."[22] Nerval had finally been given his complete freedom.

Yet even in death he knew no rest. Six weeks after the funeral a granite stone was placed on his tomb. It had no inscription. Ten years later, owing to an oversight on the part of the Society of Men of Letters who had paid for the funeral expenses, the plot in which Nerval's body lay reverted back to the city, and the body had to be moved. Gautier and Houssaye contributed the funds necessary to buy a permanent plot in the same cemetery. On March 19, 1867, Nerval's body was exhumed and his remains were placed in a child's coffin. The sight was horrifying: "The poor skeleton was in pieces, Death had done her work quickly . . . the head which had represented virile beauty did not even look like a bald cranium. Thousands of worms were suspended on it in cluster formation, and had become nearly ossified. It was difficult to disengage it; we could no longer breathe."[23]

On February 13, 1875, Houssaye, believing he was accomplishing a kind deed, had the remains of an obscure writer, Charles Colligny, placed in Nerval's coffin, thereby helping another "disinherited" man of letters find a home. Houssaye must have regretted his action later, because on March 12, 1890, he had the sepulchral stone placed on Nerval's coffin restored and had a fine column of white marble, which supported a veiled urn, carved with an inscription:

TO GÉRARD DE NERVAL
HIS FRIEND ARSÈNE HOUSSAYE

NOTES

PREFACE BY JEAN PIERRE FAYE

1. George Bataille, *Oeuvres* (Paris: Gallimard), "Et Laure: Ecrits et fragments," *Change*, 1976.

2. Gérard de Nerval, *Oeuvres* II, p. 399. [In this and following citations, the italics have been added by Jean Pierre Faye.]

3. Ibid., p. 385.

4. Nerval, I, p. 381.

5. Nerval, II, p. 390.

6. Nerval, I, p. 381.

7. Nerval, II, p. 385.

8. Nerval, I, p. 414.

9. Ibid., p. 388.

10. Ibid., p. 389.

11. Ibid., p. 375.

12. Ibid., p. 369.

13. Ibid., p. 376.

14. Ibid., p. 373.

INTRODUCTION

1. Evil, according to St. Augustine, is denied existence in a God-created world; it is given no "substance," but is looked upon as a *privatio boni*. In St. Augustine's argument against the Manicheans and the Marcionites, he writes: "*Evil therefore is nothing but the privation of good.* And thus it can have no existence anywhere except in some good thing. . . . So there can be things which are good without any evil in them, such as God himself, and the higher celestial beings; but there can be no evil things without good." Evil is, therefore, relegated to a "defect in good things" or to the figure of the Antichrist. The implications of such a concept with regard to certain philosophical trends during the following centuries were great. See C.G. Jung, *Aion* (Princeton: Princeton University Press, 1959), p. 50.

CHAPTER 1

1. Aristide Marie, *Gérard de Nerval, le poète, l'homme* (Paris: Librairie Hachette, 1914), p. 8.

2. Gérard de Nerval, *Oeuvres complètes,* I (Paris: Gallimard, Pléiade, 1966), p. 135.

3. Ibid., p. 134.

4. Ibid., p. 135.

5. Ibid., p. 937.

6. Gérard de Nerval, *Sylvie* (Paris: Société d'Édition d'Enseignement Supérieur [Pierre-Georges Castex], 1970), p. 150. (Hereafter referred to as *Sylvie.*)

7. *Oeuvres complètes,* p. 135.

8. Ibid., p. 136.

9. Léon Cellier, *Gérard de Nerval* (Paris: Hatier, 1963), p. 19.

10. Jean Richer, *Nerval expérience et création* (Paris: Hachette, 1970), p. 57.

11. *Sylvie*, p. 119.

12. *Oeuvres complètes*, p. 125.

13. Ibid., p. 10.

14. Albert Béguin, *L'âme romantique et le rêve* (Paris: Librairie José Corti, 1967), pp. 500–10.

15. Ibid., p. 501.

16. Ibid.

CHAPTER 2

1. Charles Dédéyan, *Gérard de Nerval et l'Allemagne* (Paris: Société d'Édition d'Enseignement Supérieur, 1957), pp. 26–27. *Faust* had been translated into French in 1823 by the Comte de Saint-Aulaire and, later, by Frédéric-Albert Stapfer. Critics declared both translations to be inaccurate and cumbersome.

2. Gérard de Nerval, *Oeuvres complètes*, II, "Souvenirs de Thuringe."

3. Ibid., p. 1,127 (May 31, 1854).

4. George René Humphrey, *L'Esthétique de la poésie de Gérard de Nerval* (Paris: Nizet, 1969), p. 38.

5. Una Birch, *The Disciples at Sais* (London: Methuen, 1903), p. 4.

6. Albert Béguin, *L'Ame romantique et le rêve* (Paris: Librairie José Corti, 1967), p. 68.

7. Ibid., p. 67.

8. Ibid., p. 199.

9. Ibid., p. 211.

10. Ibid., p. 204.

11. Ibid., p. 201.

12. Ibid., p. 60.

13. Ibid.

14. D. W. Walmsley, *Anton Mesmer* (London: Robert Hale, 1967), pp. 25–70. As a child at Mortefontaine Gérard had read occult books in his Uncle Boucher's attic: Lucius Apuleius' *The Golden Ass*, *Oedipus Aegyptiacus* (1562), a *Myth-Hermetic Dictionary* etc. In Antoine Mesmer's volume, *De Planetarum Inflexu* (1766), Gérard might have learned that a vital fluid penetrated all things; that stars, planets, and the flow of ocean tides affected various parts of the organism, particularly the nervous system. When this vital fluid was out of harmony "with the universal rhythm," the individual's nervous system was disturbed and mental disorder was certain to ensue. Mesmer, a healer, used magnets to treat his patients suffering from hysteria, amnesia, or other aberrations. These magnets, he believed, acted as conductors of the vital fluid which, when spread throughout the patient's body, restored nature's balance and thus good health.

15. Eric Neumann, *The Origins and History of Consciousness* (New York: Pantheon Books, 1954), p. 263.

16. C.G. Jung, *Psychological Types* (New York: Pantheon Books, 1964), p. 233.

17. Hildegard Nagel, "Goethe's Mephistopheles," *The Collective Unconscious in Literature* (New York: Analytical Psychology Club of New York, 1958), p. 33.

18. Ibid., pp. 33–38.

19. Jung, p. 256.

20. Ibid., p. 233.

21. Goethe, *Faust* (translation by Gérard de Nerval), (Paris: Joseph Gibert, 1947), p. 9.

22. Ibid., p. 49.

23. Nagel, pp. 33–40.

24. Ibid., pp. 36–40.

25. Ibid.

26. Ibid.

27. Jung, p. 596.

28. As he had before his transformation with his thinking function, as an aged scholar.

29. Jung.

30. *Faust,* Nerval, p. 10.

31. Ibid., p. 11.

32. C.G. Jung, *The Archetypes and the Collective Unconscious* (New York: Pantheon, 1959), p. 70.

33. Nerval, I., p. 135.

CHAPTER 3

1. *Entretiens de Goethe avec Eckermann.* Quoted by Léon Cellier, *Gérard de Nerval* (Paris: Hatier, 1963), p. 24.

2. Hector Berlioz' statement was paraphrased by Léon Cellier, *Gérard de Nerval,* pp. 24–25. Gérard had also written satires, odes, and elegies—to "Napoleon and France at War" (1826), "Byron's Thought" (1827). Though these were all rather romantic poems, poetry seemed to pour from Gérard, as did the glow of youth.

3. Pierre-Georges Castex, *Le Conte fantastique en France* (Paris: José Corti, 1951), pp. 121–165.

4. Ibid.

5. Gérard de Nerval, *Oeuvres complètes,* II, pp. 1,127–1,169.

6. Ibid.

7. Ibid.

8. Ibid.

9. Marcel Schneider, *La Littérature fantastique en France* (Paris: Fayard, 1964), p. 100.

10. Nerval, p. 1,143.

11. Schneider, pp. 97–103.

12. Alexandre Dumas, *Mes Mémoires,* V (Paris: Calman-Lévy), p. 117. Dumas had said that a great deal of French history was connected with the Arsenal. It had been constructed during the reign of Charles IX, blown up when Francis I was king, rebuilt by Henri IV, who then gave it to Sully, his minister of finance.

13. Ibid., p. 119.

14. Hubert Juin, *Charles Nodier* (Paris: Pierre Seghers, 1970), p. 92.

15. Michel Salomon, *Nodier et le groupe romantique* (Paris: Perrin Co., 1908), p. 112.

16. Alexandre Dumas, p. 122.

17. Ibid., p. 118.

18. Ibid., p. 120.

19. Ibid., p. 126.

20. Castex, p. 43.

21. George René Humphrey, *L'Esthétique de la poésie de Gérard de Nerval* (Paris: Nizet, 1969), p. 52.

22. Jean Richer, *Nerval expérience et création* (Paris: Hachette, 1970), p. 107.

23. Auguste Viatte, *Les Sources occultes du romantisme,* II (Paris: Honoré Champion, 1969), pp. 164–65. In his essay *On Palingenesis,* Nodier declared that God's work had not yet been fulfilled and that man would elevate himself via a series of reincarnations and ascend the more perfect spheres, whereupon he would reincorporate himself into divinity. He even claimed that in 1828 he had had a vision of the world beyond: "I finally perceived a complete and sublime creation."

24. Dumas, p. 128.

25. Solomon, p. 129.

26. Ibid.

27. Ibid., p. 133.

28. Ibid., p. 175.

29. Dumas, p. 112.

30. Solomon, p. 223.

CHAPTER 4

1. Gérard de Nerval, *Oeuvres complètes,* I, p. 782.

2. George René Humphrey, *L'Esthétique de la poésie de Gérard de Nerval* (Paris: Nizet, 1969), p. 104. In *Awakening in a Coach* (1832) linear and spacial differences vanish as they do in a dream. The poem begins as someone is riding along in a horse-drawn carriage, awakens from his sleep but not completely, just enough to see the countryside moving about: trees, fields, people seem to be jogging about at a rapid pace. Had life become chaotic? Had the earth liquefied? Certainly its consistency had altered. If the external world can change so traumatically—just by riding in a carriage—then what is reality? Is reality that which is visible? The world of appearances?

3. Ibid., p. 132.

4. Théophile Gautier, *Histoire du romantisme* (Paris: Charpentier, 1827), p. 70.

5. Ibid., p. 72.

6. Aristide Marie, *Gérard de Nerval, le poète, l'homme* (Paris: Librairie Hachette, 1914), p. 42.

7. Enid Starkie, *Pétrus Borel the lycanthrope,* (London: Faber & Faber, 1954), pp. 29–30.

8. Solomon Rhodes, *Gérard de Nerval* (New York: Philosophical Library, 1951), p. 43.

9. Marie, p. 40.

10. Gautier, p. 78.

11. Ibid., pp. 72, 96.

12. Ibid., p. 97. Nerval's play *The Prince of Fools* (1830) introduced audiences to medieval France. A troupe of jugglers try and succeed in entering a feudal manor in order to rescue a beautiful girl held captive by her father and tyrannical husband. In following sequences, an angel descends from heaven, tries to win as many souls as possible in order to bring them back to heaven. The Devil,

annoyed by the angel's excessive zeal, plucks out its feathers. A fight ensues, chaos invades the scene, giving the young man ample opportunity to escape with his beautiful love. The decors were as terrifying as the story line: the stage opened onto the mouth of hell painted a reddish color; above it was paradise.

13. Nerval, I, p. 778.

14. Three scenes of *Nicolas Flamel* were published.

15. Nerval, I, p. 50.

16. Ibid., p. 58.

17. The sub-title of Nerval's story was to be *Histoire macaronique extrait des contes du Bousingo par une camaraderie*. The word *bousingo* was designed to frighten readers since it was the name given to a group of political plotters who had attempted to overthrow the French government. Nerval and his friends enjoyed playing these pranks.

18. Such an influence on Nerval is understandable because he had translated several of Hoffmann's tales into French: *Adventures of Saint-Silvester Night, The Devil's Elixir,* etc. Nerval had always been drawn to the strange and mysterious, as were most Romantics. An article "Fantastique" has been attributed to Nerval, as had several tales: *The Dinner of the Hanged, L'Auberge Vitré,* etc. (Nerval, I, p. 571).

19. Parallels may be drawn between the manner in which Nerval handles the historical aspects of *The Enchanted Hand* and the approach used by Scott in some of his works.

CHAPTER 5

1. Aristide Marie, *Gérard de Nerval, le poète, l'homme* (Paris: Librairie Hachette, 1914), p. 60.

2. Gérard de Nerval, *Oeuvres complètes,* I, p. 798.

3. Marie, p. 58.

4. Nerval, I, p. 792.

5. Ibid., p. 793.

6. Ibid., p. 797.

7. Marie, p. 62.

8. Jean Richer, *Nerval par les témoins de sa vie* (Paris: Lettres Modernes, 1970), p. 82.

9. Ibid.

10. Arsène Houssaye, *Confessions* (Paris: Dentu, 1885), p. 286.

11. Marie, p. 102.

12. Richer, *Témoins,* p. 47.

13. Marcel Schneider, *La Littérature fantastique en France* (Paris: Faÿard, 1964), pp. 210–13.

14. Nerval, I, p. 66.

15. Marie, p. 97.

16. This painful love was immortalized by Henri Murger in *Scènes de la vie de bohème,* upon which Puccini based his opera, *La Bohème.*

17. Nerval, I, p. 69.

18. Solomon Rhodes, *Gérard de Nerval* (New York: Philosophical Library, 1951), p. 78.

19. Richer, *Témoins,* p. 46.

20. Marie, p. 93.

21. Jean Richer, *Oeuvres complémentaires de Gérard de Nerval*, I, (Paris: Lettres Modernes, 1959), p. 130.

22. Ibid., p. 131.

23. Houssaye, *Confessions*, p. 311.

24. Richer, *Témoins*, p. 4.

25. Nerval, I, p. 66.

26. Richer, *Oeuvres complémentaires*, p. 345.

27. Nerval, I, p. 68.

28. Ibid., p. 70.

29. Richer, *Nerval: Expérience et Créations* (Paris: Hachette, 1970), pp. 169–172.

30. Ibid., p. 311.

31. Ibid., p. 320.

32. Ibid., p. 804 (Sept. 27, 1836).

33. Ibid., p. 808.

34. Ibid., pp. 1,348–1,351.

35. C.G. Jung, *Symbols of Transformation* (New York: Pantheon Books, 1956), p. 424.

36. Nerval, I, p. 753.

37. Ibid., p. 754.

38. Ibid., p. 755.

39. Emma Jung, *Animus-Anima* (New York: The Analytical Psychology Club, 1957), p. 6.

40. Nerval, I, p. 757.

41. Jung, *Symbols*, p. 424.

42. Nerval, I, p. 759.

43. C.G. Jung, *The Archetypes and the Collective Unconscious* (New York: Pantheon Books, 1959), p. 70.

44. Nerval, I, p. 762.

45. Ibid., p. 757.

CHAPTER 6

1. Jean Richer, *Oeuvres complémentaires de Gérard de Nerval*, I (Paris: Lettres Modernes, 1959), p. 443.

2. Ibid., p. 446.

3. Ibid.

4. J.E. Cirlot, *A Dictionary of Symbols* (New York: Philosophical Library, 1972), p. 73.

5. Ibid., p. 215.

6. Gershom G. Scholem, *Major Trends in Jewish Mysticism* (New York: Schocken Books, 1965), p. 134.

7. Brian Juden, *Traditions orphiques et tendances mystiques dans le romantisme français* (Paris: Editions Klincksieck, 1971), p. 15.

8. Hermann Hesse, *The Glass Bead Game* (New York: Holt, Rinehart & Winston, 1969), p. 55.

9. Gérard de Nerval, *Oeuvres complètes*, I, p. 60.

10. Ibid.

11. Nerval later denied that *Leo Burckhart* was based on the life of the German dramatist August von Kotzebue despite the fact that plot and characterizations indicate the contrary.

12. Nerval, II, p. 743.

13. Jean Richer, *Nerval par les témoins de sa vie.* Paris: Lettres Modernes, 1970, p. 123.

14. C.G. Jung, *Psychology and Alchemy* (New York: Pantheon, 1953), pp. 233, 234.

15. Ibid., p. 255.

16. Ibid.

17. Her success in *The Saltimbanques* by Dumersan and Varin (1837) won accolades from most all journalists. According to the actor Adolphe Laferrière, an "unusual love relationship existed between him and Esther de Bongars." Jean Sennelier, *Un Amour inconnu de Gérard de Nerval* (Paris: Lettres Modernes, 1966), p. 73.

18. The title was later changed to "Le Roi de Bicêtre."

19. Nerval, II, p. 940.

20. C.G. Jung, *Psychology and Alchemy,* p. 112.

21. Jean-Louis Barrault said that he met Artaud on the street one day. He began imitating Artaud and Artaud was so terrified when he thought he was seeing himself that he fled in fright.

22. "The Devil's Portrait" was signed G.L.

23. C.G. Jung, *Psychology and Alchemy,* p. 54.

24. Nerval, II, p. 55.

25. Ibid., I, p. 838.

26. Sennelier, p. 112.

27. Jean Guillaume, *Gérard de Nerval. Pandora* (Namur: Secrétariat des Publications, 1968).

28. December 23, 1839.

29. Nerval, II, p. 39.

30. The first half of *Pandora* was published only in 1954.

31. Nerval, I, p. 349.

32. Ibid., I, p. 351.

33. L.-H. Sebillotte, *Le Secret de Gérard de Nerval,* Paris: José Corti, 1948, pp. 100–01.

34. The money Nerval requested from *l'Artiste* arrived on March 19th, making it possible for him to return to Paris. The necessity of meeting his commitments forced him to write more frequently for *Le Messager* and *La Presse,* and to ask his friend August Maquet to write a short story for him, *Emilie* for which he gave him the story line. The themes of suicide, fatality, and the dream factor are present in this tale.

CHAPTER 7

1. Jean Richer, *Oeuvres complémentaires de Gérard de Nerval,* I (Paris: Lettres Modernes, 1959), p. 12.

2. Auguste Viatte, *Les Sources occultes du romantisme,* I (Paris: Librairie Honoré Champion, 1969), p. 58.

3. Emmanuel Swedenborg, *Heaven and Hell* (New York: Dutton, 1911), p. 44.

4. Alice Raphael, *Goethe and the Philosopher's Stone* (New York: Garrett Publications, 1965), p. 247.

5. Ibid.

6. Nerval, Goethe's *Faust* (Paris: Joseph Gilbert, 1947), p. 13.

7. Raphael, p. 123.

8. Viatte, pp. 58–70.

9. Hans Jonas, *The Gnostic Religion* (Boston: Beacon Press, 1967), p. 157.

10. Joseph Head and S.L. Cranston, *Reincarnation an East-West Anthology* (Illinois: The Theosophical Publishing House, 1962), p. 178.

11. Nerval, p. 17.

12. Ibid., p. 14.

13. Ibid., p. 17.

14. Raphael, p. 13.

15. Ibid.

16. Hildegard Nagel, "Goethe's Mephistopheles," *The Collective Unconscious in Literature* (New York: Analytical Psychology Club of New York, 1958), p. 42.

Alchemy was said to have originated in Egypt with the Egyptian god Hermes (Thoth-Hermes Trismegistus), creator of both the arts and sciences. According to Arab legend, the secrets of alchemy were given to Moses and to Aaron by God. The alchemical theory which is of the greatest import is based on the notion of *transmutation of metals.* All substances, alchemists contend, are composed of some primitive matter of *prima materia;* which, during the course of their earthly existence becomes differentiated, alters in form and texture, due to the addition or deletion of certain specific qualities or component parts of the *prima materia.*

The idea of *prima materia* was formulated by Xenophanes, who believed in primal unity from which all creation emerged. Thales of Miletus also posited a monistic theory, suggesting that all things emanated from water, which he defined as "the foundation of the world." Such concepts were not unknown to the Egyptians, who were convinced that Osiris was water and that all things came from and were enclosed within him. Anaximander went a step forward when he declared that opposites develop from an original or primal substance. Such polarity, which is part and parcel of alchemical belief, was expressed by the Babylonians in terms of the sun (associated with gold, the masculine principle, the godhead) and the moon (the earthly, female, silvery entity, always in a state of flux and dependent upon another element for life). Empedocles went on to note the conflict inherent in primordial (indestructible) atoms, which were animated by either love or hatred, attraction and repulsion and so introduced the law of opposites basic to the universe: hot and cold, solid and liquid, the elements of earth, water, air and fire. Heraclitus assumed that the cosmos was in a state of "becoming" and that its essence was fire. The conflict of opposites introduced by Anaximander and elaborated upon by Empedocles and Heraclitus created an energetic and dynamic condition within the universe leading directly to tension. When Heraclitus spoke of fire, it was not to be understood merely as physical combustion but rather as the fire within a being, within his feelings, whether emerging from the human, mineral, or vegetable world—a philosophical fire. It was this energy or vitality that made transmutation of everything in the cosmos possible.

17. Rudolf Bernoulli, "Spiritual Development as Reflected in Alchemy and related Disciplines," *Eranos Yearbooks,* IV (Princeton: Princeton University Press, 1970), pp. 312–20.

18. C.G. Jung, *Psychology and Alchemy* (New York: Pantheon, 1953), p. 168.

19. Raphael, p. 98.

20. C.G. Jung, p. 220.

21. Ibid.

22. Ibid.

23. Ibid.

24. Raphael, p. 12. The alchemist, according to C.G. Jung in *Psychology and Alchemy,* usually led an isolated existence. He responded to his own unconscious notions or to the creative energy which emerged from his *descensus ad infernos,* a confrontation within his own depths. As the alchemist worked on his chemical experiments, he was always facing the "mysterious substance" before him. These entities were not the only things in the process of transforming; as they changed so they aroused a concomitant activity within the alchemist's unconscious. As a result, he projected a variety of characteristics on each substance with which he was dealing. Jung described the psychological tranposition of such a situation as follows: whenever man is faced with a mystery (as was the alchemist when dealing with chemical substances), he fills the void with unconscious contents or psychological projections (fantasies). In so doing, he attributes all sorts of virtues and philosophical concepts to his observations, thereby indicating a corresponding activity within his own psyche. His attempt to understand the mystery of matter may be considered as a manifestation of work going on within him, an individual desire to discover meaning in his own subliminal world.

> Although their labors over the retort were a serious effort to elicit the secrets of chemical transformation, it was the same time the reflection of a parallel psychic process which could be projected all the more easily into the unknown chemistry of matter since that process is an unconscious phenomenon of nature, just like the mysterious alteration of substances. What the symbolism of alchemy expresses is the whole problem of the evolution of the personality, the individuation process. (p. 34)

During the course of his experiments, the alchemist endowed the substance with which he was working with the names and sexes of people, animals and humans. Because he interpolated opposites into his experiments (masculine and feminine), he characterized the activities of the elements before him in terms of feeling: attratio, adulatio, nuptiae, and so forth, indicating his subjective reactions to his experiments. C.G. Jung, *Psychology and Alchemy,* p. 34.

25. The résumés and passages omitted are in act IV, for the most part.

26. Raphael, p. 141.

27. Jung, p. 197.

28. The ego is defined as the center of the conscious personality, that faculty which enables one to relate to people and circumstances in daily life.

29. Raphael, p. 152.

30. Ibid., p. 169.

31. Ibid., p. 183.

32. Ibid., p. 183.

33. Ibid., p. 195.

34. Ibid., p. 196.

35. Nagel, p. 46.

36. Flames are observed in acts IV and V and Faust watches the cottage of Baucis and Philemon burn. According to the alchemist, the vision of the philosopher's stone was preceded by a symbolic death, "the highest color can only be achieved by an increase in darkness." The fire viewed by Faust in this act is comparable to a "baptismal fire" that, according to Orphic tradition, indicates a burning away of all sins and the emergence of absolute purity, the birth of the philosopher's stone. Faust, now conscious of his sins, will come to terms with them, thereby earning redemption in the last act. Raphael, p. 215.

37. Ibid., p. 230.

38. Ibid., p. 231.

39. Jung, pp. 457–465.

40. George René Humphrey, *L'Esthétique de la poésie de Gérard de Nerval* (Paris: Nizet, 1969), p. 46.

41. Nerval, *Faust,* p. 18.

42. Ibid., p. 18.

43. Ibid., p. 21.

44. Ibid., p. 22.

45. Jean Richer, *Gérard de Nerval* (Paris: Seghers, 1963), p. 50.

CHAPTER 8

1. Gérard de Nerval, *Oeuvres complètes,* I, p. 1,336. Jean Richer concluded that, though some scholars believed Nerval's friends to be the sole author of the short story *The Golden Ass,* Nerval had written at least five chapters.

2. Marie-Louise von Franz, *The Golden Ass of Apuleius* (New York: Spring Publications, 1970), I, 4. Lucius admired Plutarch and the Neoplatonists of the period because they blended Stoicism and Pythagoreanism into their own systems and beliefs.

3. Nerval, I, p. 526.

4. Ibid., p. 528.

5. It is interesting to note that Brook Farm, established in the United States in 1841 and transformed into a Fourieristic community in 1845, proved a dismal failure and was disbanded in 1847. Fourier bitterly fought the socialist doctrines of Saint-Simon and Owen.

6. Enid Starkie, *Pétrus Borel the lycanthrope* (London: Faber & Faber, 1954), pp. 51–52.

7. Frank Paul Bowman, *Eliphas Lévi visionnaire romantique* (Paris: Presses universitaires, 1969), pp. 5–25.

8. Nerval, II, pp. 533–35.

9. Starkie, pp. 53–54.

10. Jean Richer, *Nerval par les témoins de sa vie* (Paris: Lettres Modernes, 1970), pp. 139, 52.

11. L.-H. Sébillotte, *Le Secret de Gérard de Nerval* (Paris: José Corti, 1948), p. 62.

12. Léon Cellier, *Gérard de Nerval* (Paris: Hatier, 1963), pp. 83–85.

13. Weill's article was published in April, 1881. Richer, p. 126.

14. Nerval, I, p. 1,424.

15. Richer, p. 128.

16. Jean Richer, *Nerval expérience et création* (Paris: Hachette, 1970), pp. 38–85.

17. Nerval, I, p. 899.

18. Ibid., p. 897.

19. Sébillotte, p. 63.

20. *Autobiography of a Schizophrenic Girl* (New York: New American Library, 1968), p. xiv.

21. *La Chronique médicale,* Aug. 15, 1908, p. 518.

22. Ibid., pp. 513–26.

CHAPTER 9

1. Nine years later, in 1851, a volume that would include essays and articles concerning his earlier trip to Switzerland, Vienna, and Italy as well as his present tour of Egypt, Lebanon, and Turkey would be printed.

2. Letter to Frederick II, April 17, 1737.

3. James Hillman, *Pan and the Nightmare* (New York: Spring Publications, 1972), pp. xxii–xxviii.

4. Henri-Charles Puech, "Gnosis and Time," *Man and Time. Eranos Yearbooks,* III (New York: Pantheon Books, 1957), pp. 40–43.

CHAPTER 10

1. Linda Fierz-David, *The Dream of Poliphilo* (New York: Pantheon Books, 1950), p. 1.

2. Gérard de Nerval, *Oeuvres complètes,* II, p. 68.

3. Ibid., p. 69.

4. Ibid.

5. Fierz-David, p. 4.

6. Ibid., p. 10.

7. Rudolf Bernoulli, "Spiritual Development as Reflected in Alchemy and Related Disciplines," *Eranos Yearbooks,* IV (Princeton: Princeton University Press, 1960), pp. 308–22.

8. Fierz-David, p. 24.

9. Ibid.

10. Such focusing of attention on one object also brings to mind the disciplines of the meditation practices in the Indian's *yantra,* according to Mrs. Fierz-David, p. 44. The Hindu term for the world of opposites is illusion. He experiences the real world in cosmic unity.

11. Ibid.

12. Friedrich Heiler, "The Madonna as Religious Symbol," *Eranos Yearbooks,* VI (Princeton: Princeton University Press, 1968), pp. 348–55.

13. Ibid., p. 352.

14. Nerval, II, pp. 77, 79.

15. Hugo Rahner, "The Christian Mystery and the Pagan Mysteries," *Eranos Yearbooks,* II (New York: Pantheon Books, 1955), p. 350.

16. Ibid., p. 351. "Common to all mysteries is a ritual that speaks to the feelings through powerful external techniques, through glaring light and sound effects and a polyvalent symbolism that sublimates the elementary actions into images of supersensory secrets."

CHAPTER 11

1. Gérard de Nerval, *Oeuvres complètes,* II, p. 89. The fact that Nerval entitled the section of *Voyage in the Orient* dealing with his descent into the pyramids, *The Women of Cairo,* indicates the emphasis he placed on women—the strange and alluring role they played in both Egypt and within his own psyche.

2. Ibid., p. 92.

3. Ibid., p. 93.

4. Ibid., p. 94.

5. Ibid., p. 95.

6. Ibid., p. 179.

7. Ibid., p. 181.

8. Ibid., p. 172.

9. Ibid., p. 109.

10. Ibid., p. 203.

11. Ibid., p. 132.

12. Ibid.

13. Erich Neumann, "Mystical Man," *Eranos Yearbooks,* VI (Princeton: Princeton University Press, 1968), pp. 377–86.

14. Nerval, II, p. 133.

15. Georges Nagel, "The Mysteries of Osiris in Ancient Egypt," *Eranos Yearbooks,* II (Princeton: Princeton University Press, 1955), p. 120.

16. Nerval, II, p. 168.

17. Emma Jung and Marie-Louise von Franz, *The Grail Legend* (New York: G.P. Putnam's Sons, 1970), p. 132.

18. Ibid., p. 127.

19. Plato, *Collected Dialogues* (New York: Tudor Publishing Co.), pp. 274–75.

20. C.W. Ceram, *Gods, Graves, and Scholars* (New York: Alfred A. Knopf, 1961), p. 71.

21. Ibid., p. 118. In 1820 Belzoni returned to London where he displayed the alabaster sarcophagus he had brought back from Sethos and a reproduction of the burial chamber.

22. Ibid., p. 120.

23. Peter Tomkins, *Secrets of the Great Pyramid* (New York: Harper & Row, 1971), p. 218.

24. Nerval, II, p. 226.

25. Ibid., p. 221.

26. An acolyte is first taught certain sciences, geometry and numbers, etc. astronomical sciences, the evolution of man . . . the rest of the initiation, which includes mastership of body and mind, lasted twenty-two years. Tomkins, p. 256.

27. Nerval, II, pp. 221–23.

28. Ibid. p. 224.

29. Ibid.

30. Ibid.

31. Ibid.

32. Similar to the one inhabited by Adam and Eve.

33. C. Kerényi, "The Mysteries of the Kabeiroi," *Eranos Yearbook,* II (New York: Pantheon Books, 1955), p. 44.

34. Walter Wili, "The Orphic Mysteries and the Greek Spirit." *Eranos Yearbooks,* II (New York: Pantheon Books, 1955), p. 66.

35. In the Orphic religion, time has created "the silver egg of the cosmos" and from it bursts forth the triurnal figure Phanes-Dionysus (to bring light, to shine): Dionysus-Zagreus and Dionysus-Lyseus—a bisexual divinity in whom all was contained and from which everything emanated. This unanimistic view gave rise to the belief that "the one is split into many, that the many becomes one again, and that universe, God, and man are governed by this primal rhythm." Ibid., p. 72.

36. Mircea Eliade, "Mysteries and Spiritual Regeneration in Extra-European Religions," *Eranos Yearbooks,* V (New York: Pantheon Books, 1964), p. 17.

37. Ibid.

38. Serge Hutin, *Les Sociétés secrètes* (Paris: Presses universitaires, 1970), p. 19.

39. Nerval, I, p. 923.

40. Ibid., p. 261.

41. In the Greek Eleusinian mysteries, for example, the mystai prays to the Queen of the Dead, to Persephone, for fertility. Demeter, her mother, the *Mater Dolorosa,* mourns for her daughter during six months of the year and when she finally recaptures her, expresses her joy by providing earthly abundance in agriculture. Isis mourned her husband as did other nature goddesses; Aphrodite and Adonis; Attis and Cybele, Ishtar and Tammuz. Only through death can fecundity be born. According to Orphic and Platonist belief, death brings about a liberation of the soul from imprisonment of the body. Walter F. Otto, "The Meaning of the Eleusynian Mysteries," *Eranos Yearbook,* II (New York: Pantheon Books, 1955), pp. 14–30.

CHAPTER 12

1. Gérard de Nerval, *Oeuvres complètes,* II, p. 347.

2. Betty Bouthoul, *Le Calife Hakim* (Paris: Sagittaire, 1950), p. 15. Some scholars believe the Druse came originally from China; others that they are descendants of the Count Dreux, a Crusader who had remained in the Middle East after his countrymen had returned from the wars—forgetting his land, language, and religion.

3. Nerval, II, p. 353.

4. Bouthoul, p. 110.

5. Nerval, II, p. 353.

6. Ibid., p. 355.

7. It is also interesting to note that people believed in Hakim's divinity during the millennium, a time fraught with fear and the belief that the world was coming to an end.

8. Nerval, II, p. 355.

9. Ibid., p. 356.

10. Ibid., p. 357.

11. Ibid., p. 359.

12. Ibid., pp. 360, 361.

13. Max Pulver, "The Experience of Light in the Gospel of St. John, in the 'Corpus Hermeticum,' in Gnosticism, and in the Eastern Church," *Eranos Yearbooks,* IV (Princeton: Princeton University Press, 1970), p. 262.

14. Ibid., p. 263.

15. Nerval, II, p. 361.

16. Ibid., p. 362.

17. Evelyn Underhill, *The Mystics of the Church* (New York: Schocken Books, 1971), pp. 76, 106.

18. Pulver, pp. 261, 142.

19. Nerval, II, p. 363.

20. J.E. Cirlot, *A Dictionary of Symbols* (New York: Philosophical Library, 1972), p. 150.

21. Nerval, II, p. 365.

22. Ibid., p. 366.

23. Ibid., pp. 371–72.

24. Ibid., p. 372.

25. Ibid., pp. 378, 379.

26. Ibid., p. 386. He usually appears in tales during important moments.

27. Ibid., p. 392.

28. Ibid., p. 384.

29. Ibid., p. 397.

CHAPTER 13

1. Robert H. Pfeiffer, *Introduction to the Old Testament* (New York: Harper & Row, 1948), p. 383.

2. Salo W. Baron, *A Social and Religious History of the Jews,* I (Philadelphia: Jewish Publication Society, 1952), p. 75.

3. Heinrich Graetz, *History of the Jews,* I (Philadelphia: Jewish Publication Society, 1891), p. 165. For further information on the Biblical legend and a variety of interpretations see André Chastel, "La Légende de la Reine de Saba," *Revue de l'histoire des religions,* vols. 120–124, July/August, 1939–1941, p. 163.

4. Rivkah Schärf Kluger, *Psyche and the Bible* (Zürich: Spring Publications, 1974), p. 93.

5. Héberlot de Molainville, *Bibliothèque orientale* (Paris: La Compagnie de Libraires, 1697), p. 357.

6. Gérard de Nerval, *Oeuvres complètes,* II, p. 506.

7. Kluger, p. 93.

8. Ibid., p. 109.

9. Merdowski, *The Epic of the King Shab-Name the National Epic of Persia* (Chicago: University of Chicago Press, 1967), pp. 1–17.

10. Nerval, II, pp. 517, 514.

11. Ibid., p. 506.

12. Ibid., p. 1,375. It is interesting to note that Rachel called her son Benoni "son of my suffering" because her labor pains were so great. After she died, her husband Jacob called their son Benjamin. (Gen. 35:18)

13. According to certain Kabbalistic and Talmudic scholars the world was ruled by a series of great kings. Isaac de la Peyrère in his volume *The Pre-Adamites* (1655) gives an account of these kings, their powers and their downfall.

14. A.E. Waite, *The Holy Kabbalah* (New York: University Books, 1971), p. 274.

15. Nerval, II, p. 504.

16. Ibid., p. 556.

17. Ibid., p. 537.

18. Ibid., p. 1,380.

19. Ibid., p. 552.

20. Ibid., p. 687.

21. Ibid., p. 562.

22. W.L. Wilmhurst, *The Masonic Initiation* (London: John M. Watkins, 1957), p. 78.

23. Paul Naudon, *La Franc-Maçonnerie* (Paris: Presses Universitaires de France, 1971), pp. 84–95.

24. Ibid.

25. Ibid.

26. Harold W. Percival, *Masonry and its Symbols* (New York: The Word Publishing Co., 1952), pp. 7–15.

27. Ibid., p. 10.

28. Naudon, p. 86.

29. Serge Hutin, *Les Sociétés secrètes* (Paris: Presses Universitaires de France, 1970), p. 72.

30. Percival, p. x.

31. Serge Hutin, *L'Alchimie* (Paris: Presses Universitaires de France, 1971), p. 45.

32. Wilmhurst, p. 146.

33. Hutin, *L'Alchimie,* p. 65.

34. Ibid., pp. 61, 75.

35. Chastel, p. 164.

36. Gaston Bachelard, *La Psychanalyse du feu* (Paris: Gallimard, 1949), p. 34.

37. Kluger, p. 89.

38. Ibid., pp. 94–98. Flavius Josephus refers to Sheba as queen of Ethiopia and Egypt. In Arab legends, Sheba is known under the name Bilqis or Balqis (Balkis). Bilqis was a "phonetic transformation of a himyaritic" (South-Arabic) god, Ilmukah or Illumnkuf, and because of such an association, Sheba was endowed with divine attributes. Sheba was also identified with the Spouse in The Song of Songs, symbolically interpreted as the soul seeking union with God. Christian Fathers have identified her with "The Queen of the Morning" or of the "South" mentioned by St. Matthew. "The queen of the south shall rise up in the judgment with this generation, and shall condemn it: for she came from the uttermost part of the earth to hear the wisdom of Solomon; and behold, a greater than Solomon is here." (12:42) In Revelation, a female figure, also associated with Sheba and the Virgin Mary, is alluded to as coming from afar. "And there appeared a great wonder in heaven; a woman clothed with the sun, and the moon under her feet, under her head a crown of twelve stars." (12:1)

39. Emma Jung and Marie-Louise von Franz, *The Grail Legend* (New York: G.P. Putnam's Sons, 1970), p. 192.

40. Wilmhurst, p. 110.

CHAPTER 14

1. Analogies may be readily drawn between Emma Bovary and Rodolphe and Nerval's protagonists.

2. Gérard de Nerval, *Oeuvres complètes,* I, p. 581.

3. Ibid., p. 586.

4. Ibid., p. 587.

5. Ibid.

6. Ibid., p. 589.

7. Ibid., p. 590.

8. Syzygies may be defined as opposing points in the orbit of heavenly bodies, especially the sun and moon.

9. Nerval, I, p. 596.

10. Ibid., p. 598.

11. Ibid.

12. Ibid., p. 601.

13. Ibid., p. 602.

14. Ibid.

15. Ibid., p. 614.

16. Ibid., p. 721.

17. Pascal's *Pensées* is most fitting here: "The heart has its reasons that reason knoweth not."

18. Nerval, I, p. 631.

19. Ibid., p. 631.

20. Ibid., p. 646.

21. Ibid. p. 639.

22. Ibid., p. 637.

23. Coction then has taken place; the process during which the chemical or metallic substance is perfected.

24. Nerval, I, p. 741.

25. Ibid. p. 742.

26. Jean Richer, *Nerval par les témoins de sa vie* (Paris: Lettres Modernes, 1970), p. 116.

27. Nerval, I, p. 742. Nerval had borrowed some episodes from Charles Nodier's story "Ines de la Sierras" (1837) and from Prosper Mérimée's theatre, *La Guzla* and sections from Goethe's *Faust* II. The themes for *The Montenegrins* (the heroism of a girl, a soldier's love, the courage and honesty of the native population, the emperor's benevolent attitude, the fusion of dream and reality) were handled in a banal manner.

28. As far as scholars are able to determine, Nerval either never completed or lost some of the plays he allegedly wrote at this period: *A Sleepless Night, The Black Forest, Rousseau's Death* are extant only in outline form. As for *The Hand of Glory,* only a brief synopsis remains.

29. Nerval was fascinated with the art of printing (as Balzac had been). Printing implies the dissemination of the word, the spreading of ideas, knowledge, thought—and in this respect, power. The word, therefore, permits one to become a Titan; it offers immortality to mortals—fame and fortune. *The Printmaker of Haarlem* lasted two weeks.

CHAPTER 15

1. Mircea Eliade, *Myths, Dreams, Mysteries* (London: Harvill Press, 1960), p. 43.

2. C.G. Carus, *Psyche* (New York: Spring Publications, 1970), p. 1. It is not known whether Nerval knew C.G. Carus personally, though he certainly must have heard about him. Carus was not only a physician, a painter, but also a

friend of Paganini, Liszt, Clara Wieck (who was to become Schumann's wife). He had the advantage of having known Goethe, whom he considered his *spiritus rector* and about whom he wrote a volume, *Goethe* (1843), and *Letters on Faust* (1835).

3. C.G. Jung will later develop these ideas basing his own philosophy on them.

4. Carus, p. 1.

5. Ibid., p. 63.

6. Ibid., p. 14.

7. In 1839 Nerval published certain studies on the Illuminists, a short story *Raoul Spifame* which was to be included in his volume, *The Illuminists* or *The Precursors of Socialism* (1852).

8. *The Illuminists* comprises two short stories, "Raoul Spifame, The History of the Abbé Bucquoy" which had been printed in the *National* in 1850, essays on Restif de la Bretonne, Jacques Cazotte, Cagliostro, Quintus Aucler.

9. Sheila Ostrander and Lynn Schroeder, *Psychic Discoveries behind the Iron Curtain,* (New Jersey: Prentice-Hall, Inc., 1970).

10. Nerval's essay on Restif de la Bretonne was entitled *Les confidences de Nicolas.*

11. Armand Bégué, *Etat Présent des études sur Restif de la Bretonne* (Paris: Les Belles lettres, 1948), p. 50.

12. Auguste Viatte, *Les Sources occultes du romantisme,* I (Paris: Librairie Honoré Champion, 1969), p. 253.

13. Ibid.

14. Ibid., p. 255.

15. Ibid., p. 257.

16. Ibid., p. 258.

17. Gérard de Nerval, *Oeuvres complètes,* II, p. 999.

18. Ibid., p. 1,004.

19. Ibid., p. 1,065.

20. H. Mann, M. Siegler, H. Osmond, "Time," *Journal of Analytical Psychology,* XIII, 1968, p. 36.

21. Nerval, II, p. 1,071.

22. Other similarities may be pointed out between Restif and Nerval. Both were fascinated by the art of printing, typography in particular; both loved the country, the freedom it offered, the solitude, the fields and forests; both prided themselves on their illustrious heritage; Restif claimed to be descended from the Roman Emperor Nerva. Ibid., pp. 1,109–1,492.

23. Ibid., p. 1,072.

24. Jean Richer, *Nerval, expérience et création* (Paris: Hachette, 1970), p. 450.

25. Nerval, II, p. 1,154.

26. Ostrander and Schroeder, p. 213.

27. The Oriental considers such divisions artificial, intellectual concepts, devoid of meaning.

28. Cazotte joined the Martinist order. The ideologies as enunciated by the Martinists, by Martinès de Pasqually, were based largely on the teachings of the Hebrew Kabbalists and the Gnostics of the Alexandrine schools. According to the Kabbalists, air, water, fire, breath, as well as the ten spheres (Sephiroth) that make up the cosmos, are emanations of the All Being (En-Sof). After the cre-

ation of man (when man fell into matter), the divine aspect within him had been contaminated and, therefore, had to be rehabilitated. It could be purified by means of certain disciplines: prayer, fasting, theurgical practices. In this way the Devil (evil) could be extracted from man; his material nature reintegrated into the All-Being for the Kabbalist and into Christ for the Gnostic. The Fall, it must be recalled did not only affect man, but the entire hierarchy of spirits which resided at various levels within the cosmos—between Man and God. Edward Peace Shaw, *Jacques Cazotte* (Cambridge: Harvard University Press, 1941), p. 73.

29. Nerval, II, p. 1,138.

30. Ibid., p. 1,149.

31. Shaw, p. 109.

32. C.G. Jung, *Structures and Dynamics of the Psyche* (New York: Pantheon Books, 1963), p. 449.

33. Peter Wilding, *Adventures in the 18th Century* (New York: G.P. Putnam's Sons), pp. 250–80.

34. Ibid., p. 277.

35. Ibid., p. 291.

36. Viatte, p. 37.

37. C.G. Jung, *Memories, Dreams, Reflections* (New York: Pantheon, 1963), p. 304.

38. C.G. Jung, *Structures*, p. 480.

39. Arthur Koestler, *The Roots of Coincidence* (New York: Random House, 1972), p. 87.

40. Jung, *Structures*, p. 434.

41. Ibid., pp. 436–458.

42. Ibid.

43. Ibid.

44. Jung, *Memories, Dreams*, p. 390.

45. Jung, *Structures*, p. 551.

46. *Memories, Dreams*, p. 388.

47. *Structures*, p. 519.

48. Ostrander and Schroeder, p. 154.

49. Koestler, p. 50.

50. Ibid., p. 106.

51. Ibid., p. 107.

52. Ibid., p. 61.

53. Ibid.

54. Ibid., p. 62.

55. Ibid., p. 70.

56. Ibid.

57. Ibid., p. 71.

58. Ibid., p. 74.

59. Ibid., p. 77.

60. In *The Almanach Cabalistique* (1849) Nerval included essays on what he called, the "Red Prophets": Buchez, Lamennais, Mickiewitz, Towiansky, Considérant, Leroux, and Proudhon.

Philippe Buchez (1796–1865) the founder of the Catholic Republican Party (1834), linked his beliefs, in some strange way with Catholic orthodoxy. His two idols were Jesus Christ and Robespierre. Frequently called "the archangel of the

Revolution," because he took part in several plots to overthrow the Restoration, he finally became a disciple of Saint-Simon.

Félicité Lamennais' fate was unfortunate. A priest, a defender of the monarchy, he attracted for some strange reason, the young élite liberal Catholics to his banner. Vigorous, temperamental, he founded the newspaper *L'Avenir* (1830) in which he preached an alliance between the church and the concept of liberty. Pope Gregory XVI, however, disavowed Lamennais' credo in an Encyclical Mirarivos. Lamennais suddenly found himself without disciples. In 1834 he broke openly with the church in his *Parole d'un Croyant.* Abandoned by his church, he was condemned to one year of imprisonment (1840) by the July Monarchy. Lamennais was considered a proponent of liberty and justice.

Less well known, and perhaps even more surprising a figure, was the Polish poet Adam Mickiewicz. Exiled from his native land, he settled in Paris and was put in charge of Slavic literature at the Collège de France (1840). His teachings suddenly deviated from the normal when he came under the influence of the Polish mystic André Towiansky. Mickiewicz' wife who had been mentally sick, was cured by the Polish mystic through some treatments in magnetism. The poet, grateful to him, preached Towiansky's doctrine; as a result, he was suspended from his teaching post in 1845.

André Towiansky (1799–1878) was a notary in Wilna when he showed signs of mental derangement. Sent to an institution for a short time, he was released and then left for Brussels (1837). Towiansky considered Napoléon I a messiah. He believed that the emperor's soul, after his death, was a guiding force in helping man along the right path. When Napoléon's ashes were returned from St. Helena to Paris, the emperor's soul "took advantage of the opening" of the casket and flew out. It found its way into a new home—into Towiansky—who became man's new leader. But before undertaking the task of guiding humanity, Towiansky went to Waterloo on a pilgrimage "to visit the prophet and the place" that had been sanctified by Napoleon's presence.

Victor Considérant (1808–1893) was, according to Nerval, only a "vice-prophet," a man who carried out the dictates of his leader Fourier. A believer in the notion of universal harmony, in the phalansteres as outlined in his volumes (*Social Destiny,* 1833–1834; *Exposition of the Fourier System,* 1845), he attempted to bring his theories into practice. When he tried to realize his dream, the establishment of the phalanstere, he failed. Elected in 1848 to the Constituent Assembly as representative of the people, then to the legislature, he took part in the insurrection of June 13, 1849, and was condemned by default to deportation. He fled to Belgium, and then to America, where he founded a socialist type of community in Texas. It also failed.

Pierre Leroux, whose system was inspired by both Pythagoras and Leibniz, believed in neither a God- creator nor in a Creation. God is a universal soul, a collection of intelligent monads that animate men, animals and the like. Man, the result of a permanent state of "uncreatedness" (*l'incrée*), sees only a "simulacre of existence." The intelligent being "does not die, his personality merely ceases to appear" to others. Leroux believed that human society was a communion with its laws concerning equality, property, and solidarity. In opposition to Christianity Leroux believed man to be perfectible and in this sense he was an optimist.

Pierre Proudhon (1809–1865) attempted to prove the unity of man's origins by means of the unity of language in his *Essai de Grammaire générale* (1837). He was also a fighter in the temporal realm, trying to rid society of inborn inequality. He was elected to the national assembly in 1848 but was imprisoned a year later for speaking too openly in the press. His ideas, which he expounded in *The Philosophy of Wretchedness* (1846) and in *Revolutionary Ideas* (1849), were violent. He denigrates communism, statism, Fourierism, the theory of competition; denounces "spoliation of workers by capitalists" and said, in 1840 (before Marx), that "property is thievery." Though Proudhon was considered a materialist, Nerval wrote that he defended the "very divine" principle of Christianity.

These men were of interest to Nerval because they allied politics and economics to mysticism.

CHAPTER 16

1. *The Illuminists* was published in 1852. *October Nights* included a series of short sketches which were published in the magazine *l'Illustration*.

2. Gérard de Nerval, *Oeuvres complètes*, I, p. 1,059.

3. Jean Richer, *Gérard de Nerval par les témoins de sa vie* (Paris: Lettres Modernes, 1970), pp. 207–08.

4. Ibid., p. 205.

5. February 11, 1853.

6. Nerval, I, p. 1,054.

7. L.-H. Sébillotte, *Le Secret de Gérard de Nerval* (Paris: José Corti, 1948).

8. *Sylvie* was published on August 15, 1853 in *La Revue des deux mondes.*

9. *La Chronique Médicale*, September 1, 1908, pp. 545–76.

10. Nerval, I, p. 1,052.

11. Ibid., p. 1,059.

12. Alice Raphael, *Goethe and the Philosopher's Stone* (New York: Garrett Publications, 1965), p. 124.

13. Nerval, I, May 26, 1853.

14. Richer, p. 27.

15. Ibid., p. 192.

16. Ibid.

17. Nerval, I, p. 1,064.

18. Ibid., p. 1,091.

19. Ibid., p. 1,067.

20. Ibid., p. 1,073.

21. Ibid., p. 1,067.

22. Ibid., p. 1,073.

23. Ibid., p. 1,078.

24. Richer, p. 208.

25. Ibid., p. 189.

26. John Custance, *Wisdom, Madness and Folly* (New York: Pellegrini and Cudahy, 1952), p. 61.

27. Nerval, I, p. 1,083.

28. John Custance, p. 20.

29. Jean Richer, *Nerval expérience et création* (Paris: Hachette, 1970), ch. II.

30. Nerval, I, p. 1,092, December 10, 1853.

31. Ibid., p. 1,496.

32. Ibid., p. 1,098.

33. Ibid.

34. Richer, *Gérard de Nerval par les témoins de sa vie*, p. 277.

35. Nerval, I, p. 1,094.

36. Ibid., p. 1,103. The circular images and references to circles so frequently found in Nerval's writings, particularly during the last period, indicated that he was consuming his energy. Like the primitive circle of the uroborus, he was just going around and around and never tapping his "true" depths. "I am turning in an increasingly narrowing circle," he claimed, and kept feeling that he was incapable of writing anything worthwhile.

37. Ibid., p. 1,102.

CHAPTER 17

1. *The Daughters of Fire* includes short stories which Nerval had written as far back as 1839 (*Corilla*), to the one composed in 1852 (*Sylvie*); others revised in 1853 (*Angélique*) and a group of seven of the most beautiful sonnets in the French language entitled *Chimères*. Nerval dedicated *The Daughters of Fire* to Alexandre Dumas. It was he, Nerval wrote, who had alluded to his "insanity" in an article in *Le Mousquetaire* (Dec. 2) and for this reason Nerval felt compelled to thank him for his compassion. "A few days ago, people thought I was crazy, and you devoted some of the most charming lines to the epitaph of my mind." Nerval parried the dagger thrust most astutely and forcefully, and also proved to his readers that he was not insane. How could a madman write coherently? beautifully? since some of his short stories included in this volume had already received great praise. Nerval showed himself capable of taking the situation in stride. Gérard de Nerval, *Oeuvres complètes*, I, p. 149.

2. Gaston Bachelard, *L'Eau et le rêves* (Paris: José Corti, 1942), p. 8.

3. Jean Richer, *Nerval expérience et création* (Paris: Hachette, 1970), p. 145.

4. When Nerval spoke of Mephistopheles in *Faust,* he did not look upon this "fallen angel" as a negative figure. On the contrary, it was the Devil who had helped the hero accomplish his final salvation. In his play *The Printmaker of Harlem,* the Devil provokes and prods the protagonist Costa, to pursue his work, thereby stimulating his creative energy but not until the end with the presence of his celestial daughter, does he experience a state of awareness and insight into his life and actions.

5. Richer, p. 145.

6. *Angélique* was first published in 1850 as part of a larger work, *The Faux-Saulniers,* in *Le National* (Oct. 24 to Dec. 22, 1850). The second section of *The Faux-Saulniers,* dealing with the adventures of the Abbé Bucquoy, was included in *Les Illuminés* (1852). Other sections were published in *La Bohème Galante* and in *Loreley.* Nerval, I, p. 1,249.

7. Angels, according to the *Aggadas,* were made of a "divinely harmonized" mixture of fire and water.

8. Mircea Eliade, *Aspects du mythe* (Paris: Gallimard, 1963), pp. 150–53.

9. Nerval, I, p. 151.

10. Alice Raphael, *Goethe and the Philosopher's Stone* (New York: Garret Publications, 1965), p. 48.

11. Nerval, I, p. 181, p. 165. In Nerval's discussion of libraries he mentions that the burning of the library of Alexandria had been erroneously attributed

to the kaliph Omar (A.D. fourth century) when in fact it had been destroyed by Christians intent upon ridding the world of pagan documents. Such religious fanaticism was also evident in the murder of the very beautiful Pythagorean philosopher Hypatia, who was stoned to death by Christian mobs while walking through the streets of her native land.

12. Ibid., p. 181.

13. Ibid.

14. Ibid.

15. Ibid.

16. Ibid., p. 150.

17. Mircea Eliade, *Le Sacré et le profane* (Paris: Gallimard, 1965), p. 34.

18. Ibid., p. 113.

19. Ibid., p. 154.

20. Nerval, I, p. 190.

21. Ibid.

22. Ibid., p. 189.

23. Ibid., p. 179.

24. Richer, pp. 294–95.

25. Urban Holmes, *A History of Old French Literature* (New York: F.S. Crofts, 1938), pp. 139–99.

26. Nerval, I, p. 180.

27. Ibid., p. 191.

28. Ibid.

29. Ibid., p. 192.

30. In medieval France, liturgical drama usually revolved around Christ's Passion.

CHAPTER 18

1. *Sylvie* was first published on August 15, 1853 in the *Revue des deux mondes*. An excellent commentary on this work may be found in Georges Poulet "Sylvie ou la pensée de Nerval," *Cahiers du Sud,* October 1938; also in *Sylvie* by Castex.

2. Gérard de Nerval, *Oeuvres complètes,* I, p. 245.

3. Oskar Seyffert, *A Dictionary of Classical Antiquities* (New York: Meridian, 1964).

4. Nerval, I, p. 214.

5. Ibid., p. 241.

6. Ibid., p. 243.

7. Ibid., p. 242.

8. Ibid., p. 242.

9. Esther Harding, *Woman's Mysteries* (New York: G.P. Putnam's Sons, 1971). Since the shape of the moon was subject to change throughout the month (full, crescent, invisible), it came to represent woman's fickle nature, personality changes within her character. The lunar cycle and the woman's physiological cycle were equated. Because the moon is multiple, it changes constantly, it symbolizes a fragmented nature, disjointed activities.

10. Nerval, I, p. 243.

11. Harding, p. 35.

12. C.G. Jung and C. Kerényi, *Essays on a Science of Mythology* (Princeton: Bollingen Series, Princeton University Press, 1969), p. 112.

13. Ibid., p. 110.

14. Esther Harding, p. 112. The three Marys represent her threefold nature all contained in the Great Mother archetype. In Christianity the worship of the Virgin as the "Mother of God" became popular prior to and during the time of the Crusades (11th century) when Northerners became deeply affected by the powerful influence of these female deities during the course of their travels to the East.

15. Nerval, I, p. 269.

16. Ibid., p 271.

17. Ibid., p. 245.

18. Ibid.

19. Ibid., p. 246.

20. E.O. James, *The Cult of the Mother Goddess* (London: Thames & Hudson, 1969), p. 215.

21. Ibid., p. 257.

22. Ibid., p. 257.

23. Gaston Bachelard, *L'Eau et les rêves* (Paris: José Corti, 1942).

24. Nerval, I, p. 272.

25. Ibid., p. 247.

26. Ibid., p. 241.

27. Ibid., p. 247 .

28. Jung and Kerényi, pp. 104–82.

29. Harding, p. 111.

30. Nerval, I, p. 247.

31. Harding, p. 99.

32. In some Latin hymns the Virgin Mary is referred to as both "Mother" and "Spouse" of her Son, increasing the element of mystery enshrouding her. Ibid.

33. Nerval, I, p. 247.

34. Ibid., p. 248.

35. Pierre-Georges Castex, *Sylvie* (Paris: Société d'Enseignement Supérieur, 1970).

36. Nerval, I, p. 250.

37. Ibid.

38. Ibid., p. 251.

39. Ibid., p. 253.

40. Ibid., p. 259.

41. Bachelard, *L'Eau et les rêves,* p. 67.

42. Nerval, I, p. 259.

43. Ibid., p. 272.

44. Ibid., p. 272.

45. Harding, p. 196.

46. Ibid., p. 35.

47. Ibid., p. 68.

CHAPTER 19

1. Gérard de Nerval, *Oeuvres complètes,* I, p. 294.

2. Similarities between Isis' chastity, Horus' mysterious birth, and the miracle of Mary's Virgin birth have also been presented. There are many versions of

the Egyptian myth. Some say that Isis gathered up the various parts of Osiris' body which the evil Set had cut up and strewn all over the world, restored him to life, and then gave birth to the divine child Horus. Another version relates the story of Isis who, after having been transformed into a bird, gathered some semen from Osiris' penis, impregnated herself with it, and gave birth to Horus. According to yet another account, Isis found all parts of Osiris' body except for his phallus and despite this loss, gave birth (mysteriously) to Horus. Osiris was then relegated to the underworld and was transformed into a passive principle. Henceforth, he was associated with all that was green and all that suffered. He became the symbol of the perpetual martyr since every living creature ate of his body and he bore his perpetual dismemberment in "stoic silence," never begrudging the world for its aggressive ways, always fructifying when damage to him had been accomplished. Marie-Louise von Franz, *The Golden Ass of Apuleius* (New York: Spring Publications, 1970), ch. XI, p. 4.

3. Nerval, I, p. 302.

4. Ibid., p. 303.

5. Ibid., p. 304. Robert Graves, *The Golden Ass* (New York: Farrar, Straus & Giroux, 1951), p. xxii. Franz, ch. X, p. 3.

6. Franz.

7. Ibid., ch. X, pp. 1–10.

8. C.G. Jung, *Psychology and Religion* (New York: Pantheon Books, 1963), p. 130.

9. Ibid., p. 131.

10. Friedrich Heiler, "The Madonna as Religious Symbol," *Eranos Yearbooks* VI (Princeton: Princeton University Press, 1968), p. 356.

11. Jung, p. 312.

12. Franz, ch. XI, p. 4.

13. The church has become the priest's mother-bride, not only symbolically, but physically. Ibid., ch. XI, p. 15.

14. Jung, p. 393.

15. Franz, ch. VI, p. 5.

16. Nerval, I, p. 300.

17. People are likewise startled when hearing their own voice on a microphone, recording machine, etc.

18. Cirlot, *A Dictionary of Symbols* (New York: Philosophical Library, 1972), p. 272.

19. Walter A. Strauss, *Descent and Return* (Cambridge: Harvard University Press, 1971), p. 10.

20. Franz, ch. X, p. 9.

21. Ibid., ch. X, p. 1, 10. Similar bells or rattles are used in many African tribes during their religious services to prevent demons or ghosts from carrying out their evil tasks.

22. Ibid., ch. X, p. 10, 12.

23. Nerval, I, p. 296.

24. Just as there are baptismal fonts and basins containing holy water in Christian churches and cathedrals, so there were likewise in temples devoted to Isis. Many ancient Egyptian families kept holy water in their homes because of the virtues they attributed to it. Cups containing holy water were painted on the chests of mummies thereby infusing, symbolically, the body and spirit of Osiris,

with the living substance, injecting thus the corpse with eternal life. Ibid., p. 299.

25. The same meaning may be attributed to the Holy Grail mysteries during the Middle Ages. When Christ died he left no living remains. When he came to Joseph of Arimathea, he gave him a vessel in which his blood was contained, the *anima Christa*. His soul was alive in the Holy Grail which contained the "secret of the Grail tradition" or "the hidden secret which guarantees his life on earth." Franz, ch. XII, pp. 3–4.

26. Nerval, I, p. 301. Graves, p. 264.

27. Franz, ch. IV, p. 5.

28. Ibid., ch. XII, p. 9.

29. Ibid., ch. X, p. 3.

30. Nerval, I, p. 301. Graves, p. 266.

31. Georges Nagel, "The Mysteries of Osiris in Ancient Egypt," *Eranos Yearbooks*, II (Princeton: Princeton University Press, 1955), p. 32.

32. Nerval, I, p. 300.

CHAPTER 20

1. *Webster's New World Dictionary* (New York: New World Publishing Co., 1966).

2. Edouard Schuré, *The Great Initiates* (New York: St. George Books, 1961), p. 234.

3. Ibid., p. 243.

4. Ibid.

5. Ibid., p. 268.

6. Pythagoras' writings were recorded in Lysis' *The Golden Verses*, in Plato's *Timaeus*, and in fragments written down by Philolaus Archytas.

7. Hervé Masson, *Dictionnaire initiatique*, (Paris: Pierre Belfond, 1970, pp. 302–07.

8. *The Works of Plato* (trans. by B. Jowett), (New York: Tudor Publishing Co.), p. 403.

9. Schuré, p. 329.

10. Ibid., p. 305.

11. Ibid., p. 311.

12. Ibid., p. 314.

13. Ibid., p. 315.

14. Ibid., p. 316.

15. Ibid., p. 318.

16. Ibid., p. 320.

17. Ibid., p. 329.

18. Ibid., p. 329.

19. Serge Hutin, *Les Sociétés secrètes* (Paris: Presses Universitaires de France, 1970). An association may be made between the death of the profane individual and the rebirth of the perfect creature and the "Great Work" of the alchemists; the goal of the Free-Masons, the Rosicrucians, the Illuminists and the Gnostics. Each in his own manner, seeks through expanded consciousness, to ascend through the material world to the spiritual realm, to recapture "the Lost Words of God" and become reintegrated in His luminous domain.

20. Hans Jonas, *The Gnostic Religion* (Boston: Beacon Press, 1967), pp. 42–47.

21. Alexandre Koyré, *La Philosophie de Jacob Boehme* (Paris: J. Vrin, 1929), pp. 200–400.

22. Ibid.

23. Its head and the front part of its body were those of a lion; its back parts were those of a serpent; its middle, a goat.

24. Nerval took his title from *Ivanhoe* (ch. 8.): "On his shield was drawn as his coat of arms a young uprooted oak tree, and his motto was "Desdichado," a Spanish word meaning disinherited, "fatal destiny." Excellent studies of Nerval's poem "El Desdichado" and the other sonnets in this collection are to be found in Jean Richer's *Nerval Expérience et création;* François Constans' "Deux enfants du feu" (*Mercure de France,* April 1, 1948); Georges Le Breton's "La Clé des Chimères: L'Alchimie" (*Fontaine,* No. 44, 1945). The translations of the sonnets *Les Chimères* are for the most part and with minor changes those of Geoffrey Wagner: *Gérard de Nerval: Selected Writings,* tr. by Geoffrey Wagner, copyright © 1957 by Geoffrey Wagner (New York: Grove Press, 1958; Ann Arbor: University of Michigan Press, 1970).

25. Eric Neumann, *Amor and Psyche* (Princeton: Princeton University Press, 1971), p. 111.

26. C.G. Jung, *Psychology and Alchemy* (New York: Pantheon Books, 1953), p. 49.

27. Jean Richer, *Nerval expérience et création* (Paris: Hachette, 1970), pp. 557–58.

28. Ibid., pp. 558–59.

29. Pythagoras had discovered a correlation between arithmetic ratios and musical intervals, depending upon the tension of the strings involved and the reverberations of the tones.

30. Richer, p. 559.

31. Marie-Louise von Franz, *The Golden Ass of Apuleius* (New York: Spring Publications, 1970).

32. Neumann, p. 78.   33. Ibid., pp. 78, 115, 7, 8.

34. Vergil is supposed to be buried in front of the grotto beneath the Posilipo promontory.

35. Richer, p. 562.

36. Mélusine's love ended in sadness because Count Lusignan (like Orpheus) was unable to comply with the strict regulations placed in his path.

37. Serge Hutin, *L'Alchimie* (Paris: Presses Universitaires de France, 1971), p. 91.

38. The philosopher's stone became manifest in the ruby red powder as well as in the phoenix, which was consumed and then rose from its own ashes.

39. The kiss which the lord placed in Medieval times on his vassal and the bond thereby established by the two was looked upon as an important symbol.

40. In medieval mysticism, the grotto represented the human heart or center and for this reason it was propitious for miracles (Lourdes).

41. Gaston Bachelard, *La Terre et les rêveries du repos* (Paris: Librairie José Corti, 1971), p. 146.

42. Odysseus protected his men by putting wax in their ears and tying them to a mast. Orpheus protected Argonauts from a similar fate by playing even more sweetly than the Sirens.

43. Franz, ch. VI, pp. 2–15.

44. Edouard Schuré, pp. 305–40.

45. Ibid., p. 329.

46. J.E. Cirlot, *A Dictionary of Symbols* (New York: Philosophical Library, 1972), pp. 99–100.

47. Peter Tomkins, *Secrets of the Great Pyramid* (New York: Harper & Row, 1971), p. 3.

48. J.H. Breasted, *Development of Religion and Thought in Egypt* (New York: Harper & Brothers, 1959), p. 11.

49. The divinity Ka-Mutef is regarded as enacting the same role in Egyptian religion as the Holy Ghost did in the Christian trinity. Franz, ch. XI, p. 2.

50. Gérard de Nerval, *Oeuvres complètes,* I, p. 303.

51. Leto, Zeus' love and mother of Artemis and Apollo, had been pursued by the jealous Hera from island to island and finally found shelter at Delos, a floating island which became fixed after she gave birth to her divine progeny.

52. The Amalekites were annihilated during the reign of Hezekiah (eighth century B.C.).

53. Bachelard, p. 75.

54. Gershom G. Scholem, *Major Trends in Jewish Mysticism* (New York: Schocken Books, 1965), p. 130.

55. Eric Neumann, *The Origins and History of Consciousness* (New York: Pantheon Books, 1954), p. 72.

56. Ibid., p. 244.

57. C.G. Jung, *Symbols of Transformation* (New York: Pantheon Books, 1956), p. 250.

58. Ibid., p. 219.

59. Artemis may mean *Art,* and *tem,* law.

60. Tarot fortune-telling cards of the ancients were purported to have been copies of the oldest volumes in the world, written by Hermes Trismegistus, councillor to Osiris, for the king of Egypt.

61. C.G. Jung, *The Structures and Dynamics of the Psyche* (Princeton: Princeton University Press, 1969), p. 456.

62. Richer, p. 561.

63. Cirlot, p. 146.

64. Jung, *Psychology and Alchemy,* p. 74.

65. Serge Hutin, *L'Alchimie,* p. 62.

66. Richer, p. 595.

67. Jung, *Psychology and Alchemy,* p. 75.

68. Ibid., p. 74. In alchemy, the rose stands for the earth's answer to the heavenly sun.

69. Bachelard, *La Terre et les rêveries,* p. 26.

70. Ibid., p. 27.

71. Josef Albers, *Interaction of Color* (New Haven: Yale University Press, 1971), p. 27.

72. Bachelard, *La Terre et les Rêveries,* p. 35.

73. Josef Albers, p. 8. Haptic means affecting the sense of touch.

74. The Pythagoreans were vegetarians: to kill an animal meant doing away with someone's soul.

75. Hutin, *L'Alchimie,* p. 61.

76. Bachelard, *La Terre et les rêveries,* p. 51.

77. Heterotopic eyes are those found all over bodies of beings and things.

For some excellent studies of Nerval's *Les Chimères* consult:

Paul Bénichou, *Nerval et la chanson folklorique* (Paris: Corti, 1971).

Léon Cellier, *De Sylvie à Aurélia* (Paris: Minard, Lettres modernes, 1972).

Ross Chambers, *Gérard de Nerval et la poétique du voyage* (Paris: Corti, 1969).

François Constans, *Ascendance mystique, existences mythiques, Mercure de France,* I–XI, 1952.

Georges Le Breton, "La Clef des Chimères: L'Alchimie," *Fontaine,* No. 44, été, 1945.

Marie Jeanne Durry, *Gérard de Nerval et le mythe.* (Paris: Flammarion, 1956).

Jean Richer, "Gérard de Nerval et les doctrines ésotériques," *Critique,* December, 1947.

Marc Richelle, "El Desdichado de Gérard de Nerval," *Revue des Languages Vivantes,* XVII/2.

Norma Rinsler, "Classical Literature in the Work of Gérard de Nerval," *Revue de littérature comparée,* Jan-March, 1963.

Kurt Schärer, *Thématique de Nerval ou Le Monde recomposé* (Paris: Minard, Lettres Modernes, 1968).

CHAPTER 21

1. Gérard de Nerval, *Oeuvres complètes,* I, p. 1,120.
2. Ibid., p. 1,127.
3. Ibid.
4. Ibid.
5. Ibid., p. 1,144.
6. Ibid., p. 1,159.
7. Ibid., p. 1,151.
8. Ibid., p. 1,143.
9. Ibid.
10. Ibid., p. 1,161.
11. Ibid., p. 1,158.
12. Ibid., p. 1,147.
13. Ibid., p. 1,146.
14. Ibid., p. 1,140.
15. Ibid., p. 1,151.
16. Ibid., p. 1,157.
17. Ibid.
18. Ibid., p. 1,159.
19. Ibid., p. 1,160.
20. Ibid., p. 1,162.
21. Ibid., p. 1,131.
22. Nerval's phrase "I am the other" is important because of the influence it had on Arthur Rimbaud, who built his credo around a slightly altered version of this same sentence "Je est un autre . . ." likewise indicating the mass tension he felt within him. André Breton, *Arcane 17* (Paris: 10/18, 1965) p. 157.
23. Edward Edinger, *Ego and Archetype* (New York: Putnam's Sons, 1972), p. 153.
24. *Gérard de Nerval,* trans. Geoffrey Wagner, (Ann Arbor: University of Michigan Press, 1970), p. 115.
25. Nerval, I, p. 360.

26. Ibid., p. 361.

27. Ibid., p. 362.

28. Ibid., p. 364.

29. Ibid., p. 365.

30. Ibid.

31. The Greek god of sleep Hypnos (or in Latin, Somnus) was the son of Night and the twin brother of Death (Thanatos). Both brothers were frequently depicted in art as sleeping in the arms of their mother, death (black) and sleep (white). It was in this abysmal realm that Nerval found the unity he so longed for, the calm after the storm.

32. A difference must be made between Memory (Mneme) and Souvenir (Anamnesis), the latter indicating a veritable loss which may be equated with death. Those who remember anterior existences, according to Plato, are concerned with recording their peregrinations through past lives and, therefore, are looked upon with respect and admiration. Mircea Eliade, *Aspects du mythe* (Paris: Gallimard, 1963), pp. 147–53.

33. Edinger, p. 119.

34. According to Rudolph Steiner in *Les Hiérarchies spirituelles*, angels belong to astral spheres.

35. Eden Gray, *The Tarot Revealed* (New York: New American Library, 1960), p. 184.

36. Edinger, p. 159.

37. Nerval, I, p. 363.

38. John Custance, *Wisdom, Madness and Folly* (New York: Pellegrini & Cudahy, 1952), pp. 82, 92.

39. Jérome-Antoine Rony, *La Magie* (Paris: Presses Universitaires de France, 1968), p. 25.

40. Nerval, I, p. 40.

41. C.G. Jung, *Symbols of Transformation* (New York: Pantheon Books, 1956), p. 383.

42. Custance, p. 30.

43. William James, *The Varieties of Religious Experience* (New York: Longmans, Green & Co.), 1911, p. 398.

44. Jacob Boehme, *Dialogues on the Supersensual Life* (New York: Frederick Ungar), pp. ix–xxxv.

45. John Weir Perry, *The Self in Psychotic Process* (San Francisco: University of California Press, 1953), p. 19.

46. John Weir Perry, "Acute Catatonic Schizophrenia," *Journal of Analytical Psychology*, II, 1957, p. 147.

47. John Weir Perry, "Reconstitutive Process in the Psychopathology of the Self," *Annals of the New York Academy of Sciences*, vol. 96, 1962, p. 853.

48. James, p. 162.

49. Nerval, I, p. 366.

50. Ibid., p. 368.

51. Ibid., p. 371.

52. Edinger, p. 54. The bird had been identified with the soul. In ancient Egyptian symbolism the bird with a human head indicated the Ba (the soul) or the notion that the soul flies out of the body with the arrival of death. The ancient Egyptians believed more strongly in death than in life. Their entire exis-

tence was built around a concretistic concept of death: the mummification of the body, the building of pyramids. Value was placed on the afterlife and not on life. Outside of the palace of the king there were very few elegant houses in Egypt in the early centuries. One can understand Nerval's attitude toward the bird, he who was so taken with Egyptian mythology. Marie-Louise von Franz, *Puer Aeternus* (New York: Spring Publications, 1970), p. 4.

53. Marie-Louise von Franz, *Creation Myths* (New York: Spring Publications, 1972), p. 201.

54. Marie-Louise von Franz, *The Feminine in Fairytales* (New York: Spring Publications, 1972), p. 215.

55. Mircea Eliade, *Le Sacré et le profane* (Paris: Gallimard, 1965), p. 34.

56. Marie-Louise von Franz, *The Feminine in Fairytales,* p. 221. The Yogi practices meditation with the hope of recreating what he terms his "diamond body," that is, the "immortal nucleus of the personality." Ibid., p. 222.

57. Nerval, I, p. 373.

58. Ibid., p. 374.

59. Ibid., p. 373.

60. Ibid., p. 376.

61. Ibid.

62. Ibid., p. 377.

63. Ibid., p. 378.

64. Ibid., p. 379.

65. Edinger, p. 113.

66. Jean Richer, *Gérard de Nerval et les doctrines ésotériques* (Paris: Editions du Griffon d'Or, 1947), p. 46. Other sources were also used by Nerval which Richer includes in his volume: *Le Mutardi,* an Arab manuscript translated by Pierre Vattier (1666) in which the secrets of the pyramids were revealed; *Essai sur l'homme ou l'homme microcosme* by Devismes du Valgay (1805) and *Essai sur la vie ou l'homme posthume* (1805), describing Swedenborg's theory of "universal love," the reason for the fall of certain angels and the relationships between angels and the dawn of Egyptian history. *The Book of Enoch* narrated the manner in which giants had been born from angels and how and why they frequented earthly women.

67. Edinger, p. 3.

68. Nerval, I, p. 376.

69. The Peri: "a male or female supernatural being like an elf or fairy but formed of fire, descended from fallen angels and excluded from paradise until penance is accomplished; originally regarded as evil, but later as benevolent and beautiful." Undine: "an elemental spirit of the water." Salamander: "a mythical and not clearly defined animal having the power to endure fire without harm; a being inhabiting the element fire in the medieval theory of elementals especially as formulated by Paracelsus." Ibid., I.

70. Ibid.

71. Ibid., p. 380.

72. Ibid., p. 382.

73. Ibid., p. 383.

74. Ibid., p. 384.

75. Ibid., p. 385.

76. James, p. 158.

77. Custance, p. 61.

78. Ibid., p. 61.

79. James, p. 410.

80. Ibid., p. 411.

81. Ibid., p. 411.

82. Ibid., pp. 53–57.

83. Nerval, I, p. 385.

84. Ibid., p. 386.

85. Ibid., p. 388.

86. Ibid., p. 390.

87. Ibid., p. 391.

88. Ibid., p. 393.

89. Eliade, *Aspects du mythe*, p. 148.

90. James, p. 153.

91. Nerval, I, p. 394.

92. Ibid., p. 396.

93. Ibid., p. 397.

94. Ibid., p. 398.

95. Ibid., p. 401.

96. Ibid., p. 402.

97. Ibid., p. 404.

98. Ibid., p. 409.

99. Edinger, p. 57.

100. C.G. Jung, *Aion* (Princeton: Princeton University Press, 1959), p. 51.

101. Edinger, p. 44.

102. Eliade, *Aspects du mythe*, p. 85.

103. Edinger, p. 3. The total psyche includes the conscious and unconscious. The Self is "identified as the inner empirical deity and is identical with the *imago Dei.*"

104. Ibid., p. 7. When maturity comes into being, the ego separates from the Self and must be "relativized." Many psychoses including that of Nerval may stem from such an ego-identification.

105. Franz, *Puer aeternus*, I, 2.

106. Nerval, I, p. 402.

107. Edinger, p. 253.

108. Nerval, I, p. 404.

109. Ibid., p. 409.

110. Ibid., p. 413. Blood, for primitive peoples and for Christians has a "mana function" or positive life force. A striking example of blood as a nourishing agent is in the myth of the Pelican, the aquatic bird who so loved its young that when it could find no food to give them, nourished them with its own blood, opened up its breast which they devoured. The Pelican myth was looked upon by Bosch in his *Ars Symbolica* as an allegory of Christ. For Musset, who included this myth in his poem, *Nuit de Mai*, it represented the poet. For some other fine studies on *Aurélia* consult:

Shoshana Felman, " 'Aurélia' ou 'le livre infaisable:' de Foucault à Nerval," *Romantisme*, 1972.

Edward K. Kaplan, "L'Imagination occulte chez Gérard de Nerval: Une épistémologie de la connaissance spirituelle dans "Aurélia," *Revue des Sciences Humaines*, April-June 1967.

Georges Le Breton, "L'Alchimie dans 'Aurélia': Les Mémorables," *Fontaine,* Oct. 1945.

Norma Rinsler, "Gérard de Nerval's Celestial City and the Chain of Souls," *Studies in Romanticism,* II, no. 2 (winter, 1963).

CHAPTER 22

1. Gérard de Nerval, *Oeuvres complètes,* I, p. 1,169.
2. Ibid., p. 1,174.
3. Ibid., p. 1,175.
4. Ibid., p. 1,176.
5. Jean Richer, *Gérard de Nerval et les doctrines ésotériques* (Paris: Editions Griffon d'Or, 1947), p. 102.
6. Aristide Marie, *Gérard de Nerval* (Paris: Hachette, 1914), p. 345.
7. Nerval, I, p. 1,180.
8. Ibid., p. 1,186.
9. Jean Richer, *Gérard de Nerval par les témoins de sa vie* (Paris: Lettres Modernes, 1970), p. 226.
10. Marie, p. 342. Richer, *Témoins,* p. 292.
11. Ibid.
12. Richer, *Témoins,* p. 292.
13. Ibid.
14. Ibid., p. 304.
15. Ibid.
16. Marie, p. 344.
17. Richer, *Témoins,* p. 389.
18. Marie, p. 344.
19. Ibid., pp. 338–39.
20. Richer, *Témoins,* p. 354.
21. Ibid., p. 354.
22. Jean Richer, *Gérard de Nerval* (Paris: Seghers, 1963), p. 94.
23. Marie, p. 357.

BIBLIOGRAPHY

Albers, Josef. *Interaction of Color*. New Haven: Yale University Press, 1971.
Artaud, Antonin. "Sur les chimères." *Tel Quel,* summer, 1965.
Autobiography of a Schizophrenic Girl. New York: New American Library, 1968.

Bachelard, Gaston. *La Psychanalyse du feu*. Paris: Gallimard, 1949.
———. *L'Eau et les rêves*. Paris: Librairie José Corti, 1942.
———. *La Terre et les rêveries du repos*. Paris: Librairie José Corti, 1971.
Baron, Salo W. *A Social and Religious History of the Jews*. I and II. Philadelphia: Jewish Publication Society, 1952.
Bégué, Armand. *Etat présent des études sur Restif de la Bretonne*. Paris: Les Belles Lettres, 1948.
Béguin, Albert. *L'âme romantique et le rêve*. Paris: Librairie José Corti, 1967.
———. *Gérard de Nerval*. Paris: Librairie José Corti, 1945.
Bénichou, Paul. *Nerval et la chanson folklorique*. Paris: José Corti, 1971.
Bernoulli, Rudolf. "Spiritual Development as Reflected in Alchemy and related Disciplines." *Eranos Yearbooks*. IV. Princeton: Princeton University Press, 1970.
Birch, Una. *The Disciples at Sais*. London: Methuen, 1903.
Boehme, Jacob. *Dialogues on the Supersensual Life*. New York: Frederick Ungar Pub. (no pub. date.)
Bousquet, Jacques. *Les Thèmes du rêve dans la littérature romantique*. Paris: Didier, 1964.
Bouthoul, Betty. *Le Calife Hakim*. Paris: Saggitaire, 1950.
Borgal, Clément. *De Quoi vivait Gérard de Nerval*. Paris: Deux-Rives, 1950.
Bowman, Frank Paul. *Eliphas Lévi visionnaire romantique*. Paris: Presses Universitaires, 1969.
Breasted, J.H. *Development of Religion and Thought in Egypt*. New York: Harper & Brothers, 1959.
Breton, André. *Arcane 17*. Paris: 10/18, 1965.
Breton, Georges Le. "L'Alchimie dans 'Aurélia': les mémorables," *Fontaine,* October, 1945.
———. "La Clef des chimères: l'alchimie." *Fontaine,* no. 44, summer, 1945.

Carus, C.G. *Psyche*. New York: Spring Publications, 1970.
Castex, Pierre-Georges. *Sylvie*. Paris: Société d'Édition d'Enseignement Supérieur, 1970.
———. *Le Conte fantastique en France*. Paris: José Corti, 1951.
Cellier, Léon. *Gérard de Nerval*. Paris: Hatier, 1963.
———. *De Sylvie à Aurélia*. Paris: Minard, Lettres Modernes, 1972.
Céram, C.W. *Gods, Graves, and Scholars*. New York: Alfred A. Knopf, 1961.
Chambers, Ross. *Gérard de Nerval et la poétique du voyage*. Paris: José Corti, 1969.
Chastel, André. "La Légende de la Reine de Saba." *Revue de l'histoire des religions,* vols. 120–124, July-August, 1939–1941.
Chronique Médicale (La), August 15, 1908.
Constans, François. "Ascendance mystique, existences mythiques." *Mercure de France*. I–XI, 1952. "Deux enfants du feu," April 1, 1948.
Cirlot, J.E. *A Dictionary of Symbols*. New York: Philosophical Library, 1972.
Custance, John. *Wisdom, Madness and Folly*. New York: Pellegrini and Cudahy, 1952.

Dédéyan, Charles. *Gérard de Nerval et l'allemagne.* I, II. Paris: Société d'Édition de l'Enseignement Supérieur, 1957.
Dumas, Alexandre. *Mes Mémoires.* V. Paris: Calman-Lévy (no date of pub).
Durry, Marie Jeanne. *Gérard de Nerval et le mythe.* Paris: Flammarion, 1956.

Edinger, Edward. *Ego and Archetype.* New York: G.P. Putnam's Sons, 1972.
———. "An Outline of Analytical Psychology" (unpublished).
Eliade, Mircea. "Mysteries and Spiritual Regeneration in Extra-European Religions," *Eranos Yearbooks.* V. New York: Pantheon Books, 1964.
———. *Myths, Dreams, Mysteries.* London: Harvill Press, 1960.
———. *Aspects du mythe.* Paris: Gallimard, 1963.
———. *Le Sacré et le profane.* Paris: Gallimard, 1965.
———. *Forgerons et alchimiste.* Paris: Flammarion, 1956.

Faulkner, R.O. *The Ancient Egyptian Pyramid Texts.* Oxford: At the Clarendon Press, 1969.
Felman, Shoshana. " 'Aurélia' ou 'le livre infaisable:' de Foucault à Nerval." *Romantisme, 72.*
Ferdowski. *The Epic of the Kings Shab-Nama.* Chicago: University of Chicago Press, 1967.
Fierz-David, Linda. *The Dream of Poliphilo.* New York: Pantheon Books, 1950.
Franz, Marie-Louise von. *The Golden Ass of Apuleius.* New York: Spring Publications, 1970.
———. *Interpretation of Fairy Tales.* New York: Spring Publications, 1970.
———. *Puer aeternus.* New York: Spring Publications, 1970.
———. *Creation Myths.* New York: Spring Publications, 1972.
———. *The Feminine in Fairytales.* New York: Spring Publications, 1972.

Gautier, Théophile. *Histoire du romantisme.* Paris: Charpentier, 1827.
Goethe, Johann Wolfgang von. *Faust* (translation by Gérard de Nerval). Paris: Joseph Gibert, 1947.
Graetz. *History of the Jews.* I. Philadelphia: Jewish Publication Society, 1891.
Graves, Robert. *The Golden Ass.* New York: Farrar, Straus & Giroux, 1951.
Gray, Eden. *The Tarot Revealed.* New York: New American Library, 1960.
Guillaume, Jean. *Gérard de Nerval. Pandora.* Namur: Secrétariat des Publications, 1968.

Harding, Esther. *Woman's Mysteries.* New York: G.P. Putnam's Sons, 1971.
Head, Joseph and Cranston, S.L. *Reincarnation an East-West Anthology.* Wheaton, Illinois: The Theosophical Publishing House, 1962.
Héberlot de Molainville. *Bibliothèque orientale.* Paris: La Compagnie des Librairies, 1697.
Heiler, Friedrich. "The Madonna as Religious Symbol," *Eranos Yearbooks.* VI. Princeton: Princeton University Press, 1968.
Hesse, Herman. *The Glass Bead Game.* New York: Holt, Rinehart & Winston, 1969.
Hillman, James. *Pan and the Nightmare.* New York: Spring Publications, 1972.
Houssaye, Arsène. *Confessions.* Paris: Dentu, 1885.
Holmes, Urban. *A History of Old French Literature.* New York: F.S. Crofts, 1938.

Humphrey, George René, *L'Esthétique de la poésie de Gérard de Nerval*. Paris: Nizet, 1969.

Hutin, Serge. *Les Sociétés secrètes*. Paris: Presses Universitaires de France, 1970.
———. *L'Alchimie*. Paris: Presses Universitaires de France, 1971.

James, E.O. *The Cult of the Mother Goddess*. London: Thames and Hudson, 1969.

James, William. *The Varieties of Religious Experience*. New York: Longmans, Green and Co., 1911.

Jasinski, René. *Les Années romantiques de Théophile Gautier*. Paris: Vuibert, 1929.

Jonas, Hans. *The Gnostic Religion*. Boston: Beacon Press, 1967.

Juden, Brian. *Traditions orphiques et tendances mystiques dans le romantisme français*. Paris: Editions Klincksieck, 1971.

Juin, Hubert. *Charles Nodier*. Paris: Pierre Seghers, 1970.

Jung, C.G. *Aion*. Princeton: Princeton University Press, 1959.
———. *Psychological Types*. New York: Pantheon Books, 1964.
———. *The Archetypes and the Collective Unconscious*. New York: Pantheon Books, 1959.
———. *Symbols of Transformation*. New York: Pantheon Books, 1956.
———. *Psychology and Alchemy*. New York: Pantheon.Books, 1953.
———. *Psychology and Religion*. New York: Pantheon Books, 1963.
———. *The Structures and Dynamics of the Psyche*. New York: Pantheon Books, 1963.
———. *Memories, Dreams, Reflections*. New York: Pantheon Books, 1963.
——— and Kerényi, C. *Essays on a Science of Mythology*. Princeton: Bollingen Series, Princeton University Press, 1969.

Jung, Emma. *Animus-Anima*. New York: The Analytical Psychology Club, 1957.
——— and Franz, Marie-Louise von. *The Grail Legend*. New York: G.P. Putnam's Sons, 1970.

Kaplan, Edward K. "L'Imagination occulte chez Gérard de Nerval: Une épistémologie de la connaissance spirituelle dans 'Aurélia,' " *Revue des Sciences Humaines* (April-June, 1967).

Kerényi, C. "The Mysteries of the Kabeiroi," *Erdnos Yearbooks*. II. New York: Pantheon Books, 1955.

Kluger, Rivkah Schärf. *Psyche and the Bible*. Zürich: Spring Publications, 1974.

Koestler, Arthur. *The Roots of Coincidence*. New York: Random House, 1972.

Koran (The). N.J. Dawood trans. London: Penguin Classics, 1959.

Koyré, Alexandre. *La Philosophie de Jacob Boehme*. Paris: J. Vrin, 1929.
———. *Mystiques, spirituels, alchimistes du XVI siècle allemand*. Paris: Gallimard, 1971.

Lévi, Eliphas. *Dogme et rituel de la haute magie*. Paris: Editions Bussiere, 1967.

Mann, H., Siegler, M., Osmond, H. "Time," *Journal of Analytical Psychology*. XIII, 1968.

Martinès de Pasqually, Joachim. *Traité de la reintégration*. Paris: Chacornac, 1899.

Marie, Aristide. *Gérard de Nerval, le poète, l'homme*. Paris: Librairie Hachette, 1914.

Masson, Hervé. *Dictionnaire initiatique*. Paris: Pierre Belfond, 1970.

Merdowski. *The Epic of the King Shab-Name the National Epic of Persia.* Chicago: Chicago University Press, 1967.

Nagel, Georges. "The Mysteries of Osiris in Ancient Egypt," *Eranos Yearbooks.* II. Princeton: Princeton University Press, 1955.

Nagel, Hildegard. "Goethe's Mephistopheles," *The Collective Unconscious in Literature.* New York: Analytical Psychology Club of New York, 1958.

Naudon, Paul. *La Franc-Maçonnerie.* Paris: Presses Universitaires de France, 1971.

Nerval, Gérard de. *Oeuvres complètes.* I and II. Paris: Gallimard, Pléiade, 1966.

———. *Oeuvres complémentaires.* I. Paris: Lettres Modernes, 1959.

———. *Oeuvres complémentaires.* II. Paris: Lettres Modernes, 1961.

———. *Oeuvres complémentaires.* III. Paris: Lettres Modernes, 1965.

———. *Oeuvres complémentaires.* VI. Paris: Lettres Modernes, 1960.

———. *Oeuvres complémentaires.* VIII. Paris: Lettres Modernes, 1963.

———. *Le Carnet de Dolbreuse.* Athènes (Jean Richer), 1967.

Nodier, Charles. *Contes.* Paris: Flammarion, 1961.

Neumann, Erich. *The Origins and History of Consciousness.* New York: Pantheon Books, 1954.

———. "Mystical Man," *Eranos Yearbooks.* VI. Princeton: Princeton University Press, 1968.

———. *Amor and Psyche.* Princeton: Princeton University Press, 1971.

———. *The Great Mother.* New York: Pantheon Books, 1963.

Ostrander, Sheila and Schroeder, Lynn. *Psychic Discoveries Behind the Iron Curtain.* New Jersey: Prentice-Hall, Inc., 1970.

Otto, Walter F. "The Meaning of the Eleusynian Mysteries." *Eranos Yearbooks.* II. New York: Pantheon Books, 1955.

Percival, Harold W. *Masonry and its Symbols.* New York: The Word Publishing Co., 1952.

Perry, John Weir. "Acute Catatonic Schizophrenia," *Journal of Analytical Psychology.* II. 1957.

———. *The Self in Psychotic Process.* San Francisco: University of California Press, 1953.

———. "Reconstitutive Process in the Psychopathology of the Self," *Annals of the New York Academy of Sciences.* Vol. 96. 1962.

Pfeiffer, Robert H. *Introduction to the Old Testament.* New York: Harper & Row, 1948.

Plato. *Collected Dialogues.* New York: Tudor Publishing Co. (no date).

Poulet, Georges. "Sylvie ou la pensée de Nerval," *Cahiers du Sud.* October, 1938.

Puech, Henri-Charles. "Gnosis and Time." *Eranos Yearbooks.* III. New York: Pantheon Books, 1957.

Pulver, Max. "The Experience of Light in the Gospel of St. John, in the 'Corpus Hermeticum,' in Gnosticism, and in the Eastern Church," *Eranos Yearbooks.* IV. Princeton: Princeton University Press, 1970.

Rahner, Hugo. "The Christian Mystery and the Pagan Mysteries," *Eranos Yearbooks.* II. New York: Pantheon Books, 1955.

Raphael, Alice. *Goethe and the Philosopher's Stone.* New York: Garrett Publications, 1965.

Rhodes, Solomon. *Gérard de Nerval.* New York: Philosophical Library, 1951.

Richer, Jean. *Gérard de Nerval oeuvres complémentaires.* I. Paris: Lettres Modernes, 1959.

————. *Nerval, Expérience et création.* Paris: Hachette, 1970.

————. *Gérard de Nerval par les témoins de sa vie.* Paris: Lettres Modernes, 1970.

————. *Gérard de Nerval* . Paris: Seghers, 1963.

————. *Gérard de Nerval et les doctrines ésotériques.* Paris: Editions Griffon d'Or, 1947.

Richard, J.-P. *Géographie magique de Nerval.* Paris: Seuil, 1955.

Rinsler, Norma. "Gérard de Nerval's Celestial City and the Chain of Souls," *Studies in Romanticism.*" II. No. 2, winter, 1963.

Rony, Jérome-Antoine. *La Magie.* Paris: Presses Universitaires de France, 1968.

Romantiques Allemands. Paris: Pléiade, 1963.

Salomon, Michel. *Nodier et le groupe romantique.* Paris: Perrin Co., 1908.

Schaeffer, Kurt. *Le Voyage en orient de Nerval.* Neuchâtel, La Baconnière, 1967.

Schärer, Kurt. *Thématique de Nerval ou le monde recomposé.* Paris: Minard, Lettres Modernes, 1968.

Schneider, Marcel. *La Littérature fantastique en France.* Paris: Fayard, 1964.

Scholem, Gershom G. *Major Trends in Jewish Mysticism.* New York: Schocken Books, 1965.

Schuré, Edouard. *The Great Initiates.* New York: St. George Books, 1961.

Sébillotte, L.-H. *Le Secret de Gérard de Nerval.* Paris: José Corti, 1948.

Sennelier, Jean. *Un Amour inconnu de Gérard de Nerval.* Paris: Lettres Modernes, 1966.

Seyffert, Oskar. *A Dictionary of Classical Antiquities.* New York: Meridian, 1964.

Shaw, Edward Peace. *Jacques Cazotte.* Cambridge: Harvard University Press, 1941.

Slonimsky, Nicolas. *Cyclopedia of Music and Musicians.* New York: Dodd, Mead and Co, 1952.

Starkie, Enid. *Petrus Borel the lycanthrope.* London: Faber and Faber, 1954.

Strauss, Walter A. *Descent and Return.* Cambridge: Harvard University Press, 1971.

Swedenborg, Emmanuel. *Heaven and Hell.* New York: Dutton, 1911.

Tailleux, Dominique. *L'Espace Nervalien.* Paris: Nizet, 1975.

Tomkins, Peter. *Secrets of the Great Pyramid.* New York: Harper & Row, 1971.

Trinick, John. *The Fire-Tried Stone.* London: Vincent Stuart and John M. Watkins Ltd., 1967.

Trismegistus, Hermes. *The Divine Poimander.* New York: Samuel Weiser, 1972.

Underhill, Evelyn. *The Mystics of the Church.* New York: Schocken Books, 1971.

Viatte, Auruste, *Les Sources occultes de romantisme.* I and II. Paris: Librairie Honoré Champion, 1969.

Vivier, Marie de. *Gérard de Nerval.* Paris: La Palatine, n.d.

Wagner, Geoffrey. *Gérard de Nerval.* Ann Arbor: The University of Michigan Press, 1957.

Waite, A.E. *The Holy Kabbalah.* New York: University Books, 1971.

Walmsley, D.W. *Anton Mesmer.* London: Robert Hale, 1967.

Wilding, Peter. *Adventures in the 18th Century.* New York: G.P. Putnam's Sons.

Wili, Walter. "The Orphic Mysteries and the Greek Spirit." *Eranos Yearbooks.* II. New York: Pantheon Books, 1955.

Wilmhust, W.L. *The Masonic Initiation.* London: John M. Watkins, 1957.

INDEX

Other Books by Bettina L. Knapp

Louis Jouvet: Man of the Theatre

That Was Yvette (coauthor)

Louise Labé

Cymbalum Mundi

*Le Mirliton: A Novel Based on the
Life of Aristide Bruant*

Jean Genet

Antonin Artaud: Man of Vision

Jean Cocteau

Jean Racine: Mythos and Renewal in Modern Theater

Céline: Man of Hate

Off-Stage Voices

French Novelists Speak Out

The Contemporary French Theater (anthology)

Dream and Image

The Prometheus Syndrome

Anaïs Nin

Maurice Maeterlinck